INCARNATIONAL

✠

MINISTRY

Ray S. Anderson

Essays in Honor of
RAY S. ANDERSON

INCARNATIONAL MINISTRY

The Presence of Christ in Church, Society, and Family

Edited by
CHRISTIAN D. KETTLER
TODD H. SPEIDELL

With a Foreword by
David Allan Hubbard

HELMERS & HOWARD

COLORADO SPRINGS

Published by Helmers & Howard, Publishers, Inc.
P.O. Box 7407, Colorado Springs, CO 80933 USA.

Library of Congress Cataloging-in-Publication Data

Incarnational ministry : the presence of Christ in church, society, and
   family : essays in honor of Ray S. Anderson / edited by Christian D. Kettler,
   Todd H. Speidell.
      p.   cm.
   Includes bibliographical references and index.
   ISBN 0-939443-21-X (alk. paper)   ISBN 0-939443-20-1 (alk. paper : pbk.)
   1. Pastoral theology. 2. Church work with families. 3. Clergy—Office.
4. Incarnation. I. Anderson, Ray Sherman. II. Kettler, Christian D., 1954- .
III. Speidell, Todd H., 1957- .
BV4011.I53 1990
253—dc20
                                                                    90-35852
                                                                    CIP

Printed in the United States of America.

He broke fresh ground—because, and only because, he had the courage to go ahead without asking whether others were following or even understood. He had no need for the divided responsibility in which others seek to be safe from ridicule, because he had been granted a faith which required no confirmation—a contact with reality, light and intense like the touch of a loved hand: a union in self-surrender without self-destruction, where his heart was lucid and his mind loving.

Dag Hammarskjöld, MARKINGS

Contents

DAVID ALLAN HUBBARD

✝

Foreword:
An Appreciation

R AY ANDERSON'S THIRTEEN YEARS of ministry at Fuller have been part
of his third career. He began his adult life on a farm in northeastern
South Dakota near the Minnesota border. There he and his bride, Mildred,
continued for several years the traditions of their families—working the
soil and tending the animals.

Mildred and Ray were high school sweethearts in the town of Wilmot
when World War II began. Upon graduation, Ray enlisted in the Army Air
Corps and was selected for training as a navigator. When the war ended they
married and Ray pursued studies in agriculture, especially animal husban-
dry, at South Dakota State University, graduating with a Bachelor of
Science degree. University was followed by several years of working the
land and beginning to raise a family.

Those years of turning the soil—taking care of it so it would take care of
him, as his father had taught him—were accompanied by the stirrings of
God's Spirit in his life. Reared as a Lutheran by his Scandinavian parents,
Albert and Alma, Ray awakened, as he himself put it, "to the reality of Jesus
Christ as God's Son and my Savior." With that awakening came an insistent
call to leave the farm (and even the prized new tractor) and ready himself for
Christian ministry.

The three years at Fuller (1956-59) saw the beginnings of the emphases
that have shaped Ray Anderson's ministry through the past three decades:
academic rigor—here Edward John Carnell, president during that period,
was his powerful mentor—coupled with *evangelistic outreach* in the Gospel
Team and *service in leadership* as student body president.

Graduation from Fuller ushered in the second career for Ray and Mildred:
the planting and nurture in Covina, California of a congregation affiliated
with the Evangelical Free Church of America. It was during this decade of
ministry in Covina that I first became acquainted with Ray, whom I had
met casually in his student days. His avid participation in alumni activities

and his unstinting willingness to serve Fuller impressed me deeply during the early years of my presidency. Even more impressive was his pastoral care of some of my loved ones who were going through painful transitions at the time they came under his ministry. His thoughtful preaching, sensitive counseling, and warm acceptance made a life-changing contribution to them.

Then, in 1970, came another call, persistent and cogent. Ray responded to it by leaving the pastorate, selling his possessions, and moving his family to pursue doctoral studies in theology at New College, Edinburgh. There began his friendship with Thomas Torrance, whose mentoring helped to shape the contours of Ray's third career, launched with the granting of a Ph.D. in 1972. Four years of teaching at Westmont College gave him opportunity to combine stimulating classroom presentations with significant pastoral ministries to students and faculty colleagues.

Since 1976, Anderson has been a valued member of the faculty at Fuller Theological Seminary. He has combined an extraordinary teaching load with the effective accomplishment of numerous administrative responsibilities, including terms as Assistant and Associate Dean while carrying the directorships of the Extended Education and Doctor of Ministry programs. And all the while his busy typewriter has hammered out the series of books, essays, and reviews cited in the Bibliography of the volume.

Among his remarkable contributions to the church during the Fuller years has been his passionate desire to keep theological inquiry and pastoral ministry tied inextricably together. He has demonstrated that in his leadership of the Harbour Fellowship, a church now meeting regularly for worship in a school building in Huntington Beach. He has further implemented that desire in his day by day interaction with pastors enrolled in the Doctor of Ministry program, as supervisor of their dissertations. The hundreds of D.Min. graduates are testimonies to his insight, competence, and dedication to the theory and practice of pastoral care.

For years he has teamed with his colleagues in clinical psychology and marriage and family counseling as they have engaged in the task of relating human sciences to a biblical understanding of our nature, need, and behavior as human beings. Indeed, a conviction that as Christians we should see life whole and especially that we should find fullness of life in the incarnate Christ has been one of Ray's prime compulsions. His academic title, Professor of *Theology and Ministry,* is fitly chosen.

His devotion to his professional tasks is matched by his allegiance to his family. The Anderson clan includes three daughters. Carol Purga and her husband, Tim, are the parents of three children: Lara, Joshua, and Tondi. They live at Forest Home Christian Conference Center, where Tim serves as Executive Director. Jollene is Assistant Director of the Lowell W. Berry Institute for Continuing Education in Ministry at Fuller. Ruth Evans is a registered nurse. Her husband Greg, a physician, is a resident in reconstructive surgery at Johns Hopkins Hospital in Baltimore, MD.

Ray's colleagues, students, and parishioners have found in him a notable blend of pastoral compassion, scholarly intensity, driving sense of call, and omnivorous capacity for work. The friendships he has formed in all his phases of ministry run deep and steady. Former students by the score from Westmont and Fuller rise up regularly to call him blessed.

His burning vision for what theological education ought to be has helped focus my perspective. The file folder under his name in my office undoubtedly contains a larger number of memos—on how what we do could and should be different—than that of any other faculty member. His ideas have proved stimulating even when their implementation has seemed impossible. Likewise his interventions in faculty and committee meetings are *sui generis*. He has the courage of his convictions in all the arenas in which he serves, and his very presence can be an inspiration to the practice of justice, to the reflection on truth, and to the consideration of innovation, if not revolution. No faculty could handle a whole crew of Ray Andersons. But any faculty would be the poorer without at least one.

With the contributors to the volume, and with its editors, I salute his ministry and celebrate his friendship.

CHRISTIAN D. KETTLER
TODD H. SPEIDELL

✝

Introduction

I NCARNATIONAL MINISTRY" IS certainly not a new theme for theology or the church. The heart of the faith has always been found in the eternal Word of God, who "became flesh and dwelt among us, full of grace and truth" (Jn. 1:14). From the early Christological battles of Athanasius and Nicaea, to the Reformers, to the twentieth-century theology of Karl Barth, the incarnation of God in Jesus Christ has never been far from the church's proclamation, even in its darkest hours.

It is another question, however, to ask whether or not the church has allowed the incarnation to formulate a decisive influence on its ministry in the world. Is a radical incarnational ministry perhaps a bit threatening because, in the incarnation, God comes *too close,* becomes *too personal?* Perhaps this is one reason why the church has often shied away from the hard theological thinking and costly personal practice that should flow from its doctrine of the incarnation.

The purpose of this volume arises from a desire on the part of many to honor Dr. Ray S. Anderson, a pastor and theologian who, in a unique way, has both wrestled with the issues of incarnational ministry and manifested the reality of such a ministry in his own life. Often a *Festschrift* to honor an esteemed teacher or colleague comprises a collection of largely unrelated essays which are presented to the honoree and then kindly shelved, lost in the wilderness of the library. We intend this *Festschrift* as a tribute to Dr. Anderson by presenting essays motivated by the concerns of incarnational ministry, and organized around the areas of *church, society,* and *family.* Our hope is that this organization will facilitate use of this volume as both a textbook in the theology of ministry and as a stimulus to further discussion among pastors, theologians, counselors, and laypeople concerning the nature of incarnational ministry.

The essays in this volume are as diverse as their authors: theologians, ethicists, pastors, administrators, and social scientists and practitioners. The first section of the book develops a theology for the church in ministry. The various essays underscore the critical significance of Christ's continued ministry through his church. Church ministry in the name of Jesus Christ cannot be conducted as a mere matter of technique, as if the social and behavioral sciences contributed more to the practice of ministry than theology itself. Theology that is true to the incarnate Savior will inform and enable ministers of Christ's church to understand better, and participate in more effectively, the ministry of Christ through his church.

The second section emphasizes a theology for the church in society. The nature of the incarnation attests the reality of God's presence and work beyond the institutional walls of the church. A church preoccupied with its own survival or growth may lose its soul. A church in mission and service, by contrast, witnesses to Christ's solidarity with the world, and stands in union with the incarnate one himself. Liberation, solidarity, and reconciliation are not incidental to Christ's saving work; on the contrary, they are essential to the very heart of the gospel of Jesus Christ.

The final section furthers the nascent literature of the ministry of the church to families. Marriage, sexuality, and family, like the institution of the church, should not be idealized. The incarnate one himself was single and gave his primary loyalty to God. The incarnate one was also, however, the creator and redeemer of humanity, not simply of souls. Sexuality is essential to our humanity. Marriage and family are gifts of God for our humanity. The church of Jesus Christ in society should be a family both to those with and to those without a marriage and family.

Although a collection of diverse essays cannot provide a comprehensive treatment of church, social, and family ministry, it can contribute to and encourage engagement in theological reflection oriented to ministry. A perusal of Ray Anderson's writings (see the Bibliography on page 317) reveals his contributions to an incarnational theology that thinks concretely about the ministry of Christ. These essays can only hope to do nothing more and nothing less.

Incarnational ministry is the ministry of God in becoming a *person* in Jesus Christ, the "Personalizing Person," in T. F. Torrance's words, who creates "personalized persons" by taking upon himself our humanity.[1] It seems to us only fitting that a collection of essays on incarnational ministry should come in the form of a *Festschrift* honoring a person who has embodied such a life and ministry. For countless numbers of students, first at Westmont College and then for many years at Fuller Theological Seminary, Anderson has been a model of an "incarnational minister" in both his teaching and his practice. Three facets of this ministry are especially evident in his life: (1) the incarnational minister is a *free* theologian; (2) the incarnational minister is a *pastoral* theologian; and (3) the incarnational minister is a *committed* theologian. In all three, one can see that the minister is never separated from the theologian and the theologian is never separated from the minister.

(1) "The incarnational minister is a *free* theologian." Ray Anderson is not enamored with novelty or the latest theological or ecclesiastic fad. Anyone who has ever tried to pigeonhole Ray in a particular political position will attest his independent spirit! Certainly part of that independent spirit comes from his background of growing up on a South Dakota farm and becoming a farmer himself before entering seminary. (We wonder if Ray is familiar with T. F. Torrance's comparison of Karl Barth's laborious exegetical work on the Bible while he was a pastor with the careful "exegesis" of the soil in which Barth's farmer parishioners were involved![2]) That independent, free spirit of the farmer is recalled by Ray to his students when he quotes the words his father once said to him while taking up a fistful of soil, "Take good care of the land, and the land will take care of you."

Anderson has exhibited freedom in his creative pastoral leadership, first at the Covina Evangelical Free Church, and then most recently with the adventuresome group of Harbour Fellowship, a small, informal church in Huntington Beach, California, where Ray has led worship, preached, and pastored for thirteen years — without the benefit of a denomination, large numbers, staff, or even permanent facilities — while maintaining his exhaustive teaching and administrative load at Fuller Seminary.

He has shown freedom in his patience and tolerance toward those of radically different viewpoints, without extolling tolerance as the sole virtue one maintains at all costs. A Fuller student with a heterodox Christological view once decided to proclaim his position on the seminary's "Board of Declaration." This created an immediate cacophony among some students, who demanded that this individual recant or be expelled. But Anderson, a free theologian, invited the student to his own Christology class, allowing him to present his view. (The student may have received more than he bargained for, however. What followed was a penetrating critique, slowly tearing the student's argument apart, in Socratic fashion!)

This freedom is, above all, the freedom *for God* and *for humanity,* a theme of great importance in the theology of one of Ray's greatest influences, Karl Barth. (It has been said that while other theologians can tell you what Barth *says,* Anderson's lively, pastoral interpretation makes Barth *sing*!) The tendency among many theologians is either to adopt uncritically a confessional, traditional theology — gaining a degree of security but forfeiting the critique of the Word of God over our tradition — or simply to reject all tradition for the sake of the novel and the trendy. Anderson has refused to do both, because of his theology of the freedom of the Word of God. This has allowed Anderson as a theologian to draw heavily on traditional incarnational theology, particularly in developing implications for a theology of ministry, while always maintaining the judgment of the Word of God over both tradition and innovation.

(2) "The incarnational minister is a *pastoral* theologian." In contrast to some seminary professors who were once pastors but apparently gave up their pastoral identity and sensitivity when they became professors, Anderson has never ceased to be a pastor in name or deed. This is true not only for his congregation in Huntington Beach, but also for the students under his teaching. His availability to students is well known. When a student comes to see him, Ray's theology of *grace* ceases to be simply a theory, and becomes a reality. His patience with students who have been beset by personal crises has been a source of healing and hope for many. Students regularly encounter his pastoral heart in the lecture room, where many who have come to class heavily burdened are then refreshed to hear anew the gospel of grace of the incarnation in a nevertheless highly academic lecture! Even in a theological seminary, that is a rare gift.

(3) "The incarnational minister is a *committed* theologian." The free and pastoral perspectives of the incarnational minister are simply extensions of the committed theologian, a person of faith committed to Jesus Christ. For Ray Anderson, that faith determines the form and content of his theology.

But for Anderson, faith is not simply an individual's private perception of God. As a pastor, he knows how deadly it can be to throw persons back solely on the resources of their own faith. This is condemning them to a kind of "works righteousness" even of faith which ultimately ends in frustration and despair. Rather, Anderson has seized upon the great paradigm of incarnational theology in the twentieth century offered by Karl Barth, Dietrich Bonhoeffer, and Thomas Torrance (the last was Ray's doctoral mentor at the University of Edinburgh). Such a theology is both *scientific* and *humane*. As the early Barth states, "to be scientific means to be thrown up against reality. The reality of theology is its unconditional respect for the peculiarity of its own chosen theme."[3]

Anderson's commitment to the incarnation of God in Jesus Christ has allowed him to be "thrown up against" the reality not only of God, but also of humanity. Bonhoeffer makes this connection very clear when he says, "Whoever sees Jesus Christ does indeed see God and the world in one. He can henceforward no longer see God without the world or the world without God."[4] Here lies the impetus of a scientific and humane theology for pastoral ministry. Like Barth's, Anderson's perspective comes from the context of his years pastoring a congregation. He knows what is at stake: the lives of human beings who desperately need the grace of God.

Anderson's incarnational, pastoral theology offers unique promise for contemporary evangelical theology. For a theology to be truly "evangelical"—that is, a "gospel" theology—it must begin with God's *self*-revelation, his proclamation of himself. And since that self-revelation is made manifest in the incarnation of the person Jesus of Nazareth, it is nothing less than *personal*. A truly "evangelical" theologian must manifest both sides of God's self-revelation: its scientific nature, in unconditional respect for the uniqueness of God's self-revelation, as well as its humane goal, in the communication of the grace of God to broken humanity through the life and ministry of Jesus Christ. Imperfect as all human ministers may be, Ray Anderson has been such a model of an incarnational minister, for which the editors, contributors, and supporters of this volume give thanks to God.

We would like to thank the following people who contributed greatly to the production of this volume: the *Festschrift* committee (consisting of John Altman, Bill Marquis, Tim Purga, Pat Rexroat, and Luanna Young); Harbour Fellowship, Covina Evangelical Free Church, and the Continuing and Extended Education Division and other friends at Fuller Theological Seminary; Dr. David Allan Hubbard for his foreword; Don Simpson and Kathy Yanni of Helmers & Howard, Publishers; and Diane Ferguson and Carol Mullikin of Friends University for secretarial assistance.

NOTES

1. Thomas F. Torrance, *The Mediation of Christ* (Grand Rapids: Eerdmans, 1983), p. 78.
2. Thomas F. Torrance, *Karl Barth: An Introduction to His Early Theology, 1910-1931* (London: SCM Press, 1962), p. 34.
3. Karl Barth, *The Epistle to the Romans,* trans. Edwyn C. Hoskyns (London: Oxford Univ. Press, 1933), p. 531.
4. Dietrich Bonhoeffer, *Ethics,* ed. Eberhard Bethge, trans. Neville Horton Smith (New York: Macmillan, 1965), p. 70.

PART I

✣

A Theology of
Church Ministry

1

THOMAS F. TORRANCE

✛

The Distinctive Character of the Reformed Tradition*

I T IS, I BELIEVE, in its *doctrine of God* that the really fundamental character of any church tradition becomes revealed. That is certainly true of the whole Reformed tradition from John Calvin to Karl Barth. Thus right from the start, over against the Latin patristic and medieval notions of the immutability and impassibility of God, often construed in Aristotelian terms of the Unmoved Mover, the theologians of the Reformed Church laid the emphasis upon the sovereign majesty of the mighty, living, acting, speaking God, with a closer relation between the mighty acts of God in Israel and in the kingdom and church of Christ.

This doctrine has to be understood within the context of the whole Reformation movement in which there took place a paradigmatic shift from dialectical to dialogical discourse, from abstract questions about essence to concrete questions about event, and thus from mainly static to dynamic modes of thought. A great attempt was made to abandon a way of thinking from a point of absolute rest for a kinetic mode of thinking that was appropriate to divine acts in space and time—hence the characteristic stress upon atonement and eschatology. That was not entirely successful, for scholastic Calvinist and Lutheran dogmatics soon lapsed back into rather static patterns of thought. Nevertheless, the urgent concern of the Reformation with doctrines of redeeming and saving event have ever since characterized the whole Protestant tradition.

Built into the foundations of the Reformed tradition, of course, was the primacy given to the *Word of God*, which was regarded not as some communication about God, detached from him, but as God himself speaking to us personally. God is known only through God, on the actual ground of his self-revelation and his gracious activity toward us, for it is

---

* The Donnell Lecture given at Dubuque Theological Seminary on 6 October 1988.

2

only through Christ and the Spirit that we have access to him. The God we know in this way is never dumb or inactive.

Reformed theological thinking along these lines was determined from the very start by Calvin's reversal of the stereotyped medieval questions: *quid sit, an sit, quale sit.* That imported a rejection of the essentialist approach to God that had dominated the analytical and logical thinking of the great schoolmen. For Calvin the primary question became: *Who is God?* Who is he who acts in this merciful and loving way toward us in Jesus Christ and the Holy Spirit? This is not a question in which the essence and the existence of God are held apart from one another, but one in which God is allowed to disclose who he is in his actual relation toward us, and one in which we are cast wholly upon God's own reality in presenting himself to be known by us. God is who he is in his Word of self-communication to us. He comes to us clothed with his revelation, for God and his revelation are indivisibly one. The Word of God *is* God, and God *is* his Word.

Let us recall here Karl Barth's point that twice in its long history the church has had to struggle for the central truth of the gospel.

The first time that happened was in the fourth century, when the doctrine of the deity of Christ was at stake—and thus also the doctrines of the deity of the Holy Spirit and of the Triunity of the Godhead. It was a struggle to secure the identity of God's self-revelation with God himself, which the church achieved through its formulation of the *homoousion* in asserting that the incarnate Son of God is of one and the same being with God the Father. This secured belief both in the deity of the Holy Spirit and in the doctrine of the Holy Trinity.

The second time the church had to struggle for the central truth of the gospel was in the sixteenth century, when not only the objectivity of revelation but the primacy of justification by grace, and all the saving truths of the gospel, were at stake. It was a struggle to secure the identity of God's self-giving in grace through his Word and Spirit with God himself, which the Reformation achieved through its insistence upon the identity of the gift of grace with God the giver. That is to say, at the Reformation the Nicene *homoousion* was applied both to the Word and to the grace of God proclaimed in the gospel, for in them God has revealed and communicated not just something about himself, but himself in his own personal being. Thus if the Nicene Fathers had to lay their main emphasis upon the *being* of God in his acts, the Reformers had to lay their main emphasis upon the *acts* of God in his being. It is to Karl Barth's great merit that he has brought those two emphases together in a doctrine of the dynamic being of God, particularly evident in his identification of the electing and revealing act of the eternal God with the incarnation of his beloved Son in space and time.

Let us now consider some principal features in this Reformed tradition.

PREDESTINATION AND PROVIDENCE

Predestination means the anchoring of all God's ways and works in his own eternal being and will. While the term *predestination* refers everything back to the eternal purpose of God's love for humanity, the cognate term *election* refers more to the fulfillment of that purpose in space and time, patiently worked out by God in the history of Israel and brought to its consummation in Jesus Christ.

Thus predestination is not to be understood in terms of some timeless decree in God, but as the electing activity of God providentially and savingly at work in what Calvin called the "history of redemption." Behind it all is the unvarying faithfulness or dynamic constancy of God, for in choosing humanity for fellowship with himself the electing God thereby wills to set aside everything contrary to this eternal purpose. In his faithfulness God never says "yes" and "no" to us, but only "yes." That is the way in which Calvin understood the couplet "predestination" and "reprobation." If predestination is to be traced back not just to faith as its "manifest cause" but to the *yes* of God's grace as its "hidden cause," so reprobation is to be traced back not just to unbelief as its "manifest cause" but to the *yes* of God's grace as its "hidden cause" as well—and not to some alleged "no" of God. There are not two wills in God, but only the the one eternal will of his electing love. It is by the constancy of that love that all who reject God are judged.

The gospel tells us that it is only in Jesus Christ that election takes place. He embodies the electing love of God in his own divine-human person. That is why Calvin used to insist that we must think of Christ as the "cause" of election in all four traditional senses of "cause": the efficient and the material, the formal and the final. He is at once the *Agent* and the *Content* of election, its *Beginning* and its *End*. Hence it is only *in Christ* that we may discern the ground and purpose of election in God's unchanging being, and also how election operates in God's creative, providential, and redemptive activity. In Christ the whole electing and convenanting love of God is gathered up to a head and launched into history. Before Christ, apart from him, or without him, God does not will or do anything, for there is no God behind the back of Jesus Christ.

This identity of eternal election and divine providence in Jesus Christ generated in the Reformed tradition its well-known conjunction of repose in God and active obedience to him in the service of Christ's kingdom. However, if the repose in God is referred to an inertial ground in the eternal being of God, as has happened only too often in the history of Reformed churches, then there opens up a split in people's understanding between predestination and the saving activity of Christ in space and time—e.g. in the notion of election as "antecedent to grace." That would seem to be the source of a tendency toward a Nestorian view of Christ that keeps cropping up in Calvinist theology. This is very evident in misguided attempts to construe the "pre" in "predestination" in a logical, causal, or temporal way, and then to project it back into an absolute decree behind the back of Jesus, and thus to introduce a division into the very person of Christ. It is one of Karl Barth's prime contributions to Reformed theology that he has decisively exposed and rejected such a damaging way of thought.

THE DOCTRINE OF THE TRINITY

It was well known during the Reformation that in his doctrine of the Trinity Calvin took his cue from Gregory the Theologian—that is why Melanchthon nicknamed Calvin "the Theologian" after him. But it was also the case that in formulating his doctrine of the Holy Trinity, Calvin operated with a concept of person ontologically derived from the eternal communion of love in the Godhead, which had been put forward by Richard of St.-Victor and Duns Scotus, rather than with a concept of person analytically derived from the notions of individual substance and rational nature, which had been set out by Boethius and Thomas Aquinas. That was to give Reformed theology one of its most important features.

Calvin's understanding of the nature and role of the person was to have very far-reaching implications in the whole course of the Reformed tradition—not least in respect of the doctrines of the knowledge of God and of justification by grace through personal union with Christ, together with the cognate doctrines of Eucharistic Communion and of the church as the body of Christ. But it also had a wider application to the social structure of humanity, and even a startling relevance to physical science in generating insight into the fact that relations of things to one another may belong to what things really are in themselves.

We turn first to the fact that knowledge of God and knowledge of ourselves are found to have a relation of profound mutuality, yet one in which the divine Subject and Agent always retains priority. We cannot cut off knowledge of God from the fact that he has addressed us in his Word. Therefore, our knowledge of him must include within it the proper place given by God to the human subject—but one in which the human subject refers everything to God and nothing to itself. As Calvin regarded it, this reference of knowledge back to God reflects the doctrine of election, which insists that we do not know God in acting upon him but in being acted upon by God.

Hence we must learn to distinguish what is objectively real from our subjective fantasies. Apart from such self-critical testing, a gross personalism easily takes over in which the people obtrude themselves into the place of God, making their own relations with God constitute the actual content of theological knowledge. Theological statements are thereby recast into anthropological statements. That is what happened in European thought with the Cartesian and Lockean notion of the autonomous reason when Western theology followed Boethius and Aquinas in their concept of the person as the individual substance of rational nature, instead of following Richard of St.-Victor and John Calvin in their very different concept of the person, in which the objective relations of persons with one another were regarded as belonging to what persons are.

Of quite central importance in the Reformed tradition was the emphasis Calvin laid upon union with Christ. It was typical of him that he should stress the fact that union with Christ must be thought of as coming *first*, for it is only through union with him that we may partake of Christ and all his benefits. For Calvin this concept of union with Christ was inseparable from his doctrine of the Holy Spirit, for just as incarnation and pentecost belong together in the saving acts of God, so our life in union with Christ and in the communion of the Spirit belong savingly together. The concept of a union with Christ had played an important role in the medieval Franciscan tradition, as is evident in the hymns of Bernard of Clairvaux which we like to sing. But Calvin introduced into that concept two far-reaching changes.

The first change involves what was known as the *ordo salutis*. As expounded by Alexander of Hales, the teacher of both Thomas Aquinas and Bonaventura, union with Christ comes at the end of a saving process mediated through the administration of grace. Justification and sanctification were thought of as "graces" successively infused into the faithful, deepening their relation with Christ.

With Calvin that *ordo salutis* was inverted, for it is only through union with Christ *first* that we may partake of all the saving benefits embodied in him: Union with Christ thus precedes justification and sanctification. This was another way of stating that Christ himself is not only the agent but the actual matter or substance of election—a concept well understood by people as diverse as David Brainerd and Karl Barth.

It was otherwise, however, with the Westminster Confession of Faith, in which there was a reversion to the Halesian notion of the order of salvation, and indeed to a medieval framework of thought governed by primary and secondary causes. The strange idea that, while the death of Christ is *sufficient* for all, it is *efficient* only for some, which also derives from Alexander of Hales, cannot be attributed to Calvin, for it was explicitly rejected by him, although it was reintroduced into a scholastic form of Calvinism by Theodore Beza.

The second change has to do with the place given by Calvin to the *vicarious humanity* of Christ. To be united with Christ is to be joined to him in the human nature which he assumed from us and within which he took our place throughout the whole course of redemption, which he fulfilled from his birth to his crucifixion and resurrection. The implication of this for an understanding of the saving life and activity of Jesus is immense: It laid the emphasis not only on what was called his "passive obedience," in which he submitted to the divine judgment upon us, but also upon his "active obedience," in which he took our place in all our human activity before God the Father—such as our acts of faith, obedience, prayer, and worship. To be united with Christ is to be joined to him in his life of faith, obedience, prayer, and worship, so that we must look away from *our* faith, obedience, prayer, and worship to what Christ is and does for us in our place and on our behalf.

This focus upon the vicarious humanity of Christ is a concern that ever since the Reformation has been found at the heart of theological debate in Scotland. One of the main issues at stake here has been the effect of the doctrine of "active obedience" in pointing up the saving significance of the human life of Jesus, thus opening the way for a proper theological assessment of what has come to be called "the historical Jesus."

It is rather strange, however, that this doctrine of the active obedience of Christ tended to be rejected by the Heidelberg, Bezan, and Westminster traditions of Calvinism but was taken up by Albrecht Ritschl in Lutheran theology. When its relation to the deity of Christ became loosened, however, as in a defective appreciation of the Nicene *homoousion*, it tended to further a liberal, moralistic approach to Christ and his saving significance.

Nevertheless, the doctrine of union with Christ in his vicarious human nature and priesthood remains central to the Reformed tradition and is surely one of its most helpful contributions to the Ecumenical Church.

This evangelical conception of union with Christ governed Calvin's teaching about justification and sanctification, Holy Communion, and the church as the body of Christ. With reference to the words of St. Paul that Christ dwells in our hearts by faith, Calvin pointed out that a union in being is involved here beyond the relation of faith. For us to *be* in Christ or for Christ to *be* in us has to be understood in an ontological way, and not just in a figurative or spiritual way. It is through a real union with Christ in his vicarious humanity that all that he has done for us in himself becomes ours and we are made to share together what he is. That was Calvin's doctrine of "the blessed exchange" which he took over from the Greek Fathers. It is in that incarnational and atoning way that justification has to be understood, not just in terms of imputed righteousness but in terms of a participation in the righteousness of Christ which is transferred to us through union with him.

It was also in this ontological way that Calvin understood baptism. There is *"one baptism common to Christ and his Church,"* which Christ underwent in his own life, death, and resurrection on our behalf when he made our human nature his own. And it is that one objective baptism, in which Christ has associated us with himself, that every act of baptism in the church presupposes, and from which it derives its significance and efficacy.

It is in a similar ontological way through personal union with Christ that the Eucharist has to be understood—that is, in terms of Christ's personal self-giving to us in which we partake of the whole Christ crucified and risen who mediates to us his *real presence*—not just in his body and blood but in the indivisible reality of the Savior in his personal being and atoning self-sacrifice. It is the presence of the crucified and risen Lord in the reality of his divine-human person clothed with his gospel and the power of his Spirit.

Thus Holy Communion has to do with a personal union with Christ of the most profound kind, for in it the real presence that Christ grants to us in space and time is objectively grounded in the presence of God in Christ to himself. The nature of this real presence in the Eucharist is to be respected as a mystery grounded in the mystery of hypostatic union of divine and human natures in the one person of Christ. That is why the Reformed Church has always rejected any attempt to offer any interpretation of the real presence in terms of substance and accidents, and why it rejected any explanatory appeal to container notions of space, but reverted to the relational forms of thought developed by the Greek Fathers of the fourth century out of respect for the inexplicable nature of the incarnation and the ascension.

Once more it is basically in the same realistic and ontological way that the church has to be understood as *the body of Christ*—not just in a figurative or spiritual way, but as an ontological reality, in which the faithful are made to share together in the mystery of Christ, the incarnate, crucified, and risen Son of God. Calvin rejected the idea of a twofold or two-headed church, the church as "mystical body" and as "juridical society," for Christ himself is not divided. As the body of Christ, the church is one indivisible reality in him. It is that one actual church in space and time that we know by faith to be the body of Christ. At this point Calvin was probably more influenced by Cyril of Alexandria than by Augustine or Luther.

Incidentally, this conception of the church known through faith alone is to be traced in the statements about the church as the body of Christ found in the Tridentine Catechism, where we have the earliest anticipation of the Constitution on the church promulgated by the Second Vatican Council. It was, of course, this essentially Reformed doctrine of the church as the actual, and not just the mystical, body of Christ that has informed so much of our ecumenical thinking this century. This applies also to the teaching of the Second Vatican Council which was heavily influenced by Karl Barth in his profoundly Christocentric and Christological account of the church as the body of Christ, "the earthly-historical form of the existence of Jesus Christ."

It was largely in the Reformed tradition that there developed the concept that the interrelations between persons are part of what persons are—this is what I call "onto-relations," a concept that goes back ultimately to the teaching of Athanasius and Gregory Nazianzen about the *perichoresis* of the substantive relations between Father, Son, and Holy Spirit within the eternal Godhead. While these onto-relations apply to our understanding of the Triunity of God in a unique and transcendent way, they also apply in quite another way on the creaturely level to the interrelations of human persons whom God has created for communion with himself, and which in their created way reflect the uncreated relations within himself.

REFORMED CONCEPTUALITY

With the whole movement of the Reformation there took place through the rediscovery of the mighty Word of God a profound epistemological shift from optical to acoustic modes of knowing and thinking. Thus Martin Luther drew a clear contrast between the "audible kingdom" and the "visible kingdom," with the insistence that knowledge of God is mediated to us through hearing rather than through seeing. In order to "see" God, he declared, you must "stick your eyes in your ears"!

This new approach to *auditive knowledge of God* had already been worked out by John Reuchlin on the ground of what he called "Hebrew truth," impressed upon him particularly through his study of the Old Testament Scriptures. From him it passed through the teaching of John Major in Paris to John Calvin, with whom it took the form of intuitive, evident knowledge that arises through the obedience of faith to the Word of God speaking to us in person in the Holy Scriptures. While this outlook permeated the Lutheran and Calvinist Reformations alike, our immediate concern is with the particular mode of conceptuality to which Calvin's emphasis on the inseparable relation of Word and Spirit gave rise in the Reformed tradition. Let me single out several of its main ingredients.

(1) Knowledge of God derived from his Word must be regarded as objectively grounded in God, for the Word which God addresses to us in Jesus Christ is not some Word detached from God but is consubstantial with him and belongs as Word to his eternal being. This was the point upon which Reuchlin had insisted. In the dominant medieval tradition the Thomists had criticized Anselm's teaching that there is a "speaking" as well as an "understanding" in the innermost being of God, but Reuchlin argued that this was to contradict the doctrine of the *homoousion* in the Nicene Creed. Like the Son of God, the Word is divine reality and resides as Word in the eternal being of God and proceeds from him as Word without being less God.

That was precisely Calvin's point: the Word we hear in the Holy Scriptures derives from and reposes in the inner being of God; and that is the objective ground, deep in the life of God, upon which rests knowledge of God mediated through his own self-witness. In his own eternal being God is not mute or dumb, but Word communicating or speaking himself.

That is the Word we hear in the Holy Scriptures, for God personally resides in his Word even when he communicates it to us, and when by the presence of his Spirit he effects in us intuitive, auditive, evident knowledge of himself.

(2) It follows from this that authentic knowledge of God which derives through the conjoint operation of the Word and the Spirit, and takes root in us through the hearing of faith, is *never non-conceptual*. Although knowledge of God is essentially spiritual and requires spiritual understanding to be grasped, this does not mean that it is mediated to us in some merely spiritual, non-conceptual way which requires conversion into concepts if it is to be grasped and understood. On the contrary, just as the Spirit and the Word are indivisibly one in God, so they are indivisibly one in God's self-revelation to us and in our knowledge of him.

That is the essence of Calvin's doctrine of *"the internal testimony of the Spirit"* which has been so cherished in Reformed churches. This gives expression to the fact that our knowledge of God emanates from a testimony inherent in God. The Spirit, as Calvin used to say, inheres in the truth of God's own being. Through the Spirit and the Word functioning together we are given to share in God's own self-knowledge or self-witness. That is the Word we hear through the testimony of the Spirit, but it reaches us already in the conceptual form of Word, not as something vague and non-conceptual that we must transpose into cognitive form before it can be apprehended or expressed.

By the term "internal testimony" Calvin did not refer primarily to what is internal to us but to what is internal to God—i.e. to the self-witness inherent in God's own being, but which he makes by the action of his Holy Spirit, the unique causality of his divine being, to echo within us. Hence in forming our acts of cognition we are led by the Spirit of Truth who acts critically upon the forms of thought and speech we bring to the understanding and interpretation of the Word of God, and transforms them through his creative power so that they may be appropriate to the nature of God's self-revelation.

(3) Knowledge of God governed by the Word and Spirit of God eschews intelligible as well as sensible images. Here Calvin found he had to face a double problem inherited from the development of Latin patristic and scholastic theology.

On the one hand, through Augustinian and Aristotelian metaphysics there had grown up the habit of thinking of objective realities not directly but by means of media between the mind and what it apprehends, called "images in the middle" or "significates"—reminiscent of the doctrine of "representative perception" that was later put forward by the British empiricists. Thus it was widely held that when people apprehend or speak of things they are more sure of subjective states in their minds than what lies beyond them. The primacy that this gave to images greatly accentuated the allegorical exegesis that prevailed in the Middle Ages, but it also had the effect of accentuating the habit of the human mind in projecting out of its imagination false conceptions upon God.

At the same time, matters were made rather worse by the decision of the Roman Church to abolish the second commandment, which condemns the fabrication of graven images of God. It was distinctive of Calvin's thought, even in contrast to that of Luther, that he insisted on restoring the second commandment with its prohibition of images, and set about working out its epistemological implications. All the images we invent or ideas we devise for ourselves are idols of the mind, the products of our own diseased imagination which we project upon God. However, *God is not imaginable.* Thus theological language is not to be regarded as in any way descriptive of God, but is to be used in such a way as to *refer imagelessly* to God beyond what we can imagine or conceive. The kind of conceptuality developed in the Reformed tradition thus calls into question all the fabrications and inventions that we dream up and project upon God, for all authentic knowledge of God operates with appropriate modes of conception imposed upon by us by the nature of God and his self-communication through the Word and Spirit.

This is another aspect of Reformed theology which in our own day has been powerfully developed by Karl Barth in drawing out the epistemological implication of election as the rejection of all anthropomorphic conceptions of God. Election speaks not of the projection of the human into the divine, but of the divine into the human. As such it has the effect of securing fundamental biblical and creedal beliefs from mythologizing constructions and demythologizing reinterpretations. It is worth reflecting on the observation that modern problems about mythologizing and demythologizing have arisen only on soil where the second commandment, to say the least, has not been allowed to retain its critical epistemic force.

REFORMED HERMENEUTICS

When Calvin reversed the order of the questions asked by the medieval schoolmen, he gave priority to the question *qualis sit* over the questions *quid sit* and *an sit*. Thus instead of beginning with abstract questions as to essence and possibility, he directed theological inquiry to the nature of God disclosed in his self-revelation. In that event the question *quid sit* fell away altogether, and the question *an sit* became not a question about possibility but a critical question as to whether our modes of thought are appropriate to the nature of God.

The effect of this development was to change the character of the questions. They were no longer dialectical questions designed to clarify the logical structure of a set of propositions, but open, *interrogative questions* designed to bring to light the distinctive nature of the realities under investigation—e.g. the kind of questions directed to witnesses, events, and reports in a court of law in order to force the truth out into the open. Rigorous, interrogative questions have a critical effect upon the questioners themselves, for their hidden presuppositions and prejudgments must also be brought into question if the matter under inquiry is really to be understood objectively out of itself and in accordance with its nature.

It was just such sharp questioning that Calvin found thrust upon him by Jesus, who insisted that no one could be his disciple without renouncing himself, taking up his cross, and following him. Early in his life Calvin had learned from *De imitatione Christi* of Thomas à Kempis that it was only in allowing himself and all his preconceptions to be called utterly into question before Christ and his cross that he could be genuinely open to the truth as it is in Jesus and obedient to its directing of his mind. That was the nature of the critical, evangelical, and theological inquiry that Calvin applied to the interpretation of the Holy Scriptures, all with a view to letting his mind be opened to the compelling claims and transforming power of God's self-revelation in Jesus Christ, which they are inspired to mediate to humankind.

What does this mean for hermeneutical inquiry?

Due to the way in which God addresses us personally in the Holy Scriptures, a personal relation is set up between us in which knowledge of God and knowledge of ourselves are bracketed together. Within that situation it is incumbent upon us to put our knowledge of God to the test in order to distinguish it from knowledge of ourselves. The hermeneutical principle which Calvin deployed here was "the analogy of faith," a critical movement of thought in which we test the fidelity of our interpretation by referring the biblical statements back to their ground in the Truth of God. Thereby we let the Truth retain its own majesty and authority over us, and allow ourselves to be questioned before it so that we may be delivered from distorting it through our own prejudices.

It has ever since been characteristic of Reformed theology that it seeks to bring into play here the great Reformation principle of justification by grace in which we look exclusively to Christ—and thus away from our-selves—in order to live out of him alone. Properly understood, justification by the grace of Christ applies to the whole realm of human life, to the works of the mind as well as to the works of the flesh. Our whole person, with all our knowing and doing, is questioned before God down to the roots of our being, and precisely by being put in the right with the truth by the free grace of God we are exposed as wrong and untrue in ourselves.

That is the epistemological relevance of justification: it tells us that theological interpretations and statements are of such a kind that they cannot claim to have the truth in themselves, for by their very nature they point away from themselves to Christ as the one Truth of God. In justification, as St. Paul taught us, we "let God be true and every man a liar." No one in the whole history of the Reformed tradition has felt that critical edge of justification in biblical interpretation or in theological exposition so keenly or expounded it so fully as Karl Barth: that is precisely what Barth was concerned with in his revolutionary *Commentary on the Epistle to the Romans.*

The fact that in the Holy Scriptures we come up against the sheer majesty of God in his Word made Calvin deeply conscious of a measure of "inadequacy" and even "impropriety" in all human speech about God, even the human speech found in the Bible, for all human terms and concepts fall short of the nature of God. This forced Calvin to think through the relation of language to being in a thoroughly realist way in which he refused to identify statements about the truth with the truth itself. Like Luther he found help in the patristic principle that biblical statements are to be subordinated to the objective realities they serve, and not the other way round, for the truth of biblical statements lies not in themselves but in the truth to which they refer independent of themselves. It is thus on the objective ground of the Word and Truth of God himself that all authentic knowledge of God mediated through the Holy Scriptures rests, and with reference to which all interpretation must be controlled. Hence the Scriptures are not to be understood simply in terms of their grammatical and syntactical patterns, but in terms of their intrinsic intelligibility derived from divine relation.

For Calvin, as we have noted, proper hermeneutical activity operates through open interrogative questioning which allows the objective realities to disclose themselves to us in their own rationality and truth, so that under their impact upon our minds we may develop modes of thought and speech appropriate to their nature. It is formally not otherwise with biblical hermeneutics, but here interpretation is governed by the unique nature and activity of the living God who speaks to us personally in his Word, bears witness to himself, and allows that witness through the Holy Spirit to echo in our hearts and minds in such a way that it creates in us the capacity to recognize and obey him.

It is thus that all our knowledge of God arises, through "the obedience of faith." For Calvin this meant that faithful interpretation of the Holy Scriptures is always *theological,* for biblical statements may be understood only as we discern the way in which they are locked into the truth of God's Word beyond themselves to which they are divinely inspired to direct us.

Hence evangelical theology is built up not through systematic construction out of biblical propositions, but through such a cognitive indwelling of theologians in the Holy Scriptures that the objective truths of divine revelation become steadily imprinted upon their minds. It is then on the ground of those truths and their inner connections to which the Scriptures refer, and under the guidance of the theological instinct they generate, that theologians must think it all out for themselves and bring it to coherent expression. That is why Calvin deliberately linked together his *Commentaries on the Holy Scriptures* and his *Institute of the Christian Religion* in such a way that each supplements the other in instructing the faithful in the understanding of the gospel.

Now I should like to show something of the wider impact of Reformed thought by referring to two important points in the development of scientific method.

The first has to do with an empirical approach to the discovery of the secrets of nature inaugurated by Francis Bacon in his rejection of the view that scientific knowledge can be reached through the application of logico-deductive processes to sense experience. Taking his cue from Calvin, Bacon put forward a new mode of active investigation through interrogative questioning and obedient interpretation designed to yield knowledge that could not be achieved otherwise, by letting nature disclose itself unhindered by preconceived patterns of thought imposed upon it. It was the task of natural science, as he understood it, to interpret the books of nature by penetrating their hidden patterns and developing modes of thought congruent with what was thus discovered. He sought to transfer the kind of hermeneutics that Reformed thought had developed in interpretation of the books of God to the interpretation of the books of nature. With Bacon himself, however, that remained little more than a formal program, for he was not sufficiently familiar with the mathematical language of nature to grasp and bring to adequate expression the kind of intelligibilities embedded in the physical creation.

The second has to do with James Clerk Maxwell, who projected a "new mathesis" with which to grasp the dynamic mathematical structures embodied in nature and bring them to appropriate theoretic expression. That is what he sought to achieve through the partial differential equations he developed for a dynamical theory of the electromagnetic field. It is highly significant that at this crucial transition in the scientific understanding of nature he adapted the relational concept of the person which he found in his Scottish Reformed tradition to explain how particles bear dynamically upon one another in such an intrinsic way that their interrelations belong to what they essentially are.

Clerk Maxwell thereby not only called a halt to a mechanistic and deterministic concept of nature, but put forward the idea of the continuous dynamic field as an independent reality, which Einstein considered the most important change hitherto made in our understanding of nature and in the logical structure of science. The fact that onto-relations of this kind can be applied so successfully, although in this distinctive way, to physical realities calls for a radical rethinking of interrelations in biological and social fields, but so far little progress has been made along these lines.

Throughout history there has been much more significant traffic between theological and scientific ideas than is often realized, but the lessons that Francis Bacon and James Clerk Maxwell teach us in their different ways is that Reformed theology may still have a very important part to play in our understanding of the kingdom of nature as well as the kingdom of God.

2

DONALD W. MCCULLOUGH

✝

Holy God, Holy Church

I N 1 PETER WE FIND an exhortation to the church "to be a holy priest-
hood" (2:5), grounded in the fact that it is "a holy nation" (2:9).
Accordingly, the Creed confesses "one *holy* catholic and apostolic church."
What is the nature of this holiness?

ORIGINS OF "HOLY"

Insofar as the meaning of "holy" can be determined etymologically, the
word originally had reference to *"that which is marked off, withdrawn from
ordinary use."*[1] As von Rad stated it,

> the holy could much more aptly be designated the great stranger in the human
> world, that is, a datum of experience which can never really be co-ordinated into
> the world in which man is at home, and over against which he initially feels fear
> rather than trust—it is, in fact, the "wholly other."[2]

The Holy, then, is something utterly distinct, "the great stranger in the
human world."

In the life and faith of Israel the term "holiness" underwent a significant
development. Procksch has outlined two major streams of tradition which,
though often overlapping, are distinctly discernible in the literature of the
Old Testament: the *cultic* and the *prophetic.*[3]

Israel's cultic tradition
"Holiness," in the earliest stratum of biblical literature, is linked with the
cult.[4] The word is not found in Genesis, where the cult plays no significant
role, but it does emerge in Exodus with the story of Moses. That its
substantive "always denotes a state and not an action"[5] is shown in the fact

16

that *objects* are "holy"—the ground around the burning bush (Ex. 3:5), Gilgal before Jericho (Jos. 5:15), Jerusalem (Is. 48:2; Neh. 11:1,18), the site of the temple (Is. 11:9, 56:7), the temple itself (Is. 64:10), the "holiest of holies" (Ps. 28:2). And "the more deeply we penetrate into the priestly literature of the Pentateuch, the more common the word becomes."[6] In Leviticus we read of holy offerings (2:3, 10), the unleavened bread and the holy place where it is to be eaten (6:16-17), the "most holy" guilt offering (7:1), holy linen (16:4), the holy place of atonement (16:16-17), holy convocations (23:4), the holy tithe of the land (27:30), etc. These are the "holy things" of the Lord (22:2). As the static conception of the Holy merges with the cultic, eventually "the cultus itself comes under the threat of the purely material conception of holiness."[7] This materialization of the Holy had become commonplace by the time of Jesus, as his rebuke of it seems to indicate (Mt. 23:17-19).

The cultic was not, however, completely limited by a materialized notion of holiness. The adjective "holy" is more fluid in its renderings, and with it an important development takes place. This form of the word is used of persons. As a predicate of God, it "comes to have the meaning of divine, and thus becomes an adjective for God (Is. 5:16; 6:3; Hos. 11:9)."[8] The personalization of the Holy finally comes into its own as the substantive, which originally had a purely static connotation, is applied to the name of God. Through this process of personalization, the concept of holiness fuses with that of divinity so that finally Yahweh's holiness is contrasted with everything creaturely.

To sum up the exegetical investigation to this point: In its most primitive use, "holiness" has to do with that which is separate—first, as applied to the cult, the holy things of God are perceived as set apart for his service; and second, as applied to the name and person of God, God himself is understood as set apart. Thus, the Holy is first a *religious,* not an ethical, term. It indicates something alien to ordinary human life: either the personal being of God or those things set apart by him.

Introduction of the ethical dimension

Eventually, however, the *ethical* comes into relationship with the religious. Because God has set apart not only objects for his use but a people as well, there emerges the idea of a holy people who live according to a unique standard of conduct. The so-called Holiness Code of Leviticus (17:26) is based on the statement in Leviticus 19:2: "You shall be holy; for I the LORD your God am holy." "Yahweh's holiness demands the holiness of His people as a condition of intercourse. . . . Cultic purity, however, demands personal purity."[9]

This ethicization of the Holy reaches full bloom in prophetic theology. The prophets blast with abhorrence empty cultic ritualism and call the holy people of God to live justly by correcting oppression, defending the fatherless, and pleading for the widow (Is. 1:11-17). This emphasis on the conduct of the holy people is perhaps due to a new appreciation of the moral distinctives of their holy God. Hosea, especially, recasts the idea of the Holy in a new form. Breaking completely with the cultic element of Israel's faith, Hosea presents Yahweh in moral antithesis to humanity: "I am God and not man, the Holy One in your midst" (11:9).[10] Because God's holiness opposes the uncleanness of Israel (6:10, 9:4), it has a death-dealing aspect that causes the final "stumbling" of Israel (14:1); yet his holiness also has a creative element that makes him a tree of life (14:8). In a way that is astonishing in the context of Israel's religious traditions, Hosea links the notions of holiness and love (11:1-4). "The opposition of God's holiness to Israel thus works itself out in His love."[11] The holiness of Yahweh, as the sum of his being, is precisely the creative love that heals as it tears and brings life through its slaying (6:1):

> There can be no playing down the annihilating power of holiness, and the intensity of the threat of judgment in Hosea can hardly be exaggerated. Nevertheless, in the end it is *the incomprehensible creative power of love which marks out Yahweh as the wholly "other"*; the one whose nature is in complete contrast to that of the created cosmos.[12]

Or as Procksch summed up Hosea's view, "the antithesis between God and man consists in the very love which overcomes it."[13]

In the theology of Isaiah, the concept of holiness is central. His God is "the Holy One of Israel" (5:19, 24; 10:20; 12:6; 17:7; 29:19, 23; 30:11-15; 31:1). "The Trisagion of his initial vision (Is. 6:3) remained normative for his picture of God."[14] In Isaiah's temple experience, fearfulness and awe before the "wholly other" are surely present, but the contrast for Isaiah is *moral* in character: "Woe is me! For I am lost; for I am a man of unclean lips, and I dwell in the midst of a people of unclean lips . . ." (6:5). Isaiah needs atonement, and it comes to him from the Holy God (6:7). The presence of the Holy reveals Isaiah's state of moral estrangement and at the same time effects reconciliation.

Deutero-Isaiah develops further the image of the Holy One of Israel, filling the phrase with a content not unlike Hosea's theology of holiness. For Deutero-Isaiah the thought of redemption is central. The Holy One of Israel is the Redeemer (41:14; 43:13-15; 47:4; 48:17; 49:7; 59:20). "A connection is here established between salvation and holiness."[15] Yahweh reveals his holy "otherness" precisely in his power to save, to be the Holy One *of Israel*.

If in the context of the cult the Holy tends toward distortion through materialization, in the context of the ethical it tends toward distortion through moralistic legalism. That this, too, was prevalent in Jesus' time is seen from his rebuke of it (Mk. 7:1-23).

This survey of the Old Testament understanding of holiness reveals the presence of two important aspects of the Holy. First, a religious use of the word *holy*, quite independent from moral connotations, was intertwined with the cultic life of Israel. Here the word carried with it its most primitive etymological meaning: it signified the "wholly other," the utterly separate. It was as readily (perhaps more readily) applied to things as to persons. It indicated the complete distinction between the sacred and the profane.

But as the word *holy* became associated with the God of Israel, it underwent a personalization—the consequence of which was an equation of holiness and divinity. As Israel's God revealed himself and his will more fully, the concept of holiness progressed accordingly. As God acted on behalf of his people, showing himself to be their Redeemer, a God of love, these attributes became, by association, the characteristics of holiness. Thus an *ethical* dimension was introduced to the idea of the Holy.

So the eventual Old Testament view of the Holy may be summarized this way: the Holy is utterly distinct: *the* "wholly other" is the God of Israel; his set-apartness consists in the fact that he is Redeemer, the God of love. The holiness of God, therefore, refers to the fact that God is antithetical to humanity precisely in his overcoming of the antithesis. As holy, he is the consuming fire of love.

BIFURCATION OF THE RELIGIOUS/ETHICAL DIMENSION

In the New Testament, too, we find both the religious and the ethical understanding of holiness. The religious, for example, is obviously present in the eschatological vision of the four living creatures singing, "Holy, holy, holy, is the Lord God Almighty, who was and is and is to come!" (Rv. 4:8), and the ethical stands behind the apostolic admonition to "be holy yourselves in all your conduct" (1 Pt. 1:15). But we would expect that the union of the religious and ethical aspects of holiness, seen first in the Old Testament, would find its fulfillment in Christ, the one in whom "all the fullness of God was pleased to dwell" (Col. 1:19). Indeed, in Christ God reveals his holiness, his utter separateness precisely in his will not to be separate. But theology has not always kept this Christological focus, and the result has been a continuing bifurcation in the church's understanding of both the holiness of God and its own holiness.

Otto's Idea of the Holy
A theological discussion of the Holy can hardly avoid Rudolf Otto's influential book, *The Idea of the Holy*. "It is probably the most widely read theological work in German of the twentieth century."[16] Most significant about this book is that it vigorously champions the *religious* aspect of the

Holy in contradistinction to the ethical. Whereas the Holy had usually been identified by theologians with absolute moral good, "Otto defined the holy as an independent category."[17] Not only does he set it apart from the moral, he also separates it from the rational.[18]

To describe the Holy in its ineffable character, Otto introduces a term coined from the Latin *numen*, "the numinous."[19] The numinous is the object outside the perceiving mind, to which the mind turns spontaneously when encountered.[20] It causes the "creature feeling" to arise within, "the note of submergence into nothingness before an overpowering, absolute might of some kind."[21]

The numinous has two sides to it. On the one hand, it is the *mysterium tremendum*, the element of daunting awfulness, majesty, that which evokes awe and terror in a person—the "wholly other."[22] On the other hand, there is something attractive, fascinating, about the numinous; it has a magnetic appeal. This characteristic he calls the *fascinans*. "These two qualities, the daunting and the fascinating, now combine in a strange harmony of contrasts,"[23] together representing the content of the Holy.

That a person can perceive the numinous is due to the fact that the capacity for encountering the Holy is an inherent quality in the human creature. Otto speaks of the "predisposition," the "religious impulsion," in humanity.[24] With the foundation thus laid, Otto proceeds with an empirical study of the appearances of the Holy in its earliest manifestations (magic, worship of the dead, animism, loathing of the unclean, etc.),[25] its development from the "crude" stage to higher religions (as the numinous reveals itself, thus supplying a rational element, yet without minimizing the non-rational),[26] and its fullest development in Christianity.[27]

Why can Otto assert that Christianity is the most perfect revelation of the Holy? By "intuition" we perceive the Holy in Christ:

> The Cross of Christ, that monogram of the eternal mystery, is its completion. Here the rational are enfolded with the non-rational elements, the revealed commingled with the unrevealed, the most exalted love with the most awe-inspiring "wrath" of the numen, and therefore, in applying to the Cross of Christ the category of the "holy," Christian religious feeling has given birth to a religious intuition profounder and more vital than any to be found in the whole history of religion.[28]

Otto rediscovered the religious nature of the Holy, as distinct from the ethical meanings that had often been associated with it. In doing so, he clearly underscored one strand of biblical tradition concerning the Holy: namely, its character as the "wholly other." However, inasmuch as his discussion centered on the subjective consicousness of the person, he distanced himself from even this tradition, for in the priestly conception of the Holy the word often conveyed an objective meaning, as we have seen.

The consequent sanctification of things, the material holiness of the cult, is quite foreign to Otto's thought.

For this reason, von Rad concludes that the "considerable body of Old Testament evidence concerning holiness reveals the limitations of the great work of Rudolf Otto, in which the holy is related much too one-sidedly to man and his soul."[29] That Otto did not condone the materialization of the Holy, which Jesus later condemned, is certainly no flaw in his theology. The point is, however, that he dissolved the "wholly other" into the consciousness of the perceiving subject in such a way that the *objective* nature of the Holy—the set-apartness *extra nos*—was almost completely done away with. Though the objectivity of Israel's cult often degenerated into a very static materialism, it did nevertheless maintain the separate distinctiveness of the Holy. The Holy is set apart—even from the human consciousness.

Otto is even further removed from the ethical dimension of the Holy. Indeed, he consciously tried to distance himself from this. Yet, as was shown, this is of great importance for biblical faith, especially in prophetic theology. Otto's phenomenological description of holiness established it as an independent, de-personalized category, quite apart from any *specific* religious faith, let alone any specific God. If he finally affirmed the superiority of Christianity, it was because, in his judgment, it best conformed to the specification of the Holy enabled by empirical analysis.

But for Christian faith the Holy is not an empty, independent category; it knows only the Holy One of Israel revealed in the Holy One of Nazareth. While there is always the "wholly other" dimension of holiness in biblical faith, its separateness is filled in, as it were, with a specific content: the "otherness" of God is precisely his redemptive love. Abraham Heschel, a Jewish theologian, has correctly hit upon Otto's weakness:

> The God of the prophets is not the wholly other, a strange, weird, uncanny Being, shrouded in unfathomable darkness, but the God of the covenant, whose will they know and are called upon to convey. The God they proclaim is not the Remote One, but the One who is invoked, near, and concerned. The Silent One may be the antithesis to man, but the prophecy is God meeting man.[30]

The Holy as moral cleanliness
While Otto has emphasized the religious nature of holiness, other theologians have stressed its *moral* character. Paul Tillich attributes the association of the Holy with the morally clean to the influence of Calvin and his followers:

> An almost neurotic anxiety about the unclean develops in later Calvinism. The word "Puritan" is most indicative of this trend. The holy is the clean; cleanliness becomes holiness. This means the end of the numinous character of the holy. The *tremendum fascinosum* becomes pride of self-control and repression.[31]

A glance at Heinrich Heppe's *Reformed Dogmatics* would confirm that some following in Calvin's train indeed moved in the direction indicated by Tillich.[32] However, we cannot accurately characterize this as a particularly *Reformed* approach to the Holy. A survey of standard dogmatic works shows that the description of holiness in moral categories cuts across denominational and theological lines.[33] It is present, as Tillich noted, in later Calvinism (with its concern for cleanliness), but also in the vastly different theological framework of the Ritschlian school of Liberal Theology (with its stress on the ethical).

In any event, the Holy *has* often been linked to notions of moral cleanliness, the prophetic-ethical conception of holiness stressed to the exclusion of the cultic-religious. Thus Clarke, for example, writes: " . . . the doctrine of holiness is at the deepest a doctrine of absolute and perfect moral excellence."[34] And Hall discusses holiness under the "moral attributes" of God, defining it as his "self affirming purity . . . freedom and separation from moral perfection."[35]

Certainly this understanding of holiness coincides with *part* of the biblical witness. Moral cleanliness is connected with the Holy in both the priestly and prophetic literature, but not, as we have attempted to demonstrate, to the exclusion of the religious dimension; the "wholly other" aspect never dissolves—not even in prophetic theology. Isaiah was overwhelmed with his own uncleanness in the presence of awesome majesty describable only in the symbolic language of royalty ("upon a throne, high and lifted up . . . his train filled the temple"), angelic beings ("above him stood the seraphim"), and cataclysmic violence ("the foundations of the thresholds shook")—Is. 6:1-4. The "woe is me!" of personal imperfection came from being in the presence of the "wholly other":

> It is indeed unquestionable that the idea of the holy in reference to the concept of God strongly emphasizes also moral perfection. But as holiness is reinterpreted in the direction of morality, sin is likewise interpreted moralistically and loses its religious orientation. It is therefore, as has been stated, very important that holiness retain its original and purely religious meaning. Only when the separation between the divine and the human implied in holiness is given due consideration, and the divine is allowed to appear as unconditional majesty in relation to the human, can holiness be of fundamental significance for the Christian conception of God.[36]

THE FOUNDATIONAL UNDERSTANDING: GOD'S REVELATION IN CHRIST

By stressing either a purely religious or a purely ethical conception of holiness, such theologies find themselves in the untenable position of abstractly defining the being of God apart from his full, concrete revelation in Jesus Christ.

Otto's *mysterium tremendum* was discovered by means of empirical observation of the nature of religious experience in the presence of the "wholly other." For him, the Holy is a general, a priori category, distinct from any of its specific manifestations in human history. Jesus Christ has significance for Otto because he instantiates and fills out a previously determined— hence independent—category of holiness.

But if Jesus Christ is the Word of God incarnate, the fullest and final self-revelation of God to humanity, then must we not judge all descriptions of the nature of God's being according to the knowledge of Christ, rather than gauge Christ by the measuring rod of an a priori standard somehow disclosed through human experience? Is not Otto's *mysterium tremendum* far removed from the God revealed in Jesus Christ?

Similarly, a one-sided emphasis on the ethical dimension of holiness is equally unacceptable, for it also abstractly defines God apart from his concrete revelation in Christ. If we define the being of God by such terms as "cleanliness," "stainless purity," "moral goodness," and others taken from the realm of *human* values, do we not recast God in the human image, however many adjectives we employ to show that he is infinitely better? And however much such a God may help reinforce ethical values, is not a true understanding of his character threatened by an ethical legalism—the laws of which are legislated and adjudicated by human experience?

In that God has *revealed himself* in Jesus Christ, the event of revelation is an event of grace. Does this not mean, then, that God always stands over against humankind, the "wholly other" who *because he is separate* can give to it something it does not possess of itself—that is, a true knowledge of the Holy?

Therefore, we must look for an understanding of holiness that is grounded in Jesus Christ. Since both the "religious" and the ethical dimensions of holiness find their unity in him, we cannot be satisfied with approaches that abstract one or the other apart from him. Holiness, as we have seen, has two aspects: *complete "otherness,"* as shown in the original "religious" use of the word, and *mercy,* as shown in the "ethical" application of the word. These two strands are not mutually exclusive; quite the contrary. As the concept of holiness developed, they merged to the extent that the holy-profane antithesis came to consist fully in the overcoming of the antithesis. This overcoming found its fulfillment in Jesus Christ. In the unity of his act of grace and judgment, God's "otherness" asserts itself without compromise—an "otherness" which is nothing other than love.

UNDERSTANDING THE CHURCH AS "HOLY"

What, then, is meant by the holiness of the church? Our understanding of God's holiness must guide us in this matter, for the people of God are holy only in a derived sense, only as they in some way share in the being of

God. Accordingly, theologians have tended to single out one of the strands of tradition regarding the Holy: that is, the holiness of the church has most often been described in either a cultic-religious or in a prophetic-ethical way.

Berkouwer: the church as "set apart"

In his book *The Church,* G. C. Berkouwer attempts to understand the holiness of the church in light of Otto's *The Idea of the Holy*.[37] In so doing, he clearly places himself in the train of those who have understood the Holy in the cultic-religious categories. Berkouwer refers to Otto's description of the Holy as *tremendum* and *fascinans,* and asks whether it would not be helpful "to bring the holiness of the Church into connection with the *fascinans*."[38] While recognizing the empirical difficulty of considering the historical church in terms of the "fascinating," Berkouwer nevertheless wants to uncover the genuine *fascinans* "which rests in the acceptance of the gift, the nearness of the Lord in humility, in nostalgia, and striving for the sanctification that is seen and experienced by others."[39]

What, exactly, is the *fascinans*? "In analyzing what is actually fascinating . . . the *fascinans* has usually been connected to what is new, to something surprising that was outside our horizon of expectation, and, especially, to 'what had never been before.'"[40] Berkouwer acknowledges that the church, as guardian of tradition, has all too often been associated with the opposite of newness. But the church cannot be related exclusively to the past for the simple reason that "in the New Testament, salvation is connected with unmistakable clarity to radical newness."[41] This newness is both an eschatological hope and a present reality for the church. "The old has passed away, behold, the new has come" (2 Cor. 5:17), as Paul expressed it. For Berkouwer, then, holiness is "the setting apart of the Church *in* Christ *for* newness of life."[42]

Berkouwer certainly stands on solid ground when he stresses the element of newness in the gospel. In Christ the new *has* come. But it is not clear why Berkouwer understands holiness so completely in this light. The only apparent reason is his unquestioned acceptance of Otto's definition of the Holy. The difficulty with this, as we have seen, is that such a position allows "holiness" to be defined by an external—perhaps empirically observable—concept.

Ironically, this "idea of the Holy," which above all aims to protect its "wholly other" aspect, allows the Holy itself to be imprisoned by an alien concept—a concept, moreover, discovered and formulated in the world over against which the Holy is supposed to be "wholly other." If the Holy *is* distinct from the world and its rationality (empirical or otherwise), then it must define itself in its own terms.

The Holy has revealed itself in Christ, and what we see in Christ is a holiness marked by a distinctive otherness that is the otherness of God's redemptive love. Certainly this love in Christ is new, and its gospel has much newness about it, but Berkouwer, by limiting his understanding of holiness to this, risks evacuating holiness of its content. God's "newness" in Christ has a specific content; so also does the church's "newness."

Calvin and Macquarrie: the church as "more or less" holy

With more frequency than the cultic-religious, the prophetic-ethical approach to holiness has also been used with regard to the church. Here the church's holiness is conceived of as moral and ethical purity, as freedom from the stain of sin.

Now of course the immediate problem facing this approach is the empirical fact that the church is all too obviously not free from sin. Though *by faith* we may believe it has been clothed in the righteousness of Christ, *by sight* we clearly see the bride of Christ still dressed in the soiled garments of unrighteousness. Thus holiness must be seen to be a matter of "more or less"—a quantity possessed in certain degrees.

Calvin, for example, believed the church is holy in the sense that it is daily advancing: "it makes progress from day to day but has not yet reached its goal of holiness."[43] Because Christians "zealously aspire to holiness and perfect purity, the cleanness that they have not yet fully attained is granted them by God's kindness."[44] In Calvin's view, holiness is granted to the church by God's grace in Christ in an objective, eschatological sense, but is only a present reality in part. "It is . . . true that the Church's spots and wrinkles have been wiped away, but this is a daily process until Christ by his coming completely removes whatever remains."[45] In its concrete actuality, then, the church is *less* holy than it will one day be, and in the future will be *more* holy than it is today. That it daily advances means that something is being added to it, rather like a liquid being poured into a cup. It is being filled with stainless purity.

John Macquarrie gives a more contemporary expression of this approach. Holiness, he tells us, "is very much a case of 'more or less,' and to many it will seem that the Church has often been less rather than more holy."[46] What does "holiness" mean? It means "being an agent of the incarnation, letting Christ be formed in the Church and in the world."[47] The results will be *ethical* in nature. Unfortunately, the church will not always live according to its proper moral standards, but in the end one can hope that the specific failures will be over-balanced by the life of the church as a whole.[48]

Calvin and Macquarrie, who in other respects have vastly different theologies, share the belief that the holiness of the church has to do with its ethical life. Since Christian conduct is marred by sin, they attempt to solve the problem quantitatively, measuring holiness against unholiness, and pronouncing the former to be (at least eschatologically) the dominant characteristic of the church.

As we have seen, when holiness is defined ethically, to the exclusion of the religious "otherness" that also forms part of the biblical witness to the Holy, it risks trivialization into a this-worldly legalism where the freely transcendent is bound by the chains of moralism. Consequently, the religious dynamic is lost as the vertical of the "wholly other" flattens out into the horizontal of a proper code of well-regulated behavior. Not only does this ignore a considerable body of biblical material regarding holiness, it de-claws the Lion of Judah into a tame, domesticated pet as comfortable and familiar as old slippers. Commandments, principles, and ideals may all remain, but they are defused, safe, non-threatening; the rod of moralism deflects the lightning shock of the Holy.

When holiness is quantitatively measured against unholiness, we must ask: With what sort of scales is the judgment made? Who has supplied the measuring device? In the furnace of which—and whose—values has the weigh beam been cast? How many ethical deeds are needed to cancel out an unholy deed? Certainly the legalism implied in these questions has no official place in either Calvin's or Macquarrie's theology, and, in fact, is undermined by the rest of their thought. But the questions serve to point out the slippery slope one steps out on when defining holiness in primarily ethical terms. When it is a question of "more or less" holiness, something independent of holiness itself—a value, an ideal, a principle?—will be required to judge human conduct and pronounce a verdict upon it. Consequently, the Holy is stripped of its regal robes of transcendence and forcibly wrapped in the beggarly rags of human wisdom and morality. Holiness is then lost, for whatever else one may have in hand, the Holy remains ungraspable in the radical freedom of its "wholly otherness."

Holiness as God's gift to the church

In what does the holiness of the church consist? Holiness cannot be reduced either to a bare religious notion, indicating a formal separation void of specific content, or to a purely ethical concept, where it acts as merely a cipher for a moralism judged and directed by human reason. Biblically, the Holy is *both* a religious and an ethical term. In Jesus Christ both the cultic and prophetic approaches to holiness find their fulfillment and final unity; in him, the two have become one. As the Holy One of God, Jesus Christ is the "wholly other," absolutely free and distinct from this world, the personal embodiment of transcendent grace. And yet, inasmuch as the "wholly other" is revealed in *grace,* he is shown to be "wholly for"; what sets the Holy One off *from* the world is precisely his being *for* the world.

Two important implications follow from this for the church. First, because holiness is, in its original sense, the act of God's grace in Christ, it can never be abstracted from the event of grace. That is to say, the holiness of the church is always God's *gift* to the church. And second, inasmuch as the holiness of the church is participation in *God's* gift of holiness, the distinctiveness of its being is the very distinctiveness of God himself.

God's holiness as guarantee of the church's holiness

The church is holy *because* God is holy. If it is true that God's holiness is the event of his grace in Jesus Christ, in which the "wholly other" is revealed as the "wholly for," then this means that the church's holiness is grounded in the holiness of God. What sets God off in ontological distinction from the rest of creation is his transcendent "otherness"—an "otherness" that is, in fact, his love for the world. His gracious love is the true antithesis between the divine and the human. *Therefore,* the holiness of God is the guarantee of his grace. The church exists not in *spite* of his holy "otherness," but *because* of it. His holiness is the uniqueness of his grace by which he has constituted for himself a people for fellowship. That there is a *koinonia* of persons chosen by the Father, reconciled in Jesus Christ, and empowered for praise and service in the Holy Spirit, is because God is holy, and remaining true to the distinctiveness of his being as love, he has established a sanctuary of grateful human response in the midst of the world.

The church is holy, then, not of its own accord, but because God is holy. And in the active working out of that holiness, the church has been granted a share in his holiness. Thus the Ephesian letter, in its opening paean to the God of grace, declares that we have been chosen in Christ "before the foundation of the world, that we should be holy and blameless before him" (Eph. 1:3-4.)[49] The purpose of our election in Christ is that we should be holy before him. In other words, God has established, in the act of holiness, the reality of holiness in the midst of his creation. The holy Word has created a holy echo. The church is this holy response.

For this reason all attempts to define the church's holiness in terms of certain ethical qualities it possesses in a "more or less" way must be rejected. Where holiness is established, the reign of grace effectively draws all into its domain. If the church is holy, it is by God's grace *extra nos*; its holiness is granted in an objective way, outside of itself.

And because holiness and grace can never be sundered, the church may never point to one part of its life and say, "This is holy and righteous" (as if it needed no grace), and to another part, "This is sinfully unholy" (and thus in need of grace). For if the church is holy, then it is so only in grace, and grace is the overcoming of sin by divine love. There cannot be parts of the church that are holy and thus freed from the structure of grace, and other parts that are still sinful and dependent on grace. For—and this is the critical link in the argument—the church has its being in Jesus Christ. It is his body even as he is its head. There is no part of the church isolated from him; anything separated from his being is not the church. Therefore, because Jesus is the name and personal embodiment of God's loving grace, it follows that the *whole* church is established in grace. Being the body of Christ, it exists totally in grace, and thus totally in the sphere of God's holiness.

Furthermore, because *grace* constitutes the church, the church is *in itself* the opposite of holy love: it is sinful. Grace overcomes sin by God's redeeming love in Christ. Where grace is total, sin is total. Without the barrier there would be no need for the overcoming. If the *whole* church is constituted in Christ, if the *whole* church is thus established in the sphere of grace, then the *whole* church is also guilty of sin. Such are the implications of confessing the *sancta ecclesia*. The whole church is holy, and the whole church is sinful: *simul justa et peccatrix*.

This does not mean, though, that holiness and sinfulness are coequal sides of the church. "The holiness of the Church is light, revealing its nature; the sinfulness of the Church is shadow, darkening its true nature."[50] The true being of the church is its holy life in Christ; with him it exists in a relationship structured by grace, and thus always as a fellowship of sinners grateful for the love and mercy of God. But because the holy love of God is the eternal and victorious side of this structure of grace, the sin of the church is its passing shadow. As the church, a pilgrim people, journeys on through its historical existence, it constantly moves away from the sin of its past and toward the eternally victorious love of God.

God's holiness as standard of the church's holiness

The church is holy *as* God is holy. The exact nature of the church's holiness cannot be known and measured by some sort of external ethical standard; rather, God alone defines holiness. The shape and content of the church's holiness is revealed only in the light of God's holiness. Thus to comprehend its own nature, the church most look to *the* event of divine holiness, to Jesus Christ, in whom it shares in the being of God. In him it participates in the holiness embodied in his person.

Jesus Christ, in his being and work, unites the religious and ethical conceptions of holiness woven throughout the biblical narrative. We are driven to this definition of holiness: what sets God apart as "wholly other" is the fact that he is "wholly for" humanity. God's distinctive nature was revealed in Christ, and in Christ we see a God of gracious love. So we must assert the paradoxical fact that the genuine, eternal distinction between the divine and the human, between the holy and the profane, is precisely the love that overturns and defeats the false, passing division between God and humanity.

The implications of this for the holiness of the church are far-reaching. It means the end of all attempts to understand the holiness of the church in purely religious ways. The church's separateness is not merely a formal abstraction; it has a specific content. If God's holiness is revealed in his self-giving love for the world, and if this distinguishes his being from all others, then does it not follow that the church, as holy, is also ontologically distinct *from* the world precisely in its self-giving *for* the world? As the body of Christ, it draws its life from him —

> who, though, he was in the form of God, did not count equality with God a thing to be grasped, but emptied himself, taking the form of a servant, being born in the likeness of men. And being found in human form he humbled himself and became obedient unto death, even death on a cross (Phil. 2:6-8).[51]

As the church lives by faith in Jesus Christ, and in the power of his Holy Spirit, it is holy. This means, first of all, that it really is set apart from the world. This cannot be denied without violating the root meaning of holiness. The Holy is the great stranger in this world, utterly distinct, separate. As the church is granted a share in this holiness, it cannot fail to become different — perhaps not always visibly, but different in essence, ontologically, because it has a new being in Christ. Therefore, its true nature, whether immediately evident or not, is an alien characteristic that does not grow out of the inherent goodness of its members but is given to it. We could say, then, that the church is, ontologically, an *ecstatic* community of the Holy. Its essential being is outside of itself in Christ; its life "is hid with Christ in God" (Col. 3:3).

Yet this separateness cannot mean the church is set apart in aloofness; its separation is not the neutral self-saving distance created by a Pilate who washes his hands of the godforsaken agony of the world's Black Friday. Its separateness is the distinction of being found in the Holy One who did not wash his own hands but washed the sin-stained world with the blood of his broken body, the One for whom it was not too mean a thing even to wash away the dust and sweat of his disciples' feet on the eve of his death. The church, as its Lord, is "wholly other" as it is "wholly for." The church is not the world; to the extent that it is "wholly for" it is "wholly other." Its being is not that of the world but that of the One who stands over against the world in the judgment of his grace: separate in love *for* the world; distinguished by self-giving in a world whose engines are fueled with the crude oil of self-serving; set apart by the refreshing wind of the indwelling Spirit of the Holy in a world choking in the blinding smog of self-centeredness. The church *is* different, ontologically distinct.

> But the Church is most surely preserved from becoming the world when she embodies the servant-form of the incarnate Lord, as she becomes the suffering servant and bears in her body the dying of Christ for men, as she is willing to make the world's suffering her own. And the Church most surely becomes the sinful world when she is afraid to spend her life and seeks to save it, becomes self-defensive and trusts only to her own strength, falls into spiritual pride and holds aloof from the world. . . . [52]

Even as the being of Christ stands over against the world (separate) in the gracious judgment of his self-emptying love, so the church, as it "lives and moves and has its being in him," *is* separate—separate in the concrete love it lives out on behalf of the world. Such is its holiness.

NOTES

1. Walter Eichrodt, *Theology of the Old Testament,* I, trans. J. A. Baker (London: SCM Press, 1961), p. 270.
2. Gerhard von Rad, *Old Testament Theology,* I, trans. D. M. G. Stalker (Edinburgh and London: Oliver & Boyd, 1962), p. 205.
3. O. Procksch, "*hagios,*" in *Theological Dictionary of the New Testament,* I, ed. Gerhard Kittel, trans. Geoffrey W. Bromiley (Grand Rapids: Eerdmans, 1964), pp. 89-94. My analysis of the biblical meaning of "holiness" is very much indebted to this excellent linguistic and theological study.
4. Ibid., p. 89.
5. Ibid.
6. Ibid., p. 90.
7. Ibid.
8. Ibid.
9. Ibid., p. 92.
10. Ibid.
11. Ibid., p. 93.
12. Eichrodt, *Old Testament Theology,* I, p. 281.
13. Procksch, "*hagios,*" p. 93.
14. Ibid.
15. Ibid., p. 94.
16. Heinz Zahrnt, *The Question of God—Protestant Theology in the Twentieth Century,* trans. R. A. Wilson (London: Collins, 1969), p. 48.
17. Ibid.
18. Rudolf Otto, *The Idea of the Holy—An Inquiry into the Non-Rational Factor in the Idea of the Divine and Its Relation to the Rational,* trans. John W. Harvey (London: Oxford Univ. Press, 1923; 1977 reprint), p. 5.
19. Ibid., pp. 6-7.
20. Ibid., p. 11.
21. Ibid., p. 10. Otto prefers to speak of "creature-consciousness" rather than Schleiermacher's "feeling of dependence," believing he thereby avoids Schleiermacher's subjectivism. John Harvey points out, correctly I think, that Otto's *intention* in *The Idea of the Holy* was to emphasize the objective reality of the Holy: ". . . Otto's emphasis is always upon the objective reference, and upon subjective feelings only as the indispensable clue to this. . . . He *was* . . . really opposing the subjectivist trend in religious thought" (John W. Harvey, "Translator's Preface," *The Idea of the Holy,* by Rudolf Otto, p. xvii). Nevertheless, it is doubtful that he succeeded in his task, for the larger part of his work consists of a psychological description of the effects caused by the holy object. Otto never really breaks out of the subjectivist framework, for the Holy is always defined in terms of the experience it generates in a person's perceiving consciousness. Cf. Friedrich Schleiermacher, *The Christian Faith,* ed. H. R. Mackintosh and J. S. Stewart, trans. D. M. Baillie, et al. (Edinburgh: T. & T. Clark, 1928), pp. 341-45, where the holiness of God is treated under the section dealing with the *consciousness* of sin.
22. Otto, *The Idea of the Holy,* pp. 12ff.
23. Ibid., p. 31.

24. Ibid., p. 116.
25. Ibid., pp. 117-35.
26. Ibid., pp. 134-35.
27. Ibid., pp. 170ff.
28. Ibid., p. 173.
29. von Rad, *Old Testament Theology*, I, p. 206.
30. Abraham J. Heschel, *The Prophets* (New York: Harper & Row, 1962), p. 227.
31. Paul Tillich, *Systematic Theology*, I (Chicago: Univ. of Chicago Press, 1951), p. 217.
32. Heinrich Heppe, *Reformed Dogmatics,* rev. and ed. Ernst Bizer, trans. G. T. Thompson (London: George Allen & Unwin Ltd., 1950), p. 92.
33. See, e.g., Albert C. Knudson, *The Doctrine of God* (New York: Abingdon Press, 1930), pp. 335-36 (Methodist); Edward Arthur Litton, *Introduction to Dogmatic Theology,* ed. Philip E. Hughes (London: James Clarke, 1960), p. 71 (Anglican); Ernest Swing Williams, *Systematic Theology,* I (Springfield: Gospel Publishing House, 1953), p. 187 (Pentecostal).
34. William Newton Clarke, *The Christian Doctrine of God* (Edinburgh: T. & T. Clark, 1909).
35. Francis J. Hall, *Theological Outlines,* rev. Frank Hudson Hallock (London: SPCK, 1934), p. 90.
36. Gustaf Aulén, *The Faith of the Christian Church,* trans. Eric H. Walstrom (London: SCM Press, 1960), p. 103.
37. G. C. Berkouwer, *The Church,* trans. James E. Davison (Grand Rapids: Eerdmans, 1976), pp. 325-33.
38. Ibid., pp. 325-36.
39. Ibid., p. 328.
40. Ibid.
41. Ibid., p. 330.
42. Ibid.
43. John Calvin, *Institutes of the Christian Religion,* II, ed. John T. McNeill, trans. Ford Lewis Battles (Philadelphia: Westminster, 1960), p. 1031.
44. Ibid., p. 1032.
45. Ibid., p. 1161.
46. John Macquarrie, *Principles of Christian Theology* (London: SCM Press, 1966), p. 363.
47. Ibid.
48. Ibid., p. 364.
49. See also Col. 1:21-22.
50. Hans Küng, *The Church,* trans. Ray and Rosaleen Ockenden (New York: Sheed & Ward, 1967), p. 328.
51. Ray S. Anderson has developed an ecclesiology based on a kenotic Christology. He writes: "The conformity, then, of the Christian is to the Incarnate Son of God and not to the world, but this conformity involves a solidarity with humanity— solidarity with the world—which can be expressed as the incarnational aspect of kenotic community" (p. 569). Anderson grounds the uniqueness of the church in Jesus Christ, and thus also stresses its solidarity with the world. As I understand his argument, he presents cogently, but in a different way, the essence of what I'm maintaining in this essay. On the difference between the church and the world: "The point is, the 'difference' . . . can only be expressed in solidarity with humanity" (p. 577). See Ray S. Anderson, "Living in the World," in *Theological Foundations for Ministry,* ed. Ray S. Anderson (Grand Rapids: Eerdmans, 1979), pp. 567-94.
52. Claude Welch, *The Reality of the Church* (New York: Charles Scribner's Sons, 1958), p. 207.

3

ALASDAIR I. C. HERON

✝

Homo Peccator *and the* Imago Dei *According to John Calvin*

THERE ARE, NO DOUBT, many theologians in whose work and theological vision the *imago Dei* in humanity plays only a peripheral part. The widely accepted picture of Calvin as the very epitome of that type of theology that seeks to glorify God by debasing humanity, to flatten out all creation before the overwhelming weight of the divine sovereignty, might well lead one to expect that he would be one of those who have little or nothing to say about the image of God. Yet such an expectation would be wholly wrong. The creation of humans in the image and likeness of their Maker is absolutely pivotal in Calvin's theological anthropology. Further, his treatment of this theme concentrates *in nuce* his total understanding of humanity's place in relation to God—an understanding that is both positive and negative. The theme of the *imago Dei* takes us into the very heart of Calvin's doctrine of man as created, as fallen, and as restored to his humanity through Jesus Christ. That doctrine, as I shall try here to indicate, is much more subtle, much more dialectical, and indeed vastly more "human" than the common caricatures of Calvin would suggest.

This subject has been extensively explored by Calvin scholars in the last half-century or thereabouts. It became a matter of intense debate following the controversy between Barth and Brunner in the mid-1930s; for those on both sides could and did appeal to Calvin in support of their own views as to the possibility or otherwise of some kind of *theologia naturalis*.[1] Unfortunately, while contemporary dispute of this sort can serve to stimulate fresh interest in the thought of great figures from the past, it also has a tendency to distort the questions put to them, and to issue in less than balanced accounts of their position. As the enquiry proceeded, however, a more accurate reproduction became possible, both of the overall drive and sweep of Calvin's theology and of the place of particular topics within it. His treatment of the *imago Dei* in particular has been analyzed in close detail by T. F. Torrance in his *Calvin's Doctrine of Man.*[2] The following account is especially indebted to Torrance's study. Instead of summarizing and commenting upon it, however, I will seek to follow Torrance's example and allow Calvin to speak largely for himself.

In order to make the topic manageable within the confines of a short treatment while preserving the shape it has in Calvin's own handling of it, it seems best to concentrate on his systematic exposition of the *imago Dei* in the *Institute of the Christian Religion* I.xv. First, however, something must be said by way of introduction about his chief writings and about the general pattern of his theology.

CALVIN'S THEOLOGICAL SCHEME IN CREATION, FALL, REDEMPTION

Apart from occasional tracts and treatises, and numerous sermons, Calvin's chief theological works were his *Commentaries* on most of the books of both the Old and the New Testament, and the *Institute.* The *Institute* was first published in 1536, and after much rewriting and rearrangement attained its final form in 1559. Calvin himself saw a clear connection between it and the *Commentaries*: it was intended to give a clear, systematic explanation of the whole pattern of biblical doctrine presented more briefly and fragmentarily in the *Commentaries,* thus making it unnecessary in the *Commentaries* themselves "to enter into long discussions of doctrinal points, and enlarge on common-places."[3] This connection should not be forgotten: Study of Calvin is liable to be misled if it focuses so exclusively on the *Institute* as to leave the *Commentaries* out of sight. In particular, it can lose touch with Calvin's own conscious desire to be a *biblical* theologian rather than simply a systematizer of doctrine. Certainly, Calvin very clearly was a systematic theologian, and the *Institute* a masterpiece of the systematic genre; but he never intended it to stand independently, in majestic isolation. Certainly, too, his systematizing tendencies were both a strength and a weakness, not only in the *Institute* but in the *Commentaries* as well.

Provided all this is kept in mind, however, it is in order to go to the *Institute* for the main lines of Calvin's thought and for his outlining of central themes, and to draw on the *Commentaries* for further details, as well as for occasional modifications and qualifications of his positions. Especially on the *imago Dei,* reference should also be made to the *Sermons on Job.*[4]

Similarly, it is to the *Institute* that we must look for the overall understanding of God's dealings with humankind that characterizes Calvin's theology in general, and his interpretation of the *imago Dei* in particular. That understanding is woven into the pattern of the *Institute* itself, especially in its final form of 1559. The first edition in 1536 contained only six chapters, and was laid out thus:[5]

(1) On the Law (with exposition of the Decalogue).
(2) On the Faith (with exposition of the Apostles' Creed).
(3) On Prayer (including the Lord's Prayer).
(4) On the Sacraments (Baptism and the Lord's Supper).
(5) On the five "false sacraments."
(6) On Christian liberty, ecclesiastical authority, and political government.

Virtually all this material was preserved in the later editions, but it was massively added to and comprehensively reordered.[6] From the second edition of 1539 onward, Calvin recast the whole in a pattern more closely corresponding to that of the Creed, and by the final version in 1559 the *Institute* was divided into four books:

(I) Of the Knowledge of God the Creator.
(II) Of the Knowledge of God the Redeemer in Christ.
(III) The Mode of Obtaining the Grace of Christ.
(IV) Of the Holy Catholic Church.

This broad division indicates the general sweep of the work, but it does not yet adequately convey its inner dynamic.

Precisely what that dynamic is, has been a matter of much debate in recent times. One major difficulty is that at points in the *Institute,* and particularly in Book I, Calvin seems to be struggling with several different principles of organization of the material, and not always wholly successfully. Consequently, his argument by no means always proceeds in an obviously straight line, and it is sometimes debatable whether a particular chapter (or even block of chapters) should be put, so to speak, in parentheses rather than seen as standing in direct continuity with what precedes or follows it.[7] One must therefore beware of looking for signs of subtle planning in what may simply reflect the attempt of the author by one means or another to fit in material that must somewhat be included.

But another, and more elusive, problem lies in the nature of Calvin's own thought. It is frequently subtly dialectical, combining apparent antitheses in a bipolar scheme, which has more in it of "both/and" than of "either/or." His transitions from one topic to another, at first sight distinct, may therefore nonetheless represent a genuine onward development in his argument; there may be more of a connection than first meets the eye between the successive stages in his presentation. It is with this in mind that I would offer the following suggestions: they are far from expressing all that appears to be going in the *Institute,* but are of direct relevance to its account of the *imago Dei* in humanity.

The work is built on the primary distinction between the knowledge of God the Creator and the knowledge of God the Redeemer — as the titles of the first and second books demonstrate.[8] Calvin insists very firmly on this *duplex cognitio dei.*

Since then the Lord appears, as well in the creation of the world as in the general doctrine of Scripture, simply as a Creator, and afterwards as a Redeemer in Christ, a twofold knowledge of him hence arises: of these, the former is now to be considered; the latter will afterwards follow in its order. (*Inst.* I.ii.1)

Much more is involved in this than a merely factual or purely logical difference between creation and redemption. Calvin's account of the *cognitio dei Creatoris* is the indispensable presupposition for his exposition of the *cognitio dei Redemptoris*: hence his insistence on dealing with the former in the first place. In order to bring this further into the open, we must first say a little about the general pattern of the movement through Books I and II of the *Institute,* and then add some observations on the knowledge of God the Creator as presented in Book I.

Books I and II of the *Institute* may be roughly divided into the following books:

(I.i-v) The nature of the knowledge of God the Creator and the corruption of that knowledge in fallen man.

(I.vi-x) This knowledge restored by Scripture; the authority of the Bible as the Word of God.

(I.xi-xiii) The true God and fictitious gods: the Trinity.

(I.xiv-xviii) Creation and Providence.

(II.i-v) The consequences of the Fall: depravity and the enslavement of the will and blinding of the intellect.

(II.vi-xi) Redemption through Christ in both Old and New Testaments.

(II.xii-xvii) Christology and Soteriology.

From this it can be seen how, after he has first laid the groundwork for the doctrine of God in I.i-x and outlined that doctrine itself in I.xi-xiii, Calvin casts the narrative in the form of a vast *Heilsgeschichte* which moves through creation and fall in order then to turn to the actualization of God's redemptive will from II.vi onward. The real turning point, therefore, ought perhaps to be located at the end of II.v rather than at the end of Book I. Certainly there is a closer inner connection between much of Book I and II.i-v than the division of the Books themselves might suggest. But however this may be, the pattern shows how Calvin was concerned to set redemption against the *prior* background of the fall, and that in turn against the *prior* background of creation. Creation and fall supply the essential dramatic presupposition for the message of redemption; and they have a distinct independence from it. Clearly, the *duplex cognitio dei* is not something purely formal for Calvin; it is an axiom deeply embedded in the foundations of his theology, and with far-reaching consequences for its overall shape. Just how far-reaching can be seen if we now consider more closely some of the main elements in his account of the knowledge of God the Creator.

First, as the very opening words of the *Institute* show, the knowledge of God which concerns Calvin is intimately bound up with our self-knowledge:

> Our wisdom, in so far as it ought to be deemed true and solid wisdom, consists almost entirely of two parts: the knowledge of God and of ourselves. But as these are connected together by many ties, it is not easy to determine which of the two precedes and gives birth to the other. For in the first place, no man can survey himself without forthwith turning his thoughts to the God in whom he lives and moves, because it is perfectly obvious that the endowments which we possess cannot possibly be from ourselves; nay, that our very being is nothing else than subsistence in God alone. . . . On the other hand, it is evident that man never attains to a true self-knowledge until he have previously contemplated the face of God, and come down after such contemplation to look into himself. (*Inst.* I.i.1-2)

This formal statement could of course be developed in several directions. Not without reason have some detected in here an adumbration of Schleiermacher's "feeling of absolute dependence," or of Tillich's "method of correlation," though neither of these exactly follows the train of Calvin's own thought as he goes on to draw it out. What he wants us to recognize is that authentic knowledge of God is not merely abstract or theoretical, but based on encountering God *as he is toward us*; and, conversely, that it involves on our part *an appropriate response*:

> By the knowledge of God, I understand that by which we not only conceive that there is some God, but also apprehend what it is for our interest, and conducive to his glory, in short, what it is befitting to know concerning him. For, properly speaking, we cannot say that God is known where there is no religion or piety. . . . But although our mind cannot conceive of God without rendering some worship to him, it will not, however, be sufficient simply to hold that he is the only being whom all ought to worship and adore, unless we are also persuaded that he is the fountain of all goodness, and that we must seek everything in him, and in none but him. . . . For this sense of the divine perfections is the proper master to teach us piety, out of which religion springs. By piety, I mean that union of reverence and love to God which the knowledge of his benefits inspires. For until men feel that they owe everything to God, that they are cherished by his paternal care, and that he is the author of all their blessings, so that nothing is to be looked for away from him, they will never submit in voluntary obedience; nay, unless they place their entire happiness in him, they will never yield up their whole selves to him in truth and sincerity. Those therefore who in considering this question propose to enquire what the essence of God is, only delude us with frigid speculations, it being much more our interest to know what kind of being God is, and what things are agreeable to his nature. (*Inst.* I.ii.1-2)[9]

Where God is authentically known, what is discerned are his perfection, his goodness, his love and care; and as these are apprehended, they enable and evoke the response of reverence, trust, obedience, and commitment. Here, the glory of God and the interest of humanity meet in a relation in which the creatures recognize their Creator, and in that recognition realize their own created being as given by and answering to their Maker. This is "that simple and primitive knowledge to which the mere course of nature would have conducted us *si integer stetisset Adam*" (*Inst.* I.ii.1); it is the knowledge and service of God for which Adam was intended. Further, although the course of nature has been turned into other channels by Adam's fall, so that a new message of reconciliation is now necessary to restore that primitive awareness, it still remains a *distinct* feature in our recognition of God's favor toward us:

> For although no man will now, in the present ruin of the human race, perceive God to be a father, or the author of salvation, or propitious in any respect, until Christ interpose to make our peace; still, it is one thing to perceive that God our Maker supports us by his power, rules us by his providence, fosters us by his goodness, and visits us with all kinds of blessings, and another thing to embrace the grace of reconciliation offered to us in Christ.(*Inst.* I.ii.1)

This leads us on, secondly, to Calvin's sense of the "present ruin of the human race" and its baneful impact on our natural knowledge of the Creator. To that subject he devotes *Inst.* I.iii-v. This has the curious effect that he has to consider the epistemological results of the fall before coming to any detailed account of the fall itself, and that may be why those chapters have a markedly phenomenological tone. Calvin mostly confines himself to general observations on the more or less universal failure of the human race to profit by the available means of knowledge of God, without tracking the failure back to its cause; the omission is, however, made good in Book II.ii.12-25, where the limitations of man's fallen intellect are closely analyzed.

Significantly, Calvin does not speak in *Inst.* I.iii-v of a simple obliteration of any natural knowledge of God in our present state. There remains a *sensus deitatis* "inscribed on every heart" (iii.1), while in the universe around us and in "each of his works, his glory is engraven in characters so bright, so distinct, and so illustrious that none, however dull or illiterate, can plead ignorance" (v.1).

What the fall has caused is not the mere abolishing either of inner awareness of God or of his external manifestation, but something much worse: such a corruption and vitiation of our sense of God that "though it can never be completely eradicated," it is now like a plant that "is only capable of producing the worst of fruit" (iv.4). The fruit Calvin has in mind is that of superstition and hypocrisy, the confused "shadow of religion" (iv.4) which bewilders people "in such a maze of error that the darkness of ignorance obscures and ultimately extinguishes those sparks which were designed to show them the glory of God" (ibid.).

Nor is that the worst of it, for in this distortion of the sense of God, we are entangled in a spiral of intensifying guilt and condemnation. At one level, the fact that we do have an awareness of God prevents us from "pretending ignorance" of him (iii.1), and makes us "condemned by our own conscience when we neither worship him nor consecrate our lives to his service" (ibid.). At a profounder level, our misuse of that awareness, issuing in idolatry, adds further insult to injury:

> No sooner do we, from a survey of the world, obtain some slight knowledge of deity, than we pass by the true God, and set up in his stead the dream and phantom of our own brain, drawing away the praise of justice, wisdom and goodness from the fountain-head, and transferring it to some other quarter . . . we either so obscure or pervert his daily works, as at once to rob them of their glory, and the author of them of his just praise. (*Inst.* I.v.14-15).[10]

Through these chapters, Calvin depicts with all the eloquence at his command the corruption, vitiation, and ruin of the *cognitio dei Creatoris*. And it is only such terms as "corruption" and "ruin" that can adequately convey his meaning. It is not that nothing remains of our created capacities; it is that what remains is now so perverted as to contradict its primordial nature. Consequently, both our knowledge of God and our service to God are hopelessly distorted: we wander up and down in a labyrinthine maze, chasing the confused will-o'-the-wisps of our own phantasmagorical speculations about God, the broken and shifting imaginations that witness to the real but diseased *sensus deitatis* within us. Thus we call upon ourselves both divine judgment and the condemnation of our own conscience, testifying to our alienation from God, and at the same time leaving us "without excuse" — as Calvin repeatedly insists, in conscious echo of Rom. 2:1. We still stand in a relation to God; without it we could not continue to exist at all; but as our knowledge has turned to superstition and our obedience to rebellion, that relation has turned to one by which we are brought under divine judgment. Accordingly, that self-knowledge which is bound up with our knowledge of God must itself be set in a twofold light: this is indicated already in *Inst.* I.i.1, and stated again more precisely at the beginning of Book II:

> It was not without reason that the ancient proverb so strongly recommended to man the knowledge of himself. . . . But self-knowledge consists in this, *first,* When reflecting on what God gave us at our creation, and still continues graciously to give, we perceive how great the excellence of our nature would have

been had its integrity remained, and at the same time remember that we have
nothing of our own, but depend entirely on God, from whom we hold at his
pleasure whatever he has seen it meet to bestow; *secondly,* When viewing our
miserable condition since Adam's fall, all confidence and boasting are overthrown, we blush for shame and feel truly humble . . . it is impossible to think of
our primeval dignity without being immediately reminded of the sad spectacle of
our ignominy and corruption ever since we fell from our original in the person of
our first parent.(*Inst.* II.i.1)

Thus there is not only a *duplex cognitio dei,* but a *duplex cognitio nostri (Inst.*
I.xv.1). Even in its negative aspect, this self-knowledge directs us toward
awareness of God:

For as there exists in man something like a world of misery, and ever since we were
stripped of the divine attire our naked shame discloses an immense series of
disgraceful properties, every man, being stung by the consciousness of his own
unhappiness, in this way necessarily obtains at least some knowledge of God.
Thus our feeling of ignorance, vanity, want, weakness, in short, depravity and
corruption, reminds us that in the Lord and none but he dwell the true light of
wisdom, solid virtue, exuberant goodness.(*Inst.* I.i.1)

Further, *both* aspects of self-knowledge must be drawn in if our standing in
relation to God is to be properly grasped: so Calvin introduces the account
of the creation of humankind in the image of God with these words:

We have now to speak of the creation of man, not only because of all the works of
God it is the noblest and most admirable specimen of his justice, wisdom and
goodness; but, as we observed at the outset we cannot clearly and properly know
God unless the knowledge of ourselves be added. This knowledge is twofold,
relating, *first,* to the condition in which we were at first created; and, *secondly,* to
our condition such as it began to be immediately after Adam's fall. For it would
little avail us to know how we were created if we remained ignorant of the
corruption and degradation of our nature in consequence of the fall. At present,
however, we confine ourselves to a consideration of our nature in its original
integrity. And certainly, before we descend to the miserable condition into which
man has fallen, it is of importance to consider what he was at first . . . we shall
afterwards see in its own place how far mankind now are from the purity
originally conferred on Adam.(*Inst.* I.xv.1)

In other words, a proper appreciation of our present state can only be
attained via a recognition of the state from which we have declined—a
recognition that opens up a radically critical perspective upon us as we now
are, disclosing that we are indeed ruined and corrupted.

How, then, is this dire state to be remedied? One might expect the short answer to be, "by salvation through Jesus Christ"; and that is indeed Calvin's eventual answer. But he advances toward it by intermediate stages, as we must now show.

The third movement in Calvin's argument has to do with the fresh disclosure of the true character of the Creator, which he expounds from *Inst.* I.vi onward. Here he introduces, in the words of the title of ch. vi, "the need of Scripture, as a guide and teacher, in coming to God as a Creator." After three intervening chapters on the authority and credibility of the Bible and the *testimonium internum Spiritus sancti,* he takes up the thread again in ch. x, affirming that the knowledge of the Creator mediated in Scripture is necessary to make clear to us what we fail to discern in the created world, thought it is objectively manifest there. How he sees the connection is best illustrated by the famous metaphor of the reading glasses:

> Therefore, though the effulgence which is presented to every eye, both in the heavens and on the earth, leaves the ingratitude of man without excuse, since God, in order to bring the whole human race under the same condemnation, holds forth to all without exception a mirror of his deity in his works, another and a better help must be given to guide us properly to God as a Creator. Not in vain, therefore, has he added the light of his Word. . . . For as the aged, or those whose sight is defective, when any book, however fair, is set before them, though they perceive that there is something written, are scarcely able to make out two consecutive words, but when aided by glasses, begin to read distinctly, so Scripture, gathering together the impressions of deity which till then lay confused in their minds, dissipates the darkness and shows us the true God clearly. (*Inst.* I.vi.1)

> Therefore, while it becomes man seriously to employ his eyes in considering the works of God, since a place has been assigned to him in this most glorious theatre that he may be a spectator of them, his special duty is to give ear to the Word, that he may the better profit. (*Inst.* I.vi.2)

Consistently with what we have already noticed, this *cognitio dei Creatoris* mediated and restored by Scripture is quite clearly distinguished by Calvin from the *cognitio dei Redemptoris.* The theme here is not salvation, but rather the identification of the one true God over against the false projections of our imagination:

> The course which God followed towards his Church from the very first was to supplement these common proofs by the addition of his Word, as a surer and more direct means of discovering himself. And there can be no doubt that it was by this help that Adam, Noah, Abraham and the other patriarchs attained to that familiar

knowledge which in a manner distinguished them from unbelievers. I am not now speaking of the peculiar doctrines of faith by which they were elevated to the hope of eternal blessedness. It was necessary, in passing from death unto life, that they should know God not only as a Creator, but as a Redeemer also; and both kinds of knowledge they certainly did obtain from the Word. In point of order, however, the knowledge first given was that which made them acquainted with the God by whom the world was made and is governed. To this first knowledge was afterwards added the more intimate knowledge which alone quickens dead souls, and by which God is known not only as the Creator of the world, and the sole author and disposer of all events, but also as a Redeemer, in the person of the Mediator. But as the fall and the corruption of nature have not yet been considered, I now postpone the consideration of the remedy. Let the reader then remember that I am not now treating of the covenant by which God adopted the children of Abraham. . . . I am only showing that it is necessary to apply to Scripture in order to learn the sure marks which distinguish God as the Creator of the world from the whole herd of fictitious gods. . . . God the Maker of the world is so manifested to us in Scripture, and his true character expounded, as to save us from wandering up and down as in a labyrinth in search of some doubtful deity. (*Inst.* I. vi. 1)

So Calvin proceeds in the way summarily outlined above to sketch the doctrine of God the Creator as revealed in Scripture, and this takes him to the end of Book I. Then follows the detailed account of the consequence of the fall in II. i-v. That in turn brings him to the unfolding of the doctrine of redemption, which he introduces thus:

The whole human race having been undone in the person of Adam, the excellence and dignity of our origin as already described is so far from availing us, that it rather turns to our greater disgrace, until God, who does not acknowledge man as his own work when he is defiled and corrupted by sin, appear as a Redeemer in the person of his only-begotten Son. Since our fall from life into death, all that knowledge of God the Creator of which we have discoursed would be useless, were it not followed up by faith, holding forth God to us as a Father in Christ. (*Inst.* II. vi. 1)

What then, we may ask, is the purpose of this long journey through the *cognitio dei Creatoris*? The answer seems to lie in the method Calvin has applied through the whole development. His argument proceeds in a series of ascending steps, in which each stage not only depends on what has gone before, but also looks forward to what is yet to come. Humanity's natural capacity to know God is presented and forcefully maintained, but then immediately negated as hopelessly corrupted. This lost and ruined awareness of God is then described as restored by the Word of God in Scripture, which gathers it up again and gives it solidity. But that knowledge is not of itself adequate for our salvation: what is needed is faith in God the Redeemer. In the same way, hoever, that faith does not abolish or do away with the *cognitio dei Creatoris,* nor does it subsume it under the *cognitio dei Redemptoris.* Instead, it reestablishes it in the fullest sense by setting humans once more in a proper relation to their Maker.

Thus the knowledge of the Creator is fundamental to the entire scheme; for it is at once the point of original reference (we were first created to know and serve God), the base for the critical antithesis (we have fallen from proper knowledge and obedience, and put ourselves under judgment), and an abiding element in the resolved dissonance (we are restored through Christ to a right relation to God as Creator as well as Redeemer). There is therefore ground for the conclusion that the dynamic that drives the whole forward is itself generated by the *duplex cognitio dei,* and within it, by the *duplex cognitio nostri.*

Even if it be granted, however, that it is in this way that the theological machinery of the *Institute* is set in motion, the question can fairly be asked why we should have given this amount of space to it before proceeding to close inspection of Calvin's account of the *imago Dei.* The chief reason is, in the end, very simple: Calvin's treatment of the *imago* is itself deeply marked by the theological scheme we have broadly outlined. He relates the *imago Dei* to humanity's original creation, to the fall, and to the redemption worked by Christ. And he sees the *imago* as corrupted and vitiated by the fall in exactly the same fashion as our knowledge of God; indeed, the distortion and ruin of our natural knowledge of God is itself an essential element in the defacing of the *imago Dei.*

Thus, in a sense, we have all along been speaking of the *imago Dei* as Calvin understands it, though we have not been using the term. The connections must now be brought more clearly into the open by concentrating directly upon what he writes about it. In what follows, both the relative independence of creation from redemption and Calvin's profound sense of total depravity must be kept in mind: we have not seen the last of them.

CALVIN'S ACCOUNT OF THE *IMAGO DEI*

The imago *as created*

The primary discussion of the *imago Dei* as such in the *Institute* comes in I. xv, where Calvin speaks of the original creation of Adam, because "before we descend to the miserable condition to which man has fallen, it is of importance to consider what he was at first" (I. xv. 1). He goes on to affirm that man "consists of a body and a soul; meaning by soul an immortal though created essence which is his nobler part" (II. xv. 2). It is in defense of this affirmation that he then turns to the topic of the *imago Dei:*

A strong proof of this point may be gathered from its being said that man was created in the image of God. For though the divine glory is displayed in man's outward appearance, it cannot be denied that the proper seat of the image is in the soul. I deny not, indeed, that external shape, in so far as it distinguishes and separates us from the lower animals, brings us nearer to God; nor will I vehemently oppose any who may choose to include under the image of God that

> While the mute creation downward bend
> Their sight, and to their earthly mother tend,
> Man looks aloft, and with erected eyes
> Beholds his own hereditary skies.
> (Ovid, *Metamorphoses* I)

Only let it be understood that the image of God which is beheld or made conspicuous by these external marks is spiritual. (*Inst.* I. xv. 3)

As the immediately following remarks reveal, Calvin (as not uncommonly) has a particular opponent in mind here; and (as also not uncommonly) in this case it is Osiander, who located the *imago* in Adam's body, created as an antitype of the humanity of Christ, which humanity he saw in turn as the *imago* of the Trinity. Calvin's primary objections here are to the ideas that the *imago* lies in the body, and that humanity can image forth the Trinity, or Christ the Holy Spirit; but he is also unhappy about a straightforward Adam-Christ typology in respect of the *imago.* "There is more plausibility in the imagination of those who interpret that Adam was created in the image of God because it was conformable to Christ, who is the only image of God; but not even for this is there any solid foundation" (I. xv. 3).

Such a dismissal of a connection which many others than Osiander might hold to be valid deserves some comment. Calvin's main motive seems to be his suspicion of what was a central principle for Osiander—the Scotist conviction that the incarnation would have taken place even if Adam had not fallen, and that a direct connection there obtains between creation and the incarnation. Calvin refers briefly to this matter in I. xv. 3, but deals with it much more fully at II. xii. 4ff. It is apparent from this that the only line he is willing to draw from creation to the incarnation runs through the fall, for "since the whole Scripture proclaims that he was clothed with flesh in order to become a Redeemer, it is presumptuous to imagine any other cause or end" (II. xii. 4).

Thus the dispute with Osiander throws into further relief Calvin's sharp disjunction between creation and redemption: the *imago Dei* is to be interpreted initially in terms of man's original creation, and so of his relation to his Creator; it is not too rapidly to be drawn into orbit around salvation in Christ.[11]

Calvin develops his discussion further by rejecting any sophisticated search for a subtle difference in meaning between "image" and "likeness" in Gn. 1:26, "since likeness is merely added by way of exposition . . . man being called the image of God because of his likeness to God . . . God having determined to create man in his own image, to remove the obscurity which was in this term, adds by way of explanation *in his likeness,* as if he had said that he would make man in whom he would as it were image himself by means of the marks of resemblance impressed upon him" (I.xv.3). Maintaining his insistence that these "marks" are essentially spiritual, he proceeds to give an initial summary explanation of them:

> Accordingly by this term is denoted the integrity with which Adam was endowed when his intellect was clear, his affections subordinated to reason, all his senses duly regulated, and when he truly ascribed all his excellence to the admirable gifts of his Maker. (I.xv.3)

From these brief quotations, the fundamentals of Calvin's understanding of the *imago Dei* can be drawn out. Three points in particular may be emphasized. First, the primary ground of the *imago Dei* is *God's decision to image or mirror himself* in us: "God looks upon himself, so to speak, and beholds himself in man as in a mirror" (*Sermon on Job* 10:7f.). "Man was created, therefore, in the image of God, and in him the Creator was pleased to behold, as in a mirror, his own glory" (*Inst.* II.xii.6). The *imago Dei* is not created simply or even chiefly that *man* may contemplate it, but that *God* may reflect his own glory in man. The dynamic and relational metaphor of metaphor of "mirroring" thus betters conveys Calvin's sense of the matter than any purely static conception of "an image."

Second, and conversely, our imaging or mirroring of God involves our grateful response to God's movement toward us; it is a reflection back to the giver of thankfulness for his gifts. This sense of a rhythm of communication from God to humanity and humanity to God lies close to the heart of Calvin's theology and is fundamental to his interpretation of the *imago Dei.* Certainly he can and does often also speak of it in terms of marks "engraved" or "impressed" upon humanity, and to this extent might appear to be following other, rather different lines of thought which would lead to a more static or "substantive" conception of the *imago* itself. But if there is any inconsistency here, its extent should not be exaggerated. The metaphor of "engraving" or "inscribing" is one of his favorites, and must be given its full weight, whether it is applied to the *imago Dei* in human-kind, to the marks of God's glory in the created universe (e.g. *Inst.* I.v.1), or to the *sensus deitatis* (e.g. *Inst.* I.iv.4). The underlying analogy is that of a *written communication*: that is, of "marks" that convey a meaning beyond themselves and thus serve to bear a message. In not entirely dissimilar fashion, Calvin also describes the sacraments as "seals" (e.g. *Inst.* IV.xiv.5), functioning within a comparable trajectory of communication of the Word to faith (*Inst.* IV.xiv.1).[12] In both instances, too static an interpretation of the "engraved mark" or "seal," or one that treats them in any way as self-enclosed, can only distort Calvin's intention. At bottom, then, Calvin understands the *imago Dei* in terms of a dynamic relation between God and humanity.

Third, and in further support of what has just been said, the *imago* consists less in particular qualities as such than in a certain wholeness and soundness in which we attain our full created stature. Torrance has shown how Calvin repeatedly uses three terms to describe this, *integritas, rectitudo,* and *temperatura*;[13] and their application can be gathered from the lines quoted above from *Inst.* I.xv.3, and also, among others, from *Inst.* I.xv.4, where Calvin summarily states that "at the beginning the image of God was manifested by light of intellect, rectitude of heart, and the soundness of every part." In this connection, it is also relevant that he is at pains in *Inst.* I.xv.5 to counter the view of his arch-enemy, Servetus, that the soul is itself "a transmission of the substance of God," as well as Osiander's opinion that the *imago* consists in "essential righteousness" brought about by a "substantial transfusion of Christ into us." Against them, he insists that "souls, notwithstanding of their having the divine image engraven on them, are created. . . . Creation, however, is not a transfusion of essence, but a commencement of it out of nothing," and that "man was conformable to God, not by an influx of substance, but by the grace and virtue of the Spirit" (*Inst.* I.xv.5). While the "substance" here in view is that of God (in the case of Servetus) and of Christ (in the case of Osiander), Calvin's firm stress upon the createdness of the soul and upon the activity of the Holy Spirit also weighs against any too substantive notion of the created *imago*. It is not simply the soul per se that is the *imago Dei,* but the soul created upright and responding to the God who mirrors and beholds his own goodness in it, and so also having its own integrity in that relation to the Creator.

Two further main strands in this chapter of the *Institute* must now be taken into account: first, the ruin and repair of the *imago,* and second, the closer indication of that in which it consists. Both topics are introduced together in *Inst.* I.xv.4:

> But our definition of the image seems not to be complete until it appears more clearly what the faculties are in which man excels and in which he is to be regarded as a mirror of the divine glory. This however cannot be better known than from the remedy provided for the corruption of nature. It cannot be doubted that when Adam lost his first estate he became alienated from God. Wherefore, although we grant that the image of God was not utterly effaced and destroyed in him, it was however so corrupted that anything which remains is a fearful deformity; and therefore our deliverance begins with that renovation which we obtain from Christ, who is therefore called the second Adam because he restores us to true and

substantial integrity . . . the end of regeneration is to form us anew in the image of God. . . . Accordingly Paul elsewhere shows that the new man is renewed after the image of him that created him (Col. 3:19). To this corresponds another passage, "Put ye on the new man, who after God is created" (Eph. 4:24). We must now see what particulars Paul comprehends under this renovation. In the first place he mentions knowledge; and in the second righteousness and true holiness.

Thus it is only in the light of the second Adam that the real nature of the original *imago Dei* can be grasped. At first sight this might appear to contradict what we have said above about Calvin's disjunction between the creation and the incarnation, but the contradiction is only apparent, not real. Calvin is firmly convinced of the gulf between the two, and is indeed reduced to a certain awkwardness in justifying even a retrospective understanding of the original state of Adam in the light of Christ:

> For although Paul, contrasting the quickening Spirit which believers receive from Christ with the living soul with which Adam was created, commends the richer measure of grace bestowed in regeneration, he does not, however, contradict the statement that the end of regeneration is to form us anew in the image of God. . . . Hence we infer that at the beginning the image of God was manifested by light of intellect, rectitude of heart, and the soundness of every part. For though I admit that the forms of expression are elliptical, this principle cannot be overthrown — viz. that the leading feature in the renovation of the divine image must also have held the highest place in its creation. (I. xv. 4)

At this point more clearly than any other in Book I of the *Institute,* the framework of the *duplex cognitio* threatens to rend apart the fabric of the argument being extended upon it — or, alternatively, to collapse under its weight. We cannot here pause to diagnose the inner tension in any further detail, but must observe only that Calvin seems here to be at his least successful in distinguishing and yet holding together humanity unfallen and humanity restored, human nature in Adam and human nature in Christ. But the moment of danger passes, and his argument proceeds undisturbed to further comment upon the ruin and renovation of the *imago* and the "faculties" in which it is to be discerned.

The *imago defaced and restored*

We have just heard Calvin stating that the created *imago* "was not utterly effaced and destroyed," but yet "so corrupted that anything which remains is a fearful deformity" (I. xv. 4). Hence the need of that "renovation which we obtain from Christ" (ibid.). This renovation is in its completeness an eschatological promise rather than a perfected present reality:

> Therefore as the image of God constitutes the entire excellence of human nature as it shone in Adam before his fall, but was afterwards vitiated and almost destroyed,

nothing remaining but a ruin, confused, mutilated, and tainted with impurity; so it is now partly seen in the elect in so far as they are regenerated by the Spirit. Its full lustre, however, will be displayed in heaven. (I. xv. 5)

Here in effect the entire *Heilsgeschichte* is briefly summarized—and with a marked sense of symmetry in the sequence of the four stages: created excellence; ruin and corruption; partial regeneration; ultimate restoration. The pivot of the whole, here left unstated, is of course the redemptive activity of God in Christ. So it is clear that, so far as Calvin is concerned, it would be futile to attempt to reconstruct the *imago* simply by considering humans as they now are: what they display is on the one hand its ruin, on the other its gradual repair.

Thus the *imago Dei,* so to speak, stands over against humans as they actually are: it is set over against them as the sign of what they have lost, the sign therefore of wrath and condemnation; but it is also set over against them as the sign of their promised restoration—at least, that is, if they belong to the elect. (The symmetry of the pattern thus holds *only* for the elect: for the reprobate, only the first half of the sequence is relevant, as they remain in their sins. But it will perhaps be as well here to avoid the additional entanglements of Calvin's doctrine of the eternal predestination of God—which in any case does not materially affect his understanding of the *imago*). In the first half of the pattern, this dialectical relation of humanity to the *imago* is negative: the operative contrast is between Adam as he first was and humans as they became through Adam's fall. In the second half, the dialectic is by contrast positive: the significant antithesis is between humanity as fallen and humanity as restored in Christ, and it is this which transforms the situation from one of despair to one of hope. But— and this is crucial for Calvin—the radical nature of the restoration can only be appreciated in the light of the radical nature of the fall. From this stems his anxiety to drive home the extent of the contrast between original excellence and subsequent corruption.

In view of this, it is perhaps not surprising that he can frequently make statements about the destruction and obliteration of the *imago Dei* in fallen humanity which, by contrast with *Inst.* I. xv. 4, seem to imply that there is simply nothing at all left of it. The *imago* has been "effaced" (II. i. 5); our nature has been "overthrown and destroyed" (II. iii. 2); the wicked bear the image of Satan rather than of God (I. xiv. 18). Is this simply exaggeration as compared with the less extreme statement that the *imago* "was not utterly effaced and destroyed" (I. xv. 4), or that it was "almost destroyed" (I. xv. 5)? Perhaps in part it *is* exaggeration; but another explanation seems more likely. If one conceives, as Calvin does, that the *imago* has been radically corrupted and ruined, then whether one says that it has been *wholly* destroyed or *almost* destroyed will depend on the aspect of the matter one has in mind. There is a sense in which what is corrupted and ruined is no longer itself at all; yet in another sense we may also and just as correctly say that something still remains of what it was.[14] The extreme statements about the effacing and destruction of the *imago* reveal the depth of the perversion which Calvin holds has overtaken it, even though, when viewing from another angle, we may say that something of what it once was is yet present. Like the metaphors of ruin and corruption, they point to an alteration which is qualitative rather than merely quantitative, not simply the loss of this or that element, but the vitiation of the whole, such that even what is left no longer serves its proper purpose. Calvin's conviction that this fate has indeed been that of the created *imago Dei* cannot be understated without distortion of his whole position; and it is met and balanced by his sense that what we are offered through Jesus Christ is nothing less than *total* regeneration:

> Being born again means, not the improvement of a part, but the renewal of one's nature. It follows that there is nothing in us that is not corrupted. If we must be renewed part and whole, it follows that this corruption is spread through our whole being. (*Comm. John* 3:3)

So the doctrine of "total depravity" (cf. *Inst.* II.iii) bears directly upon the *imago Dei,* as upon Calvin's doctrine of man in general. This is of course one of the aspects of his theology which has been most criticized — not least by non-Calvinists, some of whom tend conveniently to overlook the extent to which Calvin has borrowed his teaching on this, as on many other matters, from Augustine. But the outcry is not altogether surprising. Do we not seem to have here the misanthropic pessimist, the despiser of humankind who sees the glory of God as set free only through the laying of miserable humanity in the dust?

The question is not without some justification; but if left, as it so often has been, as a self-answering rhetorical question, it does Calvin immense injustice. In effect, it isolates one theme in the complex symphony of his theology, ignores its relation to others, and treats it as if it were the whole. His devastating portrayal of the abysmal consequences of the fall is integrally bound up, as we have already tried to show, with his overwhelming sense of the immense dignity for which humankind was created—and which is offered again through Christ and by the transforming power of the Spirit of God. Again, as is clear even from his introductory remarks on human misery, want, and sin in such passages as I.i.1 and II.i.1, he is convinced that genuine dissatisfaction with ourselves is a true and proper motive for turning afresh to seek mercy and grace from the overflowing fountain of God's perfect goodness, but that those who have no sense of need will be scarcely inclined to lift their eyes upward. Further, he is adamant that "Men are stripped of their glory, not to leave them grovelling in their own shame, but to clothe them with another glory that is better. For God does not take pleasure in men's shame . . . but takes away from them their false glory . . . then they may seek true glory" (*Comm. Jeremiah* 9:23-24). All this is but part of his firm and settled conviction that "there is no salvation for man save in the mercy of God, because in himself he is desperate and undone" (*Inst.* II.iii.2), and that this salvation is indeed presented to us in Christ, whose work it was

> to restore us to the divine favour so as to make us, instead of sons of men, sons of God; instead of heirs of hell, heirs of a heavenly kingdom. Who could do this unless the Son of God should also become the Son of man, and so receive what is ours as to transfer to us what is his, making that which is his by nature to become ours by grace? Relying on this earnest, we trust that we are sons of God because the natural Son of God assumed to himself a body of our body, flesh of our flesh, bones of our bones, that he might be one with us; he declined not to take what was peculiar to us, that he might in his turn extend to us what was peculiarly his own, and thus might be in common with us both Son of God and Son of man. . . . In this way we have a sure inheritance in the heavenly kingdom. (*Inst.* II.xii.2)

While this passage does not refer explicitly to the *imago Dei,* it presents us with the vital core of Calvin's soteriology, and so fills out what he means when he speaks in *Inst.* I.xv.4 of restoration of the *imago* through Christ. The connection is made explicit elsewhere when he writes: "Christ is not only the image of God in so far as he is the eternal Word of God; but even on his human nature, which he has in common with us, the likeness of the glory of the Father has been engraved so as to form his members to the resemblance of it" (*Comm. John* 17:22).

It were better to take the "happy exchange" as the key to Calvin's thought than "total depravity"! In fact, however, neither by itself is *the* key to open all his doors: total depravity does have its distinct place in the overall scheme, along with the disjunction between creation and redemption, and the doctrine of the *imago Dei* is not, for Calvin, simply an aspect of Christology, nor does it turn simply on the hinge of the incarnation, although the *restoration* of the *imago* does.

In this connection, it is perhaps significant that Calvin for the most part seems to speak less of the restoration of the *imago Dei in the humanity of Christ* than of its restoration *in us* through the work of Christ and the regeneration of the Spirit. This is no doubt bound up with his polemic against Osiander which we have already mentioned; and it is hard not to suspect a further link with the widely-criticized Nestorian tendencies in his Christology.[15] The most revealing symptom of those tendencies is not perhaps the so-called *extra-Calvinisticum* (in spite of much Lutheran polemic), but his slide into a position closely resembling the heresy of Marcellus of Ancyra, as when he seems to imply that when God is "all in all," the humanity of Christ will dissolve, Christ will cease to exercise the office of mediator, and be content once more with the glory he had from all eternity, a glory no longer trammeled by creaturehood (*Inst.* II.xiv.3; II.xv.5; *Comm. John* 14:28).

Certainly in one sense this is a weakness at the outer edge of Calvin's Christology; but it may also have a certain bearing upon the center as well, a fitting in with a tendency to treat the incarnation as a matter of temporary significance within a wider and more all-embracing horizon—such as that of the creation, the fall, and the restoration of the *imago Dei*. The disagreement with Osiander thus leaves further questions still to be put to Calvin; but in justice it must be said that these questions can also be raised from the standpoint of other dimensions of Calvin's own theology, and not least from his account in *Inst.* II.xii of the purpose of the incarnation itself.

The imago *and the faculties of intellect and will*

In the opening words of *Inst.* I.xv.4, Calvin indicates that he wishes to go on to show "what the faculties are in which man excels and in which he is to be regarded as a mirror of the divine glory"; for, "In order to know the particular properties in which it [i.e. the *imago*] consists, it will be proper to treat of the faculties of the soul" (ibid.). He proceeds to reject alike "Augustine's speculation that the soul is a mirror of the Trinity in as much as it comprehends within itself intellect, will and memory," and "the opinion of those who place likeness to God in the dominion bestowed upon man, as if he only resembled God in this. . . . The likeness must be within, in himself . . . the internal good of the soul" (ibid.). What then is this "internal good"? In brief, "the image comprehends everything which has any relation to the spiritual and eternal life" of humanity (ibid.); or, as he can put it elsewhere, "God first formed us in his own image, that he might elevate our minds to the pursuit of virtue and the contemplation of eternal life" (*Inst.* II.i.1).

Thus the *imago* has to do with the very *life* of humanity and with the *ends* to which our lives are (or ought to be) directed. The character of dynamic, vital intentionality does not therefore disappear from the *imago* when Calvin goes looking for the "faculties" of the soul in which it consists. In view of this, we may rightly expect the faculties themselves to look less like *properties* or *qualities* than *capacities*; and such proves to be the case.

A broad hint of the direction his enquiry will take is in fact given in *Inst.* I.xv.4 when, as we have seen earlier, he finds in Eph. 4:24 two prime features of the regenerated *imago Dei*: "knowledge" and "true righteousness and holiness." His typical double emphasis on knowledge and obedience, on awareness of God and service of God, is clearly manifest here; and it also underlies his account of the chief faculties of the soul, which he describes as intellect and will. He does certainly take the time briefly to consider more complex analyses offered by "the philosophers" in I.xv.6; but while he does not wholly reject these, his feeling is that "for the edification of the pious, a simple definition will be sufficient" (ibid.). So he concludes:

Let us therefore hold, for the purpose of the present work, that the soul consists of two parts, the intellect and the will—the office of the intellect being to distinguish between objects according as they seem deserving of being approved or disapproved; and the office of the will to choose and follow what the intellect declares to be good, to reject and shun what it declares to be bad . . . the soul does not possess any faculty which may not be referred to one or another of these members. (*Inst.* I. xv. 7)

This now enables him to offer a vision of our original state:

Therefore God has provided the soul of man with intellect, by which he might know and discern good from evil, just from unjust, and might know what to follow or shun, reason going before with her lamp; whence philosophers, in reference to her directing power, have called her *to hegemonikon*. To this he has joined will, to which choice belongs. Man excelled in these noble endowments in his primitive condition, when reason, intelligence, prudence and judgment not only sufficed for the government of his earthly life, but also enabled him to rise up to God and eternal happiness. . . . In this upright state, man possessed freedom of will, by which if he chose he was able to obtain eternal life . . . in the mind and will there was the highest rectitude, and all the organic parts were duly framed to obedience. (*Inst.* I. xv. 8)

Calvin's use of the "faculty psychology" of his time is thus quite minimal.[16] What he takes from it is quite capable of being stated in other terms and with the help of quite different systems of psychology. Indeed, it is hard to conceive of any remotely adequate account of human nature which would not in some fashion include those basic dimensions of cognition and volition which he takes as quintessentially and primordially human. Here again, the markedly "existential" quality of his thought displays itself, and reinforces what has already been said of the dynamic and relational nature of the *imago Dei* in his description.

At the same time, the terms and categories in which Calvin expands and develops his conception of humanity show how heavily he was indebted to the heritage of Plato and of Stoicism. Not for nothing was his first published work a commentary on Seneca! It is, surely, from that intellectual stream that he has acquired his emphasis on reason, on the direction of the will, on prudence and judgment, on soundness as consisting in integrity and rectitude, to say nothing of his contempt for the "pigsty" of Epicureanism (e.g. *Inst.* I. i. 5-6) in both its ancient and contemporary forms.

In making this (fairly commonplace) observation, I am far from wishing to jump from it to any sweeping judgments of a negative sort upon Calvin's use of Stoic language and patterns of thought. There is at least room to wonder, however, whether Calvin's confidence that it is possible to outline the nature of unfallen humanity in this way does not betray a too uncritical acceptance of a plausible and attractive account of human nature itself which may have appealed to him for other reasons than any very patent coherence with the biblical witness. If that doubt is indeed justified, it may both reinforce what we have already said about his tendency to construct his system in distinct and semi-independent stages, and indicate where constructive criticism might find leverage.

Calvin himself is certainly also much concerned to distinguish his account of humanity from that of the philosophers. His reasons, however, need to be precisely grasped. It is not, as we might be tempted to imagine, that Calvin is a sixteenth-century forerunner of modern critics of the Hellenization of the gospel. A revealing indication of this is that, having insisted on a doctrine of the immortality of the soul which most today would regard as "Greek" rather than biblical (*Inst.* I.xv.2), he proceeds to criticize the philosophers—apart from Plato—for *not* grasping it (*Inst.* I.xv.6). His anthropology represents a fusion of biblical and Platonist/Stoic elements which he believes to be simply and purely biblical. His difference with the philosophers is of another order:

> For philosophers, being unacquainted with the corruption of nature, which is the punishment of revolt, erroneously confound two states of man which are very different from each other. (*Inst.* I.xv.7)

> Hence the great darkness of philosophers who have looked for a complete building in a ruin, and fit arrangement in disorder. (*Inst.* I.xv.8)

Since the fall humans no longer possess either an undamaged intellect or an authentic free will, for in both respects the *imago* which consists in these has been defaced. Thus even where they have rightly discerned that cognition and volition are of the essence of humanity, the philosophers have erroneously concluded that humans actually retain both in their integrity, and so they "throw everything into confusion" (*Inst.* I.xv.8).

The full systematic account of the impact of the fall upon the faculties of intellect and will is to be found in *Inst.* II.ii–v. The corruption of the intellect is the theme especially of ch. ii.13–25, while that of the will is dealt with particularly in ii.26–27, iii, and v. In introducing the topic, Calvin draws upon the traditional distinction between the loss of supernatural gifts and the corruption of the natural but is careful at the same time to offer his own exegesis of it:

> Man when he withdrew his allegiance to God was deprived of the spiritual gifts by which he had been raised to the hope of eternal salvation . . . so that all things which pertain to the blessed life of the soul are extinguished in him until he recover them by the grace of regeneration. Among these are faith, love to God, charity towards our neighbor, the study of righteousness and holiness. All these, when restored to us by Christ, are to be regarded as previously abolished. On the

other hand, soundness of mind and integrity of heart were at the same time withdrawn, and it is this which constitutes the corruption of the natural gifts. For although there is still some residue of reason and of judgment as well as of will, we cannot call a mind sound and entire which is weak and immersed in darkness. As to the will, its depravity is but too well known. Therefore since reason, by which man discerns between good and evil, and by which he understand and judges, is a natural gift, it could not be entirely destroyed; but being partly weakened and partly corrupted, a shapeless ruin is all that remains. . . . In like manner the will, because inseparable from the nature of man, did not perish, but was so enslaved by depraved lusts as to be incapable of one righteous desire. (*Inst.* II.ii.12)

Thus it is not going too far to say that the repair of the natural gifts cannot be accomplished without the restoration of the supernatural as well, for in them the natural find their goal and completion. Both have their essential place in the *imago Dei,* which properly subsists only where humans receive both kinds of gift from God, and by them respond in faith, love, and obedience, thus realizing the purpose of their own making in the image and likeness of the Creator. The "natural" which remains after the fall is truncated and incomplete, and does not fully correspond to the "natural" of the original creation.[17]

This does not, however, mean that there is nothing in any sense good or noble about fallen humanity. Calvin is well aware that both intellectual and moral greatness are to be seen in us, and takes some pains to show that this is not inconsistent with the radical and total depravity of our nature (see e.g. *Inst.* II.ii.12ff.; II.iii.3ff.). What he insists is that all these achievements of mind and virtue fail to attain the heights for which we are intended, that they are to be ascribed to the grace of God continuing to work even in fallen creatures, and overall, that they do not disprove the essential vitiation of nature by the fall. At best, they point crookedly to the glorious original from which we have catastrophically declined. So he is far from denying some capacity in us, as we are, to attain to genuine knowledge of truth and to seek after goodness; but he is convinced that these do not reach far or high enough to work our salvation or repair the ruin of our nature. This must be looked for in another quarter entirely, in Christ and not in ourselves. We dare not pride ourselves upon the broken and shapeless remains of the *imago Dei* which we can seek to trace in our own being, but must look for its remaking from beyond. Otherwise, so far as Calvin is concerned, we simply repeat and reinforce the sin of Adam:

. . . he who is most deeply abased and alarmed by the consciousness of his disgrace, nakedness, want and misery, has made the greatest progress in the knowledge of himself. Man is in no danger of taking too much from himself, provided he learns that whatever he needs is to be recovered in God. But he cannot arrogate to himself one particle beyond his due without losing himself in vain confidence and, by transferring divine honour to himself, becoming guilty of the greatest impiety. And assuredly, whenever our minds are seized with a longing to possess a somewhat of our own which may reside in us rather than in God, we may rest assured that the thought is suggested by no other counsellor than he who enticed our first parents to aspire to be like gods, knowing good and evil. (*Inst.* II. ii. 10)

There is, however, another side to this same matter, and it is fitting to conclude this account of the *imago* presented by Calvin by giving it a suitably prominent place. We dare not look to ourselves and rest in what we see there; we must look to God and to God's paternal mercy in Christ. But how should we look on our neighbor? Does the *imago Dei*, even ruined and corrupted, have anything to tell us here? Calvin is in no doubt that it does — that we must look on our fellow humans with eyes that recognize the *imago Dei* in them, because that is how God wishes us to see them. Where the angle of vision is changed in this way, it is no longer of the ruin and destruction of the *imago* that we must speak, but of the dignity with which it surrounds and ennobles even the least and most unworthy, for there the discernment of the *imago Dei* is not an inducement to pride but to love, and as such is free from the dangers Calvin is so concerned to avoid. Several passages could be gathered from his writings on this, but it will suffice here to quote the fullest and most detailed that I have found:

the Lord enjoins us to do good to all without exception, though the greater part, if estimated by their own merit, are most unworthy of it. But Scripture subjoins a most excellent reason when it tells us that we are not to look to what men in themselves deserve, but to attend to the image of God which exists in all, and to which we owe all honour and love. But in those who are of the household of faith, the same rule is to be all the more carefully observed, inasmuch as that image is renewed and restored in them by the Spirit of Christ. Therefore, whoever be the man that is presented to you as needing your assistance, you have no ground for declining to give it to him. Say he is a stranger. The Lord has given him a mark which ought to be familiar to you, for which reason he forbids you to despise your own flesh. Say he is mean and of no consideration. The Lord points him out as one whom he has distinguished by the brightness of his own image. Say that you are bound to him by no ties of duty. The Lord has substituted him, as it were, into his own place, that in him you may recognise the great obligations under which the Lord has laid you to himself. Say that he is unworthy of your least exertion on his account. Yet the image of God by which he is recommended to you is worthy of yourself and all your exertions. But if he not only merits no good, but has provoked you by injury and mischief, still this is no good reason why you should not embrace him in love, and visit him with acts of love. . . . In this way only we attain to what is not to say difficult, but altogether against nature—to love those that hate us, render good for evil and blessing for cursing, remembering that we are not to reflect upon the wickedness of men, but look to the image of God in them, an image which by covering and obliterating their faults, should by its dignity allure us to love and embrace them.(*Inst.* III.viii.6)

Whatever reservations may be advanced against Calvin's treatment of the *imago Dei*—and several have at least been hinted at in this essay—here, surely, he touches the heart of the matter.

NOTES

1. The reverberations of this debate can be conveniently traced in Edward A. Dowey, *The Knowledge of God in Calvin's Theology* (New York: Columbia Univ. Press, 1952; 2nd ed. with a new preface, 1965). This aspect of Calvin's thought is also treated by T. H. L. Parker, *The Doctrine of the Knowledge of God: A Study in the Theology of John Calvin* (Edinburgh: Oliver & Boyd, 1952).

2. T. F. Torrance, *Calvin's Doctrine of Man* (London: Lutterworth, 1949); cf. also R. S. Wallace, *Calvin's Doctrine of the Christian Life* (Edinburgh: Oliver & Boyd, 1959), pp. 103ff. & 148ff.

3. Calvin's *Epistle to the Reader,* prefaced to the second edition of 1539 and again, in expanded form, to the final edition of 1559. An illuminating account of the method Calvin employed in thus separating the *Institute* from the *Commentaries* is given by T. H. L. Parker, *Calvin's New Testament Commentaries* (London: SCM Press, 1971), ch. 3. The translation followed (with some slight modifications) in this paper is that of Henry Beveridge (Edinburgh: T. & T. Clark, 1863).

4. On the *imago* as treated in the *Sermons on Job,* see Torrance, *Calvin's Doctrine of Man,* ch. 6.

5. The text is given in Calvin's *Opera Selecta,* ed. P. Barth and W. Niesel (Munich: Chr. Kaiser, 1926ff.), I, pp. 36-280.

6. A detailed account of the different editions and the changes made from 1536 to 1559 is given by Barth and Niesel, *Opera Selecta,* III, pp, vi-1.

7. So, for instance, Dowey plausibly argues (*Knowledge of God,* p. 86f.) that *Inst.* I.vii-ix "appear . . . as an excursus or footnote to chapter vi. They could be dropped, assuming that the problem of the authority of Scripture were dealt with elsewhere, without affecting the course of the argument between vi and x." Throughout his study, Dowey makes many suggestive and helpful comments about the structure and movement of the argument through the first books of the *Institute*; and while I have not necessarily followed his specific interpretations, they have stimulated such personal reflections as I offer here.

8. Cf. E. A. Dowey, "The Structure of Calvin's Thought as Influenced by the Two-Fold Knowledge of God," in *Calvinus Ecclesiae Genevensis Custos,* ed. W. Neuser (Frankfurt: Peter Lang, 1984), pp. 135-148.

9. Cf. also *Inst.* I.v.9: ". . . the knowledge of God which we are invited to cultivate is not that which, resting satisfied with empty speculations only flutters in the brain, but a knowledge which will prove substantial and fruitful wherever it is duly perceived and rooted in the heart. The Lord is manifested by his perfections. When we feel their power within us, and are conscious of their benefits, the knowledge must impress us much more vividly than if we merely imagined a God whose presence we never felt. Hence it is obvious that in seeking God, the most direct path and the fittest method is not to attempt with presumptuous curiosity to pry into his essence, which is rather to be adored than minutely discussed, but to contemplate him in his works, by which he draws near, becomes familiar, and in a manner

communicates himself to us." This stress both on the *solidity* of genuine knowledge of God and on the necessity of *direct communication* from him is one of the most characteristic features of Calvin's theology. It appears again when he proceeds, having outlined the doctrine of Christ in Book II, to "the mode of obtaining the grace of Christ"; so he begins Book III: "We must now see in what way we become possessed of the blessings which God has bestowed on his only begotten Son, not for private use, but to enrich the poor and needy. And the first thing to be attended to is that so long as we are without Christ and separated from him, nothing which he suffered and did for the salvation of the human race is of the least benefit to us. To communicate to us the blessings which he received from the Father, he must become ours and dwell in us. . . . The whole comes to this, that the Holy Spirit is the bond by which Christ effectually binds us to himself" (*Inst.* III.i.1).

10. This vigorous polemic against idolatry is another of Calvin's favorite themes. Like his doctrine of the authority of Scripture, it has of course a particular bearing upon the debates of the Reformation. Calvin's understanding of the nature and authority of Scripture is well laid out by Dowey in *Knowledge of God*, pp. 86-147.

11. Certainly Calvin does say at II.xii.6 that at Adam's creation, "Christ was even then the image of God, and accordingly whatever excellence was engraven in Adam had its origin in this, that by means of the only begotten Son he approximated to the glory of his Maker. Man therefore was created in the image of God, and in him the Creator was pleased to behold as in a mirror his own glory. To this degree of honour he has exalted by the kindness of the only begotten Son." But as he goes on to make clear in this same passage—which is all directed against Osiander—he rejects the inference "that the primary type of the image of God was *in the man* Christ" (my italics), whereas Osiander believes "that man was created in the image of God inasmuch as he was formed *on the model of the future Messiah*" (ibid.). For Calvin, the Christ who is in the strict and proper sense the image of the Father is *the eternal Son*, and only secondarily *the man Jesus Christ*—cf. *Comm. John* 17-22, which is quoted *infra*—and the creation of Adam is related to the former, not the latter.

12. Here too he can speak of "inscribing" and "impressing" of sacramental signs by the Word—*Inst.* IV.xiv.18—and of the Spirit as "engraving assurance upon our minds"—*Inst.* IV.xiv.10.

13. Torrance, *Calvin's Doctrine of Man*, p. 44.

14. To say this is not necessarily to reject Barth's riposte in *Nein!* (ET in E. Brunner and K. Barth, *Natural Theology* [London: Geoffrey Bles, 1946], p. 93): "Is the change in the human situation through the revelation of God, of which I Corinthians and Galatians 2 speak, really a *reparatio*, a restoration in the sense in which Brunner employs it when he says, 'It is not possible to repair what no longer exists. *But it is possible to repair a thing in such a way that one has to say this has become quite new*'? [Emphasis mine.] I must confess that I am quite flabbergasted by this sentence. Had one not better at this point break off the discussion as hopeless? Or should one hope for an angel from heaven who would call to Brunner through a silver trumpet of enormous dimensions that II Corinthians 5:17 is not a mere phrase, which might just as well apply to a motor-car that has come to grief and been successfully 'repaired'?" Brunner found in Calvin a rather stronger continuity on the one hand between the created and the fallen *imago*, and on the other between the fallen and restored *imago*, than Calvin's own position could support. Barth rightly saw that the transformation in each case is more radical than that—though in the controversy he laid much less weight than Brunner on the interpretation of Calvin himself.

15. For a summary discussion, see Charles A. M. Hall, *With the Spirit's Sword: The Drama of Spiritual Warfare in the Theology of John Calvin* (Zürich: EVZ Verlag; Richmond, VA: John Knox Press, 1968), pp. 86-90; also pp. 207-209 on the apparent eventual evaporation of the humanity of Christ.

16. Cf. Hall, *With the Spirit's Sword,* pp. 46-50.

17. Similarly, "man is corrupted by a natural viciousness, but not by one which proceeded from nature. In saying that it proceeded not from nature, we mean that it was rather an adventitious event which befell man, than a substantial property assigned to him from the beginning. We, however, call it *natural* to prevent anyone from supposing that each individual contracts it by depraved habit, for in fact all receive it by a hereditary law" (*Inst.* II.i.11).

4

CHRISTIAN D. KETTLER

✝

The Atonement as the Life of God in the Ministry of the Church

IN THE HEART OF his seminal essay, "A Theology for Ministry," Ray S. Anderson states the guiding thesis of his theology of ministry: "Ministry precedes theology and produces theology, not the reverse."[1] The various contributions that Dr. Anderson has made to the continuing discussion on the integration of theology and ministry consistently reflect this thesis. The theologian does not construct a speculative mansion which the church should be forced to inhabit. There is no intellectually snobbish lordship which theology should possess to determine the ministry of the church.

Anderson can be misunderstood, however, if one does not pay close attention to what he means by "ministry": "Ministry is determined and set forth by God's own ministry of revelation and reconciliation in the world, beginning with Israel and culminating in Jesus Christ and the Church."[2] So Anderson's call is not to surrender to the banalities of an obsession with techniques, fueled by pop psychology and the theologically questionable belief that the "consumers" in the church and in the world know what they "want" and so the church, as a good supplier, should deliver the product according to supply and demand. No; the ordered priority of ministry before theology for Anderson means that God's own ministry, revealed by his act of grace, first in Israel, then fulfilled in Jesus Christ, is an act of revelation and reconciliation on behalf of a needy world. God has his own ministry, and the church as the body of Christ is simply obligated to enter into and participate in the continuing ministry of Jesus Christ out of God's grace alone.

Theology then follows this participation in the ministry of God. The purpose of this essay is to examine theologically one aspect of that ministry of God, the ministry of atonement from the sins of the world, and to seek to allow the reality of God's ministry of atonement and reconciliation to inform and shape the contours and content of the ministry of the church—

what the church is to do and say. Several "dogmatic postulates" will be offered and then tested in order to suggest some modest, yet it is hoped important, conclusions.

Much of what follows seeks to build upon the provocative and evangelical epistemology of Karl Barth and Thomas F. Torrance. Wilhelm Pauck remarks that Barth's statement, "God is known by God and by God alone" is the essence of Barth's theological epistemology.[3] The statement does guide us into some of the far-reaching implications of the theology of Karl Barth, many of which are reflected in Ray Anderson's pioneering work on theology and ministry. The knowledge of God is, first of all, God's own knowledge. God possesses it. It cannot be the rightful possession of anyone else. If God is to be treated as God, it must be on his initiative if we are to truly know him.

Thus theological epistemology is always an epistemology of grace. Knowledge of God, therefore, is not gained by "works righteousness," by our attempts to know God, in the same way that salvation is not gained by the merit of our works (Eph. 2:8-9). Knowledge of God, as well as salvation, comes by God's initiative, God's grace, alone. In recent years, Thomas F. Torrance has shown repeatedly how this way of thinking is in harmony with the Einsteinian scientific method which allows the nature of what we seek to know determine the means by which we know it.[4] The connection to Anderson's thesis, "Ministry precedes and produces theology, not the reverse," is obvious: Ministry involves nothing less than the knowledge of God, if it is to be the ministry of Jesus Christ.

Despite Barth's notoriety, his contribution has been met, unfortunately, by responses similar to Wilhelm Pauck's: "What a strange idea it is, what a disturbing idea to be entertained and explained by a human mind!"[5] For as Pauck explains, this can only mean either that God is unknowable, since there is no "point of contact" between God and humanity, or that a human being can make the claim that his thoughts are identical to God's. The better alternative, Pauck says, is to construct a theology closely critiqued by the historical relativity of all theology, in the mode of Adolf von Harnack.[6] The *actuality* of the revelation of God is to become predicated on the successful investigation into the *possibility* of knowing God. Given the problem of the revelation of God in a pluralistic world with any number of highly divergent claims of revelation, from the Ayatollah to Jim and Tammy Bakker, such a historical critical approach is very attractive to the thinking person.

But as safe as this may sound for the academic, when we consider such topics as the relationship of the atonement to the ministry of the church, such a theology is found wanting. The preacher, for example, does not have the luxury of purely cold historical analysis, if one is to be a preacher of the Christian gospel. One cannot and should not qualify and relativize to death each utterance one makes, if God has truly revealed himself in Jesus Christ.[7] Christianity has never meant anything less than God's self-revelation when it has continued to be Christianity. "Ministry precedes theology"!

The *actuality* of revelation means a great deal when we consider the reality of reconciliation and atonement.[8] For if we believe that "God is known by God and by God alone," we must approach the question of what God *did* for us based on *who* he has revealed himself to be. This, in turn, can set the church free to determine its ministry based on *who* God is and what he has *actually* done, rather than what would sell in the marketplace of ideas and religions and in "self-help" books.

My proposal is that such a theological epistemology allows the doctrine of the atonement to be centered on the healing effect of the very *life* of God communicated to humanity in the life, death, and resurrection of Jesus Christ. This life cannot be known by us except through God's initiative. "God is known by God and by God alone"! And the Christian doctrine of the atonement is based on nothing less than this, for it seeks to penetrate to the root of the human dilemma: human sin, which affects not just our behavior but even our ontological core.

Certainly, other emphases on the atonement have been proposed in the history of the church. But purely external, forensic pronouncements of atonement, based on Christ paying the penalty for our sins, or a political restructuring under the idea of "liberation," are inadequate for the sake of the church's concrete ministry to actual people in actual crises of life. Such a ministry needs to be based on the *actuality* of God's revelation of grace. Only such a ministry is worthy of participating in the continual ministry of the Incarnate Son, Jesus Christ.

Both theological principles and ministry concerns will guide this investigation, which proceeds from four "dogmatic postulates" suggesting the actuality of God's gracious revelation and reconciliation in Christ. This is in order to tie more closely together who the church is and what it does with who God is and what he does, while maintaining Barth's dictum, "God is known by God and by God alone." These four assumptions are entitled: (1) "The heart of the Father as the beginning of the atonement," (2) "The incarnation of the Son as the ontological reality of the atonement," (3) "The vicarious humanity of Christ as the atoning Godward response on behalf of humanity," and (4) "The forgiveness of sins as the vivifying center of the actualization of the atonement in the life and ministry of the church." The implications of the doctrine of the atonement for the ministry of the church will be explored through use of a particular case study as a matrix in which to test these dogmatic postulates. If the ministry of Jesus Christ continues even today, indeed if revelation is *actual*, not just *possible*, then that ministry addresses the crucial pastoral issues confronting the ministry of the church. This is done not to offer facile answers to complicated situations, but to suggest how the ministry of Jesus Christ informs and directs our ministry in the church.

Our case involves Sondra, a woman of forty three who is wrestling with the effects of sexual abuse.[9] Starting at age five and continuing through age eleven, she was sexually abused by her father. When she was eleven her father was taken to court for abusing not only her but also her two brothers.

From ages eleven through twelve Sondra lived an outwardly normal life with her mother and brothers. But inwardly, feelings of shame, guilt, and family disgrace were pervasive. Sondra received no help during these years. After she left home for college she knew that she needed professional care.

For the last twenty five years Sondra has sought help from both psychologists and spiritual leaders. About ten years ago, her father died. A hard and unforgiving spirit, however, still burns within her.

Sondra has been married for twenty two years and has a teenage daughter. She sees no hope, no release from her memories. Her pastoral counselor at the local mental health clinic has told her that she needs to "become more spiritual."

What has the doctrine of the atonement to say to Sondra? And how can that truth be mediated to Sondra through the life and ministry of the church?

THE HEART OF THE FATHER AS THE BEGINNING OF THE ATONEMENT

The atonement does not begin with the willingness of the Son to suffer and die, but with the heart of the Father (J. McLeod Campbell), the heart which refuses to let the world slide into the abyss of destruction. Thus, there is one divine purpose of love which is expressed in the Father's desire to rescue humanity from its own devices.

The *actuality* of revelation and reconciliation as the ministry of God begins with Jesus Christ as the Son of God. Why not the Father? Why not the Holy Spirit? The *incarnation* of the Son makes the difference. The true "point of contact" between God and humanity is the man Christ Jesus (1 Tm. 2:5). But this Son is dependent upon the Father, according to the Gospel record. In the Fourth Gospel Jesus proclaims, "Truly, truly, I say to you, the Son can do nothing of his own accord, but only what he sees the Father doing" (Jn. 5:19; cf. Jn. 5:17, 26, 30, 36; 6:37, 44, 57; 8:16, 18, 29; 10:18; 12:49). The revelation of the Son immediately becomes the revelation of the Father. There is a mutual knowledge between the Father and the Son: "No one knows the Son except the Father, and no one knows the Father except the Son *and anyone to whom the Son chooses to reveal him*" (Mt. 11:27). Clearly this passage shows that not only is the incarnation our access to the Son, but also that the incarnation of the Son *truly reveals the Father.*

In some theories stressing the penal aspect of the atonement, the Son paying the penalty for humanity's sins at the hand of the Father's wrath has been emphasized to the point of denying de facto the unity of being between the Father and the Son. For some lay people this has had disastrous results.

This was true among the parishioners of the church of John McLeod Campbell, the great nineteenth-century Scottish theologian. McLeod Campbell had seen his people develop an idea of a great chasm between the wrathful Father and the innocent Son. In essence, God was the wrathful avenger of the sin which dishonored him and Jesus the innocent victim, appeasing this wrath. This created among McLeod Campbell's parishioners an unrelieved fear of God the Father in contrast to the loving sacrifice of the Son. How could one be sure that the awesome wrath of the Father would be stayed?

Admittedly, this was a greater problem in the nineteenth century than it would be in most churches today. However, McLeod Campbell suggests a model of how a pastor becomes a theologian in order to provide *theological* answers to the problems of his people.

In response to his congregation's anxieties, McLeod Campbell worked out his view of the atonement in his major work, *The Nature of the Atonement.*[10] He perceived that a dualism had been created by the tradition of penal substitution so that the wrath of the Father was viewed in utter antithesis to the loving, willing innocence of the Son. What had purported to be an orthodox doctrine in effect denied the *homoousion* of the Nicene Creed, that the Son is of one substance with the Father. The New Testament, McLeod Campbell argued, presents the Son as the manifestation of the heart of the Father, a heart that refuses to allow humanity to drown in its own mire but is determined to rescue his creation. This is what salvation is all about:

> The question of salvation is seen to be sharply the question of participation in that favour as it is an outgoing of a living love, the love of the Father's heart, and not as the mere favourable sentence of a judge and a ruler, setting the mind at ease in reference to the demands of the law of His moral government.[11]

What of Sondra and her past? If God is simply the Judge and Ruler, how can the forgiveness of Christ become for her a forgiveness that breaks through even the encrusted pain and bitterness of the years? From the beginning, the act of the atonement comes from the heart of the Father, so that the importance of the *homoousion* and its relation to the atonement for pastoral care cannot be overestimated. The God who meets Sondra in the face of Jesus Christ with forgiveness and mercy is the same as God the

Father.[12] There is no "God behind God." As McLeod Campbell states, there is one divine purpose of love seen in the relationship between the incarnation and the atonement.[13]

The objection is often raised, however, that it is the demand of God as Judge of sin that gives the atonement the force of a moral imperative. The judge has pronounced the verdict, so *the law* should lead one in living the Christian life.[14]

At first glance, it does appear that the judge has more "power" over the "convicted criminal" than the accused's "father" does. But is this really so? R. S. Franks commends McLeod Campbell for his insight at this point. In fact, states Franks, the demand of a judge is really less morally demanding than the demand of the father. The judge is only interested in justice being done. But the father presents a continual demand on his son because of that filial relationship. The command of a parent who is known by the child to love the child dearly, who has provided for the child in many sacrificial, costly ways, has an infinitely greater influence on the child's behavior than the cold letter of the law could ever hope to have. The heavenly Father, therefore, demands nothing less than "a complete and perfect holiness of life."[15]

This is not to rule out the Father's wrath against sin and the rightful place of the law in the Christian's life. Nonetheless, the "filial" *precedes* the "judicial" in McLeod Campbell's thought, as James Torrance observes.[16] Apart from this sense of the *origin* of the atonement in the heart of the Father, can the church's preaching, teaching, or pastoral care hope to break through Sondra's bitterness?

But, it might be asked, would a theology based on God as "Father" be truly helpful to a woman like Sondra, who has been abused by her own father? Would it not be better for Sondra simply to refer to God as "Creator" or even "Mother," as many have suggested?

A theological epistemology such as Barth's ("God is known by God and by God alone") can help us to recognize this problem while avoiding an answer that may create unwanted consequences. "God is known by God and by God alone" prohibits us from reading into God any idea of God, including our ideas of "father." This needs to be communicated to Sondra — and it can be, if we maintain that the knowledge of God the Father originates from our knowledge of the Son, Jesus Christ (Mt. 11:27). To read maleness into God because he is called Father is only to read *our* ideas of fatherhood into God. The second commandment, along with the rest of the biblical tradition, clearly forbids this (Ex. 20:4; cf. Dt. 4:15-16). Again, an epistemology of grace has great implications for what extent the healing power of the atonement can work in the personal crises of men and women. At stake here is the importance of "incarnate particularity," as Roland M. Frye puts it.[17] T. F. Torrance makes the case clearly that what is at stake is nothing less than a sure knowledge of God:

We cannot know God behind his back, as it were, by stealing knowledge of him, for we may know him only in accordance with the way he has actually taken in revealing himself to us. Hence, as Hilary has shown so well, we can only make use of the analogies and terms which God himself has posited, and which he has linked to his self-revelation so that they point beyond themselves. It is in this way we interpret expressions like 'father' and 'son'.[18]

Sondra needs to know the healing power of the Son—the genuine, historical Jesus of Nazareth, the one who reveals the heart of God the Father. A strictly penal view of the atonement, as we have seen, can project a purely forensic view of God the Father as only a judge. The solution is not to abandon the analogy, but to allow the biblical witness to define its content, as McLeod Campbell recognized. This is also true concerning the "maleness" of God the Father.

THE INCARNATION OF THE SON AS THE ONTOLOGICAL REALITY OF THE ATONEMENT

The atonement is not simply one moment of time on the cross, but the "develop-ment" of the incarnation, of the heart of the Father revealed in the Son, who has partaken of human flesh. Therefore, atonement is essentially the ontological communication of the life of God, a life that gives itself in suffering love, even to the point of death on a cross.

The heart of the Father has healing and atoning effects when it lives in the life of the Son. As McLeod Campbell puts it so well, the atonement is the "development" of the incarnation in an "indissoluble way," as a "natural, not arbitrary relationship" between the Father and the Son.[19] What we have revealed here is nothing less than the stupendous fact that, in the incarna-tion of the Son, humanity participates in "the history of the inner life of His Godhead" (Barth).[20] God communicates his own life in order to heal broken humanity. Again, "God is known by God and by God alone." As we have seen, to Wilhelm Pauck this is a "strange and disturbing" idea, but to hurting people like Sondra it could be the beginning of the way back to emotional and spiritual health.

Despite much of the current interest in "spiritual formation," "the inner life," and spiritual "disciplines," which too often focuses on our own piety, perhaps the greatest resource for spiritual formation is found rather in *God's* "inner life." It is the "inner life" of God as Trinity, one God in three ways of being—Father, Son, and Holy Spirit—that has been revealed to us in the Christian gospel. Indeed, has that not always been the amazing significance of the doctrines of the Trinity and the incarnation? Healing and reconcilia-tion come when we participate by the Spirit through faith in this "inner life" of the triune God, made manifest to us by the incarnation of Jesus Christ.

This is not to say that the inner life of humanity is unimportant. In fact, the manifestation of the inner life of God in Jesus Christ desires a radical surgery on humanity, an *ontological, internal* salvation, aimed at the root cause of the human predicament, sin. This, of course, has to *begin* with the individual's inner life. The psalmist certainly was aware of this when he prayed, "Behold, thou desirest truth in the innermost being" (Ps. 51:6). Despite contemporary obsessions in the church with "social justice" and emotional coping—and, therefore, with *external* behavioral change—*inwardness,* change at the root of ontological existence, is the beginning of following Jesus, according to the Gospels.

Jesus' teaching is plain and repeated on the folly of what we might call "surface atonement." An example would be his criticism of parading one's piety before others (Mt. 6:1ff.). In contrast to such a display, he exhorts his listeners to give attention to what truly "defiles" a person; "the things which come *out of* a man are what defiles him" (Mk. 7:15). At the heart of the Sermon on the Mount is Mt. 6, which Dietrich Bonhoeffer entitles "The Hidden Character of the Christian Life."[21] Certainly one should not ignore the external and outward manifestations of a disciple of Jesus. The Sermon is also plain concerning that: "You are the light of the world . . ." (Mt. 5:14). But does not Jesus' teaching on inwardness call us to regard the *beginning* of the atoning act of Christ as a radical surgery on what is *within the individual,* and only subsequently with implications for the external and social life? In fact a biblical paradigm seems to be repeated through Scripture that emphasizes the act of God beginning from an *individual* for the sake of the larger *community* (or from the *particular* to the *universal*). Abraham is chosen by Yahweh so "by you all the families of the earth shall bless themselves" (Gn. 12:3). The Servant in Isaiah is given as "a covenant to the people, a light to the nations" (Is. 42:6). And, of course, Jesus creates a community, the twelve, then the church, to "make disciples of all nations" (Mt. 28:19). The larger community is not to be ignored, but the ontological nature of salvation begins with the particular, leading to the universal.

Such a temporal priority of the particular before the universal addresses *the root cause* of the human predicament and seems to be typical of Jesus, in contrast with many "surface" theories of the atonement and salvation. Whether they emphasize political restructuring (liberation theology), or the satisfaction of God's defaced honor (Anselm), or emotional coping (pop-psychology projects), or the disintegration of the self into God (pantheistic mysticism), these are inadequate in dealing with sin and its legacy for the human being. That is why Scripture speaks of Christ as our *life.* "I am the *life*" (Jn. 14:6; 11:25). Paul's words are familiar: "To me to *live* is Christ" (Phil. 1:21), and "Christ who is our *life*" (Col. 3:4). In fact, Bonhoeffer can speak of Christ's life as "the origin, the essence and the goal of all life and of our life."[22] Christ not only pays the penalty for our sins, but also gives us the positive contribution of his very life.

Where is that life for Sondra? Where is she to find the life of Christ which can begin to deal with the depths of her anguish? Her pastoral counselor has told her that she needs to become "more spiritual." But the "spiritual" can be just as much a "surface" atonement, an excuse for idiosyncratic re-clusiveness, unless there is an *incarnational place* for Sondra to begin to be healed.

Jesus' presence was such a place for the disciples. The church as the body of Christ, as the community of the atonement, should be a place of "rehabilitation" for all, building upon the accomplished radical surgery performed by the life of the Son lived in our human flesh. The inwardness of the atonement means that Sondra's individuality needs to be respected and nourished. The root of sin is *within* the individual, and to bypass the individual for "structural sins" is to be concerned only for the symptoms and not the disease—typical of "surface atonements." In order for that individuality to be nurtured, the community is not to be a tyrant, but a place where Sondra can "recover" from the radical surgery of the atonement.

This understanding of community means that the church should be patient with Sondra—allowing her time to forgive her father and for her memories to be healed—and not expect her to be "healed" immediately. In fact, that very patience (grace) of the church becomes a judgment on Sondra's own sins. Perhaps the most basic issue in the contemporary discussion on the reality of physical healing gifts in the church today is *not* the question of whether such gifts remain in effect today, but rather the question of whether or not the church is prepared to be a place of "rehabilitation" for those whose healings, whether they be spiritual, physical, or emotional, may take years. This seems questionable as long as the church is obsessed with mere survival, whether through "church growth" techniques or simply in reflecting a certain political party's agenda.

In stark contrast, Ray Anderson even suggests that the church should be seen as a "hospice," a place where one can die with dignity and humanity.[23] If the radical surgery of the atonement involves the disturbing, even violent, metaphor of "dying with Christ" (Rom. 6:8), then should the church, as Christ's body, be anything less?

THE VICARIOUS HUMANITY OF CHRIST AS THE ATONING GODWARD RESPONSE ON BEHALF OF HUMANITY

The atonement as the communication of the life of God for the sake of humanity's healing and reconciliation is not only a "humanward" act but also a "Godward" act. This is only proper if the atonement reaches into the depths of human existence in order to restore the whole person to God and to others. But at the heart of the human dilemma is the inability to respond to God with the proper response of perfect obedience. The doctrine of the atonement means that in the vicarious humanity of Christ, the entirety of Christ's life, culminating in his death on the cross, provides an atoning response of perfect worship, trust, service, and confession of sins to the Father on the behalf of humanity.

The atonement of Jesus Christ reaches into the ontological depths of human existence. God is satisfied with nothing less than this. As such, the atonement nevertheless remains a mystery. For at its essence is the interplay of both our existence and God's existence, our being and God's being. This is the essence of atonement. Human existence must be involved in the atonement. As R. C. Moberly points out, atonement is not real unless it affects who I am.[24] The "legal fiction" of a purely forensic acquittal of sins does not help Sondra, whose very capacity for life, for joy, for service, for love has become severely crippled by the bitterness of the years. Nor would simply a cheap, sentimental word of forgiveness mean anything to Sondra's *being,* a being trapped in sin and death. As B. A. Gerrish notes, McLeod Campbell's view of the atonement should not be mistaken for such a Socinian view that "God's readiness to forgive makes atonement."[25] This does not mean, however, that God needs to be "propitiated" in the sense of being "moved to compassion." It does mean that an action is needed in time and space in order to help rescue humanity from its ontological state of sin.

God's existence must be involved in the atonement; but his being remains a mystery, even with the incarnation. When Karl Barth describes the significance of the virgin birth, he speaks of God's "inconceivable act of redeeming wisdom in which He completely assumes His creature in such a way that He imparts and bestows on it no less than His own existence."[26] "No less than His own his own existence" — can one even begin to fathom such a fact? God's existence in the incarnation remains a mystery; or, as a true revelation of God ("God is known by God and by God alone"), it is a revelation we cannot master in all of its depth. The miracle of the virgin birth, Barth reminds us, is a sign of the mystery of God's act in the incarnate Son. "God is known by God and by God alone"!

The atonement does not end, however, with the communication of God's existence (Barth), for it must also be an act that takes place in *our* existence (Moberly). For God has created humanity to respond to his *address,* his *Word.* As Eduard Thurneysen declares, "God not only calls him [humanity] into being, but by calling him into being he summons him."[27] Because he is summoned, this creature is able to answer. Only those creatures who are summoned by God can answer. As Thurneysen continues, "God creates man not only *by* the Word; he creates him also *for* the word."[28]

But whatever the privilege of being addressed by God, humanity faces two dilemmas: (1) *How* does the human being respond to God? (2) *Can* the human being respond to God? Indeed, the refusal of humanity to acknowledge these dilemmas may be said to be the source of religion. One of the enduring contributions of Barth's early theology is his continual reminder that religion is the sinful person's attempt to respond to God, but only on the sinful person's terms. The tragic irony of the phenomenon of religion is that what appears to be an act of devotion is, quite the contrary, an act of supreme *hubris*.[29] In fact, the very reality of God becoming human in order to offer a perfect, obedient response argues against our meager attempts at responding, filled as they are with ulterior motives.[30]

At an existential and pastoral level, Sondra's inability to forgive her father reminds us that when her psychological "character armor" (E. Becker) is destroyed, she is not able to respond as she knows she should. Sondra knows that she should forgive her father. But the bare knowledge that one *should* do something does not necessarily empower the person to do so. The Kantian moralist may dogmatically assert, "I can because I ought," yet the "post-conversion" interpretation of Rom. 7 reminds us of human inability in the face of moral knowledge: "I do not do what I want, but I do the very thing I hate" (v. 15).[31] The implications for pastoral care are profound, as Thurneysen comments: "The pastoral counselor, directed by the Word of God, must know and remember throughout the whole conversation that moral conflicts cannot be worked out morally."[32] In effect, Sondra must not be cast back on her own "morality."

For this reason, in recent years Thomas F. Torrance has written frequently on the doctrine of the vicarious *humanity* (not just vicarious *death*) of Christ as an essential aspect of the atonement.[33] The vicarious humanity of Christ is an all-encompassing term that includes the totality of Christ's atoning life, including and culminating in his death on the cross. Still, the gracious act of God on behalf of humanity is not limited simply to one moment of time on the cross. It is true that, in that moment, Christ takes our place and represents us at the extremity of our death. "The wages of sin is death" (Rom. 6:23; Gn. 3:3). The atonement does include a substitutionary *death*, but this should be regarded only in the wider context of his substitutionary *life*. For atonement is not simply the act of God in saving humanity *from* sin, death, and hell, but also the act of God in saving us *for* eternal life, with all the fullness of the meaning of that reality.[34]

This is what Sondra needs to hear from the pulpit of her church. All of her desires to forgive her father have already been fulfilled in the genuine humanity of Jesus Christ, the one perfect response to the Father in, as T. F. Torrance declares, "trusting and obeying, understanding and knowing, loving and worshipping" and, we may add, forgiving.[35] As the Epistle to the Hebrews puts it so frankly, Christ was "made like his brethren in every respect," becoming a high priest and expiation for sin, to the extent of "learning obedience" by suffering (5:8, 2:10), even with "loud cries and tears" (5:7).[36] In like manner, the atonement penetrates into every point of

Sondra's existence. As Calvin comments on Hebrews, in Christ are found all the qualities of human nature, even the "emotions of the soul . . . fear, dread of death, and the like" (Heb. 4:15, 5:7-10), yet in the context of a perfect obedience (see the reference to Jesus' "godly fear" [5:7] and obedience [10:5-10]).[37] He is therefore able to make continual intercession for humanity (Heb. 7:25).

Sondra is not alone. Christ has identified with her anguish. In some mysterious way, the terror, the fear, the guilt, the hatred, the shame that Sondra feels for her father is being felt by Christ himself. Her anguish has become his anguish. "Everything has happened to us, but in the context of the person of the Son" (Barth).[38] Will Sondra hear that in the Word preached to her on Sunday morning, or will she be preached a Christ who is only a "moral example," or a "satisfaction for sin," *external* to Sondra's being?

This point should not be misunderstood. Along with most other theories of the atonement offered through the history of doctrine, these two have truth to them, but not on their own. Apart from the vicarious humanity of Christ, a "moral example" only creates frustration at not meeting up to that example, and gives no hope to those who have failed time and time again at forgiving. In like manner, is a "satisfaction for sins" for the sake of God's damaged honor helpful to Sondra *now*, in the midst of her predicament? In his vicarious humanity, Christ takes Sondra's tears and frustrations up to the Father himself, forgiving her father for his wickedness, in order to clear the way for Sondra, so that she might forgive him herself, and start a new beginning for herself.

THE FORGIVENESS OF SINS AS THE VIVIFYING CENTER OF THE ACTUALIZATION OF THE ATONEMENT IN THE LIFE AND MINISTRY OF THE CHURCH

The actualization of the atonement in the ministry of the church is in the proclamation of the forgiveness of sins. This is the one act which only God can do, so it is rightly regarded as the unique task of the church, the body of Christ, to proclaim and live. Forgiveness of sins is the atoning manifestation of the life of God, motivated by the heart of the Father, taking deep ontological roots in humanity through the incarnation, and perfectly fulfilled by the faithfulness of the vicarious humanity of Christ.

The atonement of Jesus Christ consists of the healing and reconciling effect of his entire life, reaching its climax in his death. This life becomes healing as it takes root deep in our ontological existence, leaving no part of the human person unexposed by the light of the vicarious life of Christ. In this life, the heart of the Father is made manifest, proclaiming the amazing love of God toward sinners: the forgiveness of sins.

But this does not mean that the incarnation and the cross were "necessary" for God to forgive sins. As Eberhard Jüngel has shown, the "necessity" of God is an aberration of Western natural theology, based on a philosophical anthropocentric theology which attempts to control God by regarding him as the most necessary being.[39] So also the forgiveness of sins has been viewed as "caused" by the instrument of the cross, something external to God's own being. This is similar to the debate over whether, in the atonement, God is reconciled to humanity, or humanity is reconciled to God. Karl Barth has been criticized by some for not affirming the atonement as the means by which God's attitude toward humanity is changed.[40] But, in Barth's defense, has God's attitude ever been anything but an expression of grace, even going back to the very act of *creatio ex nihilo*?[41] Even his judgment is an aspect of his grace (Ps. 89:28-37). It is humanity that needs to be changed, not God. The incarnation, as McLeod Campbell observed, was "a peculiar development of the holy sorrow in which He bore the burden of our sins."[42] It seems more porper, therefore, to speak of the atonement as the *manifestation,* rather than as the *cause,* of the forgiveness of sins.[43]

Regardless of one's theology of the forgiveness of sins, it is hard to ignore its central place in the theology of the atonement. In the forgiveness of sins, we find the motive behind the atonement, the expression of the heart of the Father. The heart of the Father is simply God's desire to forgive our sins; and, indeed, forgiveness is an outworking of his eternal nature of love.

But some voices have recently asked whether the church today has forgotten this central place of the forgiveness of sins, and therefore has forgotten what "the church can say that no one else can say." Indeed, that is the subtitle of a recent book by John Leith, *The Reformed Imperative: What the Church Can Say that No One Else Can Say.*[44] In an age when social and political problems seem to attract the most attention from the mainline churches, Leith suggests that the church has readily surrendered its unique theological mission and competence in order to emphasize management skills, psychological therapy, and social-political pronouncements, all tasks that can be done better by others.[45] In effect, the church's ministry as participation in the one ministry of Jesus Christ has become trivialized.

Thomas Oden laments the same situation in regard to the very identity of the contemporary pastor. Pastors of today are expected to be management specialists, psychological therapists, and social workers, all professions in which they have not been trained. A crisis in pastoral identity and self-confidence has resulted, for no matter which of these functions the pastor performs, there is always a businessman, a psychologist, or a social worker who can do them better! At the same time, the pastor's unique calling as the minister of the Word and Sacrament receives second billing. A "hungry anxiety to accommodate to modernity," Oden claims, has created a "loss of clarity about ministry in our time."[46]

Such a situation has great implications for the place of the forgiveness of sins in the church. The proclamation of the forgiveness of sins is essentially "non-utilitarian" in the perception of the wider society. Like philosophy, in William James' description, it does not "bake any bread."[47] This is so, basically, because the forgiveness of sins cannot be *seen*. One can see the effects of physical healing, growth in church membership, a food bank for the homeless, or a political action committee. The forgiveness of sins is hardly so visible, since it is an action within God himself, in God's "inner life," which can be known only through God's grace. That is why Barth's theological epistemology is so strategic for the doctrine of the atonement and the forgiveness of sins. The "non-utilitarian" and "invisible" nature of the atonement is expressed well by the early Barth:

> The atonement which occurred in Him is an invisible atonement which is contrasted with any soul-and-sense relationship between us and Jesus as impossibility is contrasted with possibility, death with life, non-existence with existence.[48]

Such an emphasis on an "invisible atonement" has been criticized recently by Klaus Bockmuehl as promoting the unreality of God in the world.[49] The "non-observability" of salvation, Bockmuehl contends, plays right into the hands of the Marxists, who have enjoyed such success attracting people with their "gospel" of salvation in this world, a salvation that can be seen.[50] The alternative to Barth is a theology based on Scripture, which proclaims the acts of God in the world, and an emphasis on "experience of the reality of God."[51] As Bockmuehl points out, Barth, later in life, modified his early overemphasis on the transcendence of God, which almost totally excluded the immanence of God.[52] Bockmuehl's work rightly states that the reality of God in the world is an issue of utmost concern. A "kerygmatic" theology can easily degenerate into rhetoric without reference to the concrete reality of the past or the present.

Does Bockmuehl himself, however, forfeit the importance of the ontological change in humanity brought about by the atonement, a change which is within, and therefore (at least initially) "invisible"? Should one simply surrender de facto to the Marxist materialist doctrine by seeking the center of salvation in this world, rather than in God? Also, particularly striking is the absence of a discussion of the problem of evil in a world in which Bockmuehl so readily discerns God's acts. One might also question a reading of Scripture which seems to regard God's "acts" apart from his "being," for it is the life of God, as we have seen, that effects atonement.[53]

"God is known by God and by God alone" locates the center of the atonement in God's own being, reflecting his feelings and actions toward humanity. That is why the opponents of Jesus protested when the carpenter from Nazareth pronounced the forgiveness of sins by saying, "Who can forgive sins but God alone?" (Mk. 2:7). The forgiveness of sins is "hidden" in the heart of the Father, but made manifest in the proclamation of Jesus Christ. How difficult this is to communicate to the present generation is particularly evident when one considers how contemporary culture despises the "word," in its idolatry for the "image" of television and sexual attractiveness, as Jacques Ellul tirelessly preaches.[54] Forgiveness of sins seems cheap, second rate, irrelevant to pressing social needs, and is often regarded as "privatistic," "pietistic," or "individualistic," in contrast to "liberation," which is "communal" and "holistic." And so the slogans go on.

In a modern classic of the theology of ministry, *A Theology of Pastoral Care,* Karl Barth's long-time associate Eduard Thurneysen makes an attempt to return the forgiveness of sins to the center of pastoral care, and, indeed, to the center of the ministry of the church. Much of pastoral care, Thurneysen contends, is weak and ineffectual because it is not regarded as "a communication of the Word of God" in a particular form, and especially as "the proclamation of the forgiveness of sins."[55] For in the forgiveness of sins, Thurneysen argues, we find nothing less than the very *power* of pastoral care: that is, the power of God's grace to reclaim the sinful world through Jesus Christ.[56]

Thurneysen has been criticized for being "unnecessarily restrictive" in confining all pastoral care to forgiveness.[57] But it seems that Thurneysen is onto something important. What often happens in the church, unfortunately, is that we give lip service and nod our heads to the *past* act of Christ's forgiveness, centering only on the cross, and forget about the implications of God's *continuous* life of the vicarious humanity of Christ in the church, a life of continual forgiveness. This is where our ecclesiology needs to be reshaped by the interrelationship between the vicarious humanity of Christ and the forgiveness of sins. Without going back to sacerdotalism, the church, as the body of Christ, needs to acknowledge that Christ has chosen to use the church as the expression of his vicarious humanity, for the sake of both the church and the world.

A fascinating example of how the vicarious humanity of Christ and the forgiveness of sins in the life and ministry of the church are woven together is found in the story of the healing of the paralytic and the pronouncement of the forgiveness of sins by Jesus (Mk. 2:1-12, Mt. 9:1-8, Lk. 5:17-26). In Mark's version, Jesus is "preaching the word" to many (v. 2) when a paralytic is brought to him by four men. "And when Jesus saw *their* faith, he said to the paralytic, 'my son, your sins are forgiven'" (v. 5). (This is, interestingly enough, said *before* the event of Calvary!)[58]

Some commentators follow Vincent Taylor and Calvin in explaining "their faith" in Mk. 2:5 as including the faith of the paralytic as well.[59] Eduard Schweizer, however, in agreement with the ancient exegetes Victor of Antioch (fifth century) and St. Ephraem Syrus (fourth century), stresses the faith of the carriers alone as a sign that the act was entirely a work of God.[60] In fact, Ephraem notes the benefits of the "vicarious humanity" of the four carriers for the sick man: "See what the faith of others may do for one."[61] The possibility is there that "their faith" refers to the faith of the four men alone.

This argument is strengthened when one examines the six other stories of individual healing in Mark. In three out of the seven stories, some help is given by others to the one who is to be healed. (1) Concerning Peter's mother-in-law, *the disciples* "immediately . . . *told him* [Jesus] of her" (1:32). (2) "And *they brought to him* a man who was deaf and had an impediment in his speech and *they besought him* to lay his hand on him" (7:32). (3) Concerning the blind man at Beth-Saida: "And *some people brought to him* a blind man *and begged him* to touch him" (8:22); cf. the crowd healing of 1:32.

This does not mean that "the vicarious humanity of Christ in the Church" restricts the Holy Spirit to work in one way. God is still free to act as he chooses. The healing stories in Mark that stress individual effort at seeking Jesus and the faith of the one who is to be healed remind us of that fact (1:40-45, 5:25-43, 10:46-52, and the crowd healing in 3:10). The combination of both elements in the crowd healing in 6:56 is particularly striking in this regard: " . . . *they laid* the sick in the market places, and *besought him that they might touch the fringe of his garment.*" Perhaps this should be a reminder that "the vicarious humanity of Christ in the church" is not an excuse for a "state socialism" in the church which denies the dignity and rights of the individual. Rather, the purpose of the vicarious humanity of Christ is to create a *basis* for individual faith.

Having seen "their faith," Jesus pronounces the forgiveness of sins for the paralytic. To the onlookers, Jesus was certainly not meeting the "needs" of the paralyzed man! But to prove that "the Son of Man has authority on earth to forgive sins," the paralytic was physically healed (vv. 10-12). In contrast to much talk today about a "holistic" approach to salvation, Jesus seems to give a priority to the forgiveness of sins over meeting physical needs. Now, one must quickly say that the physical need was met in time, but not at the expense of the forgiveness of sins. But can such a distinction between "spiritual" and "physical" be warranted, without making the church rich in words but poor in deeds?

In answer to this question, a reminder of a little noticed excursus in Barth's *Church Dogmatics* may be in order. No one can accuse Karl Barth of being simply a "privatistic" theologian, unconcerned with social or political ills. His stalwart opposition to Hitler's Germany speaks loudly against any such accusation. Nevertheless, in his discussion of the virgin birth, Barth has a very interesting excursus in which he defends the importance of the doctrine of the virgin birth by establishing its place as a "sign" of the incarnation, which is "the thing signified." The "sign," Barth claims, should never be confused with "the thing signified." The saving fact is the incarnation, not the miracle of the virgin birth. The forgiveness of sins and the physical healing of the paralytic are similarly related, he points out. The healing is a "sign," but it is not to be given priority over the pronouncement of the forgiveness of sins, "the thing signified."[62]

In Ray Bradbury's short story "Bless Me, Father, for I Have Sinned," a priest named Father Mellon is awakened at midnight on Christmas Eve by a peculiar urge to go down to the confessional of the church and wait. What he finds is an elderly penitent eager to spill the accumulation of sixty years of sins on the priest. The sins are personal, the kind that one would likely keep to oneself for years.

The last confession particularly jolts the priest. It involves a runaway dog named Bo, greatly beloved by the man when he was a young boy. For three days and three nights the dog had been gone, and the boy had given up hope. Then on Christmas Eve, at two in the morning, the boy heard the scratching of paws at the door. Bo was back! He grabbed the dog with great joy, calling his name over and over again. Then he suddenly stopped: "How dare he run away from me?" the boy asked himself. In hatred, the boy turned to the dog and beat him, while Bo just stood and took it all. "Oh, Father," the man cries to the priest, "he couldn't forgive me. Who was he? A beast, an animal, a dog, my love."[63]

The priest turns to the man and says that he, too, had the same thing happen to him. His dog had run off. He had hated his dog for leaving him. And upon the dog's return, he had beaten him. He had never told this to anyone, until now. A feeling of camaraderie develops, and the priest invites the man to share a glass of wine with him. But when he opens the confessional door, he finds the confessional empty. He has been talking with himself.

Even the priest needed a concrete person, a representative of the vicarious humanity of Christ, to hear his sins so that he, too, could receive forgiveness. So great was his need that he had to create the existence of that other person. "Confess your faults one to another" (Jas. 5:16) is a call for the vicarious humanity of Christ to be operative in the church. While the Roman Church may be in error to restrict confession only to priests, Dietrich Bonhoeffer points out that oral confession is an imperative based on the vicarious humanity of Christ in the church: "Christ became our Brother in order to help us," Bonhoeffer says. "Through him our brother has become Christ for us in the power and the authority of the commission Christ has given to him."[64]

The atonement lives in the church when forgiveness of sins is given flesh in the presence of the brother or sister in the church—and not necessarily that of the pastor or priest. Eberhard Bethge recounts that one day in the Finkenwalde seminary, Bonhoeffer, who had encouraged his students to confess their sins to one another, asked one of the students to hear his own confession.[65] Like the priest, Bonhoeffer realized the need to know the forgiveness of sins through the touch of humanity, a humanity participating in the vicarious humanity of Christ.

The church could do many things for Sondra: provide psychological therapy, economic sustenance, or a community of service. But does not Sondra need to hear and feel and experience what the paralytic heard, "My son, your sins are forgiven," with all the implications of that stupendous announcement? The continuing life of God as the atonement can be communicated to Sondra through the church's acts of preaching, teaching, pastoral care, and fellowship. In these acts, the vicarious humanity of Christ continues to live in the church, the body of Christ, as we saw with the four men who carried the paralytic to Jesus: "And Jesus saw *their* faith." The paralytic was unable to carry himself to Jesus. The atonement continues to be powerful in the church when the message of forgiveness through the life of God is still proclaimed, even when we cannot believe, even when we need someone to believe for us.

Can the church dare to do this for Sondra? It can, if it allows its knowledge of God to come from God alone ("God can only be known by God and by God alone"), and therefore steadfastly determines to know no other gospel and no other ministry than the ministry of Jesus Christ. This can be done, not out of the church's own strength, but because the vicarious humanity of Christ, the manifestation of the life of God sent by the heart of the Father through the incarnation into the ontological depths of humanity, continues to live in a church that lives by nothing less than the forgiveness of sins.[66]

NOTES

1. Ray S. Anderson, "A Theology for Ministry," in *Theological Foundations for Ministry*, ed. Ray S. Anderson (Grand Rapids: Eerdmans, 1979), p. 7.
2. Ibid.
3. Karl Barth, *Church Dogmatics*, ed. G. W. Bromiley and T. F. Torrance, II/1 (Edinburgh: T. & T. Clark, 1936-68), p. 47. Cf. Wilhelm Pauck, *The Heritage of the Reformation* (London: Oxford Univ. Press, 1961), p. 354.
4. Thomas F. Torrance, *The Ground and Grammar of Theology* (Charlottesville: Univ. Press of Virginia, 1980), p. 8.
5. Pauck, *Heritage*, p. 354. Pauck shares the belief of Harnack that because of this "strange idea," Barth will inevitably think that he is the recipient of inspirations and found his own sect (!), ibid., p. 359.
6. Ibid., pp. 358-59.
7. Proclamation is the "presupposition" of theology, "its material and its potential goal, not its content or task." Barth, *Church Dogmatics*, I/1, 2nd ed., p. 51.
8. See also Barth on the priority of the reality of revelation over its possibility, *Church Dogmatics*, I/2, pp. 1-44. For Barth, this is integrally connected with his doctrine of God, as Torrance explains: "God is not another activity but *the* Actuality or Reality through which and in which our own actuality and that of the world is

actuality—the *causa prima, ens realissimum,* and *actus purus,* the One Actuality that lies behind and is present in every other actuality." *Karl Barth: An Introduction to His Early Theology, 1910-1934* (London: SCM Press, 1962), p. 154.

9. This case was provided by Sue Muhlenbruch, a graduate student in ministry at Friends University.

10. John McLeod Campbell, *The Nature of the Atonement,* 3rd ed. (London: Macmillan, 1867).

11. Ibid., p. 220.

12. T. F. Torrance tells of his moving experience as a chaplain on the battlefield when a young man, dying, asked him, "Will God really turn out to be what we believe him to be in Jesus Christ?" The importance of the *homoousion* for pastoral ministry could not be more vividly portrayed. T. F. Torrance, *The Mediation of Christ* (Grand Rapids: Eerdmans, 1983), p. 70.

13. McLeod Campbell, *Atonement,* p. xix.

14. This is a common deduction from Calvin's use of the law in the life of the believer. *Institutes of the Christian Religion,* ed. John T. McNeill, trans. Ford L. Battles (Philadelphia: Westminster Press, 1960), 2.7.12-13; 2.9.3.

15. R. S. Franks, *The Work of Christ* (London: Thomas Nelson, 1962), pp. 671-672.

16. James B. Torrance, "The Contribution of John McLeod Campbell to Scottish Theology," *Scottish Journal of Theology* 31 (August 1973):311.

17. Roland M. Frye, *Language for God and Feminist Language: Principles and Problems* (Princeton: Center of Theological Inquiry, 1988), p. 6.

18. T. F. Torrance, *Reality and Scientific Theology* (Edinburgh: Scottish Academic Press, 1985), p. 201 n. 3; cf. p. 4.

19. McLeod Campbell, *Atonement,* p. xix.

20. Barth, *Church Dogmatics,* IV/1, p. 215.

21. Dietrich Bonhoeffer, *The Cost of Discipleship,* trans. R. H. Fuller et al. (New York: Macmillan, 1963), p. 172. Davies and Allison note a parallel between Mt. 6:1-6, 16-18 and Rom. 2:28-29: "For he is not a real Jew who is one outwardly, nor is true circumcision something external and physical. He is a Jew who is one inwardly and real circumcision is a matter of the heart, spiritual and not literal. His praise is not from men but from God." They conclude that the two passages reflect the pervasiveness of a "common Christian tradition," which was indebted to ancient Judaism. W. D. Davies and Dale C. Allison, Jr., *A Critical and Exegetical Commentary on the Gospel According to Saint Matthew,* 1 (Edinburgh: T. & T. Clark, 1988), p. 576.

22. Dietrich Bonhoeffer, *Ethics,* ed. Eberhard Bethge, trans. Neville Horton Smith (New York: Macmillan, 1955), p. 218.

23. Ray S. Anderson, *Theology, Death, and Dying* (Oxford: Basil Blackwell, 1986), p. 157.

24. R. C. Moberly, *Atonement and Personality* (London: Murray, 1971), pp. 137-38.

25. B. A. Gerrish, *Tradition and the Modern World: Reformed Theology in the Twentieth Century* (Chicago: Univ. of Chicago Press, 1978), p. 82.

26. Barth, *Church Dogmatics,* I/1, p. 201. The parallels between Barth's thought and the thought of the Greek Fathers on deification (*theosis*) are obvious. Cf. Timothy Ware, *The Orthodox Church* (New York: Penguin Books, 1963), pp. 236-42.

27. Eduard Thurneysen, *A Theology of Pastoral Care,* trans. Jack A. Worthington, et al. (Richmond: John Knox Press, 1962), p. 59. Cf. Barth, *Church Dogmatics,* III/2, pp. 147ff.; Ray S. Anderson, *On Being Human: Essays on Theological Anthropology* (Grand Rapids: Eerdmans, 1982), pp. 33-43.

28. Thurneysen, *Pastoral Care,* p. 59.

29. Karl Barth, *The Epistle to the Romans,* trans. Edwyn C. Hoskyns (New York: Oxford Univ. Press, 1933), pp. 136, 206, 229ff., 276, 332, 368.

30. The extent of Christ's vicarious humanity may even extend to vicarious *repentance.* See the discussion in Christian D. Kettler, "The Vicarious Repentance of

Christ in the Theology of John McLeod Campbell and R. C. Moberly," *Scottish Theology of Theology* 38 (1986):529-43.

31. Thurneysen, *Pastoral Care,* p. 285.

32. Ibid., p. 142.

33. Torrance's doctrine of the vicarious humanity of Christ is particularly emphasized in *The Mediation of Christ,* especially in ch. 4, "The Mediation of Christ in Our Human Response." Cf. James B. Torrance, "The Vicarious Humanity of Christ," in *The Incarnation: Ecumenical Studies in the Nicene-Constantinopolitan Creed,* ed. T. F. Torrance (Edinburgh: Handsel Press, 1981), pp. 127-47; Christian D. Kettler, "The Vicarious Humanity of Christ and the Reality of Salvation" (unpublished Ph.D. dissertation, Fuller Theological Seminary, 1986), pp. 110-156 provides a summary and discussion of Torrance's doctrine.

34. Rudolf Bultmann, "Zaō," in *Theological Dictionary of the New Testament,* ed. G. Kittel and G. Friedrich, trans. G. W. Bromiley (Grand Rapids: Eerdmans, 1964), I, p. 865.

35. Thomas F. Torrance, *God and Rationality* (Oxford: Oxford Univ. Press, 1971), p. 145.

36. According to C. Spicq, the identification of Christ with humanity in every respect best expresses the content of the epistle. *L'Epître aux Hèbreux,* I (Paris: J. Gabolda, 1952), p. 52.

37. John Calvin, *The Epistle of Paul the Apostle to the Hebrews and the First and Second Epistles of St. Peter,* ed. David W. Torrance and Thomas F. Torrance, trans. William B. Johnston (Edinburgh: Oliver & Boyd, 1963), pp. 25-26.

38. Barth, *Church Dogmatics,* IV/1, p. 222.

39. Eberhard Jüngel, *God as the Mystery of the World,* trans. Darrell L. Guder (Grand Rapids: Eerdmans, 1983), pp. 24-25. Such a tradition of the "necessity" of God contrasts sharply with the biblical doctrine of the contingent relationship between God and the world. "The baffling thing about the creation is that it came into being at all, and now that it has come into being it contains no reason in itself why it should be what it is and why it should continue to exist. Indeed God himself was under no necessity to create the universe." Thomas F. Torrance, *Divine and Contingent Order* (Oxford: Oxford Univ. Press, 1981), p. vii.

40. David F. Wells, *The Search for Salvation* (Downers Grove, IL: Inter-Varsity Press, 1978), p. 60.

41. Barth, *Church Dogmatics,* III/2, pp. 94ff.: "Creation as the External Basis of the Covenant."

42. McLeod Campbell, *Atonement,* p. 136.

43. Does this necessarily imply universalism? Not particularly, if one remembers the judgmental nature of forgiveness. As James Torrance points out, the proclamation of forgiveness implies that the forgiven person is guilty. When one says "I forgive you," this is not only a word of love and reconciliation, but also of judgment. Whether the guilty party accepts that word is another question. "The Vicarious Humanity of Christ," pp. 142-43.

44. John H. Leith, *The Reformed Imperative: What the Church Can Say that No One Else Can Say* (Philadelphia: Westminster Press, 1988).

45. Ibid., pp. 14, 21.

46. Thomas D. Oden, *Pastoral Theology: Essentials of Ministry* (San Francisco: Harper & Row, 1983), p. 3.

47. William James, *Pragmatism* (Indianapolis: Hackett Publishing Co., 1981), p. 8.

48. Barth, *The Epistle to the Romans,* p. 160.

49. Klaus Bockmuehl, *The Unreal God of Modern Theology* (Colorado Springs: Helmers & Howard, 1988).

50. Ibid., pp. 108, 132-35.

51. Ibid., pp. 117, 142.

52. Karl Barth, *The Humanity of God,* trans. Thomas Wieser and John Newton Thomas (Atlanta: John Knox Press, 1960), p. 39.

53. In my dissertation, I argue that this desire to locate the center of salvation in the world resulted in a slew of modern anthropocentric soteriologies. As an alternative, Torrance's doctrine of the vicarious humanity of Christ is suggested as a way to take seriously salvation in the midst of humanity and the world (vicarious humanity), while maintaining its origin and reality in God's inner life. Kettler, "The Vicarious Humanity of Christ and the Reality of Salvation," op. cit.

54. Jacques Ellul, *The Humiliation of the Word,* trans. Joyce Main Hanks (Grand Rapids: Eerdmans, 1985).

55. Thurneysen, *Pastoral Care,* pp. 52-53.

56. Ibid., p. 67.

57. Derek J. Tidball, *Skillful Shepherds: An Introduction to Pastoral Theology* (Grand Rapids: Zondervan, 1986), p. 235.

58. Jesus says plainly that the sins of the man are forgiven at that moment, *pace* some writers such as R. S. Wallace: "He is asserting that he *has* the power to forgive only because he himself is on the way to meeting the full cost of forgiveness in the death he has come to achieve." R. S. Wallace, *The Atoning Death of Christ* (Westchester: Crossway Books, 1981), p. 23.

59. Vincent Taylor, *The Gospel According to St. Mark* (New York: St. Martin's Press, 1966), p. 194; John Calvin, *A Harmony of the Gospels, Matthew, Mark and Luke,* I, ed. David W. Torrance and Thomas F. Torrance, trans. A. W. Morrison (Grand Rapids: Eerdmans, 1972), p. 258.

60. Eduard Schweizer, *The Good News According to Mark,* trans. Donald H. Madvig (Atlanta: John Knox Press, 1970), p. 61.

61. Cited by H. B. Swete, *The Gospel According to St. Mark* (London: Macmillan, 1905), p. 34.

62. Barth, *Church Dogmatics,* I/2, p. 189. Barth's discussion of the hierarchy of the soul over the body is also interesting, given the contemporary tendency to homogenize the two and, in effect, ignore the importance of the soul. In contrast, Barth maintains the priority of the soul without ignoring the body and while considering the total person. Ibid., III/2, pp. 338-40.

63. Ray Bradbury, "Bless Me, Father, For I Have Sinned," in *The Toynbee Convector* (New York: Bantam Books, 1988), p. 153.

64. Dietrich Bonhoeffer, *Life Together,* trans. John W. Doberstein (San Francisco: Harper & Row, 1954), p. 111.

65. Eberhard Bethge, *Dietrich Bonhoeffer: Man of Vision, Man of Courage,* ed. Edwin Robertson (New York: Harper & Row, 1977), p. 384.

66. Earlier editions of this article were read by Dale Allison, Diane Ferguson, Bruce Parmenter, Todd Speidell, and Donna Van Haren. Their constructive comments were greatly appreciated.

5

GEOFFREY W. BROMILEY

✢

The Ministry of the
Word of God

THE QUESTION

IT HAS BEEN almost a commonplace, especially since the Reformation, to call the Christian ministry the ministry of the Word of God. The Reformation confessions made this equation very clearly and forcefully. *Von den Dienern des Wortes Gottes* is the title of Article XXV of the First Helvetic Confession (1536). The Belgic Confession (1561), too, refers to the clergy as ministers of God's Word (XXXI). The Second Helvetic (1566) confidently perceives a possibility of preaching "the very Word of God" in the church (I).

But how can human beings dare claim that they minister the divine Word? This question, which haunted the young Barth at Safenwil, will not easily go away. Is it not arrogance or self-delusion to think or say that speaking human words or performing Christian acts, whether in worship, a church program, or personal service, is a proclaiming of God's Word?

There are ways, of course, to ignore the problem or to make light of it. We can trivialize the Christian ministry. We can reduce it to human terms. We can view it as a mere profession with its own possibilities of service and advancement. We can integrate it into a system of human education with the special role of passing on spiritual and moral truths and precepts. We can take a humanitarian stance and use the ministry to further human betterment, to challenge and correct abuses, to promote progressive insights, to provide relief for human misery.

Or, allowing for the divine dimension, we can assume too quickly that our human words and acts are a valid ministry of God's Word. How simple it is to slip into an assumed prophetic role as though the denouncing of this or that vested interest or dubious policy had automatically the sanction of a "thus saith the Lord"! How equally simple it is, when contending for an inerrant scripture, to fall into the obvious fallacy—obvious at least to others—that in virtue of this advocacy all the words that we utter in ministry will necessarily be God's Word!

For those who ignore it, or who find for it a self-evident answer, Barth's question will have little relevance. It will not be a decisive factor in their practice of the ministry. Yet the question as such does not go away simply because it is suppressed or given too facile an answer. It is still the most urgent and radical of all the questions that arise in Christian ministry.

THE WORD OF GOD

An aspect of the question that greatly concerned Barth but has not always received adequate attention relates to the meaning of the phrase "Word of God." Some take it that the words simply refer to the Bible. In some sense a ministry of God's Word will be for them a biblical ministry. Others think in terms of preaching or of proclamation in its various forms. As they see it, the words and works of Christian preachers, teachers, counselors, and witnesses are the Word of God. Others prefer a more generous but also a more vague definition and equate the Word of God with the gospel. Simply ministering the gospel is ministering God's Word.

The Reformers, who spoke much of God's Word, also used the term in many different ways, as Luther scholars have shown in studies of Luther's varied usage. The text of Article XXV of the First Helvetic describes a ministry of the gospel for forgiveness, conversion, establishment, comfort, and admonition. The Gallican (1559), too, relates the ministry of the Word to the gospel through which we "enjoy Christ" (XXIV). The Belgic has in view "the pure doctrine of the gospel" that is preached in true churches (XXIV). The Reformers, then, identify the Word of God with the gospel and its proclamation by preaching and teaching. They recognize that the proclamation took at first a spoken form (Gallican II, Belgic III, Westminster I.i). They are keenly aware that Jesus himself never gave the Word written form and that he sent out his disciples to preach (Second Helvetic I).

Nevertheless, the Reformers also make a clear equation of God's Word with holy scripture. The First Helvetic says already (I) that scripture is the Word of God embodying all that belongs to the true knowledge, love, and glory of God. The Gallican and Belgic (II and III) refer to the committing of God's Word to writing in the books of scripture, the "written Word of God." The Anglican Articles reject rulings that are "contrary to God's Word written" (XX), "repugnant to the Word of God" (XXII, XXXIV), or "repugnant to the plain words of scripture" (XXVIII). The Second Helvetic confesses "the canonical scriptures of the holy prophets and apostles of both Testaments to be the true Word of God" through which "God himself speaks to us," so that when "this Word of God is now preached in the church . . . the very Word of God is preached" (I).

Reverting to the question of Barth, we note that his acceptance of the normative role of scripture, and his attempt to work out a biblical dogmatics and ethics for the guidance and correction of Christian proclamation and practice, rest on the perception that God's Word is both the living Word of proclamation and the written Word of scripture. It is not enough to go out to the world claiming to have a message from God. It is not enough to pass on a supposed divine message that has simply been picked up in church services, Sunday school classes, Bible studies, or theological lectures and seminars. It is not enough to pass on the platitudes, to fling out the challenges, to communicate the innovative insights that often pass as the contemporary ministerial currency. If Christian ministers are doing their real job, they can do it only as authentic ministers of God's Word. If they cannot claim to be this, they have no business in the Christian ministry at all. But to make the claim, they need a standard by which to tell whether their proclamation goes out to the world with any credibility to themselves and others — as God's Word. As Barth sees it, and the Reformers before him, that standard is holy scripture.

More narrowly, then, Barth's disquieting question is whether his own proclamation, and that of his church and age, can stand by this criterion. Do we really know, indeed, what the written Word of God is saying, what holy scripture is all about? If not, how can we with any honesty present ourselves to our people and the world as ministers of the Word of God? And even if we do, are we truly conforming our ministry to this normative ministry so that in fact, and not merely in word, it is the ministry of God's Word?

But there is more to it than that, for scripture shows us that as well as the Word proclaimed and the Word written there is also and primarily the Word eternal and incarnate. Here is an aspect of the ministry of the Word of God that has seldom commanded the direct notice it clearly merits. Even the Reformers do little to relate the ministry of the Word in any immediate way to the incarnate Word. From Luther on they undoubtedly equate the gospel with Christ. The Gallican Confession, as noted, speaks of enjoying Christ through the gospel (XXV). The Second Helvetic refers to the gospel of Jesus Christ, which is both the gospel that he proclaimed and also the good news of the fulfillment of the divine promises in Christ (XIII). For the Reformers Christ is the center of scripture and the basic theme of Christian proclamation. Bullinger, in discussing the Word of God in his *Decades,* can even note that primarily Christ himself is the Word of God, but without integrating this insight in his main development of the subject. Not until we come to Barth's exploration of the doctrine of the Word in his concern for the ministry of the Word do we find a comprehensive treatment that does full justice to the Word revealed or incarnate, relating it to the Word written and the Word proclaimed in triune perichoresis.

Yet little enough has been done to follow up this presentation in either the doctrine or the practice of ministry. True, the general implication that Christian ministry is Christ's ministry would hardly provoke dissent, and most ministers have some sense of at least some of the ramifications. What has not been so obviously grasped is that Christ's ministry is itself the ministry of the Word of God and that the ministry of the written Word and the proclaimed Word must be integrated into this primary ministry, first as that of the inspired and normative prophetic and apostolic witness, then as the ongoing, living testimony which the church must give in every age and place in the power of the Spirit.

THE MINISTRY OF THE INCARNATE WORD

In asking the question concerning the ministry of the Word, we often forget the threefold nature of the Word and its ministry and rush on too hastily to our own role as ministers of the Word of God, and the problems associated with that role. We thus overlook the more important fact that primarily and properly the ministry is the Word's own ministry. This is preeminently true in the case of the incarnate Word. Christ the Word came into the world to minister. He "came not to be served, but to serve" (Mt. 20:28). He was among us "as one who serves" (Lk. 22:27). He gave his disciples a striking illustration of even menial service (Jn. 13:3ff.). He had, of course, his own specific ministry during his earthly years from Bethlehem to Golgotha and Olivet. But Christ also continues his ministry through his disciples and by his presence in and through the Holy Spirit. It is *his* Word that they speak, *his* acts that they do, and in *his* name that they minister. *Their* ministry is *his* ministry.

The First Helvetic points in this direction when it calls the church's minister God's co-worker (*Mitarbeiter Gottes, cooperarios Dei,* Art. XVI). Calvin says similarly that Christ's anointing was not merely for his own teaching but for the ongoing ministry of his body (*Inst.* II.xv.2). Bullinger has a sense of the same truth in the Second Helvetic when he describes Christ as the one "who illuminates inwardly by giving men the Holy Spirit" (I). Westminster makes the same link between the ministry of Christ and the inner work of the Spirit when it states: "To all those for whom Christ hath purchased redemption, he doth certainly and effectually apply and communicate the same . . . persuading them by his Spirit to believe and obey" (VIII.viii). In this connection Westminster also includes an important reference to the ongoing intercessory ministry of Christ (cf. Belgic XXXVI). Barth, of course, follows up the general theme of Christ's continuing ministry, pushing it almost to extremes in his account of the prophetic Christ as the true witness (*CD,* IV.3).

Even today, however, the church and its ministers have been slow to appreciate the implications in spite of some promising ventures. How many debates about Christian ministry begin openly with the truth that is no doubt ultimately presupposed: namely, that no church at all has an autonomous ministry of God's Word, that all that any church can do is participate in the ministry of Christ the incarnate Word? What would it do for Christian intercommunion and unity if the churches and their theologians, ecclesiastics, workers, and members gave precedence to the fact that for all the denominational differences and their relative seriousness, the ministry of Christ alone confers authenticity on all ministry and gives it the only authentication that finally counts? What would be the ramifications in planning, strategy, technique, training, and evaluation if more thoughtful attention were paid to the reality that first and foremost the ministry is the Word's and not ours? Only secondarily and derivatively can we be ministers of the Word of God. Primarily and properly the incarnate Word is his own minister.

This means, of course, that the ultimate commissioning for ministry is his. The churches rightly ordain and institute and commission. Biblical models exist for this (Acts 13:2f.; 1 Tm. 4:14). The Reformation confessions stress it (Gallican XXXI; Belgic XXXf.; Anglican XXIII; Second Helvetic XVIII). The churches also recognize, however, that human appointment derives its authenticity only from divine appointment. The incarnate Word instituted ministry by calling disciples as God had previously called Moses and the prophets. Nor was this only a once-for-all appointment. An inner call as well as outer appointment is still required of ministers of God's Word. For the First Helvetic Christ himself is the church's true head and pastor, and he gives the church pastors and teachers who preach the Word at his command (XVIII). One might refer this statement, of course, to the original institution, but the Belgic clearly insists that a minister of God's Word must not "intrude himself by indecent means, but is bound to wait till it shall please God to call him" (XXXI). Ordination services refer regularly to an inner as well as an outer call.

The divine commissioning lies behind the validity of ministrations by unworthy ministers inasmuch as they act in God's name and "minister by his commission and authority" (Anglican XXVI; cf. Second Helvetic XVIII). Yet if Christ's commission gives welcome reassurance, it also raises questions and challenges. The ministry as such has divine authorization, but do specific ministers really have their own call and commission? Do these ministers, or any Christians performing acts of ministry, really display a sense of commission by acting under the orders of the Word and showing in both word and deed that their ministry is his? Do they say what he wants them to say and do what he wants them to do? Again, have the churches the wisdom to see that many whom they do not officially ordain, or who do not fit into ordinary patterns of ministry, may still have Christ's commission and may thus participate legitimately in the common ministry? Is it sufficiently appreciated that the ministry of Christ the Head implies the ministry of the whole body, the taking up of all believers in different ways and according to their different gifts, into the ministry of the incarnate Word? Much of the laxity, the self-will, the indolence, the arbitrariness, the contentiousness, the misplaced activity, and the ultimate futility of Christian ministry might be obviated were it more clearly understood that all our ministry rests on commissioning by the Word into the Word's own ministry.

The authority and power of ministry also rest on the fact that it is primarily the ministry of the Word himself. The Reformers note this especially in connection with the power of the keys, which they relate not merely to penance but to the total gospel of remission and renewal. Augsburg (1530) takes the lead by saying of absolution: "It is God's voice, and pronounced by his command" (Part II). The First Helvetic equates the power of the keys with the authority to "preach the Word of God and feed the Lord's flock" (XVI). No individual or group has independent authority to pronounce forgiveness or even to accuse of sin and bring under judgment. Christians often like to think they have power to do both. Condemnations and easy assurances fly from pulpits. Delegated authority easily comes to be viewed as intrinsic authority. The claim to be Christ's vicars, to have the right to act in his stead, supposedly provides vindication. It may well do so, but only if the delegation is taken seriously. For judgment and pardon belong to God and his Christ. Authority to pronounce either the one or the other derives from Christ alone.

Similarly it is to Christ's ministry by the Holy Spirit that converting and renewing power belongs. The Reformers stress this point. In the famous word of Augsburg, the Spirit "worketh faith, where and when it pleaseth God, in those that hear the gospel" (V). Faith is a free gift of God (First Helvetic XIII). "We are enlightened in faith by the secret power of the Holy Spirit" (Gallican XXI). The Spirit "brings us in all verity by his own operation" (Scots [1560] XII). Christ "illuminates inwardly by giving men the Holy Spirit" (Second Helvetic I). If God works outwardly through his ministers, inwardly he persuades "the hearts of his elect unto belief by his Holy Spirit" (Second Helvetic XVIII). Christians may press others with cogent arguments, move them by eloquent addresses, manipulate them by clever techniques, influence them by efficient organization, capture them by attractive personality, but they cannot alone do the one thing that finally counts: i.e. give the inner enlightenment and bring about the inner conversion that mean eternal salvation. God uses their ministry as a means to this end, but the power of Christian evangelism and edification is the power of the Word's own ministry by the Spirit and in high-priestly intercession.

A question also arises concerning the authority of the churches to establish doctrines and practices. This issue called forth some of the fiercest words of the Reformers as they opposed the specific dogmatic innovations and pastoral requirements of the medieval church and papacy, resisted the imposition of Roman control over the national churches, disputed the rights of popes to depose rulers and dispose of kingdoms, and questioned the absolute authority of councils. Primarily the Reformers were subjecting the church's authority to the written Word, granting it no power to ordain anything contrary to scripture, and allowing it to make its own decisions only in indifferent matters (Anglican XXI). Churches and their leaders naturally accept this authority readily in theory, but history shows that they find it hard to accept in practice. Even though they do not indulge openly in such swollen claims as those of the *Dictatus Papae,* they stretch their sphere of legitimate authority to the limit, acting and speaking as if the supreme Minister were an absentee, paying lip service to the Spirit, but apparently confident that their own decisions and utterances automatically enjoy the Spirit's sanction. In every age one of the most urgent needs of Christian ministry is that the churches, their leaders, their synods, and their members should realize that the incarnate Word into whose ministry their own is incorporate, and from whose absolute authority their own relative authority derives, is indeed the living Lord of the church, who is not merely present on occasion (in the Eucharist!), and the invasion of whose prerogatives can bring only confusion, disruption, and failure.

The same applies, of course, to the authority of individual ministers, many of whom seem to be under the illusion that they have autonomous authority, as though the author of real authority were not still a living author to whom they are subject. Unquestionably the authority that derives from the incarnate Word confers an incomparable assurance. It is divine authority. But to speak and act with this authority is a heady experience if there is no sense of the paradox, or the miracle, that human words and acts can be the divine Word and act. Unheard of arrogance and folly can be the result.

Nor are the consequences any the less disastrous when in an abuse of office ministers act as if divine authority were not an issue at all, when they simply air their own opinions, forge their own judgments, and initiate and execute their own programs among people who look to them as ministers of God's Word. If the ministry is properly the ministry of the incarnate Word, it has the valid authority which that Word confers, but it is itself always subject to the authority of that Word.

The incarnate Word provides the model of ministry by his own ministry not merely of word, sacrament, prayer, and act, but also of disposition and character. For Jesus' ministry was a matter of attitude as well as act. We see in him the features of authentic ministry: dedication, self-sacrifice, faithfulness, resoluteness, tenderness, patience, and humility. He came to do the will of him that sent him (Jn. 6:38). He resisted the ways of power and self-seeking (Mt. 4:1ff.). "He set his face to go to Jerusalem" (Lk. 9:51). He did not break the bruised reed or quench the smoking flax (Mt. 12:20). He gave his life a ransom for many (Mt. 20:28). He lived a life of consistent service which was a pattern for the power-hungry and status-seeking disciples (Mt. 20:20ff.). A ministry that is genuinely the ministry of the incarnate Word will conform to this model.

But how depressingly different the reality often is as Christians forget that their ministry is really his. Not without some truth could Emil Brunner describe Christianity as the world's greatest fiasco. Past and present, we see in the churches and their ministries either the very opposite of the qualities that mark the ministry of Christ or their perversion: either power-seeking, ambition, ruthlessness, severity, and bellicosity on the one hand; or servility, compliance, cowardice, compromise, and indolence on the other. If history seems to record outstanding achievements as well as monumental failures, only a closer inspection enables us to discern in the sorry story a ministry that bears the imprint of the ministry of the incarnate Word. If Christians, and especially ordained Christians, are to be in truth what they are supposed to be—ministers of the Word of God—then they must ask themselves, perhaps more seriously than ever before, what they are summoned not merely to say and do, but also to *be,* in a ministry that is primarily the ministry of the incarnate Word.

Nor may we treat this solely as an individual matter. It has also a structural dimension. From early days, as the churches have grown in numbers and influence, they have developed organizations and institutions that contribute to impairment of the servant character of their ministry. Whether their structures be papal, episcopalian, presbyterian, or congregationalist, whether they be autocratic, oligarchical, synodal, or bureaucratic, the churches have opened their doors to the evils against which Jesus so plainly warned his disciples. They have given dangerous power and wealth to some while treating others as pawns on an ecclesiastical chessboard, as employees to be hired and fired at will, or as a "laity" that will provide resources (especially money!) for programs over which they have little control. The problems of growth admit of no simple solutions, but the time has surely been long overdue for the churches to stop adapting their structures to secular models and to start conforming them to the pattern of Christ's own servant ministry, so that in this regard and at this level, too, their ministry can truly be, and be seen to be, the ministry of the incarnate Word.

THE MINISTRY OF THE WRITTEN WORD

If it is true that the ministry is primarily and properly the Word's own ministry, this applies to the written Word as well as to the incarnate Word. A distinction arises here, for we have seen that in their inner relationship the incarnate Word obviously has primacy. Hence the ministry of the written

Word is itself taken up into that of the incarnate Word. God caused the Word to take written form in order to teach us that he has shown his benevolence to us through his Son (First Helvetic V). He also enables the written Word to perform its function by means of the Holy Spirit, whose inner witness gives it its dignity and authority (Belgic V), and whose illuminating makes it possible for us to perceive it to be God's Word (Westminster I. vi). Nevertheless, within this ministry of Christ and the Spirit, the written Word has its own ministry into which the ministers of the Word of God are integrated as they participate in the ministry of the Word incarnate.

The written Word has this ministry as an ongoing perceptible entity — more easily perceived than Christ himself! — in Christian life and history. Barth magnificently stresses this point in his discussion of the authority and freedom of the Word in *CD* I, §§ 20-21. At times Christians may ignore scripture, domesticate it, treat it cavalierly or capriciously, obscure it, or rob it of its full power or true sense by additions, interpretations, deletions, or corruptions. But scripture as a written text has its own life and reality distinct from the life and reality of those who handle it. It has, therefore, its own power of rising up again to confront, challenge, correct, reform, and instruct the churches and their leaders and members. In an age of decay the written Word can be the motive power of a reformation; in an age of rationalism it can be the driving force behind an evangelical revival; in an age of ecclesiastical rigidity it can be the inspiration behind a movement of renewal; and in every age it can be the agent of individual faith, upbuilding, and consecration. The written Word has its own ministry, enhanced in modern times by the invention of printing and recording, and the distribution of the scriptures in hundreds of different languages across the continents.

The written Word has this ministry in its normative function as the original, divinely inspired, prophetic and apostolic testimony to God's revealing and reconciling Word and work. All subsequent ministry, to be authentic, must be tested and informed by this ministry. As the Formula of Concord (1577) trenchantly states, holy scripture is "the judge, norm, and rule, according to which, as by the (only) touchstone, all doctrines are to be 'examined and judged'" (Compendious Rule III). It is "the oldest teaching, most perfect and supreme" (First Helvetic I). It is the "rule of truth" by which all things should be "examined, regulated, and reformed" (Gallican V). It is the "infallible rule" by which to try the spirits, the "truth of God" that is "above all" (Belgic VIII). It is the voice of the church's own "spouse and pastor" over which the church "takes not upon her to be mistress" (Scots XIX). In it the church "has all things fully expounded which belong to a saving faith, and also the framing of a life acceptable to God" (Second Helvetic I). Speaking in it, the Holy Spirit is the "supreme judge, by which all controversies of religion are to be determined . . . and in whose sentence we are to rest" (Westminster I.x). In virtue of its unique status the written Word has its own unique ministry as Christ exercises his own ministry through it in the power of the Spirit.

The written Word performs its ministry as it is read and heard congregationally and individually. Most Christians across the centuries have facilitated its work by regular Old and New Testament readings at worship. Always valuable, these are especially so when there are those who cannot read the Bible for themselves. This is why it is so important that obstacles should not impede this public ministry. One such obstacle is the use of venerable but alien or antiquated texts and translations. Another is the use of unskilled or inadequately prepared readers, as though this were an unimportant exercise. Another is the simple familiarity that robs passages of their dynamism. Another is the reduction of readings to a few verses, or even the selected omission of verses, which is especially odd and reprehensible in churches that make much of fidelity to an inerrant Bible. The basic problem, perhaps, is the idea that reading the written Word is merely a tradition, and a failure to see it as a vehicle for the Word's own essential ministry whereby we may come to a saving knowledge of God and to growth in Christian faith, character, and service.

The ministry of the written Word is that of communicating the gospel to the churches and individual believers, and through them to the world. It tells the story of God's dealings with us. It presents the message of Christ and therefore of forgiveness and renewal, with all that this implies by way of doctrine, personal and social ethic, character, and the ordering of the community and its life and work. Primarily its ministry is positive. It teaches us what to believe, to do, and to be. The Reformers with their eye for abuses tend perhaps to stress the negative function. The written Word is the judge that shows us what to correct or oppose or abolish. "In controversies of religion or matters of faith, we cannot admit any other judge than God himself pronouncing by the holy scriptures what is true, what is false" (Second Helvetic II). But the written Word does show us what is true as well as what is false. The negative function is the reverse side of the positive. What we first expect from the written Word which illuminates and converts us in the power of the Spirit is knowledge of the gospel, instruction in the new life in Christ, and direction for the affairs of the church and its ministry. Only in the light of what scripture says positively, and with a view to amendment, do we seek its negative evaluation of the life, teaching, and character of ourselves, of others, of the church, and of the world at large.

The need for this positive and negative ministry of the written Word is always and everywhere apparent. Even believers whom it has enlightened have much to learn about the dogmatic and ethical implications of their faith, about Christian lifestyle and character, and about the proper structuring of the churches and fulfillment of their task. Ignorance abounds, as do also misguided and often obstinate opinions, beliefs, interpretations, speculations, and agendas. If many Christians do not yet have enough knowledge of scripture to hear what it is saying, many, too, refuse to hear it or be instructed by it, setting themselves up as its judges instead of letting it be the judge, picking and choosing from it what seems good to them, or simply preferring their own notions and practices. Unquestionably we must read the written Word discerningly if it is to do its work, but one of the most foolish and destructive courses in Christian history is the hampering of its ministry by a sorry failure to listen to it with the requisite openness and obedient humility; or by an arrogant refusal to accept the normativity of its precepts and precedents; or by a subtle erosion of its message with the help of relativizing, demythologizing, contextualizing, or an airy appeal to the moving of the Spirit in detachment from scripture.

Opposition or evasion, however, does not negate the Word's own ministry. Obstructed in one age, place, or person, it works in another. Dissected, reshuffled, and mauled by scholarly know-alls, it retains its substance and power. Defeated on the surface, it tackles the roots. Outshone by dazzling novelties, it steadily radiates the light of eternal truth which lasts when the flashy brilliance of its critics and competitors fades. Shouted down by noisy theorizers, it speaks its simple, saving message which as the Word of the Lord endures forever. Those who ally themselves with its ministry can be confident. They may be ignored or scorned as reactionary and old-fashioned. They may be tactically outmatched and outmaneuvered. They may experience what seem to be failures and defeats. But they share in a ministry which, inspired and empowered by the Spirit as witness to the incarnate Word, can never be finally arrested or overthrown, but always accomplishes that for which God himself has ordained it. As Zwingli stated so powerfully in his *Clarity and Certainty of the Word of God,* God infallibly does what he says. Because the written Word is *his* Word, we can trust it to do its work of converting, renewing, directing, instructing, judging, and correcting, notwithstanding all our human failures to heed it, to obey it, to believe it, to rely upon it, or to enter as fully as we should into its ongoing ministry.

THE MINISTRY OF THE PROCLAIMED WORD

Just as the incarnate Word and the written Word have their own ministries, so, too, does the proclaimed Word. This is not so obvious. We tend to think of this Word more narrowly as the Word that we proclaim today. Reflection shows us, however, that this Word is a past as well as a present Word. As a past Word it confronts us, like scripture, as an objective, historical entity with its own reality and ministry. We might sum up this past Word of proclamation under the word "tradition." It embraces the creeds, the confessions, the writings, the rites, the ceremonies, the practices, the policies, the institutions, and the actions of the church's past in the many shifting circumstances of human life and history.

As the ministry of the written Word is not autonomous but relates to that of the incarnate Word, so the ministry of the proclaimed Word relates integrally to the ministries of both the incarnate Word and the written Word. Deriving its authorization, authority, and power, and indeed its basic content, from the incarnate Word, it does so by the mediation and under the scrutiny of the written Word. Oral tradition in the dynamic sense undoubtedly played an important part prior to the writing and fixing of the canon, but authentic tradition and the canon do not diverge. The proclaimed Word has a valid ministry, then, only insofar as it serves the incarnate Word in accordance with the written Word and in exposition and application of it.

A first glance might suggest that many Reformation statements discount this ministry of the past Word of proclamation. The Belgic Confession bluntly refuses to "compare any writings of men, be they ever so holy," with scripture (VII). The Scots argues that "without just examination dare we not receive whatsoever is obtruded unto men under the name of general councils" (XX). The Anglican Articles realistically admit that general councils "may err, and sometimes have erred, even in matters pertaining unto God" (XXI, cf. XIX). The Second Helvetic states: "We suffer not ourselves, in controversies about religion, to be pressed with the bare testimonies of fathers or decrees of councils, much less with the received customs, or with the multitude of men being of one judgment, or with prescriptions of long time" (II). "All decrees of councils, opinions of ancient writers, doctrines of men, and private opinions" are subject to examination (Westminster I.x).

Nevertheless, the Reformers were qualifying this ministry rather than negating it. So long as the proclaimed Word neither opposes scripture, nor obscures it, nor adds to it, they would accept this Word and profit by it. Luther, Zwingli, Calvin, Bullinger, and Anglicans such as Cranmer and Jewel all quote the fathers. The Gallican (V), Belgic (IX), Anglican (VII), and Second Helvetic Confessions (XI, XVII) endorse the three historic creeds. The Second Helvetic accepts the witness of the early councils (XI), and the Scots says: "We do not rashly condemn that which godly men, assembled together in general council lawfully gathered, have proponed unto us" (XX). The condemnation of such heresies as Sabellianism, Arianism, Nestorianism, and Eutychianism is approved (Gallican VI; Belgic IX; Scots V; Second Helvetic XI). The Belgic Confession commends the true church for its constant defense of the doctrine of the Trinity (IX). The Second Helvetic boldly claims: "We retain the Christian, sound, and Catholic faith, whole and inviolable" (XI). The approach to patristic writings is similar: "We do not despise the interpretations of the holy Greek and Latin fathers, nor reject their disputations and treatises as far as they agree with the scriptures" (Second Helvetic II).

Finding much of value in the past Word of proclamation, the Reformers claim a right of dissent only from things "differing from, or altogether contrary to, the scriptures" (Second Helvetic II). This might be the vigorous dissent of Knox: "If then the interpretation of any doctor, kirk, or council repugn to the plain Word of God, written in any other place of scripture, it is a thing most certain that there is not the true understanding and meaning of the Holy Ghost" (Scots XVIII). Or it might be the more modest dissent of Bullinger, who applauds the fathers because they, too, "with one consent, will not have their writings matched with the canonical scriptures, but bid us allow them so far forth as they either agree with them or disagree" (Second Helvetic II).

Under the normative authority of the primary witness in the written Word, the proclaimed Word has a valuable ministry of insight, direction, warning, and example. Past interpretations, decisions, and actions open many windows on the substance, meaning, and implications of the divine revealing and reconciling that reached its climax in Christ. They offer helpful hints for the presentation of the gospel, the living of the Christian life, and the shaping of the church and its mission. By the mistakes they condemn and the mistakes they commit they mark off many dead ends of theological and ethical thinking, of liturgical and devotional development, of organizational practice, and of missionary and pastoral strategy. With their success and failures in many different settings they provide models of thinking, worship, life, proclamation, and structure as the churches move into different ages, countries, cultures, and circumstances.

In relation to the past Word of proclamation, the churches face the dangers of canonization on the one hand and iconoclasm on the other. It is undoubtedly tempting to be able to appeal to patristic or conciliar authority as definitive and sacrosanct; it saves much effort in thought and debate. Quoting Augustine, Thomas, Luther, or Calvin, or dismissing an opposing view as Docetic, Modalist, Nestorian, or Pelagian, gives much satisfaction. Yet it is equally tempting to reject past authority altogether. The mistakes of the fathers and the problems raised by ancient definitions, decisions, and policies are plain enough. Demolishing the past, believing that wisdom begins with one's own generation, offering insights without knowing or asking whether some ancient doctor might not have advanced or discredited them years ago, developing lines of thought or practice without taking into account prior objections or alternatives or warnings — all this confers a heady sense of originality, freedom, and vitality. But if canonization easily results in sterility, no less easily iconoclasm yields superficiality.

The past Word of proclamation has a ministry that it discharges only if there is cautious acceptance, such as we see in the Reformers. The proper role of this ministry is within the ministries of the incarnate Word and the written Word. What has been said and done before does not bind us absolutely. Nevertheless, it has much to teach us, insofar as it proclaims

Christ authentically according to the prophetic and apostolic witness. Indeed, even where we see it to be inauthentic, we can and should learn from its mistakes of interpretation, inference, and practice, developing the discernment that is needed if our own ministry of proclamation is to avoid the similar mistakes that so easily threaten us.

THE MINISTERING OF THE WORD

The ministry of the proclaimed Word is, of course, present as well as past. This fact brings us to our own living participation in the ministry of the threefold Word. It confronts us with our own responsibility as ministers of the Word of God. What does it mean to be taken up into the ministry of the Word? How are we to discharge the task?

We might define the task as that of ministering to the Word and of ministering it to others. We minister first to the incarnate Word and minister it to others. We do so by serving Christ and by presenting Christ as Savior and Lord. In Christian ministry we serve others too—non-Christians, fellow-Christians, congregations, authorities of various kinds—but we are true ministers of the Word of God only if we serve Christ first and are servants of others for Christ's sake (cf. 1 Cor. 3:5, 4:1; 2 Cor. 4:5). Similarly, we may present Christ in different ways, from different angles, with different implications, and to different detailed ends, e.g. in evangelism, instruction, worship, scholarship, philanthropy, social action, or examples, but we are true ministers of the Word of God only if we do present Christ and thus participate in Christ's own ministry.

Sermons that bypass Christ, teaching that gives a false picture of Christ, worship that fails to exalt him, scholarship that obscures his real nature and work, philanthropy that becomes self-glorification, social action that is a mere advancing of causes, examples that display a Christianity which in no way commends Christ—these may all carry the name of Christ, but only imperfectly, if at all, are they a ministering of the Word of God. The title without the reality is an empty shell which the churches may tolerate but the futility of which history itself—let alone the last judgment—brings to light. "Sirs, we would see Jesus" (cf. Jn. 12:21) is a request that has found its way into many pulpits, and it is a request that all Christians would do well to meet as in different forms they give themselves to this ministry, ministering to the incarnate Word and ministering it to others.

We are ministers of the written Word as we minister to this Word and minister it to others. We do this by enabling the written Word to do its own work and by so opening it up that its message goes out plainly and forcefully to the church and the world. This involves many specific tasks in addition to the public and private reading to which we have already referred. There are the basic tasks of copying, printing, and distribution.

There is the delicate task of accurate but idiomatic translation. There is the task of establishing a sound text, that of fixing the meaning of the Greek and Hebrew, that of exposition, that of understanding the themes and contents in the narrower and broader context, that of pressing home the message and its implications in sermons, addresses, lectures, and study groups, and finally that of appropriate application in the life and acts and practice of the churches and their members. The discharge of this ministry will itself be a ministering also of the incarnate Word inasmuch as that Word is the central subject of the witness of the written Word. To present holy scripture is in fact the most direct and effective way to present Christ.

Authentic ministry of the written Word is not, then, a ministry of the written Word alone. Scripture is not just an academic textbook whose contents Christians must learn if they are to pass successfully the last examination. Christ is, of course, presented in texts. The texts are important. There is a genuine need of study, thought, and learning. Dedication to the texts is required for progress in the meaning of faith, the demands of discipleship, and the implications of service. Yet simply to teach these things without bringing people to Christ or helping them to true faith and obedience is not to render true service to the written Word. The goal of the Spirit, the Inner Teacher, is always to lead to Christ by way of the outer ministry of the written Word.

A supposed ministry of the written Word that does not let it speak its own message can hardly contribute to the presenting of the incarnate Word. We have referred already to obscure translation, incompetent readers, and inadequate lections. We might mention also the unseemly wrangling about interpretation that results more in confusion than in enlightenment; the speculative scholarship that substitutes career-advancing hypotheses for objective research and makes of what ought to be ministry an academic game; and the illusion that we can judge the Bible, that we may pose the questions that it ought to answer, or that we may accept, amend, expand, or discard at will its own questions and answers. In ways such as these we prevent the written Word from doing its own work, from making its own points, from passing its own judgments, from putting its own questions, and from giving its own answers, We truly minister to the written Word and minister it to others only as we give it free course in proclaiming its own vital message. Our primary task it to let it say what it has to say, to teach ourselves and others how to let ourselves be told what it has to tell.

We are ministers of the past Word of proclamation as we minister to this Word and minister it to others. We do this by making it available, by studying it, by teaching it, by relating it to present conditions, by enabling it to contribute to our own thinking, writing, preaching, and practice. We sift this Word, testing it by the written word, but we also learn from it. We learn from it theologically by gaining from it insight into things that we did not see before, or did not see clearly or fully before. We learn from it biblically by letting it correct or supplement our understanding of the written Word. We learn from it practically by receiving instruction from it on the ramifications of discipleship, the methods of ministry, the legitimate options of lifestyle, and the proper structures of community and mission. By opening up the past, and by opening ourselves and others to it, we participate in its ministry, integrating our own ministry into it and thereby furthering also the ministries of the written Word and the incarnate Word.

In what forms do we minister the Word of God today? In answering this question we must avoid entanglement in false and destructive antitheses. History has seen heated debates between those who give precedence to word and those who give precedence to sacrament. Both word and sacrament, however, have behind them the precept and precedent of Christ. The Reformers saw this when they linked the two in their description of the true church (Augsburg VII; Gallican XXVIII; Scots XVIII; Anglican XIX; Second Helvetic XVII). To set them in opposition, therefore, is meaningless and disruptive.

The same applies to the antithesis of evangelism and social action which has done so much damage in the present century. Christ's own ministry was one of both word and work. The early church took this as a model as it combined the remedying of many abuses with intensive missionary efforts. So did the Reformers, who pushed through many practical programs and reforms. So did the great evangelicals, whose social agendas went hand in hand with a vigorous evangelistic, missionary, and pastoral program. Why, indeed, should we have to choose? Individuals may have to devote more time and effort to this task or that, but surely they can do so without disparaging others, and surely the churches can see that their own word-act of ministry must correspond to the word-act of God and of Christ, the act embodying the word, the word expounding the act.

Authentic ministry is multi-faceted. If emphasis often falls on word or sacrament or social action, we certainly must not forget the equally important ministry of worship, which is divine service. This in turn includes intercession, in which we integrate our ministry into the intercessory ministry of the risen Christ, and which is essential to all else that is done by way of ministry. Important, too, is the ministry of Christian life and character upon which the pastoral epistles lay such stress in describing qualifications for the ordained ministry. If Christians do not show themselves to be a "letter from Christ" which all can know and read (2 Cor. 3:2f.), ministry may be discharged with great energy and competence but it loses much of its credibility and force.

Ministry is also inclusive. The churches use the title "ministers of the Word of God" more particularly for those whom they ordain to preach and teach and administer the sacraments and offer pastoral care. In fact, however, all Christians are ministers of the Word of God in scores of different ways. They all share in the ministry of the threefold Word. They all present Christ, communicate scripture, and pass on tradition. They do it by service in the churches, by supporting Christian agencies, by fellowship in the body of Christ, by personal witness of word and act and life. Ordinary Christians often do much more than is realized by those who are clergy-oriented or those who see them mostly as a means of funding. Yet more needs to be done to end the unhealthy idea that ministry is a matter for professionals and to achieve a proper balance and cooperation of clergy and people. A more intensive mobilizing of the whole community for ministry will undoubtedly give the ministry of God's Word an added richness and power and enhance rather than diminish the special contribution of those who are called and set apart specifically to be ministers of the Word.

When we say that the task of proclamation today is to present Christ, to expound and apply scripture, and to pass on tested tradition, the question arises: What precisely is involved, and what is the specific question?

A first answer to this twofold question lies in the modern term "contextualizing." Contextualizing is a necessary task, but it also carries with it, as noted earlier, a potential for disaster. The necessary task is that each generation in each country, class, and culture must minister the Word of God in such a way that the people of that generation, country, class, and culture can understand and appropriate it. The potential for disaster is that in making the required transposition they will lose or weaken or pervert the true substance of the gospel.

Living proclamation has the responsibility of achieving the difficult balance between relevance and fidelity. Churches that compromise fidelity, often excusing themselves by a tenuous appeal to the freedom of the Word and Spirit, can easily enough find relevant words, acts, attitudes, practices, structures, and methods. History shows, indeed, that where there has not been adequate vigilance churches have even slipped unwittingly and unwillingly into the relevance that erodes fidelity. On the other hand, churches that have no care for relevance also find no great difficulty, for they simply retain traditional words, acts, attitudes, practices, structures, and methods. History shows again that where the need for relevance is not strongly felt churches can often slip unwittingly and unwillingly into the fidelity that jeopardizes it.

The Word in its ministry is constantly marching into new ages and spreading to new cultures and continents. As it does so the forms must change, the substance remain. Scripture itself has to be put into new languages, or new forms of old languages, but with no sacrifice of its meaning and message. Similarly the gospel in its totality must be translated into new forms of word and thought and life and structure, but again with no sacrifice of its enduring content. The churches constantly face the problem of the Nicene and Chalcedonian fathers as they had to put trinitarian and Christological reality into the contemporary philosophical vocabulary without illegitimately Hellenizing the gospel as some critics have supposed. They face the same problem that confronted the medieval church when it tried to establish Christian structures in the Germanic world without the illegitimate secularization that we detect so easily in retrospect. Do we not have a solemn warning against false contextualizing in the structures of our modern churches? Does not electronic evangelism show us how fine is the line between valid use and abominable abuse? Can we not see from such ventures as those of Asian and African theology, with the pressing dangers of pagan intrusion, what a delicate operation it is when the Word must be a living Word but also the same Word if it is to be genuinely God's Word?

The second answer to the twofold question, *What is involved and where is the problem?* lies in the relation between the human Word and the Spirit who is truly free, yet not free in the sense of being at the beck and call of freely floating human thoughts and fancies. This relation depends on our obedience. Are we setting our relevant human ministry within the perichoresis of the ministry of the Word incarnate, written, and proclaimed? Do we here and now present Christ according to the normative biblical witness and with due regard to tested tradition? If we do not, no facile talk about the moving of the Spirit will give our ministry of word and work validity as the ministry of the Word of God.

Yet even though we seek obediently to integrate our ministry into the Word's own ministry, can we ever take it for granted that we are really ministers of the Word of God, that our words and works are God's Work? Do we not still have to reckon with our ignorance and inadequacy: "Who is sufficient for these things?" (2 Cor. 2:16)? Indeed, are we not servants whom the Master may use as he chooses and pleases, not as we ourselves decide and plan? Is not God's Word spoken only when he himself speaks it? Even though we do all, does it not depend on God alone whether or not he speaks it?

We certainly need to say and do what we are commanded to say and do as we make the difficult transition to our own time and place. In the last resort, however, humility must accompany obedience. And humility casts us back upon the ministry of prayer in which we are taken up into the intercessory ministry of the risen Word. We need to pray that God will show us how rightly to say and do what we ought to say and do, that he will be pleased to use our feeble words and acts, that he will take whatever is right and good in them and that he will overrule all that is wrong and bad, so that in the power of his Spirit they may be his own mighty Word and act.

Thrown back upon prayer, however, we make this prayer not in the desperation of a last resort, but in expectant hope. Christ not only intercedes for us; he also instituted this ministry of ours and empowers it with his Spirit. Thus we may say: "Our sufficiency is from God" (2 Cor. 3:5). We no less than Paul, in our different ways, are ministers of the Word of God. For all our foibles, faults, and failings, we can be letters from Christ. It may be said of our works, too, that people see them and glorify our Father in heaven (Mt. 5:16). Some at least will accept our word, not as ours, but "as what it really is, the word of God, which is at work in believers" (1 Thes. 2:13). In the words of the Second Helvetic (I): "The Lord itself has said in the gospel, 'It is not you that speak, but the Spirit of my Father speaketh in you'" (Mt. 10:20). This is not a blank check. God is not endorsing all that the churches and their various ordained and ordinary ministers may say and do and be. But it *is* a ground of hope.

God adds his seal and power to authentic ministry. We can take nothing for granted. We cannot afford to be complacent. No autonomy is ours. All power is not given to *us*. Nevertheless, within the ministry of the Word itself, in the power of the Spirit and the prayer of obedience and humility, our human ministry can be in truth the ministry of the Word of God.

6

COLIN E. GUNTON

✟

Baptism and
the Christian Community

T HE THEOLOGY OF MINISTRY has rightly been identified by the editors
of this volume not only as one of Ray S. Anderson's distinctive
contributions to theology, but as an area of which contemporary theology
is notoriously neglectful. This essay is an indirect discussion of ministry in
that it treats a topic that is causing great concern for the church's ministers:
baptism. The theme will not, however, be baptism in the abstract, but
baptism in the context of a particular and concrete problem of ministry.
That context is perhaps unique in the history of our troubled and divided
Western church, and therefore requires some introduction.

THE PROBLEM IN ITS CONTEXT

What is now the United Reformed Church in Great Britain was formed in
1972 as a union of Congregationalists and Presbyterians from England and
Wales. It has since been re-formed with the addition to it of a number of
congregations of the Churches of Christ, and therein lies its uniqueness.
For the union represents the coming together in one church of communities
holding different positions on the administration of baptism: the one
paedobaptist, the other practicing only the baptism of believers. In the new
church all congregations are expected to offer both forms of baptism; no
minister, however, is compelled to administer baptism in a form that
conscience forbids.

Essential to such an arrangement is the commitment to respect the form
of baptism administered by those whose convictions are different. The
church's constitution is insistent that entry to the church is by baptism,
which may be administered only once to any person. Thus all baptisms in
both forms administered in the new church and formerly administered in
its constituent parts are recognized as real baptisms. The commitment to

recognize what was once rejected may be supposed most difficult for those whose convictions have been that baptism is to be administered only to those able to confess belief. But it is *respect* that is required, not abandonment of convictions. Thus the United Reformed Church is a testing ground for the acceptance of differences within community that will be required of all who hope to grow together with formerly separated branches of the church.

For the most part the respect for different forms of baptism has been given, and in ways which, it is hoped, will form a model for ecumenical relationships in the future. However, as often happens in such matters, the expected strains and stresses have appeared at other places than might have been expected. Into the picture have come the forces of what has come to be called restorationism,[1] with its strong stress on both the failure of the mainline churches and a call to individual renewal, a call that often denies the validity of the baptism that converts may have received as infants. Inevitably, the pressures make themselves felt in the traditional denominations, particularly in calls for what is sometimes referred to as "rebaptism." Many churches are feeling the pressures; but they bear with particular force on a church that affirms the necessity to respect the reality of both forms of baptism in the one community.

The pastoral problem arising from requests for "second" baptism forms the immediate context for this discussion. But, like all movements which renew or trouble the church—and sometimes both—restorationism does not come out of the blue. Along with its cousin, pentecostalism, its genesis can be seen to be in part a reaction to widely acknowledged weaknesses in the shape traditional Christianity has taken. A frequent object of its criticism is institutionalism, against which so many movements of protest have been directed (only to fall into it themselves in due time). But institutionalism is, it seems to me, the obverse of an equal failure, which is only too evident in both restorationism and so many of the political fashions of recent decades. It is, of course, *individualism*. In that respect, it is easy to recognize the pedigree of so many recent revivalist movements, for example as in a statement cited by Alan Sell from Robert Mackintosh's nineteenth century *The Insufficiency of Revivalism*:

> Evangelicalism does not wish to be distracted by any wider moral outlook than the desire to save one's own soul in the first place and, secondly, to promote the salvation of the souls of other individuals. . . . Infant baptism is the great rock of offence to the triumphant revival (because it places the infant individual within a covenanted fellowship).[2]

It is the heirs of the evangelical revival who succumb most easily to temptations of individualism, for reasons which that quotation makes only too clear. And yet those of us who are suspicious of evangelicalism should beware of casting too many stones in that direction. We too live in a glass house of our own making, and it can be argued that our current disorder derives at once from sloppy pastoral practice and an inadequate theology of baptism which is itself deeply stained by individualism. I shall begin by sketching in broad strokes some of the historical roots of the problem.

The enthusiasts for rebaptism, like those for some recent political movements of a strongly individualist stamp, bear likeness to the spiritual descendants of the Age of Reason. Karl Barth pointed out long ago that rationalist and pietist are but two sides of the same coin because both place the human individual in the center: the reason or experience of the individual is decisive over against, and if necessary in opposition to, the traditions and life of the community as a whole.[3] This is very important for a theology of baptism, because, as I hope to show, while baptism is in part the concern of the particular *person,* it is not primarily a matter for the person as *individual* but for the person in relation to other people in the community of salvation, the covenant people of God. Baptism cannot, and should not, be treated in isolation from the life of the community of faith.

And yet the root cause of recent difficulties is that we live at the end of a long history, beginning well before the Enlightenment, in which baptism has been treated individualistically and in abstraction from the life and worship of the covenant community. The present outbreak of enthusiasm for "rebaptism" does not appear out of thin air but is a response to the particular way in which the sacrament has been used in the life of the church for many centuries. Dominating the history is the phenomenon of Christendom, that now almost completely departed era when to be a Christian could often mean little more than being born in Europe. In the centuries after the conversion of the emperor Constantine early in the fourth century there developed a society in which Christianity became the official ideology. To be baptized under such arrangement came to involve little more than undergoing a social rite of passage. Against such practice, traces of which still remain, it is scarcely surprising that protests have arisen.

In parallel with the social development, and in a complicated relation to it, there arose an equally inadequate theology of baptism. It was based on a pessimistic view of the human condition, owing more to a form of platonic philosophy than to the gospel. It taught that to be a human being was to inherit, by virtue of the process of human descent from Adam, a stain— "original sin"—which meant that without the baptism which was supposed to remove that stain, one was destined for hell. The points about this which we should note in particular are three. The first is that there developed from it an essentially negative conception of baptism, which was conceived more as a means of avoiding an unpleasant fate than as entry into a rich inheritance. Of course, such teaching was never in practice unmixed with more positive, gospel contents, but it went very deep into the consciousness of Western society, as is revealed by the fact that fear of the consequences of a lack of baptism still operates as a motive in parents seeking baptism for their children. Baptism came to be as much a pro- phylactic handed out to individuals by an institution as the means of entry into the community of salvation.

The second point to note is that underlying the development I have sketched is an inadequate conception of a sacrament. The popular and grossly misleading definition of a sacrament as "an outward and visible sign of an inward and spiritual grace" falsely divides the world into two, the inner and the outer, and supposes that a sacrament is something that, although it makes no visible difference to the outside of a person, causes something to happen "inside." Thus baptism comes to be conceived as an inner cleansing from the stain of original sin, performed "efficaciously" by an official representative of the church.[4]

The third point follows directly, and it is that we have inherited a very individualistic conception of baptism as rather that which is performed on individuals to save them from an inherited stain or a hellish fate than that by which each of them is brought into a new relation with God through the medium of the covenant community. It must be remembered, of course, that the two latter points are caricatures, and that the Reformers and others protested against the abuse of both baptism and the Lord's Supper; but these caricatures have continued to affect our thinking and practice. Because they have been present, they have prevented an adequate theology from emerging and so contributed to the present disorder.

Before I move to what I hope will be a somewhat more adequate theology, two more items of ground-clearing are in order. First: In the light of the misuse of baptism by tradition, it is understandable that some have come to argue that only "believers" ought to be baptized—or, more radically, that the official baptism dispensed by the churches is not "real" because it is merely a social rite of passage. The protest is a proper one against the secularizing of baptism, which turns it into more a social rite of passage than a truly churchly ordinance. Despite this, I would wish to argue that the protest takes the wrong from, for it perpetuates the individu- alism of the tradition. It is not the baptism of infants that is the problem, but the indiscriminate baptism of those whose parents have no living relation to the covenant community, or, more strictly, of those for whom there is no likelihood that baptism is truly initiation into the life of that community.

Second: There is nothing to be gained by arguments about whether the primitive church did or did not practice infant baptism. The arguments are inconclusive, and likely to remain so. In any case, that is not the point; at issue is whether the *logic* of the gospel justifies the practice of baptizing those who have little or no choice in the matter. By the "logic" of the gospel I mean not something deduced from, for example, the words of scripture, but the way in which the content of the gospel can be seen, perhaps after years of reflection, to invite or require a certain response or course of action.[5] As an example, we could take one discovery of what the logic of the gospel involves that took far too long to make. The primitive church appears to have condoned the practice of slavery.[6] Yet later generations came to believe that the logic of the gospel prohibits the institution. The question for us is similar: What does the logic of the gospel have to say to us about the nature and practice of baptism?

THE NATURE OF BAPTISM

Baptism takes its reality from the death of Jesus on the cross. We baptize because Christ died on the cross for the sins of the world. That is the element we may not ignore or play down, because it is the place of our redemption. It is said that when Luther experienced his trials of faith, he would pace the room exclaiming: "I have been baptized." His baptism had not been an "experience" for him, as we so often want to make it. Rather, it determined his experience because it was grounded in the historic event that provided the framework for his existence. The cross was something that happened apart from his knowledge or wishes. Indeed, it happened when, to use Paul's expression, we were helpless. That is its significance: that before we can possibly be in a position to know or appropriate its meaning, something has been done for us and for all the world.

It is in the light of that absolute givenness of the cross that we must interpret other features of biblical talk of baptism. There are two of particular note. The first is the command to baptize recorded at the end of Matthew's Gospel. It is now widely believed that the dominical command to baptize in the name of the Father, Son, and Holy Spirit is not a report of actual words of the risen Jesus, but the invention of the early church. While it seems to me that this is a matter of opinion, because the truth cannot be known either way, what is not in question is that the practice of baptism is justified because Christ died and rose. Such "invention" as there was must be seen as the obedient response to what the church believed to be the logic of the gospel. The rightness of baptizing is not dependent upon the outcome of a historical investigation into the origins of a particular text. Rather, we accept it as a command from God because it is the means whereby we enter into relation to the saving death of Christ.

Second is the baptism of Jesus by John in the Jordan. Here I would want to argue that although the baptism of Jesus is relevant to our understanding and practice of baptism, we should not move directly from that to our own experience and practice. Jesus' baptism by John gains its significance from the fact that it was the baptism of this particular person in his relation to the people from whom he came. The significance of *this* baptism is—among other things—that it signified Jesus' identification of himself with Israel under the judgment of God represented and proclaimed by John, and that it points forward to his acceptance by death of the judgment of God on human sin. It is therefore an anticipation of his death on the cross, as the words of Jesus recorded by Luke (12:50) make clear. Jesus dies as the representative of humankind under judgment, as the passion stories, perhaps Mark's especially, show us. His death, accordingly, is the death of all (2 Cor. 4:14). Thus while the baptism of Jesus is an essential element of the theology of baptism, we do not baptize because Jesus baptized, but because he went to the cross which was foreshadowed in his baptism.

What, then, are we to make of the baptism of Jesus and its completion on the cross? Two aspects are especially significant: the public nature of what happened, and its communal or corporate dimensions.

The baptism and crucifixion of Jesus are not interesting by virtue of some experiences he may be supposed to have undergone, but for what they mean in the context of his life and ministry, and what that means also in the context of the history of Israel and all humankind. They are public events, signaling the way by which God takes place among us to achieve our redemption: that is to say, our reconciliation with God and restoration to the path of true life. It is in *this* man that all the nations of the earth shall be blessed.

In addition to their public significance, the baptism and death of Jesus are of communal significance. As we have seen, the baptism of Jesus takes place in relation to the sin and judgment of Israel. Jesus is what he is by virtue of his relation to the people from whom he comes and to whom he is called. His death and resurrection universalize the relationship: that is to say, reveal its significance for all humankind. After that, it is around him, the crucified and risen, that the covenant people of God are reconstituted by the action of the Holy Spirit. To be brought into relation with him is to be made a member of the people of God.

And the means whereby we are brought into relation with him is baptism.[7] Just as Jesus' baptism bound him up with Israel, and his death with the whole human race under judgment, so our baptism binds us to Christ and the covenant people of God reconstituted in him. That, I want to suggest, is the primary significance of baptism. It is not first of all the expression of the faith of an individual or some invisible inner cleansing, but is public and communal: it is the means by which a person is brought into relation with Christ through the medium of his body, the church. The crucial link is between the once-for-all death of Christ on the cross and the baptism which appropriates that death for the member of his body. The logic is that as Christ died once, so can there be only one baptism into his death. Almost universally, the church has accepted that logic. Even those of Baptist persuasion who believe that it is right to baptize as adults those who have been baptized as infants recognize the logic by claiming that the baptism of an infant is not a real baptism.[8]

The practice of "rebaptism," as it has taken place in recent years, therefore raises the question of "validity." Here I want to make two points. The first is to repeat that the basis of the rite, and so of its validity, is the death of Jesus on the cross. There is nothing automatically valid about the saying of particular words over and the application of water, in whatever way, to a person. But, second, given that the words have been said and the water used in a public ceremony we deny the reality of that baptism at our peril, because by doing so we risk unbelief in the promise of God that underlies the use of the words. If the baptism was performed in the light of the promise, then we are bound to say that the baptized has been brought into relation to Christ. What right have we to deny it? We may like neither the pastoral practice of indiscriminate baptism nor the fact that many baptisms are performed out of the context of the regular worship of the local community. But that does not license us to decide that the baptism was not a "real" baptism.

Baptism is a churchly and public rite before it is an individual or experiential one. It is therefore not just for the "saved," and certainly not for those alone who have been through a certain kind of experience, but for all who are called to share the life of those who are on the way to salvation. Once we lose the criterion of the public and churchly character of the sacrament, we are on the slippery slope of a merely subjective or experiential judgment. We must confess that so many baptisms have not, in practice, expressed the churchly dimension adequately. But is that warrant to deny that they were baptisms?

THE BAPTISM OF INFANTS AND
THE DOCTRINE OF THE CHURCH

Up to this point, I have argued that baptism brings us into relation with God through the medium of his community, the body of Christ. It follows that any other supposed or second baptism is not a baptism, because one cannot be brought into the body of Christ when one is already there. Baptism, of whatever kind, can be performed only once because by it we are incorporated into Christ. On this basis, churches whose practice is to baptize only believers and those who baptize infants also can share one element of unity at least. Both build upon the same bedrock: that as Christ died, once for all, for the forgiveness of sins, so there is but one way into his church: by the once for all baptism by which we are incorporated in him.

That said, however, I wish in the rest of the essay to argue very strongly for the rightness, indeed necessity, of the baptism of the infant children of those who are active worshiping members of the community of faith. I agree that there are arguments on the other side, and that some doubt, particularly as we come to terms with past abuse of the sacrament, must always remain as to whether the decision to baptize infants was the correct one. But the reaction against past abuse seems to me to result in an impoverished conception of the church, so that it is important to present those who hold that only believers should be baptized with the strongest possible defense of the opposing position. The question is: Whom should we expect to enter the life of the community by baptism? In other words, Who is called to share the life of those who are on the way to salvation?

As I have already suggested, such a question cannot be answered simply by proofs of whether or not children were baptized in the early church, partly because all such debate is inconclusive. But there are a number of general considerations that can be brought to bear. The first concerns the church's continuity with Israel. It is, of course, a continuity containing differences. The basis of the church is not nationhood, but relation to Christ its head. And yet insofar as the church is like Israel, a people, is there any reason why children should be excluded? J. S. Whale, in a brief discussion of this very matter, quotes a sentence of J. V. Bartlet: "The idea that a parent, especially the *paterfamilias,* should stand in a religious relation to God, merely as an individual, and distinct from his own flesh and blood, would never occur to the ancients, least of all to a Jew." He goes on to cite the evidence that is crucial for this discussion. In 1 Cor. 7:14 Paul affirms that in a mixed marriage the Christian partner makes the other partner and the children "holy." The logic of such a conception of the solidarity of the family for our doctrine of church membership is spelled out in passages like those of Eph. 6, where children are instructed to obey their parents "in the Lord." As Whale observes, this clearly means that they are regarded as members of the household of faith.[9] And if they are, does not that at least suggest that they are baptized?

Such arguments from New Testament theology are not, it seems to me, in themselves enough to establish the case, particularly in view of my own argument above that it is the logic of the gospel, not simple appeals to scripture, that must guide us. The weight of the case hangs rather on the kind of entity that we believe the church to be. Is the church to be conceived simply as a community of converted adults? Are we going to deny that the children of Christian people are members of the convenant community? And what of the mentally handicapped and those who will never reach an "age of reason" that enables them to make the prior decision upon which baptism is supposedly to depend? The logic of the gospel here presses very hard. If children are called to be part of the covenant people, how may they enter it except by baptism, which is, according to universal church confession, the way of entry into the church? But if they are not, we are in danger of a dangerously impoverished view of the church, that it is only for those who are of the "age of reason": adult or near-adult believers who have qualified themselves for membership by virtue of a particular experience or decision.

So far, my basis has been heavily Christological. Baptism is incorporation into the body of Christ, which is the church. To follow up the question of who may be in the church, let us turn to matters pneumatological. Here, the dogmatic basis is the Holy Spirit as agent of our incorporation into Christ through the medium of the community of faith.

Who, then, is brought into the body by the Spirit, and how? There are two answers I wish to avoid. The first is that *anyone* may be brought into the church by baptism: that is to say, that baptism may be administered indiscriminately to anyone, because the saying of particular words and the administration of water achieves an automatic pouring out of the Spirit. That seems to me to be a dangerously magical view of the matter, making the gifts of the Spirit at the disposal of the church or her representatives. Equally important, it evades the character of baptism as incorporation into a living community of belief.

The second answer I wish to avoid is the equal and opposite view that baptism may be administered only to those who have been through a certain experience. Do we have the right to say that a sharing in the Spirit's gifts and graces—that is, membership of the community—is granted only to adult believers? Again, the question can be put ecclesiologically. Insofar as the church is the community of those who give to and receive from each other in the Spirit the riches of the gifts and graces they have received, it must be asked whether we have nothing to receive, within the body of Christ, from children and those without the full capacity for reason and decision. Do only adults have the gifts and graces of the Spirit? Unless we can deny this, do we not have a dangerously impoverished view of the church? Are not our children "in the Lord" so that unless we are prepared to receive from as well as give to them we deny ourselves some of the gifts of the Spirit? (See here Mt. 21:16: "Out of the mouth of babes and sucklings thou hast brought perfect praise.")

In saying all this I do not wish to deny that in a culture which in large measure has taken leave of its Christian heritage the church will increasingly expect to gain new members by conversion. In what it is now fashionable to call a "missionary situation," a major—if not the chief—means of entry into the body of Christ will be by the baptism of believers. Indeed, advocates of the legitimacy of infant baptism should be prepared to affirm gladly that the prior form of baptism is that of adult believers, and that of infants is derivative from it. Yet none of that seems to me to entail that the *sole* way of receiving the Spirit's gifts and sharing his call should be through adult confession. Baptism is the appropriate sacrament to administer to those who are converted out of our pagan society, but there seems to me no compelling reason why we should so limit the capacity of the Spirit to bring sheep into the fold. Who is to say that the Spirit may work in only one way? If children are brought by their parents to share in the life of worship, work, and play that is the calling of the Christian community, are we to deny that as the working of the Spirit, too?

Here we return to the matter of individualism. It is easy, though wrong, to conceive of the Spirit as primarily the possession of individuals. It need not be denied that particular persons are given distinctive gifts, and indeed it is the glory of the church that in it all are called to exercise some form of ministry. Nor can it be denied that faith is the greatest of the Spirit's gifts. But it is not the only gift, and it should not be forgotten that there is a strong stress in the New Testament that the Spirit works in the *church*: his is a churchly rather than an individual sphere of activity in the sense that particular gifts are given for the building up of the life of the people of God. The *charismata* are for building up the community. This means that to baptize is not so much to confer a gift upon an individual as to bring a person into the sphere of the Spirit's working, into the place where his or her gifts may be exercised for the glory of God. The Spirit is the Spirit who creates the community of the Last Days, that worshiping body that is brought into the presence of the Father in the Son and by the Spirit.

Baptism, therefore, brings persons into relation with that community, so that they are now by means of a sacramental action brought within a new pattern of relationships: relationships that are what they are by virtue of their derivation from and orientation to the triune God. This is surely the point of Paul's "if anyone is in Christ, there is a new creation" (2 Cor. 5:17). I do not believe that this refers to some invisible inner change or (as in some forms of pietism) an instant transformation in the individual brought about by conversion. Indeed, it is not meant individualistically at all. By "in Christ" Paul means nothing other than in membership of the body of Christ, the church. There is, indeed, a new creation because of the addition to the community of "someone": some unique and particular person.

But that means something for the church as well. By virtue of the addition of a new member, the church is by each baptism reconstituted. That is the new creation of which Paul speaks. By virtue of its relationship to Abraham, it is the same church: the one historical people of God called and elected to praise him on earth. But it is also a different church, for the addition of a unique person to its membership means that new patterns of relationships, and therefore a new reality, have come to be. If that reality does not include our children and young people, then our notion of community and of the way God works toward and through it is indeed an impoverished one.

It is finally on the necessity that the church be a complete—catholic— community that I would rest the case for the membership, and therefore baptism, of all called by the Spirit, in all the many and various ways in which he does it, to share in the life of the people of God.

PASTORAL PRACTICE

The kind of pastoral practice that would follow from the argument of this paper can be set out briefly. The first implication is that if we believe what we say about baptism being the way of entry into the body of Christ, we should treat all who are baptized as members with us of the covenant community. It does not, of course, follow that we should treat all exactly the same, regardless of age, any more than we have the same expectations of every member of a family. Baptism is about membership in a community of worship, not about function within it.

The second implication is that we should not baptize any child whom we do not expect to enter into a living relation with the community of worship. Many requests for rebaptism would lose credibility if as a matter of pastoral practice some such criterion had operated in the churches of Christendom, and the baptized had truly been brought to share in the life of the community. Another way of making the same point would be to say that the promises made in services of baptism should be taken on all sides with complete seriousness, and not asked of those who are unlikely to be able or willing to keep them.

The third implication is that if we believe what we say about the inclusion of infants in the life of the covenant community, we should actively encourage the baptism of the infants of active Christian people. If we do not, we are depriving our children of the status they have under the gospel and are impoverishing both the life of the church and our conception of what it is to be the church. Recent controversy has sometimes led advocates of infant baptism to be apologetic and defensive about the practice. Yet if it is, as I believe, an implication of the logic of the gospel and obedience to the promises of God, then we should be glad to welcome our children into the community. Infant baptism may be derivative of the primary form, but that is not to say that it is second best. There is one baptism for the forgiveness of sins, in whichever form it is administered.

It is the neglect of the seriousness of baptism as a churchly action, the treating of it in an individualist and institutionalized way, that has led to the pastoral scandals of Christendom. Baptism has been treated as a rite dispensed to the individual by an institution, rather than as the means by which the person enters a new sphere of relationships which, by virtue of the new member, are themselves changed. And that has implications beyond the life of the church: it means much for the ministry of the church to those outside the life of the worshiping community. One of the ways in

One of the ways in which we may enable our own society to emerge from the stranglehold of individualism is in developing, under the gospel, forms of life in which each person is accorded that uniqueness that is the gift of existence in true community. In that way the church may be, as Calvin taught that it should, the sacrament of society: a living reminder to society of its true nature. Treating baptism with due seriousness is at the very beginning of such a process: It is the first of the ways by which the church may learn to be the church of God on earth and so a reflection of the light of the world.

NOTES

1. Andrew Walker, *Restoring the Kingdom* (London: Hodder & Stoughton, 1985).
2. Cited by Alan Sell in *Theology in Turmoil* (Grand Rapids: Baker, 1986), p. 140.
3. Karl Barth, *Protestant Theology in the Nineteenth Century: Its Background and History,* trans. Brian Cozens et al. (London: SCM Press, 1972), pp. 84f.
4. It is here that individualism and institutionalism are two aspects of the same ecclesiastical phenomenon. Baptism on such an account is something performed for and upon an *individual* by an institution. One symptom of the coincidence of the two is the English practice, now coming increasingly into question, of performing private baptisms, with only family and friends present, outside the context of the life of the worshiping community.
5. I have tried to spell out something of what this might mean in *Yesterday and Today: A Study of Continuities in Christology* (London: Darton, Longman & Todd, 1983), pp. 125-35.
6. For a major, early, and important exception see Trevor Dennis, "Man Beyond Price: Gregory of Nyssa on Slavery," *Heaven and Earth: Essex Essays in Theology and Ethics,* ed. Andrew Linzey and Peter J. Wexler (Worthing: Churchman Publishing, 1986), pp. 129-45. It is an account of "a root and branch attack" on slavery by Gregory of Nyssa.
7. The statement about means should not be taken undialectically, as has been pointed out to me by several readers of the paper. Baptism should not be conceived as taking the place of the divine action, but has the character it has "because God uses the human practice . . . in order to establish the relationship that includes us into the community of his covenant people" (Christoph Schwoebel). Similarly, as a *symbol* baptism both is and is not what it represents (Susan Durber): it therefore both makes and does not make us members of the church.
8. Those who would use sleight of hand in the matter sometimes speak of the infant rite as a "christening" in order to justify a later repetition of something like the same thing.
9. J. S. Whale, *Victor and Victim* (Cambridge: Cambridge Univ. Press, 1960), pp. 130f.

7

A L A N E. L E W I S

✞

Unmasking Idolatries:
Vocation in the Ecclesia Crucis

CHRIST

NOT THE LEAST OF Ray Anderson's many services to those engaged in Christian ministry as pastors, students, and teachers was his editing in 1979 of *Theological Foundations for Ministry*.[1] That was a heavyweight anthology in several senses, and immensely valuable, gathering lengthy excerpts on the subject of ministry from some of the most significant of modern theologians. The contributions varied not a little in content and outlook, but they shared some general methodological assumptions, in particular that of a Christocentric—and therefore also trinitarian—hermeneutic of ministry.

Anderson's own introductory essay to this collection superbly elucidates the critical implications of making Jesus Christ himself the dogmatic starting point. The church's only ministry is the ministry of Christ, as he in turn shares, through filial obedience, in the ministry of the Father.[2] And Anderson does not spare us the judgment thus pronounced on our illusions of independence and self-actualization. Especially contradicted, if the church exists and ministers only within God's reconciling act of self-revelation, are the characteristic subjectivism and pragmatism of modern theology. Our post-Enlightenment assumptions rob ecclesiology of any objective ground beyond the church's inner experience and social form, and reduce ministry from participation in the life and action of the triune God to institutional practices of verifiable utility.

Therefore, Anderson prophetically insists, "every pragmatic principle of ministry must be subjected to the critical dogmatic test: Has it gone through the death and resurrection process?" (p. 21). Self-subvertingly, the theology of ministry must yield to judgment and demise, to the discipline of "unteaching," that it might prove teachable again by God's iconoclastic, renovating Word of revelation. Only as the church acknowledges the impossibility of her own life, theology, and ministry, can she recover the actuality, and so understand the possibility, of being the church of Jesus Christ. Such is the evangelically compelling, if humanly and professionally repellent, imperative that Ray Anderson has issued: the *death*—and only on the precondition of that death—and the resurrection of the theology of ministry. What follows outlines a hesitant response to this imperative with reference to one key sub-theme of that theology.

CROSS

If the theology of ministry is to subject itself to death, it must do so at the cross of Jesus Christ, that point of God's ultimate "unity with perishability."[3] Here alone begins the *Christian* doctrine of God; for the Trinity is the interpretation of the event wherein God proceeds to union with God's opposite, while remaining God.[4] The death of Jesus Christ is revealed by the gospel as that moment in the trinitarian history of God in which Father and Son are separated, yet remain bound in love by the Holy Spirit. "The material principle of the doctrine of the Trinity is the cross of Christ. The formal principle of knowledge of the cross is the doctrine of the Trinity."[5] This *theologia crucis,* theology of the cross, constitutes the radical "un-teaching" of tradition, as that has allowed philosophical assumptions uninformed by the biblical revelation of the crucified God to be the basis of an uncritical "theology of glory."

For example, the mutual interpretation of the Trinity and the cross opposes the metaphysics of *being* with the gospel of God's *becoming,* which conceives that God *comes* to being precisely through surrender to estrangement and non-being. This recovers the once questionable doctrine of *kenosis* by not emptying God of Godness or rescinding transcendence in the incarnation and the cross, but rather intuiting God's very fullness and self-fulfillment through that event of divine self-emptying.[6] In the very absence of God from the cross, its godlessness and victory for evil, God is yet more present, visible in darkness, audible in silence. Grace abounds not where evil is removed, but in its midst, giving increase to sin and opposition and only thus flourishing beyond it (Rom. 5:20).[7]

Now if *kenosis,* divine self-emptying, truly is the means by which Christ's risen lordship is realized and God's Godness fulfilled, the friends and servants of Christ surely comprise an *"ecclesia crucis,"*[8] a church of the cross—a kenotic community in Christ, participant through him in God's own kenotic ministry. To live as the servants of the triune God, whose history of love and grace is fulfilled through the hazards of negation and identity with opposites, the church must likewise risk her own surrender of identity. The cross demands that the church lose her apartness and distinction from humanity at large. Of course, in so doing she will affirm and find herself, clarify her radical difference from a world that reads such self-surrender as sheer folly. To participate in the ministry of God, we must proceed into solidarity and oneness with others, standing where our suffering and guilty neighbors stand, as God through Christ has stood and died and been buried alongside us, only thus revealing who God is.[9]

CULTURE

What unteaching and repentance are prompted by this imperative of ecclesial *kenosis*. How perversely have God's people failed to share and mirror God's own self-giving to and for the world. Instead of confirming our transcendence as the community of renovated minds, in cruciform oneness with the least and broken of the world, we have rather been conformed to the world (Rom. 12:2), blessing and mirroring its mighty and triumphal. Thus has kenotic ministry been pathologically inverted; for the church has not emptied herself of self-promoting pride, to find herself in lowly fellowship with those beyond her boundaries. Rather, she has emptied herself of that very servitude that makes her different, through self-destroying imitation of the world's success and plenitude.

The pursuit of false gods, which promise fertility and plenty, predates the Hebrew Scriptures which repeatedly denounce this disavowal of human need, insufficiency, and receptivity—and with it the cognate refusal to be identified with the poor and the enslaved, who have no option but to trust and depend on their Maker for survival. Yet has this worship of fullness and abundance, this myth of self-sufficient independence and limitless prosperity, ever been pursued more wholeheartedly—and self-destructively—than here and now? Contemporary materialism has brought to birth, in Arthur McGill's unforgettable phrase, "bronze people"[10] who cherish illusory dreams of immortality and physical perfection in cowardly evasion of death's reality and the depredations of decay and age. Collectively, yet so individualistically, we worship idols of beauty, health, and property, sanctified by a culture of having and accumulating. Forlornly optimistic, society expects the direct or vicarious experience of fullness and success to anesthetize the gnawing pain of emptiness and need, to keep at a distance the menacing monsters of sickness and dependence, and every hint of negativity.[11]

Ray Anderson has rightly evoked Barth's admonition that "it is always the task of the church to give account of its theology in light of the contemporary situation and the dogma of Christ's ministry of reconciliation."[12] It is in our situation of acquisitive, bronze optimism that theology must let its understanding of the gospel die and be reborn, and allow its "dogma of Christ's ministry" to reshape the church's practices in ministry.

Mercifully, there are plenty among us now only too aware that the pro-phetic, iconoclastic conflict between the Crucified One and the idols of the age has to be waged inside the church as well as outside. A new Brief Statement of Reformed Faith, nearing adoption by the Presbyterian Church (USA), attests that "the Spirit gives us courage . . . to unmask idolatries in church and culture."[13] Silently acknowledged there is not only the sin of idolatry within the church, but the fact that Christians may honor the *same* false gods as those who profess no allegiance to the lordship of Christ crucified. Indeed the indictment overhanging Western Christianity and its mores and traditions is that our gospel has functioned as "the official religion of the officially optimistic society."[14] Christian theology itself—that is, an uncrucified theology of power and glory—has bestowed legit-imacy, if not sanctity, upon the "cultural triumphalism" that aims in all things for mastery, fullness, and the avoidance of reality.

The death of this theology is contained within the resurrected *theologia crucis*. And Scripture's own test of whether God's people are truly teach-able, are ready to learn the wisdom of the cross amid its foolishness, is ministry. How people act in mission, what means and forms and postures they adopt to serve the ministry of God, betrays whether or not God and God's ways are understood. Ministry is theology's polygraph, its infallible lie-detecting test, revealing the truth of what the church believes and the identity of whom she worships—the God of the cross or the false deities of her cultural ideology. The ministerial test is encapsulated in the dominical imperative: the Gentiles practice domination and control, as those with power lord it over others; it shall *not* be so among the followers of the soon-to-be-crucified Jesus, who must embrace his servanthood (Mk. 10:42-45). Naturally, one crucial aspect of this "Gentile" test is how we interpret and practice the *call* to ministry.

CALL

There is no imperative more urgent for the renewal of ministry today than recognition of the synonymity of *vocation* and the *cross*. Their separation underlies much of the church's triumphal past and present bondage to social norms. God's call and Christ's cross are not only mutually conditioned: they are the same reality. God calls humanity and the church through the crucified and risen Son; and there is no vocation that is not Christologically determined. We owe to Barth, especially, clarification of the difficult, but necessary, thought—"in contradiction to all human ideas about the divine nature"—that within God there is both a first and a second, a superior and subordinate, a sender and a sent, one who chooses and one who is chosen.[15] Of course, this ordering and differentiation express no conflict, but a unanimity of mind and will and love between the Father and the Son, substantiating rather than contradicting their equality and oneness. It is as very God that the Son is chosen and sent—and comes.

On the one hand, then, the cross reveals in time that God is eternally identified with the godless and the godforsaken, choosing and accepting as God's own the rejected and the unacceptable; and on the other, it confirms that God alone empowers the obedience of the chosen and the service of the sent. This is why the church's ministry originates so exclusively in Christ and his ministry toward the Father. To say that the Son is the eternally faithful servant of the Father's will implies that in reality only God knows how to be obedient and come to fullness and fulfillment through self-humbling service and subordination. From the lowliness of the divine Son we may learn the way of being truly human; and only in him is grounded the ecclesial possibility of kenotic, self-renouncing ministry.

When in saying Yes to the crucified Christ God says Yes to God, that is a gracious and demanding word to all humanity, and especially to those chosen to serve the Father, through the Son and in the Spirit, for humanity's sake—and that of all creation. Christ is the "mirror" of our election, as Calvin put it, both as the called—in whom we too are chosen (Eph. 1:4)— and as the one who calls. In oneness with the Father, the Son decides for us and comes to make our election visible in time and space and flesh. Brooking no opposition, waiting for no volunteers, Christ declares in speech and person a divine word that performs what it utters.[16] "You did not choose me, but I chose you" (Jn. 15:16). This insistent, commandeering grace, which enlists in ministry all who hear its promises and summons, and which so contradicts our idolatry in church and society of volunteerism and free choice, is "the word of the cross" (1 Cor. 1:18), translated into vocation. God's choice of Jesus, and thus of us, is an effective act of love which is not to be resisted, or treated as half a call awaiting our independent answer for its completion.

Even so, God's grace is always vulnerable and risky, open to abuse, frustration, disappointment, at the perilous disposal of the loved and chosen. The Spirit of the crucified serves the Father's ministry by creating a community of the called and sent, gathered into fellowship and unity and empowered with gifts for action, witness, and praise. Yet that entrusts Christ's ministry of reconciliation to men and women who have it in them, through fallenness or weakness, to resist and betray the demands of grace. How easily the church may frustrate the mission of the Trinity and recrucify the Lord! Misplaced enthusiasms, dissipated energies, or plain unfaithfulness and self-concern render the good news inaudible to worldly ears and rob the coming kingdom of all credibility. And even when Christ's chosen ones within the church are approaching faithfulness and dedication, their very insignificance to unbelieving eyes robs their ministry of attractiveness and the promise of "success." True obedience in the *ecclesia crucis* offends and shocks the world no less than the very different disobedience of an *ecclesia gloriae*. For the faithful are, as such, conformed to Christ's own self-expenditure, rejection, suffering—that servitude in obedience to the cross (Phil. 2:7-8) which so threatens the human ego and alarms the "Gentile" mighty.

CLERGY

Sadly, our history of clericalism, with its patriarchical hierarchy, reveals how often the church has simply inverted the dominical imperative to be unlike the Gentiles, and cut the crucial biblical link between vocation and the cross which summons her to iconoclastic forms of ministry sharply differentiated from the world.

The oft-told tale need not be retold here of how *diakonia* in the image of Christ, the great *diakonos* and lowly, kenotic *doulos,* ceased to be the *raison d'être* and identifying mark of the whole *ecclesia,* or even the ground of authority for its collective leadership. Rather, a "diaconate" took shape on the fringes of leadership, rendering assistance to those of greater power, whose ministry *per impossibile* was defined in other terms than service. Thus the church which confessed the lordship of the crucified messiah, who had disclosed that self-surrender to emptiness and negativity was God's own and only way to triumph and fulfillment, allowed authority and rule within Christ's body to be severed from servanthood and suffering, and even, in defiance of her own canons, from the community of praise and service altogether.[17] "Gentile" models of imperial panoply and social stratification—*dominium, potestas,* and *ordo*—were indelibly conferred upon a distinct, exclusive, hierarchic class. This surrendered both the essential lack of differential among the members of Christ's body—all one in him irrespective of gender, race, or class—and the necessary difference and critical tension between those who hear God's call from the cross and those who decline it.

The *ecclesia crucis,* formed in memory and hope around the slain victim of Caesar's power, became the victorious church of empire, conforming her own life to Caesar's structures and worshiping no longer the vulnerable crucified God, but a divine archetype of absolutist monarchy.[18] And, negating the biblical identity of vocation and the cross, "call" was withheld altogether from the people of God's elect community: the "laity" being set against the "chosen," with those "clergy," along with others in special orders of "religious" life, alone receiving God's "vocation."

Of course, the Reformation struck vital blows against this disastrous disjunction of ministry from service, of call from community, of the church from the crucified Lord. Luther's powerful reinterpretation of Paul's gospel as *theologia crucis*[19] concluded a massive "unteaching" of medieval theology with its God of absolute power and coercive, causal will. Instead, Luther found God's power and presence in the hiddenness of human suffering and demonic contradiction, and he thereby healed the severed connection between the cross and the call.[20] As all justified sinners are priests in Christ within the community of faith, God's call demolished the internal walls erected by papacy and sacerdotalism—including the wall between the religious and the secular. Whoever we are, whatever our sphere, we may gladly hear God's call to service, and answer it with our work of hands or heart or mind, no matter the lowliness of our station or the hardship of our condition. Vocation is the summons to every Christian to endure the cross in fellowship with Christ's fleshly afflictions and spiritual conflicts.

Yet Luther's way of reconnecting vocation with the cross actually served to deaden some of the ministerial dynamic he was unleashing. For the first time vocation was identified with *work*, since every form of labor, every social or domestic status, represented God's vocation or *Beruf*. Luther misinterpreted 1 Cor. 7:20—"every one should remain in the state in which he was called"—to refer to occupations and social niche, and read Paul's exposition of Christian freedom as prohibiting mobility and demanding resignation to one's social lot.

Granted, Luther restored some functional flexibility and diaconal content to the ordained ministry. Those whose *Beruf* was that of office, *Amt*, were the servants of the congregations assigned to them, and could relieve them of public responsibility for proclamation of the gospel.[21]

Nonetheless, while so democratizing vocation that everyone within the church served God through a call, Luther had also transferred into the realm of everyday activity some of the immutability and permanence of vocation's earlier clerical activity. And by identifying call with work— albeit the work of believers within the universal priesthood—Luther encouraged the separation of vocation from *ministry,* and fostered the de-theologizing of vocation. Now everyone in bourgeois society, without reference to *divine* call or *Christian* service, may voluntarily choose a "vocation," and determine an individual future through pursuit of private interest and success in career, profession, trade.

Despite his differences from Luther, Calvin did not halt—and perhaps gave impetus to—this secularization of vocation. On the one hand, Calvin did not trumpet (though he did not deny) "the priesthood of all believers," but retained the notion of God's direct calling to "the ministry" of some within the church. Ordination signified more than functional and terminable ordering by the congregation; rather, it enacted the church's confirmation of a once-for-all call of God to dominically-instituted forms of government and rule.[22] To be sure, this restored service to ministry, inasmuch as the authority of those ordained to Word and Sacrament was strictly derivative and *ex officio,* not personal or priestly *potestas.* Their authority came from the Word they preached and celebrated; and as servants of the Word they were subject to and not mediators of the authority of Christ, the church's only head.[23]

Even so, the role of those called to this ministry was interpreted through state and gubernatorial analogies drawn from an authoritarian political history; and it would be hard to deny a de facto survival in the Calvinist tradition of clericalism—what T. F. Torrance scathingly calls "Protestant sacerdotalism,"[24] and others would now indict as a cult of male personality.

As for those within the church not called to "holy ministry," Calvin, like Luther, was anxious to interpret their lives and occupations as equal responses to God's call and as means of discipleship, stewardship, and service. And he imposed slightly fewer restraints on social mobility, interpreting 1 Cor. 7:20 as not preventing movement from one occupation or station to another, provided confusion was avoided and God-given boundaries respected.[25]

Yet Calvin's application of vocation to profane employment, like Luther's, so significant for the breakdown of barriers between religious and secular life and partially those between clergy and laity, clearly is one major factor in the development of modern secular vocation. Calvin bade Christians interpret their quotidian activities as means for responding to God's electing grace with thankfulness to the Creator and responsibility toward the world. But now vocation is too often the means by which autonomous men and women express their imagined self-sufficiency in pursuit of success and personal beatitude, exploiting scientific skills and humanly-devised techniques.

Of course, technology and enterprise have borne rich fruit in the development of modern society; but many find today's work-based culture a source of deep estrangement—being denied employment, or bored, exploited, dehumanized, dissatisfied within it. This crisis requires the church to rethink her theology of work and the relation of work to vocation. But is also highlights the relation of vocation to ministry, and of call to the cross. The question is whether the church, having inadvertently encouraged the secularization of vocation, now adapts its own ministry and understanding of call to the secular pattern, once again imitating "Gentile" models of power and wisdom. That possibility will be explored through a series of questions: Who are called to ministry? To what are they called? and By what means?

PERFECTIONISM

The god worshiped by the "bronze people" throughout our culture and frequently in our churches is busy at the banishment of every blemish on the human condition: the abolition of sickness and injustice, war and death. While utopia tarries, the officially optimistic society abounds with positive

techniques for avoiding every negativity—failure, handicap, and need—
that would interrupt the idealistic dream. Perfectionist millenial fantasies
belong more to the social mainstream than to its lunatic fringe.[26] And
society idolizes, often chooses and elects to honor, privilege and power,
those whose flawless public image—cosmetic, athletic, moral, or financial—is an earnest of the well-being that awaits us all.

The God of the cross, however, is revealed as yielding to negativity and
triumphing through failure, not its avoidance, and as inaugurating a
tearless, painless, deathless future only through sacrifice, suffering, and
stigmatization.[27] Therefore vocation in the *ecclesia crucis* must be practiced
by means that do not sanctify but abrogate the perfectionist cult. These
means, surely, must include criteria for recognizing those called to public
ministry who reflect God's strange choice, not of "the best and the
brightest" or the fullest, but—in the *locus classicus* of the relation of vocation
to the cross—"not many wise . . . powerful . . . of noble birth" (1 Cor.
1:26ff.).[28] Throughout Scripture, calls to leadership in the ministry of
God's people regularly pass over the eloquent and apt, the mature and
dependable, taking risks, rather, with a mumbling Moses, a venal David, a
youthful Jeremiah, a mendacious Peter, and hostile Saul. And Paul dis-
covers that not fluency and plausibility, but folly, fear, and trembling; not
charismatic show, but bodily affliction; not righteousness, but primacy
among the sinful—these are the credentials of his apostolicity or any other,
in the ministry of Christ who was crucified in weakness (2 Cor. 13:4).[29]

One legacy of our clerical past and our beholdenness to bourgeois mores
has been the expectation that ministers attain moral heights, spiritual
profundity, and psychic equilibrium. These perfectionist demands are not
infrequently destructive to those and their families on whom they are laid.
They are also hypocritical: designed to exempt non-clergy from the rigors
of discipleship.[30]

However, it is no antidote to the quest for, and sometimes self-promotion
of, bronze preachers to fill the pulpits of bronze religiosity (and an absurd
inference from the theology of the cross), purposely to welcome into
ministry as called of God the mentally, slow, morally compromised, and
spiritually shallow. God's choice of powerless, foolish nobodies (1 Cor.
1:27f.) does not counter one ideology of power with another of weakness
and ineptitude. Paul denied inferiority (2 Cor. 11:5): he had his credentials—intellectual, moral, homiletical—even though they justified no
boasting or self-confidence. And in age that celebrates mediocrity, a society
of closed minds, moral relativism, and packaged politics, it may be that the
"fools and weaklings" whose calling most scandalizes social values are
precisely the best, intellectually, morally, spiritually: persons whose "humanness" is expressed in integrity and responsibility rather than through
public frailties of the psyche or the flesh.

This still leaves questions about those who *feel* themselves to be the best and proclaim themselves fit for service in the pulpit, at the Table, by the bedside. Whatever their objective gifts, those biblically called are subjectively aware of their unworthiness and lack of preparation, distressed by the insistence of God's commandeering summons, burdened by the prospect of the task, and clear-eyed about the risk God takes in choosing them. Only those are truly qualified for ministry who feel least so, reluctant, hesitant, Christ's fools indeed and possible betrayers, potential recrucifiers of their Lord.

Likewise the *ecclesia crucis* as a whole is not excused from her own risks in the callings she identifies and confirms. Prophetic courage, imagination, and adventure are asked of the community: the risk of bringing to authority and leadership those whose presence and position might surprise, puzzle, shock the world—not by their weakness but by their differentness. How can the church of the cross confront prejudice against gender, age, disability, race in the name of the God who dies in shame and emptiness, outside the law, unless those who represent our own society's strangers and outsiders are widely acknowledged as elect within God's kingdom, called to leadership, entrusted with authority? Only where an alien presence is welcomed and empowered is there visibly a church without barriers or differentials. And the church's differentness from the culture that dreams its perfectionist illusions will be clear when she lets herself be sometimes led by those whose bodies bring to remembrance the impairment of us all, or whose race, ethnicity, or status make inescapable the grim truth of an imperfect, crooked world.

POWER

The question of who are appropriately called within the *ecclesia crucis* leads to questions concerning what they are called to: how vocation is translated into action. This first prompts the question of power—source of such contemporary puzzlement and ambiguity in society at large. A postmodern culture struggling to overthrow discredited forms of domination understands the continuing necessities of power. Power corrupts and revolutions devour their own children; yet lack of power is no cause for celebration. The exercise of power must be renovated, not renounced.

Likewise the theology of God crucified, the weakness of the cross, the divine bias to the poor and impotent, makes no idol or ideology of powerlessness. The gospel does not abhor power but *reconceives* it radically, saying that cruciform weakness is itself powerful—divinely, creatively, resurrectingly so. Ministerially, then, the question is not *whether* but *how* power is distributed and used within the church; and that indicates not the rejection but the renewal of authorized leadership, by those whose vocation and gifts are communally recognized. The logic of the cross may relativize ordination but surely does not imply its termination.

The contemporary church almost universally is coming to acknowledge that the call to God's whole people takes precedence over the call of some to lead and represent the ministry of all.[31] That helps to reconnect vocation and the cross; for it recognizes the community of faith in its entirety as chosen in Christ the crucified to bear witness to God's gracious claim on all humanity. God's reliance upon non-entities and fools, which so confounds the world in its own folly and self-destruction, is equally the sign that God loves all the world, even its least and most recalcitrant. Therefore, the sacrament of baptism, often bestowed on little ones and always upon sinners, has an "ordaining" consequence, enlisting for service all God's chosen people, so that all humanity may see and hear the promise and demand of grace.[32]

Still, it would surely sacralize powerlessness rather than reconceptualize power in the light of the cross to confine ministry to what is done for Christ—so much and indispensable as that is—under the sign of baptism. The power of the Spirit of Christ crucified—which justifies sinners, gives life to the dead and hope to the hopeless—must be released, its word announced, its energies channeled, its dynamic acted out inside the church structures and beyond them. This requires courageous, visible, vigorous *leadership* in ministry—pastoral, kerygmatic, prophetic, even bureaucratic. Nothing is served by withholding authority and space from those with gifts to permit this release of Christ's own power; but everything is lost if those empowered for such responsibilities usurp the authority of the Word and Spirit of the cross and, separately or collegially, pretend to a clerical autonomy which incapacitates the baptismal ministry of those they lead.

Such is the challenge to churches that continue to ground ministerial authority de facto less in humble, kenotic service rendered than in priestly privileges exercised, juridical seats occupied, legislative votes cast, managerial decisions made. The church dare not be squeamish about power nor evasive of its ambiguities. But by inventing new, liberating forms of power—of mutual dependence and reciprocal subordination in the image of Christ crucified and the community of the Trinity itself[33]—the *ecclesia crucis* may incarnate emancipating leadership with a world inured to the demonization of power and longing for power's redemption.

PERMANENCE

Besides the traditional (now obsolescent) distinction between "ordinary church members" and the clergy ordained to "full-time Christian service"—which gave the lie to the Protestant theory that all Christians serve

God in answer to vocation in their daily life—nothing in practice has more separated "ministers" from others than the permanence of their ordination. The setting *apart* for ministry seems to set them *in* a special relationship with Christ, whose lifelong indissolubility, in latent analogy to marriage, gives their calling a mystique and loftiness far transcending that of simple faith and service in the community at large. The medieval theology of orders was radically transformed and de-sacramentalized by the Reformation; but the assumption stood that the call to be servant of God's Word evoked a lifelong commitment of one's whole person.

That evangelical insistence, however, partially preserved the "indelible character" of Roman ordination,[34] which to this day bedevils priests who marry, yet despite the fiction of laicization and their pastoral inactivity remain priests, theologically trapped in quasi-bigamy.[35] Is one indication of "Protestant sacerdotalism" not our association of "leaving the ministry" with moral and spiritual failure, and the violation of vows designed to keep clear the gulf between clerical vocation and merely Christian calling?

From one perspective, the presumption that ordination is permanent is a healthy expectation of commitment, integrity, and perseverance, now more necessary than ever when all relationships seem contractual and terminable. As some pursue the perfect spouse in "serial monogamy," other bronze escapists, perhaps, are in quest of the ideal profession through a series of vocations and career steps that may include ministry along the way. Yet lifelong ordination can also perpetuate hierarchy and be an inflexible instrument of moralizing and legalism, causing undeserved guilt and shame for those who make transitions out of full-time ministry, and frustration and despair for some who are afraid to. Equally, in the eyes of many now, it is a patriarchal relic, uninformed by the experience of women, who understand career in more flexible and fluid terms that allow for natural transitions from and into tasks and periodic shifts of concentration.[36] Of course, the pragmatic and experiential tensions surrounding permanence must be addressed, if not resolved, at the theological level.

The cross, we have said, as an event of self-disclosure in the history of the Trinity, reveals not a God of static immutability, but one who comes to being in the dynamic constancy of self-giving in reciprocity with others. Thus the God of the cross is unchangeably evoking and reacting to creaturely change, the divine mission unvaryingly at the mercy of humanity's wavering responses and the church's fluctuations in reliability. Only in the context of such divine mutability and dependence can God's call to individuals be understood: a gracious choice and summons, pressing and decisive, yet riskily exposed to rejection and betrayal.

This requires of the theology of call the most profound reflection on the interaction between divine sovereignty and human freedom.[37] Is the lordship of God's grace contradicted, or expressed and clarified, through risky accommodation to the processes and changes of human life? The assumption that a divine call comes just once, and that for a lifetime, is surely an inappropriately static and rigid imposition upon the God of the cross. Rather, does not God call repeatedly,[38] as tasks and times and contexts change, gifts alter and develop, re-encountering us, sometimes to affirm us anew in forms of ministry to which we are committed, often moving us from one location for such service to another, and sometimes into quite new modes of service? And may the risk of God's free grace not embrace the possibility that some will decline or surrender their vocation altogether?

The God who permits sin to increase, and abounds in grace beyond the magnitude of evil, may certainly leave space for the making of vocational mistakes, for our corrections of direction, and for the disappointments of sheer human fallibility. And surely the purposes of vulnerable love are fostered, rather than impeded, when assignments reach completion, energies burn out, vision finally fades, and some wholly dispensable servants pass on their tasks to others equally responsible and gifted.[39] Karl Barth expounds vocation in terms of constant transition from one moment to the next;[40] and perhaps the theology of ministry can come to interpret transitions within and out of ministry as no less reflective of the sovereign vulnerability of God's vocation as any original life-shaping summons into ministry. Of course, leadership in service brings special responsibilities and demands for tenacity and durability, especially in an age of cowardly, utopian illusion; yet if the gap between leader and led, so hostile to the effective ministry of all Christ's people, is to narrow, the rigidity of that distinction must be theologically indicted, and the propriety of flexible transitions back and forth affirmed.

PROFESSIONALISM

If the boundary between the ordained and unordained becomes more fluid, how would that affect the modern understanding of pastoral ministry as one of the "professions"? The analogy between clergy and other trained professionals seems irresistible today, and of course is frequently encouraged on the church's part. Yet, as we said, the bourgeois development of such professions coopted the theological concept of calling, and secularized vocation into an autonomously-chosen career exercised not with the Spirit's gifts but with rationally-tutored skills. In substituting the concept of professional minister for that of office or order in the service of the Word, the church, it could be said, is imitating one more worldly model of power, indeed the very model that is the profanization of the church's own identity and understanding as the *called* community. And there are good grounds for the judgment, based not least on the training of ministers in recent decades, that their alignment with other specialized professions is self-conscious, and presupposes acceptance of dominant cultural values, including the quest for status and prestige.[41] Does this mark the demise of *prophet,* for example, as a model of ministerial activity and self-understanding? Indeed, to what extent is professionalism in church and culture another idol to be unmasked by prophetic confrontation with the cross of Christ?

Of course, the ministry of Christ crucified can only be continued and his presence incarnated in our world if his church encounters and infiltrates social reality as it actually is. Mission in a technological society would not be faithful if it washed its hands of technology; and modern ministry clearly requires information and technique commensurate with the complexity of the lives, communities, and problems to which Christian care and witness are directed. It is no antidote to the idolizing of professionalism to doxologize instead the ineptitude of antiquarian amateurs! Once again, Paul, that Pharisee nonpareil, makes no apology for his knowledge and his skills (2 Cor. 11:6, Phil. 3:4ff.). It is precisely *not* their absence that makes him a fool in and for the crucified Christ. Pedigree, training, status, even moral blamelessness and spiritual gifts—all these Paul has, and they have utility and value, not to be despised. However, he himself is not what he *has,* but what he *hears*; and his true identity, heard and received in faith, is strictly that of Christ (Gal. 2:20). Being no longer the "I" which has so much, he does not boast about all that, but lives as if he has nothing, having lost it all for Christ (Phil. 3:7f.). And finding his new real self in Christ he must live as if he were indeed Christ: that is, share Christ's suffering, bear Christ's stigmata, imitate Christ's death—and only thus be united with Christ's triumph (Phil. 3:10f., Gal. 6:17, Rom. 8:17).

This is where the emptiness of the cross confronts the culture of fullness at the point of its glorification of the professional. Those conformed to Christ crucified must live in the world—now so technical and complex— but *as if* that world no longer is. In eschatological freedom, they marry as if single, mourn as if rejoicing, acquire as if penniless (1 Cor. 7:29-31). What endowments, skills, possessions they have, which may be many, do not determine who they are; they know, and show they know, that abundance and acclaim cannot cancel human neediness, and they utilize responsibly, avidly, their expertise and knowledge with a demeanor that leaves transparent their own incapacities and limitations. Those whose ministry as *persons* is effective are not unprofessional or shoddy, contemptuous of training: they excel in skill and maximize available means of meeting human need; but they do so as if they were the needy ones, counsel as if as broken as the client, comfort as if themselves in mourning, shelter the homeless as if dependent and demeaned.

Increasingly, men and women hear the call to public "full-time" ministry when already immersed in other professions or secular employment. Then many make concrete and costly the meaning of this "as if" Christian way of life, becoming fools for Christ by literally giving up as lost, prosperity, prestige, and "prospects." The sacrifices and hardships often entailed by ministry as "second career" constitute an eloquent critique of the values hallowing career as a ladder of self-improvement and advancement to personal kudos and success. Of course, once trained these ministers will practice pastoral skills back in the midst of the technical society, rubbing shoulders again with the other professions. At times pastors find it difficult to define their own role among those ranks of specialists; at others, it is all too clear how they differ from those who can seal their own personhood off from their public role, and limit their concern for others to narrow areas of competence.

And right here people who engage in public ministry for the sake of Christ exert radical, but creative, judgment upon modern culture. For surely the most bitter harvest of the Enlightenment has been the dualism that divorces the public from the private, science from morality, the objective from the spiritual, knowledge from feelings and beliefs. By contrast, where the professional and the personal cohere and blend; where the provider and receiver of technique remain fully human to each other, not divided and bureaucratized into active, resourceful agent and passive, needy object; there the tragic bifurcations of contemporary life are therapeutically confronted. Actively denied, whenever Christian life and ministry body forth unity and wholeness, is that radical schism in "modernity" between the transcendent and the immanent, divine purpose and human freedom, which leaves us so estranged from our Creator, and therefore from ourselves and one another.[42] It is the person of Jesus Christ who—so impossibly, on post-Enlightenment presumptions—actualizes the unity of flesh and spirit, eternity and time, divine and human; and in him that healing of estrangement has occurred, of which all Christian mission is intended to give evidence (Eph. 2:11-22). The reconciliation of person and profession, as of every other rift, has been concluded "in the blood of Christ": that human death where, at their points of greatest difference, God's Godness and creaturely mortality become inseparably one.

PRIVATISM

So those who lead ministry in the *ecclesia crucis* are called to be professional precisely in ways that subvert dominant norms of professionalism from which the personal—let alone the prophetic—is on principle excluded. This assertion, however, can be wrongly understood to endorse rather than deprecate one remaining facet of typical vocational practice in the church today. That relates to the final question: By what means are those called to leadership so identified and set upon the path to ordination? One element of the "recruitment" process illuminates well the church's own temptation to sacralize our culture's dualistic instincts.

A pastoral or kindred ministry makes relentless demands on personal resources of endurance, wisdom, and compassion. Clearly, only those should embark on such a life who sense amid their inadequacy some commensurability between what will be asked of them as persons and what they have to give as persons, and are convinced that the challenge of matching the one to the other can no longer be resisted. Probably no voice sounds in the ears; but a conjunction of inheritance, education, and experience conspires to compel a humble recognition: "This is what I must do!" With an intuition that verges on, but—let us hope!—falls short of certainty, they conclude with exquisite reluctance that they have heard God's call. Nevertheless, the *necessity* of some such personal experience, as a precondition of suitability for ordained ministry, ought not to be confused with its *independence* from and *priority* over other criteria, decisions, and participants in the process of "vocation." Some traditions woodenly divide the essentially dynamic, interactive event which constitutes "calling" into a static sequence of discrete components. This may give not only chronological but theological and adjudicative primacy to personal convictions over the responsibilities and judgments of the wider church community; and it frequently casts this primary self-assessment in explicitly private, interior, even arcane, terms.[43] It is deeply ironic that the "secret" or "inner" call has had and retains such preeminence in Reformed schemas of vocation, when Calvin himself refused it prominence, emphasizing the objectivity of the Word over inwardness in the call of election, and the outward, public call of the church with respect to ministry. In the latter case, Calvin says, "I pass over that secret call of which each minister is conscious," and does exactly that![44]

The subsequent preoccupation, on the contrary, with just such interiorized calls betrays the degradation of Reformed instincts into radical individualism, the apotheosis of Protestantism. In its pietistic forms that has reinforced, while seeking refuge from, the Enlightenment's revolt of autonomous reason which banished faith and revelation to private arenas of morality and feeling. The ensuing dualism, with its privatization of meaning and value and collapse of public discourse, is unconsciously mirrored in the churches when subjective certainty takes precedence over public scrutiny, with deep resentment often felt when the community fails to corroborate an individual's self-verifying sense of call. Vogel warns of "self-absorption" and "visionary rapture" when someone tries to discern God's call in the solitary "inner room," isolated from the neighbor.[45] After all, internal certainty can attend any "career choice";[46] and it is hard to distinguish subjectively between offering oneself—as volunteer or as commandeered—for ecclesiastical service and embarking on secular "vocation."

What does radically differentiate the former, and make *private* calling so unapt, is precisely the fact that ministry is not private but communal in very essence. There is only the ministry of the church as a whole, just as that in turn occurs only as the ministry of the triune God. And thus there is also one calling only: the individual's "call" is not discrete and separate; it has truly *occurred* only when heard and confirmed by the community. Those who are called to Christ's ministry—the baptized or the ordained—are who they are and do what they do, not as private individuals but in and through the fellowship, on which they depend and in whose service alone their being and purpose are realized. Of course, the notion that persons can only *be* in communion,[47] and only act *inter*dependently, is the most unthinkable thought in Western society! It commits the foulest heresy against the "official religion" of optimistic, self-sufficient individualism and the assumed sanctity of the private will. Yet the Christian gospel consists of just that "heresy," and indicts that religion as a tragic, cancerous falsehood, now destroying both persons and communities on a huge scale.

Faith asserts that our current idolatry of the solipsistic self was already unmasked on Jesus' cross. For there it was disclosed once and for all that true humanness is realized in utmost solidarity with others; and, yet more wondrously, that it is so just because the fulfillment of being, self, and will through solidarity is God's own way and possibility. Because *God* lives in the interdependence of community, and has *died* in communion with us, humanity is liberated from narcissistic self-destruction for the wholeness of persons-in-togetherness.[48] Ministry in union with the triune God of the cross must unmask *this* as the hidden, urgent, saving truth for our culture, through personal relations of transparent mutuality and prophetic corporate acts of kenotic oneness with the world. And it might help unmask the truth of selfhood-through-community inside the church, if we agreed that calling, like ministry itself, is one and indivisible.

NOTES

1. R. S. Anderson, ed., *Theological Foundations for Ministry* (Grand Rapids: Eerdmans; Edinburgh: T. & T. Clark, 1979).

2. Cf. G. W. Bromiley, *Christian Ministry* (Grand Rapids: Eerdmans, 1959), and R. S. Paul, *Ministry* (Grand Rapids: Eerdmans, 1965).

3. E. Jüngel, *God as the Mystery of the World* (Grand Rapids: Eerdmans, 1983), pp. 184ff.

4. See Jüngel, ibid., and *The Doctrine of the Trinity: God's Being Is in Becoming* (Edinburgh: Scottish Academic Press, 1976); and K. Barth, *Church Dogmatics* (Edinburgh: T. & T. Clark, 1936-69), esp. vols. I/1 and IV/1.

5. J. Moltmann, *The Crucified God* (London: SCM Press, 1974), p. 241; and see pp. 240-49; also *The Trinity and the Kingdom* (San Francisco: Harper & Row, 1981).

6. See Ray Anderson's profound treatment of *kenosis* in *Historical Transcendence and the Reality of God* (Grand Rapids: Eerdmans, 1975), ch. V.

7. See my article, "The Burial of God: Rupture and Resumption as the Story of Salvation," in *Scottish Journal of Theology* 40 (1987):335-62.

8. D. J. Hall, *Lighten Our Darkness: Toward an Indigenous Theology of the Cross* (Philadelphia: Westminster, 1976), p. 222; cf. E. Käsemann, "The Pauline Theology of the Cross," in *Interpretation* 24 (1970):151-77.

9. On "kenotic" community and ministry, see Anderson, *Historical Transcendence,* ch. VII.

10. A. C. McGill, *Death and Life: An American Theology* (Philadelphia: Fortress, 1987), p. 26, *et passim.*

11. Besides the social critique of Hall and McGill, see D. W. McCullough, *Waking from the American Dream* (Downers Grove, IL: InterVarsity, 1988).

12. Anderson, *Theological Foundations,* p. 21.

13. *The Presbyterian Outlook* (13 February 1989).

14. Hall, *Lighten Our Darkness,* ch. III; cf. McGill, *Death and Life,* p. 39.

15. Barth, *Church Dogmatics,* IV/1, p. 199; and see pp. 157–210; cf. II/2, pp. 94–145.

16. See O. Weber, *Foundations of Dogmatics* (Grand Rapids: Eerdmans, 1983), II, p. 500.

17. Specifically, the Sixth Canon of the Council of Chalcedon (451 A.D.), prohibiting "absolute ordination." See E. Schillebeeckx, *Ministry* (New York: Crossroad, 1981), pp. 38ff., and *The Church with a Human Face* (New York: Crossroad, 1985), pp. 154ff. See also G. Hunt, "Vocation and Ministry," in *Theology* 87 (1984):190ff.

18. Cf. Moltmann, *Trinity and Kingdom,* esp. ch. VI.

19. See W. von Löwenich, *Luther's Theology of the Cross* (Belfast: Christian Journals Ltd., 1976), and A. E. McGrath, *Luther's Theology of the Cross* (Oxford: Blackwell, 1985).

20. See G. Wingren, *Luther on Vocation* (Philadelphia: Fortress, 1957), pp. 50ff., *et passim;* see also R. L. Calhoun, "Work and Vocation in Christian Ministry," in *Work and Vocation: A Christian Discussion,* ed. J. O. Nelson (New York: Harper & Brothers, 1954).

21. See G. Haendler, *Luther on Ministerial Office and Congregational Function* (Philadelphia: Fortress, 1981).

22. See J. Calvin, *Institutes of the Christian Religion,* ed. J. T. McNeill (Philadelphia: Westminster, 1960), Bk. IV, ch. III.

23. See J. Leith, *John Calvin's Doctrine of the Christian Life* (Louisville: Westminster/ John Knox, 1989), p. 179.

24. T. F. Torrance, *Theology in Reconstruction* (London: SCM Press, 1965), p. 167; cf. J. C. McLelland, *A New Look at Vocation* (Toronto: Ryerson Press, 1964), esp. pp. 5ff.

25. See R. S. Wallace, *Calvin's Doctrine of the Christian Life* (Edinburgh: Oliver & Boyd, 1959), p. 159; cf. W. J. Bousma, *John Calvin: A Sixteenth Century Portrait* (Oxford and New York: Oxford Univ. Press, 1988), p. 74.

26. See J. H. Moorhead, "Searching for the Millennium in America," in *Princeton Seminary Bulletin* VII (1987).

27. See my article "God as Cripple: Disability, Personhood and the Reign of God," *Pacific Theological Review* XVI (1982).

28. See Weber, *Foundations of Dogmatics,* II, p. 498.

29. See F. D. Bruner, *A Theology of the Holy Spirit* (Grand Rapids: Eerdmans, 1970), esp. pp. 303ff.

30. See C. S. Calian, *Today's Pastor in Tomorrow's World,* rev. ed. (Philadelphia: Westminster, 1982), p. 95.

31. See, e.g., "Ministry," in *Baptism, Eucharist and Ministry,* Faith and Order Report No. 111 (Geneva: WCC, 1982), and "Joint Statement on Ministry," in *An Invitation to Action* (The Lutheran-Reformed Dialogue Series III).

32. On the relation between baptism and ordination, see T. O'Meara, *Theology of Ministry* (New York: Paulist Press, 1987), ch. 7, *et passim;* R. S. Paul, *Ministry,* pp. 127ff.; and J. R. Evans, "Vocation and Ministry: What Happens at the Font of the Church?" in *Austin Seminary Bulletin* 102 (October 1986).

33. See, e.g. J. Moltmann, *The Church and the Power of the Spirit* (New York: Harper & Row, 1977), esp. ch. VI; and *Trinity and Kingdom,* esp. ch. VI; H. Küng, *Why Priests?* (Maryknoll, NY: Orbis, 1988), pp. 106f.; and C. M. Campbell, "Imago

Trinitatis: The Being of God as a Model for Ministry," in *Austin Seminary Bulletin* 102 (October 1986).

34. See Weber, *Foundations of Dogmatics,* II, p. 574; cf. M. Warkentin, *Ordination: A Biblical-Historical View* (Grand Rapids: Eerdmans, 1982), p. 62.

35. See J. P. Mackey, in *Why I Am Still A Catholic,* ed. R. Nowell (London: Collins, 1982), pp. 135ff.; and P. Hebblethwaite, in *The Experience of Ordination,* ed. K. Wilson (London: Epworth Press, 1979), pp. 59ff.

36. See esp. L. N. Rhodes, *Co-Creating: A Feminist Vision of Ministry* (Philadelphia: Westminster, 1987).

37. O'Meara, *Theology of Ministry,* p. 182.

38. See H. Vogel, *Consider Your Calling* (Edinburgh: Oliver & Boyd, 1962), p. 14.

39. On "creative" departures in ministry, see C. E. Norwood, *The Call* (London: Independent Press, 1949), pp. 86ff.

40. Barth, *Church Dogmatics,* III/4, pp. 607ff.

41. See G. T. Miller, "Professionals and Pedagogues: A Survey of Theological Education," in *Altered Landscapes: Christianity in America, 1935-1985* (Grand Rapids: Eerdmans, 1989), pp. 189ff. Discussions of ministry that presuppose the professional ministry include: J. D. Glasse, *Profession: Minister* (Nashville: Abingdon, 1968); and R. A. Hunt and J. A. Hunt, *Called to Minister* (Nashville: Abingdon, 1982).

42. See L. Newbigin, *Foolishness to the Greeks: the Gospel and Western Culture* (Grand Rapids: Eerdmans, 1986); and C. Gunton, *Enlightenment and Alienation* (Basingstoke: Marshall, Morgan & Scott, 1985).

43. One such scheme, which seems highly influential today, is that of H. R. Niebuhr: the Chrisian call; the secret call; the providential call; the ecclesiastical call. See *The Purpose of the Church and Its Ministry* (New York: Harper & Row, 1956), pp. 64f. It is not always noticed that Niebuhr himself applauds developments away from the primacy of the "secret call" (p. 66). Cf. R. G. Cox, *Do You Mean Me, Lord? The Call to the Ordained Ministry* (Philadelphia: Westminster, 1985), ch. I.

44. Calvin, *Institutes,* IV, III, 11. See Weber, *Foundations of Dogmatics,* II, pp. 501ff., 573ff.

45. Vogel, *Consider Your Calling,* p. 13.

46. Weber, *Foundations of Dogmatics,* II, p. 573.

47. See J. Zizioulas, *Being as Communion* (London: Darton, Longman & Todd, 1985).

48. On this understanding of personhood, Ray Anderson himself has written with fine perception; see esp. *On Being Human* (Grand Rapids: Eerdmans, 1982), ch. 4. Cf. also E. Moltmann-Wendel and J. Moltmann, *Humanity in God* (London: SCM Press, 1984).

PART II

✝

A Theology of
Social Ministry

8

JAMES B. TORRANCE

✝

The Ministry of Reconciliation Today: The Realism of Grace

I F THERE IS ONE WORD that more than any other summarizes the deepest need of our time it must be *reconciliation*. That is the burning issue in Lebanon, Israel, South Africa, and Northern Ireland. It is the constant concern of every marriage counselor and an issue within all our churches. It is surely significant in our day that this is the word that sums up so comprehensively the heart of the gospel of grace. "God was in Christ reconciling the world to himself, and has committed to us the ministry of reconciliation" (2 Cor. 5:19). Is it not therefore the supreme task of the church to unpack the significance of this in our day, not only to summon people to be reconciled to God—to accept that reconciliation which God has provided in Christ (Rom. 5:10-11)—but to be reconciled to one another in Christ?

What is reconciliation? In the general meaning of the word, it is to restore to friendship two people, two parties, or two nations who are estranged from one another. It means overcoming alienation, hostility, misunderstanding, to create unity. The good news of the gospel is that that is what God has done for us in Jesus Christ, and is seeking to do in us and through us in the world today as we bear witness to the gospel in the divided societies of our time.

The word is a particularly rich one in the New Testament. It is the Greek word *Katallage,* meaning literally an "exchange." So Calvin speaks of the *mirifica commutatio,* the "wonderful exchange" that God has made for us in Christ. Christ has come and taken our enmity, to give us love in exchange; our alienation and hostility, to give us his friendship in exchange; our sin, our condemnation, our death, to give us forgiveness, righteousness, and eternal life in exchange. "Oh the sweet exchange!" exclaims the anonymous author of the Epistle to Diognetus in the ancient church when he contemplates the cross. The joyful ministry to which God has called us is to proclaim the good news of what God has done for us in Christ nineteen hundred years before we were born, and to summon people to receive Christ today with all the blessings that are treasured up for us in him. In theological language, the imperatives of the gospel—"Be ye reconciled to God and one another"—flow from the indicatives of grace. We hold out to the world that love and friendship, that forgiveness and righteousness, that life and liberty, which alone can create true community, and which are found in him and joyfully received in faith. We are commanded to be reconciled to God and one another because of what God has done for the world in Christ.

I want to reflect on this in the light of some of my own experiences in recent years, especially in Northern Ireland and South Africa, for in these lands we see a mirror of ourselves and find a context where we see the powerful relevance of the gospel of reconciliation—the meaning of grace.

In the week of prayer for Christian unity in 1986 and again in 1987 I was invited by a group of Roman Catholic priests to live in the Clonard Redemptorist monastery in the Falls Road area of West Belfast in Northern Ireland, to preach at a series of Protestant/Catholic rallies in the Roman Catholic church there and in different Presbyterian churches in the city, as well as address other meetings, all on the subject of unity and reconciliation. The Falls Road area is one hundred percent Roman Catholic, nationalist, and anti-Protestant. The British Army has built a wall thirty feet high to divide it from the Shankhill area, which is one hundred percent Protestant, loyalist, and anti-Catholic. Every hundred yards in the Falls Road was a British soldier with a machine gun, while an army helicopter overhead monitored the possible activity of I.R.A. gunmen. We have the tragic scene of apartheid in Northern Ireland. How does one preach the gospel of grace and reconciliation in such a context?

On my second visit in January 1987, I preached at a rally in the Falls Road on John chapter seventeen, on our Lord's high priestly prayer for unity. I told them that the previous year the question was put to me very bluntly. "How can you, a Scottish Presbyterian minister and Reformed theologian, worship with Roman Catholics?" My answer was that God does not accept us because we offer Protestant worship, or Roman Catholic worship, or some beautiful Anglican liturgy, or "free prayers"! God accepts us by grace alone, not because of any offering we sinners can make, but only for what we are in Christ and on the ground of that one offering which he has made once and for all—for what we are in the person of him who intercedes for us. There is only one true priest in his church, Jesus Christ, and only one offering truly acceptable to God—the one he has provided for us, for all nations, for all times. That is the heart of Reformation teaching, as Calvin expounded it in his *Commentary on the Epistle to the Hebrews*.

If, therefore, Christ, our great High Priest, invites me by grace to participate through the Spirit in his intercessions for unity and communion with the Father (for that is what worship is) in spite of all my sins and failures and misunderstandings, and also invites our Roman Catholic brethren by grace to participate through the Spirit in his intercessions in spite of their sins and faults and misunderstandings, am I going to say, "Lord, I am not coming with these people! They are not acceptable to me!"? That would be a betrayal of the meaning of grace. It is only by grace that any of us can worship "in the name of Christ." The church as the body of Christ is a "royal priesthood," called out of all nations to participate by grace through the Spirit both in Christ's intercession to the Father on behalf of the world and in Christ's mission of reconciliation from the Father to the world. Our worship and mission of reconciliation to the world are the gift of sharing in Christ's worship and mission. "Therefore, holy brothers, who share in the heavenly calling, fix your thoughts on Jesus, the Apostle and High Priest whom we confess" (Heb. 3:1, NIB).

For four hundred years, from the time of the Reformation, the Reformed churches have stressed *sola gratia* on the vertical plane, that God accepts us freely and unconditionally for what we are in Christ by faith alone, be we Jews or Gentiles, male or female, black or white. But so often we betray this gospel by not working it out on the horizontal plane, by failing to *accept one another* as freely and unconditionally as God in Christ has accepted us. The New Testament knows no divorce between the vertical and the horizontal. The apostolic message is: "Accept one another as Christ accepted us to the glory of God" (Rom. 15:7). "Quench not the Spirit. . . . Be generous to one another, tenderhearted, forgiving one another as God in Christ forgave you" (Eph. 4:30, 32). "Be forbearing with one another, and forgiving, where any of you has cause for complaint: you must forgive as the Lord forgave you. To crown all, there must be love, to bind all together and complete the whole. . . . You were called as members of a single body" (Col. 3:13ff.).

In the definitive passage on grace and reconciliation in Eph. 2, the Apostle says: "By grace you have been saved through faith . . . His purpose was to create in Himself [in Christ] one new humanity out of the two [Jew and Gentile] thus making peace, and in this one body to reconcile both of them to God through the cross, by which He put to death their hostility." Our Christian dogmatic starting point for all ethical, social, and political action and reflection is the indicatives of grace. *We have been made one new humanity in Christ,* therefore . . . !

What are the things, then, that obscure this gospel of grace and prevent us from accepting one another (e.g. people of other races and denominations) as freely and unconditionally as God in Christ has accepted us and made us "one single new humanity"? I select a few points from Northern Ireland and South Africa.

SECTARIANISM

Belfast must be one of the most evangelized cities in the world! Yet the tragedy is that it must be the most sectarian city in the world.

What is sectarianism? As I see it, sectarianism arises when two things happen: first, when any group or church makes an absolute identification between their formulations of the truth and the Truth, and then, second, says, "We shall only accept you IF you accept our formulation of the Truth!"—and the gospel of grace is betrayed by what is sometimes an arrogant self-righteousness, which can even lead to the active persecution (by violence or "godly discipline"!) of those who do not agree with the group. God does not accept us on the ground of our *formulations* of the doctrines of grace (or our assent to the truth of the doctrine of "justification by faith alone"). He accepts us by *grace* for what we are by faith in Christ. Why then should we impose a condition of acceptance on others, which God does not?

What we see in much of Protestantism, we have seen also in Rome. For four hundred years, from the Council of Trent to Vatican II, Catholic Rome was dominated by that kind of sectarianism—"We shall only accept you IF you accept our Roman dogmas"—until Pope John XXIII, on 11 October 1962, had the courage to say that "The *Substance* of ancient doctrine held in good faith is to be distinguished from the *formulations* in which it is clothed." This "realist" break with "nominalism" opened the door to reformation, to reformulation, to Vatican II. Prior to that, Protestants were "heretics and schismatics." But since then Rome has called us "separated brethren," accepting us for what we are in Christ.

But it is that kind of sectarianism we witness today among many Protestants in their attitude toward Rome! Catholics are dismissed as unacceptable "heretics." Only when we can both meet as "separated brethren," living by grace and seeking together the Truth as it is in Christ, can there by any hope of reconciliation.

It is particularly sad when Christians in the Reformed tradition who allegedly take their stand on "the doctrines of grace" substitute their formulations of grace for the reality of grace itself, and make their acceptance of others conditional on doctrinal conformity. Then grace is betrayed.

(This of course raises the epistemological and hermeneutical question of the relationship between "truth of statement" and "Truth of Being." They are not to be confused, but are not to be separated. The fundamental function of dogmatic statements is to point beyond themselves to the Truth of God, "the Truth as it is in Christ," the gospel of grace.)

This does not mean that we condone any doctrine we regard as false, e.g. apartheid. We must always seek to be true to the Truth and seek careful dogmatic interpretations of the gospel. But the first step on the road to reconciliation is to recognize that the Truth is in Christ, not in us. We see through a glass darkly, not yet face to face.

CIVIL RELIGION OR NATIONALISM

Nothing can more entrench the sectarian spirit than different forms of "nationalism" and "civil religion," as we see in many parts of the world today, in Islamic as well as Christian countries.

What is nationalism? Sociologists recognize it is notoriously hard to define. There is surely nothing wrong in being proud of one's nationality. But "nationalism" as a "civil religion" arises when three things are fused together: (1) our politics—be it Republicanism or Unionism in Northern Ireland; (2) a romantic, exclusive, ethnic loyalty to our own nation or *Volk*; (3) religion, be it Catholic or Protestant (or Islamic). Then the "nationalist" or "loyalist" party feels it has divine sanctions for its policies and those who do not accept its terms can be ruthlessly excluded, and the road is set for violence. From the Christian point of view, the tragedy is that what controls behavior toward others is not the gospel of grace and reconciliation, but political commitment and romantic ethnic loyalty—be it pro-British or anti-British. Of course nationalism so often arises out of situations of injustice and tyranny, and feeds on the resulting fear, frustrations, and anger.

It was against the nationalism of the so-called German Christians that the Barmen Declaration of 1934 was drawn up by the Confessing Churches to say that there is no area of life that does not belong to Jesus Christ, to whom alone we owe exclusive loyalty. It was against that same kind of nationalism of the white nationalist government in South Africa that the black Dutch Reformed Church drew up the *Belhar Confession* of 1982 to break down the barriers between "black Christians" and "white Christians" in a cry for justice. In Northern Ireland, there would appear to be two kinds of "Irish Christians" on either side of the sectarian divide—nationalist Christians and loyalist Christians. For this reason a group of leading Roman Catholic and Protestant churchmen, in June 1986, produced A Declaration of Faith and Commitment by Christians in Northern Ireland, modeled on the Barmen Declaration, calling for Catholics and Protestants to give their supreme loyalty to Christ in a common concern to work for justice for all.

The ideology of apartheid in South Africa was hammered out on the anvil of "Afrikaner Civil Religion." The Nationalists who came to power in 1948 were (1) Republican in their politics, (2) romantically Afrikaner and traditionally anti-British, and (3) Dutch Reformed Calvinists. "Afrikaner civil religion," with all its accompanying mythology and folklore, was fed by historical memories of the Boer Trek of 1838, Blood River, "the day of the Covenant" 16 December 1838, and bitter memories of the Anglo/Boer wars. When the Germans failed to defeat the British in the 1914-18 war, the Afrikaners—Diederichs, Cronje, Malan, Moeller, and others—went to study in Germany and brought back the neo-Fichtean romantic concept of the *Volk* and grafted it onto Afrikanerdom, laying the ideological basis for the Nationalist party. All this gave to the Afrikaners a sense of messianic destiny to solve the problems of South Africa. Like the old Israel after the Exodus, they were a holy nation, who had lived by the Bible and the sword, fighting the Matabele, the Zulus, and the British.

The question for the church in Northern Ireland and in South Africa is: what controls the behavior of the Christian nationalist or loyalist? So often it is not the gospel, not the message of reconciliation, but political aspirations, romantic ethnic loyalty to the *Volk* with its accompanying folklore, and sectarian religion—be it state religion, individualistic pietism, or scholastic Calvinism. Politicians are at their wits' end to know how to solve the problems of Northern Ireland.

Perhaps the real solution is in the hands of the Christian church. Only the gospel of grace can liberate Christians from animosity, prejudice, and sectarian hate. When we give our exclusive allegiance to Jesus Christ, he takes us up into his all-inclusive love and lifts us out of those sectarian barriers by which we exclude one another. It is for the church to disentangle herself from romantic racist attitudes, from arrogant sectarianism; perhaps then politicians can work together to find solutions. If this is true in Northern Ireland, it is certainly true in South Africa. But how can a Nationalist government, which is the embodiment of Afrikaner civil religion, ever have the liberty to seek true justice for all ethnic groups?

In Northern Ireland we see the tragic fusion of sectarianism and civil religion in extreme forms in the formation of "Ulster Clubs" under the cry of "For God and for Ulster." In similar fashion we see the same fusion in the "Afrikaner Resistance Movement" (AWB) led by Eugene Terreblanche under the cry of "My God, my Volk," the successor to the earlier quasi-Nazi organization, the *Ossewabrandwag*. Mrs. Thatcher was confident that by the Anglo/Irish Accord a political solution could be found to the problems of Northern Ireland, but she failed to realize the power of sectarian civil religion on both sides of the sectarian divide.

ECONOMIC FACTORS — VESTED INTERESTS

Economic factors are clearly a third force that keeps people from accepting one another as freely and unconditionally as God accepts us.

Apartheid is clearly an ideology to be understood in economic as well as ethnic terms. In sociological terms, such an ideology (1) serves vested interests; (2) interprets (distorts) reality (and the Bible) to protect vested interests; (3) is passionately believed by sincere people. Afrikaners rose to wealth and power by the economic trinity of land, security, and cheap labor. They see all three threatened in the present revolutionary situation. This is what lies behind the present emergency situation. Even where there is talk of abolishing apartheid, it is replaced by the ideology of the national security state, the allegation of the influences of "communism," to defend the same vested interests.

The cost of discipleship for the Christian can be to see that our loyalty to Christ must transcend our concern for our vested interests. The call for such is made in a multi-racial manifesto in 1987 entitled "Evangelical Witness in South Africa—Evangelicals Critique Their Own Theology and Practice." Such discipleship inevitably involves the call to suffer, a point made powerfully by the Lutheran theologian Prof. Dr. Klaus Nurnberger of UNISA in a powerful article: "By Grace Alone: The Significance of the Core Doctrine of the Reformation for the Present Crisis in South Africa,"[1] where he argues that the gospel means "unconditional, suffering acceptance of the unacceptable," and shows what this means in the South African scene.

LAW AND THE POWERS OF EVIL

The problem of reconciliation is unquestionably the problem of love: how to get people to love and accept one another freely and unconditionally. But love without justice, as the South African anti-apartheid *Kairos* document so rightly asserts, is sentimentality. There can be genuine reconciliation in society only when injustice is brought into the open and dealt with. Likewise there can be no true justice without freedom. Love, justice, and freedom are the anatomy of true reconciliation, and are mutually dependent.

But the demand for justice without love *can* become demonic, as our Lord shows in the Sermon on the Mount. The Apostle in 1 Cor. 15:56 makes the same point in asserting that "the strength of sin is the Law." What does this mean? I think that it means in part that the powers of evil in this world exploit guilty situations and often do so in the name of "Law." It is so often in guilty situations, where there comes a God-given cry for justice, that sinister forces can exploit people and enslave them in the name of "justice." The best way to fight malaria is to clean up the swamps where the mosquito breeds. So the best way to deal with "terrorism" in so many parts of the world is to clear up the guilty social conditions where it breeds. Likewise in the name of "law and order" (which of course society requires), the forces of reaction and repression can silence those with legitimate grievances, and do so in terms of "state religion" and the "security forces," as the *Kairos* document so rightly sees. Likewise the demand for "civil rights" can be a God-given cry for justice where there is social evil and discrimination. But again even this can be used for destructive purposes and become an instrument for hate.

Jesus battled against evil in this form. This evil put him to death on the cross in the name of Law—Jewish law and Roman law. But it was over evil in this form that he triumphed in his death and resurrection, in reconciling the world to God and liberating humanity.

The tragedy of the Christian church is that she so often fails to hear the cry for justice in guilty situations—but that same cry is heard by others who can exploit it in tragic ways. What so often prevents Christians from hearing that cry for justice is the fear of losing our vested interests. In the ministry of reconciliation, it is the duty of the Christian church on the one hand to listen to the Word of God, the gospel of grace and reconciliation, but on the other to listen to the cry for justice of the poor, the exploited, and the oppressed, to fulfill our prophetic function in the world by seeking to give to all their humanity—in seeking love, justice, and freedom for all.

The *Kairos* document sees clearly that there can be "no reconciliation without justice." The present struggle in South Africa is a struggle for that *justice* and *liberty,* without which reconciliation is impossible. But here there is a weak part in the document where, in order to stress this, it wrongly says (p. 12) that forgiveness is conditional upon repentance—that we are not expected to forgive the unrepentant sinner! *No.* Forgiveness (70 x 7), as love in action, is always unconditional, as in our Lord's response to Peter and in his attitude toward Zaccheus. But such forgiveness unconditionally demands repentance and must be *received* in repentance if there is to be genuine reconciliation, and such reconciliation will doubtless require reparation (as in the case of Zaccheus). In Calvin's language, the Bible teaches "evangelical repentance," not "legal repentance." Repentance is the necessary response to forgiveness, not its "condition." That, the Reformers saw, was the fallacy in the medieval sacrament of penance. The blacks should not say, We shall only forgive you IF you hand back the land (etc.). But the whites, in receiving black forgiveness, must repent and hand back the land. Reparation is not a condition of grace, but it may be a necessary response to grace. Not to forgive unconditionally is to be inhuman. But not to repent and see that justice is done is equally inhuman. The gospel calls us to give to one another our humanity, as God has restored it to us in Christ. But is it for the whites to "tell" the blacks to forgive them? We can only ask others to forgive us when we freely admit our guilt and make amends. We need one another to be human, and the white cannot presume on black forgiveness while not ensuring that justice is done.

THEOLOGICAL FACTORS

When one reflects on Northern Ireland and South Africa one can see a deep dualism between the concern for evangelism and the concern for social justice. In South Africa, the two great wings of white Christianity are *Evangelicalism,* in the pietist tradition of Andrew Murray, the Aberdeenshire Scot who was six times moderator of the Dutch Reformed Church, and the *Calvinism* (and neo-Calvinism) of the Dutch Reformed Churches. Both wings have done much to evangelize the blacks, have them baptized, and put into black churches. But too often they do not give to them their humanity. Why is there this divorce between evangelism and humanization? The weakness on the Evangelical side is the tendency to privatize the gospel, and divorce the vertical from the horizontal, personal faith and holiness from social holiness. The weakness on the Calvinist side, in the tradition of the Canons of the Synod of Dort and the Westminster Confession of Faith, is to limit the mediatorial headship of Christ to the elect (the church) and hence to interpret race relations not Christologically but in terms of *their* notions of "natural law." Then the church and society derive their structures, not from Christ, but from "orders of creation," "ethnic diversity," "pluriformity of nature," etc. So by a misuse of Calvinism, and the neo-Calvinism of Abraham Kuyper and his school, with the notion of "independent spheres of sovereignty," theological justification was sought by the nationalists for "separate development."[2]

As I see it, both wings, the Evangelicals and the neo-Calvinists, have an *inadequate understanding of the incarnation.* To hold out Christ to the world, in preaching and at the Lord's Table, is not only to hold out forgiveness and eternal life in Christ; it is to give to all their humanity. All races, be we Jews or Gentiles, black or white, male or female, are meant to see in Christ *our* humanity assumed, sanctified, offered "without spot or wrinkle" to the Father, and held out to us to be received in faith, for God's purpose in Christ was "to create in himself one new humanity" (Eph. 2).

When the whites took Christ to Africa, the blacks found salvation and eternal life in Christ. They found more. They discovered the dignity and beauty of their black humanity. But when they say to the white Christians—the custodians of "civil religion"—"Give to us our humanity!" they are told, as Archbishop Tutu was by the Eloff Commission, "Stay out of politics!"

NOTES

1. In *Transformation* 3, no. 2 (April-June 1986):41-48. Cp. "Evangelical Witness in South Africa: Evangelicals Critique Their Own Theology and Practice," in *Concerned Evangelicals* (Donsonville, 1985).
2. It is significant that during the American Civil War for the emancipation of

slaves, Calvinists fought Calvinists, Presbyterians fought Presbyterians, and the Presbyterian Church split in two. What was the theological difference? They all held to the federal Calvinism of the Westminster Confession and the old Princeton school. They all held to the doctrines of the double decree and Christ's mediatorial headship over the elect. What divided them was two different views of natural law. The Northerners believed that God by nature has made all (black and white) equal with rights to life, liberty, and the pursuit of happiness. No, said Dabney, Thornwell, Palmer, and the Southern Calvinists. God has made some white, some black; some masters, some servants; and in terms of their views of natural law found biblical justification for slavery.

In the nineteenth century, the great missionary societies in South Africa built up indigenous churches in the interest of maximum growth, with separate Zulu, Xhosa, Venda, Indian, and colored churches, so that each tribe and ethnic group could head the gospel and worship God in its own language. But then the Lutheran missiologist Gustav Warneck gave theological justification to this, saying this was right because it was in accordance with "the orders of creation"! One can understand why Karl Barth and his colleagues said *"Nein!"* in the 1930s in Nazi Germany, when the "German Christians" used the concept of "orders of creation" to justify the Aryan anti-Semitic policies of their time. Again, one can see the powerful significance of the Barmen Declaration of 1934 and the concern of the confessing church to interpret every area of life in terms of the headship of Christ as mediator for all. In a strange way in South Africa, Lutheran notions of "the orders of creation" combined with certain Calvinist notions of natural law to provide a non-Christological "biblical" justification for apartheid. Both operate with a dualism between nature and grace, natural law and the gospel, the "civil" and the "spiritual." But in fact on this approach grace presupposes nature, perfects nature in such a way that justification for "separate development" is offered in both state and church. But surely this denies the headship of Christ as mediator over every area of life, and militates against an authentic ministry of reconciliation.

9

TODD H. SPEIDELL

✦

Incarnational Social Ethics

I F THERE ARE TWO SIDES to humanity," Ray Anderson proclaims, "Christ will be found on the wrong side."[1] Jesus embodied the unreserved presence of God with sinners. "Those who are well have no need of a physician," Jesus declared, "but those who are sick. Go and learn what this means, 'I desire mercy, and not sacrifice.' For I came not to call the righteous, but sinners" (Mt. 9:12f.). Christ's incarnate humanity — his entire life, death, and resurrection among and for sinners — provided a basis for and reality of reconciliation. He stood in our place and acted on our behalf to heal our humanity. His vicarious humanity — i.e. his substitutionary life *and* death — reconciled us to one another as well as to God. Social reconciliation, I shall aver, is both an indicative and an imperative of the gospel of Jesus Christ.

CHRIST'S INCARNATION AS
GOD'S IDENTIFICATION WITH SINNERS

Jesus does not simply sojourn among us, declares Athanasius, but also heals as a physician who touches our existence with his own being.[2] He bears, not merely cures, our sins (Mt. 8:17, Is. 53:4, 1 Pt. 2:24). "Christ does not heal us by standing over against us," writes James Torrance, for he heals our humanity in solidarity with us, as the sanctifying presence of God. He is, Torrance continues, "the True Priest, bone of our bone, flesh of our flesh," who bears upon his divine heart our sins and injustices and who effects in his vicarious humanity our reconciliation.[3]

If the divine power of heaven had preserved its dignity by not coming into contact with diseased humanity on earth, then our sickness would not have received its cure and we would not have been healed. But God assumed human life from birth unto death, asserts Gregory of Nyssa, healing "all that lies between."[4] "For that which he has not assumed he has not healed," writes Gregory of Nazianzus in opposition to Apollinarianism, "but that which is united to his Godhead is also saved."[5] God in Christ assumed humanity in its wholeness to heal and sanctify our broken existence.[6]

He freely acted as the powerful one who assumed the form of weakness, the eternal one who revealed himself in space and time, the Lord who came to us as a servant. The exaltation of Christ (Phil. 2:9ff.) is not in spite of, but because of, his humiliation (Phil. 2:6ff.). Paul's exhortation to unity (which precedes the kenotic hymn) should and may be obeyed because the Philippians have the mind of Christ, whose humility was grounded in the being of God.[7] Because God revealed who he is in Christ, we therefore ought to be who we are in Christ, not merely by emulating his example but by participating in the vicarious obedience of the humiliated one, Jesus Christ.

Christ lived and died as the one on behalf of the many. The Old Testament concept of the one and the many implied a "corporate personality": one who acted on behalf of others both in a Godward and in a humanward movement.[8] Adam was the one who summed up the history of old humanity; Christ was the one who embodied the reality of new humanity.[9] Christ assumed and sanctified Jewish flesh, the one Israelite on behalf of the many, which served as "a mirror held up" to the faces "of all peoples."[10] He redeemed our unfaithful and disobedient humanity in and through his own humanity. The enfleshment of the Word, writes Irenaeus, summarized "the long history of the human race" to save and reconstitute humanity.[11]

Christ is the truth about both God and humanity. He has satisfied in his humanity what God intended for us. He has realized both God's promise— "I will be your God"—and God's command—"and you shall be my people." He is, asserts Barth, both "the promise and the command, the Gospel and the Law, the address of God to man and the claim of God upon man."[12] In him, the command is also a promise, because God in Christ fulfills what he commands, hears what he speaks, and accomplishes what he wills.[13]

Gospel and law are neither confused nor separated but fulfilled in Christ. He is the content of the gospel and the fulfillment of the law. God for us is the basis of what God wants with us and from us.[14] God's commands are weakened when they become the demands of a human "ought," for the law is weakened by the flesh, but what the law could not do on its own, God did for us in Christ (Rom. 8:3).[15] Christ's vicarious obedience for us has fulfilled (but not abrogated) the law; hence, we shall (both a command and a promise) acknowledge and love and obey God.[16]

Our participation in the ministry of the incarnate one, who lived his life concretely in a particular place for others, lays a priority on localized love: first to family, then to neighbors and friends, and finally to "distant neighbors."[17] Christians in the U.S. must address race relations in their local churches before denouncing apartheid in South Africa.[18] They should engage in local forms of service before global (and often abstract) discussions of justice and equality. When they do respond to the global dimensions of Christian social responsibility, they will then do so with integrity; they will do so with a sense of the humanity of their (even distant) neighbor.

God thus binds humans to himself and to one another in the vicarious humanity of Christ, the one on behalf of the many. The incarnation testifies to God's identifying presence with us, healing what he assumes. The cross presupposes the incarnation, God's solidarity with sinners to sanctify human life and existence. The incarnation leads to the cross, for God identifies with sinners from birth unto death, healing "all that lies between."

CHRIST'S CRUCIFIXION AS
GOD'S CONFRONTATION WITH SINNERS

Christ's death on the cross "reveals the full seriousness of the human situation."[19] Human nature is radically sinful from the center of its being throughout the whole of its existence.[20] No "attractive realism" or "Christian humanitarianism" will do, for God's grace overthrows all human attempts to establish the kingdom of God on earth (cf. Lk. 4:5ff.).[21] Christ identifies with humans, then, to confront them with God's grace for sinners.

The crucified Christ continues God's solidarity with estranged and lost humanity to effect the *reality* of reconciliation. This understanding should be distinguished from a contemporary Anabaptist view of the cross. Jesus' baptism is the inauguration, declares John Howard Yoder, and his cross the culmination, of God's kingdom, which creates "a new possibility of human, social, and therefore political relationships"—that is, "a new kind of community leading a radically new kind of life."[22] Only at one point, asserts Yoder, is Jesus "consistently" and "universally" our example: at the cross.[23] Jesus' "motto of revolutionary subordination" and "social style" of "new community" reject violence, for Christ's submission to the cross is "the model of Christian social efficacy."[24]

"Jesus' story *is* a social ethic," Stanley Hauerwas also suggests, and "people who are willing to take his cross as their story . . . become the continuation of that ethic in the world."[25] The church, he continues, exemplifies the ethic of Jesus as a "contrast model" to the world, tells the story of Jesus, and continues the truth of God's kingdom.[26] The cross in Anabaptist thought is "a way of life to be lived among people," based on the "principle" of "the way of the cross."[27] The church, then, applies "the kingdom idea" to practical life in the context of a Christ/world dualism by being an alternative community.[28]

The crucified humanity of Christ, however, should not be treated as a possibility of our radical discipleship; rather, it effects the reality of reconciliation in his humanity. "And a cross without its humanity," Anderson writes, "is a cross without its power of reconciliation. . . . But the truth of the Gospel is not that humanity has been put on the cross; it is rather that the cross has been sunk deep into humanity."[29] "The clue, therefore, to social justice," he asserts, "is not the justice of God as an abstract principle but his humanity as an historical and continuing power of reconciliation."[30] The crucified Christ stands in solidarity with humanity, not merely as an example of confrontation with the world to be imitated by us but as the reality of new humanity in which we may and must participate.

Christ gives us himself, not merely a radical ethic of confrontational discipleship. He confronts us with his true humanity, in which we have the actuality of restored humanity, not simply slogans of peace and justice nor pronouncements against social sins. He stands "against us" precisely because he is "for us."[31] He substitutes his life and death in our place, representing us to God in his whole atoning life and death.[32] The vicarious work of Christ as "the Judge judged in our place," declares Barth, effects atonement for us; otherwise, "everything else will be left hanging in the void as an anthropological or psychological or sociological myth, and sooner or later it will break and fall to the ground."[33]

The atonement originates in the Fatherhood of God and the Sonship of Christ, McLeod Campbell argues, and results in our life of sonship and daughterhood.[34] Our proper response to Christ's atoning work, he continues, is filial "trust in a Father's heart," not "trust in the judicial grounds" of a legal title. Our "filial confidence," rather than "legal confidence," indicates a response of sonship and daughterhood to the heart of God revealed in Christ.[35]

Evangelical repentance posits God as Father and humans as brothers and sisters, based on the Godward and humanward aspects of the atonement. Christ offered his life on our behalf to heal our estranged and hostile humanity; in him, we know God as Father and others as brothers and sisters.[36] There is one grace of the gospel. Christ is both the Son of the Father and the Brother of humanity; our relations toward God and one another are healed in the crucified Christ.

The movie *Places in the Heart* portrays a young black boy who accidentally kills a white sheriff. The townspeople, in turn, brutally and shamelessly kill the boy. A black man passes through town looking for work. He and the sheriff's widow provide mutual help for each other, the man needing work to survive and the widow needing help with her crops to save her property from foreclosure. In the end, the local church celebrates the sacrament of communion: the townspeople, the white sheriff's widow, the black man — even the white sheriff and the black boy — are all present, passing the bread and the cup to one another.

Christ has made us fellow citizens, no longer outsiders vs. insiders. He has created peace between us, not merely peace of mind. He has abolished our enmity and restored our humanity in himself, in his true humanity. Christ "has broken down the dividing wall of hostility," declares the author of Ephesians, and has created in himself one new humanity "through the cross" (Eph. 2:14ff.).

The crucifixion of the Jewish, circumcised, male Jesus of Nazareth, Anderson suggests, ends racial, religious, and sexual prerogatives. Jesus brought his Jewish, circumcised, and male flesh to the cross and thereby abolished these criteria of inclusion.[37] Jesus Christ is the new criterion for social relationships between men and women, Jew and Gentile, black and white.

The eschatological freedom of being in Christ, in whom there is neither male nor female (Gal. 3:28), Leonhard Goppelt argues, does not obliterate our humanity, for there is also an eschatological tension of living within one's present state (1 Cor. 7:20).[38] We are male and female in Christ, and therefore one, and yet we are still male and female. Christ radically qualifies our maleness and femaleness, breaking down hostilities, prerogatives, and self-assertion, and liberating humans to be reconciled as males and females.

Our concrete humanity cannot be simply set aside. (Cf. Letty Russell's assertion that we should explore "experimental life-styles that seek to overcome old dichotomies that we have inherited: clergy/laity, male/female, rich/poor, black/white, gay/straight"; she lists several "alternatives" and "new forms of human sexuality," such as "communal marriages, serial mating, single parent arrangements, cluster families, polygamy, homosexual arrangements."[39] Her abstract understanding of "partnership" undermines our ontological differentiation as male and female and reduces sexuality merely to biological differentiation.) Christ, the Creator and Redeemer, holds out his true humanity to us, so that we may be who we are in him as male and female. He rejects (traditionalist and feminist) abstractions of what it means to be male and female, for he qualifies our concrete humanity with his own true humanity.

The crucified Christ is the "end" of humanity in a double sense: the discontinuity of sinful criteria ("end" as *terminus*) and the continuity of created humanity ("end" as *telos,* based on the *eschaton* of Christ's true humanity). The crucified Christ confronts hostility, discrimination, oppression, and exclusion; he imparts his true and new humanity as a basis for and reality of social reconciliation.

CHRIST'S RESURRECTION AS
GOD'S RE-FORMATION OF SINNERS

Christ's double movement of humiliation and exaltation, suggests Barth, portrays the Son of God going into the far country and the Son of Man returning home, bringing along the humanity he assumed to present it to the Father and give it new life.[40] The resurrection, argues T. F. Torrance, unveils the cross as "the recreation and final affirmation" of humanity.[41] The resurrection, he continues, demonstrates to us "the *wholeness* of our redemption in a *whole* Christ," and hence concludes our adoption through Christ as his fellow sons and daughters of the Father.[42] In his death on the cross Christ destroyed the disobedience of old humanity, and in his resurrection Christ fulfilled the obedience of new humanity.[43]

"The risen Christ," Jürgen Moltmann reminds us, "is and remains the crucified Christ."[44] A social ethic based merely on the resurrection would degenerate into enthusiasm. "The radical solution," Bonhoeffer warns, sees only the ultimate and ignores the penultimate. One is either "for Christ" or "against him." Whether withdrawing from the world or improving the world, the radical hates the world as it is. "The radical cannot forgive God His creation."[45]

The compromise solution, on the other hand, sets apart "the last word . . . from all preceding words," Bonhoeffer continues, so that the penultimate is not threatened by the ultimate.[46] The compromiser hates the ultimate and excludes it from penultimate matters. "The Christian spirit of compromise," he declares, "arises from hatred of the justification of the sinner by grace alone."[47] "Radicalism hates the real," he summarizes, "and compromise hates the word."[48]

The penultimate precedes the ultimate and yet is only validly determined by the ultimate. "Method," warns Bonhoeffer, "is a way from the penultimate to the ultimate. Preparation of the way is a way from the ultimate to the penultimate," for Christ himself prepares the way.[49] Feeding the hungry should not serve as a technique for preaching the gospel, for example, but proclaiming the incarnate one binds us in solidarity with the hungry, the homeless, the naked, the sick, and the imprisoned. Both the ultimate and the penultimate have "seriousness and validity" and a closely allied task, which is "to fortify the penultimate with a more emphatic proclamation of the ultimate, and also to protect the ultimate by taking due care for the penultimate."[50]

"The *pro-missio* of the kingdom," Moltmann agrees, "is the ground of the *missio* of love to the world."[51] The mission before the mission, the gracious work of God in Christ, leads the church in service. God's ultimate word of justification orients and prepares the way for penultimate acts of service and mission. But the "eschatological proviso" of the resurrection is the crucified Christ, not an *eschatologia gloriae*.[52] The crucified God provides hope as a realistic foundation for social transformation in the midst of present contradictions and in the expectation of the promised future.[53]

Barth and T. F. Torrance criticize, however, the eschatological emptiness of an abstract concept of "hope."[54] The community of the incarnate, crucified, and risen Christ lives as the continued presence of Christ himself, whose Spirit empowers the church's mission between Christ's ascension and advent. (Also consider Moltmann's "trinitarian" theology of the cross, which neglects the role of the Spirit and, in the end, merely relies on psychoanalysis and socialism to provide a hermeneutic of psychological and political liberation, respectively.[55] Christ's Spirit enables the church to participate in the risen Christ's service to the Father, who sends the church into the world.

CHRISTIAN ETHICS AS *PARTICIPATIO CHRISTI*

Jesus Christ enacts God's love for his creation, his judgment upon sin, and his restoration of the fallen order. A Christian ethic based solely on the incarnation would lead to compromise; based solely on the cross or resurrection, it would lead to radicalism or enthusiasm. "In Jesus Christ," asserts Bonhoeffer, "we have faith in the incarnate, crucified and risen God." "There could be no greater error," he insists, "than to tear these three elements apart. . . . "[56] The incarnate, crucified, and risen Christ has upheld God's covenant with humanity by identifying with us sinners, confronting our rebellious nature, and re-forming who we are.

In Christ, God himself was present reconciling all things to himself (Col. 1:19f.). The vicarious humanity of Christ provides an objective reality of reconciliation, over against a subjective potentiality of making ourselves good. Christian ethics must not become an autonomous subject separate from theology, for in his humanity Christ both reveals God to us and reconciles us to God and one another. Christian ethics, therefore, presupposes intrinsic ontological grounds for reconciliation in the humanity of Christ, rather than abstract, independent, or universal moral laws.

Christian social ethics must attest the concrete reality of reconciliation in Christ. He does not merely leave his life and teaching for us to copy and embody in this world—as if we, rather than his Spirit, continue his presence and work in this world—but he continues to re-*present* himself as the ongoing reality of social reconciliation and true humanity. We do not need to become poor, pacifist, and powerless *like him*—unless Christ freely chooses to lead us into this lifestyle. Rather, we must be who we are—poor or rich, black or white, male or female—*in him*.

Christ presents himself in the depths of human need—the hungry, the thirsty, the naked, the sick, the imprisoned (Mt. 25:31ff.). The stranger among us, the homeless and psychologically debilitated, may be the place of Christ's presence among us. The Gospel of Matthew does not exhort us simply to be like Christ—ministering to the needy "as Jesus would" (which implies that he is not actively present but merely serves as a model for our social action)—but attests that Christ discloses himself through the stranger. We must be where Christ is, and act where he acts. By meeting the stranger, by entering into a distinctively human relationship with those to whom the government may or may not dispense services and programs, we will meet Christ himself and find our own humanity.

God in Christ, asserts Barth, "is not good *for himself*"; he "is really good *for us.*" For he "does not stand on that pretended frontier," Barth continues,

> where a smaller lack of goodness can regard itself as good in the face of a larger lack of goodness. He removes this frontier. He also removes the frontier that separates God's goodness from the lack of it which characterizes us all. He proclaims the forgiveness of sins. He opens the closed door of righteousness from within instead of rejoicing at being within and hiding himself behind the door. He brings the unrighteous in instead of talking to them through the closed door and taking pleasure in their being outside. . . . He thus spends his life, pours it out, and finally pours out his very blood for the hardened, the dejected and the hostile: not asking what he will get out of it; not asking anything, but simply acting for those who do not deserve it, turning to them as the Lamb of God which really takes away the *sin* of the world, which really *takes* it *away* (cf. John 1:29). This, then, is the divine goodness in the human goodness of Jesus of Nazareth: goodness which this man does not for a moment possess without giving it away.[57]

Christ gives his sanctified humanity to us, so that we may partake of him and his goodness. Christian ethics must offer no abstract good, but rather the goodness of God revealed in Christ and given to us by the Spirit. The will of God, insists Bonhoeffer, is "not an idea, still demanding to become real," but a reality in Jesus Christ; nor what exists, which would simply require "submissive acquiescence," but a reality both in and against what exists.[58]

"The problem of Christian ethics," however, "is the realization among God's creatures of the revelational reality of God in Christ. . . . "[59] The Spirit of Christ both commands and enables us to participate in the revealing and reconciling work of God in Christ. Our participation in Christ's self-giving solidarity with the world attests the primary reality that Jesus Christ gives his life for the world; hence, we exist as Christ's witnesses and servants in the world.

The love of neighbor, Barth argues, does not mean that we repeat or replace Christ's action of love, but that we witness to the reconciling action of God in Christ by meeting "our neighbors truly and honestly only as lost ourselves, i.e., exactly as we are, and not in the role of saviors." There is one Savior, he continues, who does not permit us to shield ourselves from our neighbor with our presumed goodness, but who commands us to "be fundamentally open to others," precisely as sinners to fellow-sinners.[60] God shows us our neighbors as brothers and sisters.

God binds us together in filial relations in the vicarious humanity of our Brother Jesus Christ. Legal demands for social justice may provide rights, but not affirmation; legally assured conditions, but not personal relations;

equality, but not respect; liberty, but not freedom. Affirmative action, for example, may be an expedient measure to correct societal injustices, but the gospel calls us beyond (even though including) rights to reconciliation and response-ability, because God has bound us to one another in Christ. We need each other as male and female, Jew and Gentile, black and white, and so on, to hear the gospel of Christ's reconciling work.

The basic form of humanity is social, reflecting the very image of the triune God. Christ offered his life among humans as a service to the Father and in the Spirit. He, as the one on behalf of the many, gave himself for the life of the world. He humanized our sinful and divisive social existence in his humanity, and enabled us to be who we are and are becoming in him.

Our cohumanity, our being in communion with others, requires human distinctives of social reconciliation. Cohumanity, Barth suggests, implies a mutual seeing and being seen, so that we see each other eye-to-eye. To look the other in the eye and to let the other look into our own eye reveals the twosided openness and disclosure of humanity, to see and be seen in a mutual and personal way. This mutual human look exposes the dangerous tendency to depersonalization: systematization in the social sciences (and theology!), the centralization of political economy, and the impersonalization of bureaucracy.[61]

Cohumanity also indicates a mutual speaking and hearing, so that we communicate mouth-to-ear. To speak as an expression of the self and to hear the other's self-expression manifests human communication, which addresses the other and is addressed by the other in a mutual penetration of personal being and knowing.[62] A human encounter of reciprocity does not allow talking past each other—"two monologues do not constitute a dialogue"—but with and to one another, for otherwise our words are "inhuman and barbaric," empty words which betray empty people.[63] The Jewish-Christian dialogue, for example, can neither permit one partner to discount in advance the other's position, which would violate respect and force the other to surrender his or her "soul as a condition of dialogue,"[64] nor allow either partner to withhold judgment or evade the other's judgment.[65] Ecumenical and interfaith dialogue must include both genuine hearing and criticism.

Cohumanity also affirms a mutual assistance and being assisted, so that we help each other hand-to-hand. To reach out my hand and to receive your hand expresses a concrete awareness of you as my fellow-human. We do not help each other as God, but only in a relative—though definite—way. Nor ought we to portray the unhealthy altruism that "helps" but does not stand by the other, for we must offer and receive the concrete solidarity of truly human help.[66] (Barth should lay more emphasis on the aspect of being helped, which he states but does not develop, for mutuality—being with the other—extends beyond charity—giving to the other.)

Cohumanity, finally, suggests a mutual gladness of seing and being seen, speaking and hearing, receiving and offering help, so that we encounter one another heart-to-heart. To be glad means to live in correspondence with one's determination as a covenant-partner of God and one's fellow humanity. A neutral position in which one can choose between "gladly" and "reluctantly" indicates inhuman aloofness—"neutrally" is thus the real alternative to "gladly"—but true freedom gladly exists with the other.[67] Gladness with the other neither loses oneself in the other nor uses the other for oneself, but affirms the freedom to be oneself with the other and to be with the other in mutual openness, communion, and action.

The Elephant Man, a movie depicting the deformity of John Merrick and the inhumanity of society, limns the reality of human healing and reconciliation. The doctor who rescued "the Elephant Man" from the circus and displayed him as a medical abnormality discovered that he was not an idiot but a human being. The doctor himself became transformed and discovered his own humanity. The woman who visited John Merrick treated him as a fellow human being—looking him in the eye, speaking with him, touching his hand, and enjoying his company. This human encounter healed him—not as a miraculous physical healing, but as a recovery of the humanity of which he had been robbed (perhaps the greater miracle). Despite the lack of physical healing, he died in peace.

Christ assumed our humanity to make us whole. He did not "merely help His fellows from without," Barth declares, "standing alongside, making a contribution and then withdrawing again and leaving them until further help is perhaps required." On the contrary. He gave "Himself to them" and made "their state and fate His own cause. . . . "[68] He affirmed and transformed our humanity in his humanity as the very work of God himself.[69]

God assumed our humanity in Jesus of Nazareth, healed our humanity with his own being, and gave our sanctified humanity back to us. The Spirit of Christ commands and enables us to participate by grace in the vicarious humanity of Christ. We must (and may!) live in the reconciled reality of our cohumanity in Christ by acknowledging the humanity of our neighbor.

The incarnate Christ, who has assumed and healed our humanity, calls us to believe and repent in response to his reconciling work. The church cannot call the world to social repentance when it has not repented of its own social sins and its own agenda to improve the world. Instead of making endless pronouncements on the way the world ought to be, the church must first believe and practice the reality of social reconciliation in Christ.

The church does have a message to the world, which should be expressed in a renewed social practice. The church may issue a summons to the world to stand with it in evangelical social repentance; believing, confessing, and re-*present*-ing God's reconciling work in Christ. It cannot trivialize the impact of the gospel on human life by limiting its message to a list of social concerns. The church must stand with and for those in need, that the church itself may continue to meet Christ in the midst of life (Mt. 25:31ff.).

"What shall we do?" questioned those who heard Peter's sermon at
Pentecost (Acts 2:37). It was asked as a response to the preaching of the
gospel. It ought not be asked easily, serving to placate a social demand, to
support a moral agenda, or to relieve the questioner of reponsibility.
"Repent, and be baptized every one of you in the name of Jesus Christ. . . "
Peter replied (Acts 2:38). There is no technique or method to control the
message of the gospel; there is no artificial application, simplistic solution,
or political program that can comprehend the claim of Christ on our lives.
The question is not a simple or naive question of social concern, but an
evangelical summons to social repentance and renewal: *be who you are and are
becoming in Christ.*

NOTES

1. Ray S. Anderson, *Historical Transcendence and the Reality of God* (Grand Rapids:
Eerdmans, 1975), p. 252.
2. Athanasius, "On the Incarnation of the Word," in *Christology of the Later Fathers,*
ed. Edward R. Hardy (Philadelphia: Fortress, 1949), pp. 97f.
3. James B. Torrance, "The Vicarious Humanity of Jesus Christ," in *The Incarnation: Ecumenical Studies in the Nicene-Constantinopolitan Creed, A.D. 381,* ed. Thomas F.
Torrance (Edinburgh: Handsel Press, 1981), p. 130.
4. Gregory of Nyssa, "An Address on Religious Instruction," in *Christology,* ed.
Hardy, pp. 304f.
5. Gregory of Nazianzus, "Letters on the Apollinarian Controversy," in *Christology,* ed. Hardy, p. 218.
6. Ibid., pp. 219f.
7. Karl Barth, *Church Dogmatics,* IV/1, ed. Geoffrey W. Bromiley & Thomas F.
Torrance, trans. Geoffrey W. Bromiley (Edinburgh: T. & T. Clark, 1956), pp. 187ff.,
193.
8. Aubrey R. Johnson, *The One and the Many in the Israelite Conception of God,* 2nd
ed. (Cardiff: Univ. of Wales, 1961), pp. 33f.
9. H. Wheeler Robinson, *Corporate Personality in Ancient Israel,* rev. ed. (Philadelphia: Fortress, 1980), p. 37; Jean de Fraine, *Adam and the Family of Man,* trans. D.
Raible (Staten Island: Alba House, 1965), pp. 274f.
10. Barth, *Church Dogmatics,* IV/1, pp. 171f.
11. Irenaeus, "Against Heresies," in *The Christological Controversy,* trans. & ed.
Richard A. Norris (Philadelphia: Fortress, 1980), p. 49.
12. Ibid., p. 53.
13. Ibid., p. 47.
14. Karl Barth, *Community, State, and Church* (Gloucester, MA: Peter Smith, 1968),
pp 76ff.
15. Ibid., p. 87.
16. Ibid., pp. 81f.
17. The phrase is Karl Barth's, *Church Dogmatics,* III/4, trans. A. T. Mackay et al.
(1961), pp. 285ff.
18. For a brief discussion of black-white relations in the church, see my essay, "The
Incarnation as the Hermeneutical Criterion for Liberation and Reconciliation,"
Scottish Journal of Theology 40:2 (1987), esp. pp. 256f.
19. Barth, *Church Dogmatics,* IV/1, p. 219.
20. Ibid., p. 492.
21. Ibid., p. 262.

22. John Howard Yoder, *The Politics of Jesus* (Grand Rapids: Eerdmans, 1972), p. 63.
23. Ibid., pp, 97, 134.
24. Ibid., pp. 190, 250.
25. Stanley Hauerwas, *A Community of Character* (Notre Dame: Univ. of Notre Dame, 1981), pp. 40, 44.
26. Ibid., pp. 50ff.
27. Guy F. Hersberger, *The Way of the Cross in Human Relations* (Scottdale, PA: Herald, 1958), pp. 33, 43.
28. Robert Friedmann, *The Theology of Anabaptism* (Scottdale, PA: Herald, 1973), pp. 41, 43.
29. Ray S. Anderson, "The Little Man on the Cross," *Reformed Journal* (Nov. 1982):16.
30. Ibid., p. 15.
31. Barth, *Church Dogmatics,* IV/1, pp. 256f.
32. Ibid., p. 259.
33. Barth, *Church Dogmatics,* IV/3, p. 273.
34. John McLeod Campbell, *The Nature of the Atonement* (London: Macmillan, 1878), p. 295.
35. Ibid., p. 299.
36. Ibid., pp. 315f.
37. Ray S. Anderson, "The Resurrection of Jesus as Hermeneutical Criterion" (Part I), *TSF Bulletin* 9 (Jan./Feb. 1986):10.
38. Leonhard Goppelt, *Theology of the New Testament,* 2, trans. John Alsup, ed. Jürgen Roloff (Grand Rapids: Eerdmans, 1982), pp. 146, 157.
39. Letty M. Russell, *The Future of Partnership* (Philadelphia: Westminster, 1979), p. 132; idem, *Human Liberation in a Feminist Perspective—A Theology* (Philadelphia: Westminster, 1974), pp. 151f.
40. Barth, *Church Dogmatics,* IV/2, p. 100.
41. Thomas F. Torrance, *Space, Time and Resurrection* (Grand Rapids: Eerdmans, 1976), pp. 56, 58.
42. Ibid., pp. 66, 69.
43. Karl Barth, *Church Dogmatics,* II/1, ed. Geoffrey W. Bromiley & Thomas F. Torrance, trans. T. H. L. Parker et al. (Edinburgh: T. & T. Clark, 1957), p. 626.
44. Jürgen Moltmann, *Theology of Hope,* trans. James W. Leitch (New York: Harper & Row, 1967), p. 171.
45. Dietrich Bonhoeffer, *Ethics,* ed. Eberhard Bethge (New York: Macmillan, 1955), p. 129.
46. Ibid., p. 127.
47. Ibid., pp. 129f.
48. Ibid., p. 130.
49. Ibid., p. 141.
50. Ibid., p. 142.
51. Moltmann, *Hope,* p. 224.
52. Ibid., pp. 159f.
53. Ibid., pp. 84, 86.
54. Karl Barth, *Letters, 1961-1968,* ed. Jürgen Fangmeier & Hinrich Stoevesandt, trans. & ed. Geoffrey W. Bromiley (Grand Rapids: Eerdmans, 1981), p. 175; Torrance, *Resurrection,* pp. 25f.
55. Jürgen Moltmann, *The Crucified God,* trans. R. A. Wilson & J. Bowden (New York: Harper & Row, 1974), pp. 243, 246; chs. 7, 8.
56. Bonhoeffer, *Ethics,* pp. 130f.
57. Karl Barth, *Ethics,* ed. Dietrich Braun, trans. Geoffrey W. Bromiley (New York: Seabury, 1981), pp. 339f.
58. Bonhoeffer, *Ethics,* p. 212.

59. Ibid., p. 190.
60. Barth, *Ethics,* pp. 343f.
61. Karl Barth, *Church Dogmatics,* III/2, ed. Geoffrey W. Bromiley & Thomas F. Torrance, trans. Harold Knight et al. (Edinburgh: T. & T. Clark, 1960), pp. 250ff.
62. Ibid., pp. 252ff.
63. Ibid., pp. 259f.
64. Eugene B. Borowitz, *Contemporary Christologies: A Jewish Response* (New York: Paulist Press, 1980), p. 34.
65. Helmut Gollwitzer, *An Introduction to Protestant Theology,* trans. D. Cairns (Philadelphia: Westminster, 1982), p. 122.
66. Barth, *Church Dogmatics,* III/2, p. 260ff.
67. Ibid., pp. 265ff.
68. Ibid., p. 212.
69. Ibid., p, 220.

10

WILLIE J. JENNINGS

✛

Conformed to His Image:
The Imago Dei *as a Christological Vision*

> If we listen to the Biblical witness regarding the image of God, we find it filled
> with actuality, and with earnestness. We can hear a note of eschatological
> earnestness which is evidently the earnestness of our ordinary life. The image
> of God stands before us in the contexts of guilt and restoration, of being lost
> and being found.
>
> G. C. Berkouwer, *Man: The Image of God*

> It is from this standpoint that the realism of the Pauline doctrine of the image
> of God is to be understood—the realism of the whole primitive Christian
> conception, for which the image and the reality are not two different things
> but the reality is present in the image. The community, Christians, are also
> present in all that Jesus Christ is, and therefore in the fact that He is the image
> of God. As they are present, their knowledge of the matter is not indirect but
> direct, not theoretical but practical, and therefore realistic.
>
> Karl Barth, *Church Dogmatics*, III/1

IN THE CORPUS OF Christian doctrine, the concept of the *imago Dei* has
served as a way of affirming both the majesty of God as the Creator and
the integrity of humanity as God's creation. The concept of the *imago Dei*
does this by pointing to a fundamental relation between God and humanity. The nature of this relation has been the focus of much discussion and
disagreement. I do not plan to review the history of these discussions here.
Nor do I wish to rehearse the development of the notion of the *imago Dei*.[1]

In this essay, I will suggest that the concept of the image of God actually
helps us define the relation between God and humanity when it is interpreted Christologically. Jesus Christ, as the principal and definitive image
of God, shows us what it means to be created in God's image. When we
interpret the *imago Dei* through Jesus Christ, we are confronted with the
call to be conformed to Christ's image. Therefore the image of God can

only be recognized and acknowledged through participation in the church. Only as the church can we understand ourselves as created in the image of God. Through the concept of the *imago Dei,* the church gains a vision of its participation in the ministry of Jesus Christ to the world.

JESUS CHRIST AS THE GROUND OF THE *IMAGO DEI*

By proclaiming that our humanity has been restored in Jesus Christ, we, as Christians, are proclaiming to the world that we know what it means to be created in the image of God. Because this acknowledgment is intrinsic to our proclamation of the gospel, the notion of the *imago Dei* can lead us into a full realization of the goodness of creation. Most traditional discussions of the image of God have focused their energy on determining how all humanity has been created in the image of God. They attempt to establish the ways in which the image is present in all people and the extent to which the fall has damaged the image of God. But these kinds of *imago Dei* discussions have not been very helpful to the church, because they inappropriately direct our attention toward abstract notions of humanity and God. Such notions tend to ignore the all-important work of Jesus Christ in creating and restoring our humanity.

Locating the image of God first in Jesus Christ, who through the church conforms us to his image, in no way denies the important affirmation that all humanity has been created in the image of God. Rather, a strongly Christological understanding of the image affirms that Jesus Christ has established true knowledge of God and humanity. And this knowledge is the ground upon which we should build our understanding of the *imago Dei.* Furthermore, this knowledge is only brought to light through the church, as those people who have been called to be conformed to the image of the Son of God. Thus to speak of Jesus as the image of God means that we are turned toward his life as the reality of salvation.

Jesus restored creation and reconciled humanity to God. The concept of the image of God is important because it is rooted in this soteriological conviction. By affirming the centrality of Jesus Christ within the *imago Dei,* we can establish two motifs that help to create a vision of the church's ministry to the world. The first motif acknowledges that Jesus is both our Redeemer and Creator; the second affirms that Jesus is our Reconciler who lived his life for others. These motifs help to create a vision for ministry by reminding the church that Jesus Christ challenges all our definitions of humanity, and defines for us what it means to be human.

As the image of God, Jesus the Redeemer is our Creator
Fundamental to Christology is the belief that in Jesus we see the Son of the Father through whom all things have been created (Col. 1:15ff.). This same

Jesus took upon himself fallen humanity: that is, Jesus became just like us in order to redeem us from sin. As Athanasius says, "He became a man, He did not come into man."[2] In Jesus Christ, we see God our Redeemer restore his creation. In making our redemption a reality, Jesus established his absolute claim on creation as its Creator. Thus in Jesus Christ, we come to see ourselves as part of God's creation, called to live in obedience and service to God.

Because the renewal of all creation and the restoration of humanity is centered in Jesus Christ, in him we gain the ability to perceive true humanity correctly: in Christ we come to know what it really means to be human. This perception was sickened by disobedience and broken fellowship with God. John Calvin noted that knowledge of God and knowledge of self are interrelated. Yet, as Calvin states, " . . . this knowledge is either smothered or corrupted partly by ignorance, partly by malice. . . . "[3] This deformed perception of our humanity is often ignored in discussions of the *imago Dei.*

Failure to acknowledge this deformity often becomes an expression of idolatry, because it points to our stubborn desire to believe that all people have basically a good perception of their true humanity: that is, that everyone knows what it means to be human. To confess that Jesus embraced our fallen humanity is to recognize that there is no part of us that is hidden or not in need of the redemptive love of God. As Gregory of Nazianzus argued against Apollinarius, " . . . that which he [Jesus] has not assumed he has not healed; but that which is united to his Godhead is also saved. . . . "[4] Our salvation is the salvation of every aspect of our humanity, including our thinking and perceiving (Rom. 12:1-2).[5]

The fact of our humanity is a given, yet awareness of what it means to be human is not. We are faced with a plethora of definitions here. Perception is bound up in differing communities and societies, each of which tends to define "a human person" in a particular way.

One reason why we have always had so many different definitions is because "humanity" is an abstract notion. In fact, its abstractness is part of its attraction. Martin Luther reminds us that we always want to define humanity (and God) according to our own needs and desires—i.e. our own image. This means that our definitions tend to be self-serving expressions of self-worship (*homo incurvatus in se*).[6]

The vacuous nature of the notion of humanity allows it to play a significant role in concealing and supporting destructive social practices. All societies and communities define the nature of humanity in accordance with their accepted customs, mores, and beliefs. These codes are bound up with the society's political practices and economic relations. Thus any definition of humanity with widespread societal acceptance is normally congenial with the dominant discourse (i.e. the prevailing ways of talking about truth and reality) of the community.

In his celebrated work *Habits of the Heart,* Robert Bellah tells us that the dominant forms of discourse in American culture and society are utilitarian and expressive individualism. These forms of individualism assert the fundamental priority of the individual over against the society. Within this form of discourse the accepted mode of argument and rationality is that which agrees with the a priori rights of individuals to pursue their own interest and have the freedom of self-expression. Bellah and his research team point out that this dominant discourse of individualism undermines other forms of discourse by reshaping them to fit within its prevailing vocabularies and categories of reason.[7]

Bellah's work indicates that the dominant discourse of a society always serves an ideological function. It is ideological because it is generated by and nourishes the prevailing political, social, and economic relations of society.[8] By helping to sustain the accepted status quo, ideological discourse plays a major role in concealing and promoting practices of domination and oppression. During the Reagan era we saw how the dominant discourse of individualism was reinforced by, and helped nourish, the self-serving political and economic practices of individuals, including many government officials. Bellah laments the fact that the discourse of individualism constantly distorts those moral discourses which attempt to help us understand what kind of people Americans ought to be.

The danger the church faces is that our discussions of the *imago Dei* often become incorporated into the ideological discourses of our society. Such discourses already have a (normally implicit) working definition of what it means to be human. As Bellah's work shows us, Western society has produced a discourse that affirms the ability of individuals to pursue their own interests as central to a definition of humanity. In a sense, a definition of humanity that is grounded in individualism would promote self-seeking people who see social, economic, and political resources as existing only to enhance their own self-expression. Thus all those who do not have these "inherent abilities"—i.e. those who do not seek their own welfare through hard work and determination—may be considered less than human. And those who deny the importance of these abilities must then be accused of denying the humanity of others as well as their own humanity.

Often a society's declaration to believe in the "integrity of humanity" displays an entire system of manipulation and control of those who do not mirror their definition of humanity or those who disagree with their definition. In human history, reason, morality, gender, class, and race have all been likely candidates for the basis of our humanity. Yet these candidates have always depended upon societal, cultural, or national interpretation. Those in a particular society, culture, or country who did not display the ability to reason, or the moral capabilities to obey the "laws of the land," were inevitably considered in some sense "less than human." Likewise, it has always been difficult to consider fully human those people who are not of the same gender, class, or race as those in a position to influence the prevailing definitions of "humanity."

Human history is replete with examples of human beings who are designated subhuman. This should warn us that the concept of the *imago Dei* always stands in danger of supporting all kinds of manipulation and oppression. In his work *Prophesy-Deliverance,* Cornel West reminds us that with the Enlightenment and the development of the structure of modern discourse, Africans and other people of color were considered subhuman because they lacked the proper intelligence, beauty, and morality.[9] These characteristics found their home in the mores of Western civilization. Even today, West notes, "the idea of black equality in beauty, culture, and intellectual capacity remains problematic and controversial within the prestigious halls of learning and sophisticated intellectual circles."[10] Thus the *imago Dei,* in Western society, stands in danger of expressing not the image of God but the image of Western society.

Such a danger increases when we attempt to define the image of God non-Christologically. Definitions that are not properly focused through Jesus Christ inevitably look to some aspect of our culture or national character as the location of the image of God in us. We then define our humanity from this cultural or national location. If the concept of the *imago Dei* is to be freed from the ideological discourses circumscribing the notion of "humanity," then we must become aware of how our societies, cultures, and nations define the "integrity of the human." As Christians, we must ask ourselves whether the attempt to affirm the inherent qualities of the human leads to capitulation to some ideological discourse. The power of ideological discourses can be overcome as the church, guided by its Christology, affirms the *imago Dei.* Jesus Christ radically challenges the power of all definitions of humanity.

The concept of the *imago Dei* can help us stand against the power of ideological discourses only as we understand it as grounded in the life of Christ. As the image of God, Jesus brings us into conformity to his image. Therefore we are turned to the world, not to be defined by its discourses, but to declare the restoration of the creation by the Creator and to challenge the ideological power of fallen humanity. In light of our knowledge of the triune God revealed in Jesus Christ, societal, cultural, and national defini- tions of humanity are severely brought into question. Because Jesus has brought all definitions of humanity into judgment by the light of his own humanity, we, as the church, have no choice but to stand vigilant against the modes of ideological discourse that have the power to manipulate us. Failure to do so is a denial of our confession that Jesus is our redeemer and creator.

As our redeemer and creator, Jesus claims absolute authority in our lives. His authority is expressed in his call to us to be born again: that is, to enter into a new definition of our humanity (Jn. 1:12-13). The new life we gain in Jesus is by necessity the death of the old life. This challenge of all definitions of our humanity is expressed in the death and resurrection of Jesus. Just as the death of Christ destroyed the power of all ideological definitions of humanity, so too the resurrection of Christ restored our humanity and defined for us what it means to be human.

As the image of God, Jesus is the One for others

Friedrich Schleiermacher, in his work *The Christian Faith,* argued that the distinction made between the person and work of Christ tended to be counterproductive. Although in our efforts to understand our redemption it is important to affirm both the person and work of Jesus, Schleiermacher believed that knowledge of Christ is also knowledge of what he has done.[11] Although I would disagree with his construal of the person and work of Christ, Schleiermacher does help us see the importance of the union of the person and work of Christ. This inseparable union helps us understand the second motif intrinsic to the notion of the *imago Dei.*

By living his life for others, Jesus healed our broken and distorted relationships. Through his life, death, and resurrection, he reconciled the world to God (2 Cor. 5:18-19). As the biblical drama teaches us, the world lives in disobedience to God. Our disobedience is the source of our broken fellowship with God and our abusive practices toward each other. Racism, sexism, political-economic oppression, and war can all be read as part of the biblical drama's witness to our rebellion against God. These manifestations of our rebelliousness point to the ways in which we distort human relationships and abuse ourselves as part of God's creation.

Jesus displayed a way of life that moved in a direction opposite to our lives of disobedience. By his love for God, his Father, and by his love for others, Jesus reestablished the true meaning of our humanity. This reestablishment took place as he fully entered into a cultural, social, economic-political matrix; Jesus was a first-century Palestinian Jewish male born and raised in a situation of poverty and political oppression. To share in these human realities was the prerequisite for Jesus to be "fully human." Such realities help to form our identities and shape our human relationships. In being fully human and living among us, Jesus was confronted with the way we force our relationships along courses inevitably leading to forms of domination.

Jesus overcame all forms of domination by reordering our human relationships. His life was a challenge to the allegiances we form through our social and political agendas. And for his challenge to our agendas, we put Jesus to death. Because he destroyed the walls of oppression standing between nations, peoples, and women and men, walls we so carefully built and so diligently maintained, we were left with only one option: murder. Killing has always been our most decisive and exalted manner of securing our way of life.

Through his resurrection, Jesus took from us the greatest obstacle to the reordering of human relationships enacted by his life, the power of the fear of death. The fear of death—that is, the fear of life-threatening reprisal— has held us from challenging the forms of domination that shape our relationships. But it was the power of his relationship with the Father in the Spirit that raised Jesus from the dead. And it was for the sake of restoring our fellowship with God and renewing our relationship with each that Jesus became our Reconciler. As our Reconciler, Jesus has brought us access to the living God and the true definition of our humanity. To be human is to live as women and men in fellowship with the God of Jesus Christ and through obedience to Jesus Christ, to live in loving relationship with one another (Mk. 12:29-31).

This definition of humanity does not seek an essential formula to which everyone would agree. Rather, by embracing a Christological definition of humanity, we are (1) faced with the reality of the restoring and reconciling work of Jesus Christ, and (2) summoned by the Spirit of Christ to respond to God by a life of repentance. It is through the church that we live out the true meaning of our humanity. As members of the body of Christ, we have the opportunity for transformation of our lives and relationships by the Spirit of Christ. The life of Jesus, in its profound renewal of creation, is the pattern through which we realize the defeat of the forms of domination that wish to shape our relationships.

The challenge facing the church is whether it will continue to succumb to the forms of domination that shape relationships in every culture, society, and nation. Because the church is embedded in cultural and political matrices, it always stands in danger of following the dominant modes of constructing allegiances. Just as we must challenge the prevailing definitions of humanity, so too we must allow the new definition of humanity we have gained through Christ to shape our relationships. It is in following Christ and his pattern of life that the church gains the power to transcend all patterns of oppression. Following Jesus' pattern of life keeps the church, in its attempts to overcome forms of domination, from falling into yet another form of ideological manipulation: ecclesial idealism.

Ecclesial idealism is the propensity, especially in the Western world, to reject as theologically insignificant, race, culture, and gender for defining our humanity. Such a rejection implies that being Christian has no relation to our concrete social locations in the world. This kind of idealism has allowed the church in the West to support many forms of cultural and political imperialism. The need to bring cultural and societal "advancement" to other cultures, regardless of the abuses we inflict, remains a powerful motif in the West. Stemming from this same notion, many churches believe that we can address the problems in race relations, the oppression of women, and the oppression of homosexuals only by accepting some form of idealism: i.e. that being black/white or male/female are insignificant; they are socially and culturally constructed definitions that must be discarded. Yet for the church to reject race, culture, and gender as crucial for our definitions of humanity is to undermine the humanity of Jesus and the very humanity that Jesus came to restore.

Jesus called into question the patterns of relationship defined by race, class, and gender. He called these things into question *by* being fully human, *by* entering into race, culture, and gender. Jesus was not human apart from being born a Palestinian Jewish male. Yet within these cultural and historical realities, Jesus revealed to us our true humanity. As the church, we have been reconciled to live our lives within race, culture, and gender, because we cannot know our humanity *apart* from them. Christ has come to us where we live to reconcile us to God. Because we have "put on Christ" through our baptism, as Paul tells us, we have entered into a new definition of our humanity that does not follow the forms of domination created by our sinfulness (Gal. 3:28).

THE IMAGE OF GOD: A CHRISTOLOGICAL VISION

A Christological definition of humanity refuses to define what it means to be human apart from our relationships with one another. Yet this definition also refuses to define our humanity apart from our fellowship with God in Jesus Christ. To declare that we have been created in the image of God is to realize that we have been crucified with Christ and we live our lives through his life (Gal. 2:20). But doesn't the concept of the *imago Dei* affirm that all humanity has been made in the image of God? Could we not say that the image of God can be seen wherever there are relationships characterized by self-giving love? Could it not be argued that to deny non-Christians the characteristics of humanity is, in fact, to deny their humanity?

Such objections fail to realize that the humanity of non-Christians can be truly affirmed only in the exact same manner as it is affirmed for Christians: in Jesus Christ. Only by proclaiming that all of humanity has been restored through the living Lord can we declare that all humanity is created in the image of God. To affirm the integrity of all humanity as the image of God is to call people to live as members of the body of Christ. It is as members of the church that people can recognize their true humanity. To attempt to affirm humanity without also issuing this call is to suggest that our own affirmation of ourselves means something outside of Christ. This self-authenticating affirmation inevitably undermines the missionary task and our calling to participate in the ministry of Christ.

I began this essay by suggesting that through the concept of the *imago Dei* the church gains a vision of its participation in the ministry of Jesus Christ to the world. I have used the notion of "vision" not to outline a strategy for carrying out ministry, but to provoke our imaginations. Knowing that we have been created in the image of God ought to stir us to imagine what this likeness should mean for the way we live our lives. Yet looking like God is looking like Jesus. Therefore, to imagine ourselves as the image of God is to gain a radical awareness of a new definition of what it means to be human, a definition that stands over against the powerful voices of our world.

Nevertheless, it is for the sake of the world that Jesus gave himself. In his life and through his death, Jesus brought to an end the uncontested power of the images we create of our humanity. And by his resurrection, Jesus has forever established a new image of our humanity, an image fashioned upon the very reality of God. Yet as the Scriptures teach us, the image we have gained is bound up with the image of the first Adam, but grounded in the life of the second Adam, Jesus Christ (1 Cor. 15:45-50). Through our baptism, we have put on Christ and have gained entrance into his ministry to the world (Rom. 6:1ff.). Thus our life of service to Christ is engulfed in an all-encompassing vision. It is a vision gained by accepting our true humanity in Jesus Christ, in whose image we have been made.

NOTES

1. For discussions of the *imago Dei,* cf. Joan E. O'Donovan, "Man in the Image of God: The Disagreement between Barth and Brunner Reconsidered," *Scottish Journal of Theology* 39 (June 1987):433-59; G. C. Berkouwer, *Studies in Dogmatics—Man: The Image of God,* trans. Dirk W. Jellema (Grand Rapids: Eerdmans, 1962); Karl Barth, *Church Dogmatics* (Edinburgh: T. & T. Clark, 1958), III, 1/2; Vladimir Lossky, *In the Image and Likeness of God,* ed. John H. Erickson et al. (Crestwood, NY: St. Vladimir's Seminary Press, 1985); Ray S. Anderson, *On Being Human* (Grand Rapids: Eerdmans, 1982).
2. *Against the Arians III,* cited by Maurice Wiles and Mark Santer in *Documents in Early Christian Thought* (Cambridge: Cambridge Univ. Press, 1985), p. 53.
3. John Calvin, *Institutes of the Christian Religion,* 2 vols., ed. John T. McNeill, trans. Ford Lewis Battles (Philadelphia: Westminster, 1960), 1:47.
4. *Letters on the Apollinarian Controversy,* trans. Charles Gordon Browne and James Edward Swallow, *Christology of the Later Fathers,* ed. E. R. Hardy (Philadelphia: Westminster, 1954), p. 218.
5. T. F. Torrance, "The Mind of Christ in Worship: The Problem of Apollinarianism in the Liturgy," *Theology in Reconciliation: Essays Towards Evangelical and Catholic Unity in East and West* (Grand Rapids: Eerdmans, 1976), pp. 139-214.
6. Martin Luther, *Lectures on Romans,* trans. & ed. Wilhelm Pauck (Philadelphia: Westminster, 1961), pp. 23-27.
7. Robert N. Bellah et al., *Habits of the Heart* (Berkeley: Univ. of California Press, 1985).
8. Raymond Williams, *Marxism and Literature* (Oxford: Oxford Univ. Press, 1977), p. 55. Cf. Fredric Jameson, "On Habits of the Heart," *South Atlantic Quarterly* 86:4 (Fall 1987):543-65.
9. Cornel West, *Prophesy-Deliverance: An Afro-American Revolutionary Christianity* (Philadelphia: Westminster, 1982), pp. 47ff.
10. Ibid., p. 47.
11. Friedrich Schleiermacher, *The Christian Faith,* 2nd ed., trans. H. R. Mackintosh and J. S. Stewart (Edinburgh: T. & T. Clark, 1986), pp. 426ff.

11

ADRIO KÖNIG

✠

Covenant and Image: Theological Anthropology, Human Interrelatedness, and Apartheid

APARTHEID AND HUMAN INTERRELATEDNESS

S IMPLY TO PUT APARTHEID exclusively over against human interrelatedness — apartheid *or* interrelatedness — would be an oversimplification. It
is true, rather, that apartheid interplays dialectically with human interrelatedness: in one sense fully acknowledging it and even using it as a point
of departure, but in another sense rejecting and even destroying human
interrelatedness.

Apartheid does not simply mean dividing and separating groups of
people from each other. There are many examples the world over of groups
of people who are separate. Some of the separations are quite inoffensive
and even good; others are harmful and even bad. There are, for example,
separate countries and states, and there are more-or-less spontaneous
groupings of people even within the same society into specific cultural
groups, interest groups, sexes, etc. But although the advocates of apartheid
have often claimed that these distinctions justify the system of apartheid,
there is virtually no relationship between them.

The system of apartheid
Apartheid is a system of artificial, enforced division and separation of black
and white. This separation has been dramatically enforced to the disadvan-
tage of the blacks.

The separation of apartheid is, however, only a *partial* one, as the groups
still share many vital interests. They still live in the same country under the
same government; they share the same judiciary, police force, defense
force, economic system, educational system; they use mainly the same
infrastructure, e.g. transport systems; over seventy five percent share the
same religious convictions; almost everybody in South Africa (SA) knows
the same language (English), even if it is not their mother tongue. Many

162

other common factors can be enumerated. This is the first crucial point: *apartheid is the forced separation between people who are bound together by many vital common interests.*

All forms of separation between people are not necessarily bad. What makes the separation of apartheid so bad is that it is enforced, and that it benefits one group and harms the other group. It is actually not separation, but a marginalization of the blacks away from the center of the country. Thus apartheid is essentially the exploitation, humiliation, and oppression of certain people over against the inclusion and advantage of the other group, who knowing or unknowingly plays the role of the oppressor.

Forced separation harms people of color in many ways. It deprives them of a normal voice in government, which means that they can put very little or no pressure on the government to serve their interests. Until recently, it excluded them from the general cultural life (theaters, restaurants, museums, public halls, and sport facilities). It limits them to the inferior part of the infrastructure (inferior buses, trains, etc.), and where they are allowed to make use of the same public roads, they are prohibited access to normal public facilities such as restaurants and toilets. They are forced to live in inferior residential areas, far from business centers and industrial areas where they usually work. They must fulfill the same standards of education but under a separate education department with only a fraction of the equipment and expertise available to whites.

It is not only the physical separation and harm that has had a destructive influence on people of color. The emotional facets of this discrimination have virtually destroyed them. They have become foreigners in the country of their birth—called "non-whites," identified by what they are not, but by what others are. Every black person was made to call every white person "boss" or "missies" (madam), a signal of respect for whites—but no white laborer ever had to use these terms.

The philosophy of apartheid

Apartheid does not stand over against the interrelatedness of people, but interacts dialectically with it. Primarily, apartheid supposes that people are interrelated, but not as individual human beings. Rather, humanity is basically divided into groups, and the members within each group are interrelated. Because interrelatedness is confined to the group, groups stand opposed to each other and threaten each other, so that they have to be kept apart to prevent friction.

Heavy emphasis is placed on both aspects (interrelatedness and separation). On the one hand the group and its interrelatedness is emphasized. The real "group" that was at stake was never an issue of theoretical reflection and neat formulation. Initially, it was the Afrikaner group, white people who spoke Afrikaans and identified with a common history. Later, English-speaking whites were included; and still later, all whites. Initially, only this group of whites was identified over against the so-called non-whites, or all those who would not be legally classified "white." Later on three groups were identified with the "non-whites": blacks, coloreds, and Indians.

According to the philosophy of apartheid, group members are strongly interrelated among themselves, but groups stand exclusively opposed to each other so that contact between groups should be minimized—because free social contact would cause friction and clashes. However, well-defined labor contacts were freely allowed, provided that there was no social interaction and that it did not take place on an equal level but that whites were always in a position of authority.

The interrelatedness of the group members on the one hand, and the inability of groups to assimilate on the other, was built on a philosophical religious notion that every group (generally called *volk* or nation; in some contexts "race") had its own identify, its own particularity (a "soul") which it received from God and which it had to protect against mixing with other people. This separateness of each nation (*volk*) was related to the biblical notion of sanctification so that a part of the call to sanctification was the maintenance of racial purity. The existence of each separate group (people, race) was thus seen as the will of God—in either his plan for creation or in his providence. The entrenchment of apartheid was sanctioned and legitimized in more or less this way. Besides these broad theological lines, other specific scripture references were also utilized. Two specific references are important: the tower of Babel (Gn. 11), where God separated the people into two different nations so that, it is assumed, we have to accept that it is his will that people stay apart; and Acts 17:26—"From one man he made very nation of men, that they should inhabit the whole earth; and he determined the times set for them and *the exact places where they should live*" (NIV). The last phrase was interpreted to mean (enforced) separate residential areas.

A second line that featured often, but never functioned strongly in official documents, is the identification of the Afrikaner people with Israel and the non-whites with the heathen in Canaan during the exodus and conquest. This notion, *inter alia,* provided the grounds for the prohibition of "mixed marriages" (between white and black), but it never led in public and official circles to the notion that blacks should be exterminated. This may possibly be explained from the fact that a fairly strong pietistic spirituality existed in the Dutch Reformed Church, the "Afrikaner" Church, which was nursed from fairly early on in the history of the white people in SA by German and English mission organizations. This influence led to a great deal of mission work among people of color—who were synonymous with heathens. In fact the Dutch Reformed Church had always, in spite of its justification and support of apartheid, embarked on great missionary enterprises. Gradually the Dutch Reformed Church created a whole family of other Dutch Reformed Churches among people of color. ("A separate church for every nation" was the theological principle behind this.) The Dutch Reformed Church often pleaded for all kinds of support and development under people of color—as long as it did not threaten the interests of whites.

What is important in this argument is the role and meaning of the interrelatedness of people. The interrelatedness of people was not denounced; in fact, it played a very important role. However, it was not the interrelatedness of *humanity* as such but the interrelatedness of the members within each specific group. It was this group interrelatedness in particular that divided humanity into groups. Nations or races had to stay apart according to divine providence. The function of the interrelatedness of people was thus, rather, to divide humanity into permanent groups who had to live at a distance from each other on a social and religious level with contact only on the labor level. This contact was always to be structured clearly beforehand with whites in a superior position.

It is important to remember, however, that this model was very seldom presented by spokespeople for apartheid as the principle according to which the whole population of the globe should be organized. Especially when the criticism against apartheid from abroad in the sixties grew stronger, it was said more and more that the situation in SA was unique, that it had a unique population constituency and that apartheid was only a necessity here. It was often said that we leave other countries and people alone to solve their problems in their own manner, and that it was exactly that which we expected of other countries—the freedom to work out our own solution for the problems of SA. It was called the policy of non-involvement in each other's internal affairs.

HUMAN INTERRELATEDNESS

The aim of this contribution

The position I present in the following pages is that apartheid has a wrong view of the interrelatedness of people. There are strong traditions in the Old Testament emphasizing the interrelatedness of *all* people, and these traditions are reinforced by the advent of Jesus Christ and the witness of the New Testament—especially about the church. The separation that group interrelatedness brings between people (and especially between groups) is a reality that should be opposed and overcome. It is not a part of God's plan for the world, but rather of his problem with the world. God began with one person who incorporated and represented the whole of humanity. When Israel failed, God again introduced one Man representing and incorporating the new humanity. In this way all human beings are in principle interrelated.

This study is thus not in the first place a study in ecclesiology (about the unity of the church), but in anthropology (about the unity of humanity). However, the unity of the church should also be considered because God prepares the new humanity within the church.

To explain the interrelatedness of humanity I will use two concepts: *covenant* and *image*. Human beings live in a covenant relationship both with God and with other humans, and human beings are created as the image of God.

Human beings as covenant beings — and human interrelatedness

Humans are covenant beings. This not only means that we de facto live in relationships but that it belongs to our essence. The two relationships that are developed here are our relationship with God and our relationship with other humans. There are also other relationships, for example our relationship with nature. However, this relationship will not be discussed in detail here.

Throughout the Bible there is a special relationship between God and human beings. Almost all that God does is directed toward people, and human beings are completely determined by their relationship with God. In certain theological circles it is common to say that the human person is essentially the-person-*before*-God (Barth, Brunner, Berkouwer). Our relationship with God is our innermost being. If we call this relationship between God and human beings the covenant, then human beings are essentially covenant beings.

This essential relatedness also pertains to people among themselves. The tendency in most biblical traditions is to speak of people in the plural, especially in terms of the relationships in which they stand. In fact, the emphasis on human beings in the plural is so strong that here and there we find an emphasis to the contrary, on the responsibility of the individual (e.g. Jeremiah and Ezekiel), without, however, ever lapsing into individualism.

The Bible is first and foremost concerned with interrelated human beings, not with individuals. In fact the concept of "man" is actually a collective concept. In the beginning God created "man" as people, as male *and* female (Gn. 1:27). God concerns himself especially with *humanity*, with the *nation* Israel, with the *church* as the community of believers. The apostles had to make disciples of the *nations*.

This essential interrelatedness of human beings is also emphasized by the work of God to bring people *near* to himself and to each other. One of the most exciting prophecies of the future, found in some of the prophets, is that all the nations will come to Jerusalem to live *together* in peace. And when the Holy Spirit was poured out, Luke emphasizes that there were representatives of the whole world present in Jerusalem. The Epistle to the Ephesians (2:12f.) interprets Christ's crucifixion as a reconciliation and unification of two hostile groups: the Jews and the Greeks (representing all of humanity). And finally, believers from all nations are going to live *together* in the new Jerusalem.

God wants to be close to people, and he wants them to be close to him and to each other. In fact, "near" tends to become a concept of salvation in the Bible, and "far" a concept of judgment. According to the prophets God is *far* from Israel because of their sins, but *near* to his faithful children and to those who suffer and are wronged. In the New Testament he comes so *near* to us that he becomes a human being in Jesus. It follows that there is never salvation when God is *far* from people or when people are separated. In fact it is sin that causes people to live in enmity, strife, and dissension. Sin causes division (Gal. 5:19-20). Against this the Spirit *binds people together* in love, kindness, and gentleness (v. 22). In fact not one of the "works of the flesh" binds people together in trust, and nothing in the fruit of the Spirit estranges people from one another. *Sin divides, but the Spirit unites.*

Related to these truths, there are important structures in the way God deals with people. Humanity is to such an extent interrelated and reflects such a unity that God can deal with all people through one person. Through the sin of Adam all people came under the judgment of God. Through the obedience of Christ all are justified by God. People who believe in Christ are joined with him in such a way that they have been crucified with him, are risen with him, share in his resurrection life, and will appear again with him in glory, while now they are hidden with him in God (Rom. 6, Eph. 2, Col. 2—3). This same structure is reflected in the fact that God's covenant with Abraham is at the same time a covenant with his descendants (and is not made individually with each member of his descendants when they are born). The children of believers today are still in the same way included in the covenant through their parents and therefore are baptized by certain churches. We speak of the corporative and the representative structures of the gospel.

It is the emphasis on these structures of communion, fellowship, and unity in the biblical message that makes it a covenant message, God a covenant God, and human beings covenant beings. It is the will of God that he and humanity, and humans mutually, should live closely together and be covenanted to each other. Actually there is something objective, given, ontological in this *communion* between God and humanity and between people mutually. This is how God *made* us and what he *intended* for us. When he calls us to be faithful, friendly, kind, etc., it is exactly to realize this—our essential nature of universal interrelatedness.

In this light it is a pity that some recent theological designs are still inclined to individualism. Think of Barth's emphasis on the "two-togetherness" of people, *two* people in relationship with one another (*CD* III/2, p. 242 ff.), that has been continued by Jüngel (*Entsprechungen,* p. 300; *Gott als Geheimnis der Welt,* pp. 484ff., and the entire par. 12—trans. by Darrell L. Guder as *God as the Mystery of the World* [Grand Rapids: Eerdmans, 1983], pp. 353 ff.). In the Bible there is no special preference for *one* person in relation to *one* other person, but rather for the communion of people and groups of people, in which individuals and groups have various relationships with other individuals and groups, and humanity is thus a network of relationships of mutual commitment. In fact the individual is not born from only one other individual, but from two. Thus even biologically every individual already has a relationship with at least two other people.

Let us summarize. God has made people to live in fellowship with him and with each other. God has joined people corporatively and representatively together. God has reconciled people to himself and *to each other* through Jesus, even if they were the greatest of enemies. Through the Spirit God bears the fruit of love, kindness, and peace in the lives of people. If all this is true, then apartheid is an appalling matter, separating by force people who even share the same land and infrastructure. This negates the reconciling, relating, uniting work of God, and the innermost being of human persons as covenant beings, interrelated in mutual fellowship.

It is true that people have a "natural" inclination to form groups. This inclination can take different forms. Some can be reasonably harmless. In the U.S. whites tend to marry whites and blacks tend to marry blacks—but this trend toward group formation may not be absolutized so that people are not allowed to have the choice of associating with people of other groups. From a Christian point of view, "natural" trends are not necessarily good; "for I am prone *by nature* to hate God and my neighbour" (Heidelberg Catechism, answer 5) and according to Eph. 2:3 we are "*by nature* children of wrath." The appeal to the natural inclination to group formation as an argument to justify apartheid lacks, therefore, any credibility.

Human beings as the image of God—and human equality of worth

The fact that we are created in the image of God means at least two things. In the more formal sense, the mere fact of all human beings created in the same image implies that all humans have equal value. And in the more material sense, the content of this image implies for all humans a specific responsibility.

People have the same value simply because they are all created in the image of God. We must first give our attention to this. Early in the Old Testament it is given as the reason why people must not kill one another (Gn. 9:5-7). The fact that human beings are created in the image of God (Gn. 1) comes almost as a surprise and against the whole trend of Genesis 1—and is therefore given special emphasis. The theme of Genesis 1 is that there is nothing divine except God himself, not even those things that were usually considered gods by Israel's neighbors, such as light, the sun, the moon, and the stars. All are *creatures,* created by God. Only God is God. Human beings also do not emanate from God, as in some creation stories of the nations surrounding Israel. We are creatures like the rest of creation. There is nothing divine in us. This, then, is a specific trend in the creation story: there is a clear distinction between God and *all* of creation; God alone is divine and all else is created.

In this context it comes as a surprise, then, that human beings are put so close to God—in fact, as close as possible without making them divine. They are created in the image of God; they somehow (have to) reflect what God is like.

This fact obviously implies that all humans have an equal value—all being created in the same image—but also that they all have an exceptionally high and distinct value, being so close to God over against the rest of creation.

In this way the universal interrelatedness of all human beings is once more emphasized. On the level of the image, as on the level of the covenant, there seems to be no trace of distinctions within the human race. Humanity as such is interrelated, not only specific human beings or even specific groups.

It is important, however, that one distinction develop: the special care that is to be taken of the destitute, the weak, the sick, the oppressed, indeed of all who have specific disadvantages—particularly because in principle they are of equal value with all other humans, but in practice suffer a setback.

God leads us in this concern, especially according to the tradition of the prophets. God cares so much for people in need that it becomes a name for him: the God of the widows, orphans, and strangers. Accordingly, the prophetic criticism was seldom sharper than when it was directed against social injustice and the oppression of those with fewer rights such as widows, orphans, and strangers (e.g. Amos and Isaiah).

Israel even had a whole set of special laws and practices pertaining to the poor, the best known of which are probably the Sabbath Year (every seventh year) and the Jubilee Year (every fiftieth year). It is not necessary to go into any detail here, but it is clear that a very important part of the motivation for the special years and the system of laws pertaining to them was to help the poor, to give them a fresh start in life with the opportunity to regain a position of equality with all other Israelites. It pertains i.a. to the emancipation of slaves, the remission or suspension of debts, and the return of land to the original owner. Special provision was thus made for the poor specifically because they had lost their position of equality.

In this connection the king and his responsibilities are important. The king rules in the name of God and therefore must reflect the will of God in the way he rules. His rule must serve the common good and must pay special attention to those in need. Vivid images for this are used in Ps. 72:6, 7, 12-14.

May the king be like rain on the fields,
like showers falling on the land.
May righteousness flourish in his lifetime,

and may prosperity last as long as the moon gives light. . . .
He rescues the poor who call to him,
and those who are needy and neglected.
He has pity on the weak and poor;
he saves the lives of those in need.
He rescues them from oppression and violence;
their lives are precious to him. (TEV)

On the strength of the fact that all people are equal, those who are poor, wronged, and oppressed are singled out for special care by the king and the government. They have to receive special attention and privileges because they have fallen behind. The communal interrelatedness of all people effects a special relationship toward those groups who suffer.

If this point of view is applied to apartheid, it is clear that apartheid is directly opposed to the biblical command. The apartheid system has indeed given special attention to the poor and oppressed—but precisely the wrong attention. It has created a whole system of special laws for the poor and oppressed (black people), but to their detriment and further impoverishment and oppression. Instead of helping strangers the way the king and the people had to, apartheid instead turned millions of people into strangers in the very land of their birth. Instead of taking special steps to uplift the poor and destitute, and to protect them from exploitation by the rich and powerful, apartheid entrenched the rights of the rich and the powerful against the poor and excluded the poor from meaningful economic, social, and political activity. Blacks were forbidden to do certain better-paid work, to live in suburbs near their jobs, to possess fixed property in the economically important parts of the country, etc. White education was free; the blacks had to pay for their children's education. The areas of the country that were given to them had little or no infrastructure, and in no instance was the land allotted to a particular black group capable of accommodating and supporting that group.

So again it is clear that apartheid is an example of the wrong interrelatedness of people. Its interrelatedness is of one specific group over against other groups, to the protection and self-enrichment of this group, oppressing those people of whom special care should have been taken.

Human beings as the image of God—and human responsibility
Apart from this more *formal* aspect of the special and equal value of all human beings, and the special care that the weak and the oppressed should get to help them to equality, there is also the *material* aspect of the content of the *imago Dei* which human beings are created in. What is this image exactly?

In earlier centuries there was a predominant trend to divide human being into (at least two) different parts, more or less in accordance with Platonic anthropology. The soul was seen as the more important part over against the body, and it was virtually universally accepted that only this more important part was created in the image of God. In more recent times the conviction that the human person is a unity has asked for new interpretations of the image. Many came to the fore, some rather mundane — e.g. that as opposed to animals, human beings walk upright and, it is sometimes added, can therefore look upward to God.

This is not the place to discuss the pros and cons of the different interpretations. I believe that the interpretation I offer will generally be accepted among evangelicals as at least an aspect or an implication of our being the image of God.

In the Bible, especially in the admonitions in the New Testament, God and Christ are used as examples for the behaviors of believers. The best known is the "as" formula: love, walk, forgive, be merciful, be holy *as God* or *as Christ*. Added to this, there are many other ways of saying the same thing, e.g. that Christ's nature should be formed in us (Gal. 4:19) and that we should have the mind or attitude of Christ (Phil. 2:5f.). These imply that we should reflect the values of Christ, his way of acting and reacting, his ethical and religious standards. My contention is that this is at least part of, or one implication of, our being his image. Being the image of God has not so much to do with appearance, with looking like God, as it has to do with action, with behaving like him. One may call this a *functional* interpretation instead of a more ontological interpretation of the image.

This again, I believe, links closely with the tendency in the Bible to emphasize the deeds of God and his involvement in the world and history, rather than his being or essence. In fact, after having stated that we were created in God's image, Genesis 1 directly refers to our acts and responsibilities, and not to our being or our appearance. "Be fruitful and multiply, and fill the earth and subdue it; and have dominion over . . . " (Gn. 1:28). In other words, we should be and reflect the image of God in our way of living.

But even this is a rather formal statement. What would the content of our life then have to be? Of course a reflection, an analogy if you like, of the content of God's life. And as we cannot come closer to a characterization of God's life than by saying that God is love, then obviously we should *live in love* (Eph. 5:2). This is the reason why Jesus summarizes God's will for our entire lives in two commandments of *love*.

We have to live in love. Love has to control our lives. This is the essence of our acting and our responsibility. And this pertains to all our relationships. It is obvious that we have to love God and our fellow human beings, but we also have to apply this to nature. Our commission to control nature and to develop culture from it implies that we treat nature with loving care. In our time this means especially that we will care for the environment and that we will ensure that our children and their descendants will still be able to live on this planet.

It is obvious that our love for nature will be different from our love for God or our love for fellow human beings.

This distinction emphasizes a particularly important point. Not only our relationship with nature, but every relationship in which we stand, calls for its own special form of love. This works in almost the same way as in the case of justice. Justice has no fixed content that can merely be applied to every situation. What is right in a specific situation depends on the nature of the situation. It is the same with love, except that there are general characteristics of love, like caring for and taking an interest in the object of one's love.

In our love for other human beings we analogically reflect God's love for us. We can therefore deduce from the general character of God's love what the content of our love should be.

We can say at least five important things about God's love for us. (1) God's love has an *object*; (2) God comes *close* to this object; (3) God *knows* this object; (4) God *does* something for us; and (5) God is even willing to *suffer* for us. Thus an object is entailed, and then closeness to, knowledge of, action, and sacrifice for this object. Our love for others has to show something of these characteristics. And as is already clear, this love will again emphasize our closeness and interrelatedness as human race.

(1) God's love has an object. God's love for us, and therefore our love for others, is first a relational concept. Love always has an *object*. Self-love is impossible because Jesus revealed the love of God in giving his life, and one cannot give one's own life for oneself. Self-love is egotism and as such not love. Jesus summarized the law in *two* commandments of love, not in three of which the third is purported to be self-love. A third commandment of self-love would also no longer be a true summary of the Ten Commandments, because the Ten Commandments do not include commandments about one's relationship with oneself. People naturally need self-respect and a good self-image. We are helped to love others by a positive acceptance of ourselves. However, neither self-respect nor a positive self-image is *love,* at least not if we want to work with a biblical concept of love. The biblical authors did not use the concept of love for our attitude toward ourselves, and they did this because of the character of love. Love must have an object.

(2) God comes close to this object. God's love for us, and therefore our love for others, brings *closeness.* Obviously we cannot always be close to everyone that we love, or ought to love. We can also love at a distance. But we do not really love if we resist coming close. Love works very much like the unity of the church. All Christians everywhere cannot always worship together. But if we resist coming close to certain believers, we can no longer say that we are one with them. Because of its character love has to do

with fellowship, communion, and sharing. God is a *covenant* God and we are *covenant* beings.

(3) God knows this object. We must have knowledge of the object of our love, whether it is God, our fellow human beings, or nature. It is impossible to know what the nature of our love should be if we do not know *whom* we have to love and what the relationship between us ought to be. Picture a marriage in which the husband is convinced that he really loves his wife while the wife complains that he does not love her. There has been a breakdown in knowledge, and therefore in communication and love.

(4) God does something for us. Love is more than a feeling or a conviction. It is *action*. The well-known text about the love of God for us, Jn. 3:16, witnesses to this: God so loved the world that he *gave*. . . .

(5) God is willing to suffer for us. Love is even willing to sacrifice. The same Jn. 3:16 tells us what God gave: his only Son! It was his greatest sacrifice. This was the zenith of God's love, but his love has always, even in Old Testament times, included this readiness for sacrifice. If our love does not include this willingness, it is no longer a reflection of the love of God.

All together, these characteristics very strongly emphasize the interrelatedness of all human beings. To know, to come close to, to act and even sacrifice on behalf of, all presupposes close interrelatedness.

Again, this love has no limits. God's love is not a love for Israel over against the nations, but a love that wants to reach the nations through Israel. It is not a love for the church over against the world, but a love that aims at the world through the church.

Yet again this love has its favorites, being especially directed to the godless, the sinner, the downcast, the poor, the sick—never at the expense of the "righteous" and rich, but rather to call them to repentance, even through judgment. So being a love for all, it has to favor the unloved ones and take special care of them.

When we consider apartheid in the light of these characteristics of love, we must obviously reject it vehemently. Instead of directing love to others, especially the poor and those who suffer, the creators of apartheid have concentrated on their own group and its self-preservation. This is why there have so often been attempts within apartheid circles to justify self-love biblically.

In the same way, biblical love that wants to be near to others, that wants to be involved and have fellowship, has been seriously lacking. In society and in the church the general tendency has been to keep blacks at a distance and to allow them near only when their services are needed, and then only in labor relationships where whites are in control as the supervisors and the blacks are servants. In many cases whites would not even allow them to attend worship services in white churches.

One of the worst sore points in apartheid is the lack of knowledge people have of one another. Because God loved us, he came close to us, became a human being like us and shared our lives. Because of this he knew our circumstances and could really help us. The system of apartheid, however, divides two groups of people from each other and leaves them without the necessary knowledge of one another.

For several reasons this lack is fatal for two groups who share the same country, economy, and government. One special problem is that the whites who rule the country and have the vote seriously lack knowledge about how the apartheid system has really disrupted the lives of blacks. This has resulted in the whole legal system being completely onesided in the interest of the whites. Furthermore, the government was never forced to listen to the cries of blacks because they did not have the vote. This position still holds. It is a difficult question whether government officials who work directly with blacks and even in black areas do in fact have sufficient knowledge of black suffering. Even so, an ideology always blinds its adherents.

Furthermore, government officials cannot easily give a negative report to their superiors. Through the years those who did, and other white and black public figures and organizations who have drawn attention to the suffering of blacks, have been branded Communist. From the beginning of the century until the sixties the African National Congress was a black nationalist organization with a strong Christian motivation that tried to negotiate the cause of the blacks with the government. But they were made out to be Communists because they rejected the policy of apartheid. So in the early sixties they chose the way of violence, and indeed some of them did turn Communist.

Various factors, but especially the distance created by apartheid, caused either a lack of knowledge among the legislators, or a lack of motivation to make use of the knowledge they had. Inevitably this meant that there was no motivation for action showing real love and aiming at fundamental justice, action that would really change the overall position of blacks. The apartheid policy itself was considered biblical — the contribution of the Afrikaans churches and theology — so that every call to oppose apartheid was stamped "liberal" (a very negative label in government circles) and even "Communist."

CONCLUDING REMARKS

In light of the concepts of covenant and image it has become evident that we must view humanity as one interrelated human race. Naturally there will be degrees of interrelatedness because some groups have very little in common (i.a. because of distances, varying cultures, and other differences). However, two points have to receive close attention.

First, the world community is in a process of growing interdependence —

and this is good. This is what God intends for humanity. Second, resistance to interdependence is heavier when people (and groups) already have many mutual interests. It is less harmful for SA not to trade with Japan than with countries in Southern Africa. (Ironically apartheid forced us into the opposite situation.) Furthermore, the forceful dispersing of people who share the same country, history, infrastructure, government, etc. is the greatest injustice against the plan of God with humanity.

God related human beings in various ways because he wants us to share our lives. In the twentieth century this interrelatedness has become stronger because the world has become smaller — "a global village" — and some of the most serious problems are those that face humanity as a whole and can only be dealt with by joint action.

On a smaller scale this is also the case for SA. The time that the white group can solve the country's problems is finally over — if there ever was such a time! The time that people of our country can be artificially divided into groups is also past. The time has come for all South Africans to develop a joint loyalty and become one nation in spite of all the differences. The time that the church has to set a living, visible example is long overdue. In the church God wants to show the world that it does not matter whether someone is Jew or Greek, man or woman, black or white.

This article is gratefully dedicated to Ray Anderson, who has inspired my reasons for choosing this theme: first, because people and relationships are very important in his theology. Second, because a few years ago he worked for some weeks as a guest professor in our department (Systematic Theology and Theological Ethics, University of South Africa). He impressed us in many respects. The one outstanding impression that I retain is his responsible analysis and evaluation of our situation. Ray is not a group-directed person, but someone who takes full responsibility for his views. He does not jump on anyone's bandwagon, but takes time and trouble to gather insights.

It was soon evident to us that Ray would not be satisfied with the mere superficial criticism against the policy of the SA government, but that he would search deeper and therefore ultimately understand better — and develop a more responsible resistance.

With his visit Ray Anderson enriched our department at Unisa, and as a department we thank him that he was willing to identify with us to such an extent.

12

JOHN W. DE GRUCHY

✢

No Other Gospel: Is Liberation Theology A Reduction of the Gospel?

THE CHARGE OF "reductionism" has a long history in Christian theology. The ancient Arians were accused of reducing the full divinity of Jesus so that while he was more tham simply a man he was not truly God. Others went in the opposite direction and denied the full humanity of Jesus, which ultimately meant that he never really suffered the agony of death on the cross. In more recent history, Protestant liberal theology, in its struggle to come to terms with modernity, reduced the gospel in order that it might fit better into the thinking of modern, secular, and scientifically informed people. Hence Adolf von Harnack's contention that the essence of Christianity is "the Fatherhood of God, the brotherhood of man, and the infinite value of the human soul."

Reductionism, in whatever form, means the undermining of historic Christianity. In fact, it creates another "gospel" which, as Paul told the Galatians, is no gospel at all (Gal. 1:6-7). The criticism that liberation theology reduces the gospel is therefore a far-reaching one because it implies that the gospel proclaimed is not the gospel of Jesus Christ. The critics of liberation theology insist that it reduces the gospel in a variety of ways but at bottom line makes the gospel subservient to an alien, atheistic, and revolutionary ideology. A far-reaching criticism indeed.

THE CRITICISM AND THE CRITICS

The first element in the critique is the charge that liberation theology is not ideologically neutral but biased in favor of the poor and oppressed. A second is that right action (orthopraxis) is given priority over right belief (orthodoxy), which means, the critics argue, the undermining of the truth claims of the gospel as God's revelation. Right action thus becomes a substitute for right belief, or at least a criterion for establishing the truth. A third element is that liberation theology redefines sin in terms of social oppression rather than of alienation or separation from God. It confuses the symptoms of sin with its root cause. As a consequence, the struggle between faith and unbelief is understood as the political struggle between the oppressed and poor (the "righteous"), on the one hand, and the rich oppressor on the other.

All of this means that salvation is reduced to socio-political liberation, and therefore something we achieve through our own effort, rather than through God's grace in Jesus Christ crucified and risen. The church becomes equated with the poor and the oppressed, and the coming of the kingdom of God is equated with the establishment of a socialist state, through violent revolution if need be. My focus will be the central charge of reductionism.

The critics of liberation theology vary a great deal in their understanding of the issues involved in their critique. There are those who have an admirable grasp of the debate and knowledge of the literature, and whose evaluation of liberation theology arises out of a deep concern for the truth and a commitment to social justice.[1] There are, however, not least in South Africa, right-wing religious and political propagandists whose ideological motives are crystal clear but whose knowledge of the debate is murky, misinformed, and superficial. They are not really interested in the truth of the matter; their intention is to score political points in the interests of preserving the status quo.

Forgetting for a moment the misrepresentation or misunderstanding implicit in much of this latter kind of criticism, there is a major problem facing both serious critics and any person responding. Liberation theology is an increasingly diverse movement. When it first surfaced in the early seventies it was largely confined to Catholic theologians in Latin America. Even then there was considerable diversity of approach among its various exponents. But since then liberation theology has broadened into a world-wide movement which includes an even greater variety of theologies. There is even variety within each grouping, whether it be black theology in South Africa, feminist theology in North America and Europe, or Minjung theology in East Asia. It is a flexible and dynamic movement that seeks to be open to what the Word of God is saying to the contemporary church in a variety of oppressive contexts.

Thus generalizations about liberation theology, or, let us even say, black theology in South Africa, become more and more problematic. Criticisms that may apply with some validity to some Latin American liberation theology may have no relevance whatsoever with regard to black theology in South Africa. Furthermore, many of the earlier criticisms of liberation theology are no longer valid. Indeed, even the critics within the Vatican have largely changed their opinion and, with some reservations (related to the issues we are dealing with in this essay), have expressed qualified support.[2] But even so, as Juan Luis Segundo, himself a Latin American liberation theologian, readily admits, it would be naive and unrealistic to deny that "there could be and surely often are superficial, boastful and excessive features."[3]

Liberation theology is not beyond criticism, and it would be foolish to assert vehemently that those critiques we are examining have not been valid of some liberation theology in the past, or that they are without any substance in the present. Such a response would not serve the interests of truth or the gospel. It would be a miracle if any theology were beyond criticism, for theology, after all, is not revelation, but a human attempt to understand and reflect on the mystery of God's saving grace and truth in Jesus Christ. Only faith expressing itself in love can grasp the height and depth of such knowledge; every attempt to describe it must, in some way, reduce its wonder and power.

My concern is not primarily to defend liberation theology but to ensure that what is true in its understanding of the gospel is not submerged under the words of its critics, but clarified and affirmed. In the process it will become evident that some critics are far more guilty of reductionism than liberation theology. It should also become evident that liberation theology, like all fresh movements in the life of the church, has arisen precisely in order to counter the reduction of the gospel and to enable the renewal of the church and its mission. Whatever its faults, liberation theology does not seek to proclaim another gospel, but to reclaim the gospel of Jesus Christ in all its power and fullness.

NO NEED FOR APOLOGY

Liberation theology does not reduce the gospel to a political ideology, but neither does it claim to be politically neutral. On the contrary, liberation theology is clearly committed to the struggle for social justice and the liberation of the poor and the oppressed; indeed, it is increasingly becoming theology which is done by poor, disadvantaged, and oppressed people themselves as they assert their God-given dignity and claim their rights as human beings. If the critics find that wrong, then there is not much we can do about it because, as far as liberation theologians are concerned, that assertion is consonant with the biblical message and the gospel. No apology is required.

A striking fact of liberation theology is the extent to which it is engaged in the study and interpretation of the Bible. It is beyond the scope of this essay to examine its interpretation of the Bible in any depth, but we can affirm that few contemporary theologies are as committed to doing theology in conversation with Scripture. Of course, not everyone (including fundamentalists at one end of the spectrum and liberals at the other) will agree with the way in which liberation theologians interpret the Bible (and there is variety among them also), but that does not mean their approach is wrong.

The Bible itself provides good reason to believe that it is meant to be read from the perspective of the underdog rather than of the mighty and the powerful; after all, much of it was written in support of the former and in judgment of the latter. It is simply a fact that the Bible says more about oppression, and Jesus said more about economics, than about prayer! This does not make prayer and spirituality unimportant, but it does raise the question whether those who oppose theologies of liberation in the name of biblical piety and evangelical or orthodox theology have, in fact, really examined the biblical evidence. As has been perceptively been noted:

> The real problem is that some "evangelicals," like old-time liberals, have operated with a truncated Bible, despite their formal acknowledgment of its authority. They have rung the charges of John 3:16 and Acts 16:31—"Believe on the Lord Jesus Christ and you shall be saved"—but have conspicuously ignored the social significance of the Magnificat and the Beatitudes. They have reveled in passages like Isaiah 1:18—"Though your sins be like scarlet, they shall be as white as snow"—but they have paid little attention to a major motif in the prophets as summarized in Amos 5:24—"Let justice roll down like waters and righteousness like an ever-flowing stream."[4]

Such reductionism of the biblical message, characteristic of some of the critics, is rightly rejected by liberation theologians.

This leads us to ask the critics, especially the propagandists: are they really willing to engage in an honest study of the Scriptures, and to try and discern what the good news concerning Jesus Christ really means for people who are poor, disadvantaged, and oppressed? And, concomitantly, what it means for those who are wealthy and powerful? In the past, and even today, the Bible has been misused in South Africa to justify racism and apartheid. Certain "prooftexts" are continually used, for example, to ensure that no one questions or opposes the actions of those in authority. Nothing could be more ideologically committed than that! But there is little evidence that right-wing critics really take Scripture seriously as a Word addressed to injustice in our situation, or as a Word that is "good news to the poor." Liberation theologians do not claim to be the only true and authentic interpreters of the Bible, but they do claim that much of Christendom has failed to heed the challenge of Scripture in its manifold attack upon injustice and oppression, and in its proclamation of hope and transformation.

But let us return to the question of ideological commitment and captivity. I have said that liberation theology does not claim to be politically neutral, which implies that it is in some way ideologically committed. The problem is that the word *ideology* is understood and used differently, so we really need to be sure about the way in which the critics of liberation theology understand it before responding to their charge.[5] Those who criticize liberation theology because it reduces the gospel to a political ideology clearly understand ideology as a closed system of ideas and values in terms of which people interpret and relate to reality, but because the ideas and values are derived from false perceptions, it distorts reality and sanctions wrong actions. This is a good working definition of ideology understood in its pejorative sense, and this is what we shall mean by ideology in what follows.

Let me state quite unequivocally that if any theologian—whether a liberation theologian or some other kind—allows some political ideology (understood as a closed system) to determine the meaning of the gospel, then the gospel has been surrendered. Liberation theologians are certainly open to this temptation, but so are their critics.

So I would want to ask the critics of liberation theology: is their understanding of the gospel as ideologically free as they suppose? This is patently not the case with regard to the religious and political propagandists. Their "right-wing" version of Christianity is by no means uncontaminated by political motivation or ideological partiality. Perhaps they ought to check for planks in their own eye before addressing the transgressions of liberation theologians. One difference between the liberation theologians and many of their critics is that the former are more self-aware and self-critical on this issue than the latter. Indeed, many of the critics show no awareness of the extent to which their own positions are ideologically bound and reductive of the gospel.

Thus liberation theologians are the first to admit their bias toward the poor and the oppressed, but they believe that their bias derives from and is confirmed by the testimony of much of the Bible. They are committed to the liberation of the oppressed precisely because they believe that this is an integral part of the gospel of Jesus Christ "according to the Scriptures." That is not reducing the gospel to a political ideology, but allowing it to be the good news of God in all its fullness for the poor and disadvantaged in society. Any other understanding of the gospel is certainly not the good news of Jesus Christ.

DOING THE TRUTH

In his Latin American journal, Henri Nouwen describes a visit he made to the Centro Bartolome de las Casas in Peru. He writes:

> What is most striking about this center of higher studies is that it stays close to the daily life of the people. It practices theology by reflecting critically on socio-

economic, political, and ecclesiastical events, and by evaluating them in the light of the Gospel and the teachings of the Church.

He then goes on to make this assessment:

> What makes liberation theology so original, challenging, and radical is not so much its conceptual content as its method of working. A true liberation theologian is not just someone who thinks about liberation, but someone whose thought grows out of a life of solidarity with those who are poor and oppressed. The most impressive aspect of the Centro Bartolome de las Casas is that those who come and work there are men and women whose knowledge has grown from an intimate participation in the daily life of the people who struggle for freedom.

This leads Nouwen to make an observation that is of fundamental importance in trying to understand liberation theology:

> . . . the center reveals one of the oldest of truths: that *theologia* is not primarily a way of thinking, but a way of living. Liberation theologians do not think themselves into a new way of living, but live themselves into a new way of thinking.[6]

In many respects, this is the heart of the matter, for liberation theology is not proposing another gospel to replace that of historic Christianity, but another way of understanding, appropriating, and expressing that gospel.

One of the most significant aspects of liberation theology is that its proponents are not liberal theologians. This, I believe, is a very important fact to remember. Liberal theology is, I would agree, a reduction of the gospel to make it fit modernity — hence the attempt by Harnack and many others to extract the "essence of Christianity" from the tradition and recast it in terms that make sense to their contemporaries. This has usually meant a denial of biblical authority, a movement away from the historic creeds, and the downplaying of the uniqueness of Jesus Christ. Liberal theology is, in fact, a peculiarly Western theology which emerged in positive response to the Enlightenment and in tandem with the secularization of Europe. Two of its characteristics are its excessive individualism and its privatization of the gospel, so that Christianity is reduced to something largely inward and personal. Liberation theologians reject such reductionism out of hand.

Of course, orthodox Christianity means different things within the different historic Christian traditions, but each by its very nature is wary of any reduction of the historic Christian faith. Thus in Latin America, for example, the Catholic theologians of liberation strongly affirm the historic creeds and Catholic tradition. Numbered among liberation theologians are many whose roots are firmly planted within evangelical and Pentecostal

Christianity. Neither Latin American liberation theologians nor South African black theologians are rehashed liberal theologians; indeed, few have gone through a liberal stage. Most, if not all, see their task much more as a rediscovery and restatement of historic biblical Christianity, rather than its liberal reduction, especially when the latter reduces Christianity to a privatized form of religion which denies the liberating power of the gospel in society.

But what of the relationship between right belief and right action? Does liberation theology reduce Christianity to moral or ethical action? It is thoroughly biblical to insist that knowledge of God is inseparably bound up with doing what is right. In his criticism of Shallum, the son of King Josiah of Israel, the prophet Jeremiah reminds him of his father's goodness and makes this telling point: "He defended the cause of the poor and needy, so all went well. 'Is that not what it means to know me?' declares the LORD" (Jer. 22:16). The knowledge of God, which is what theology is primarily about, is here directly related to taking sides with and defending the interests of the disadvantaged in society.

Related themes run throughout the Old Testament, particularly in the prophetic writings. In fact, Micah sums up God's requirements by telling Israel "to act justly and to love mercy, and to walk humbly with your God" (Mi. 6:8). "Walking with God," in other words, is inseparable from doing justice. This is, of course, simply making more specific and concrete the command that sums up every commandment: to love God with heart, mind, and soul, and one's neighbor as oneself. Jesus himself strongly affirmed this tradition, and in the parable of the Last Judgment (Mt. 25:31ff.) he took it to its logical conclusion. Paul, in his exposition on faith, hope, and love, gave priority to love over everything else (1 Cor. 13). And the Fourth Gospel (notably ch. 8) and the letters of John and James make the most striking affirmation that knowledge of the truth or faith in God have to do with the way in which we live and act in society. Nowhere is it more clearly stated that by doing the truth we discover what it means, and, as a corollary, that what we believe is ultimately discerned in what we do and who we are.

Does this mean that orthodoxy is unimportant or that the gospel is in some way reduced to a certain kind of behavior? To affirm the priority of right action in no way denies the importance of right belief. After all, liberation theologians, with perhaps the odd exception, are not saying that right action takes the place of right belief, but that right belief is discovered in reflection on Scripture in the midst of "doing the truth"—which, of course, includes the struggle for justice. Right belief is not something that emerges in intellectual isolation from witnessing to the gospel and struggling for what is right and just. Moreover, it would be counterproductive for liberation theologians to argue that what we believe does not matter. Wrong beliefs about God and human beings (for example, the idea that white people are superior by nature to blacks) have led to slavery, apartheid, and much else besides.

The question that needs to be addressed to the critics, then, is whether or not they have reduced Christianity to belief alone, to belief separated from right action—indeed, to some beliefs that lead to wrong deeds.

Christians through the centuries, in reflecting on the biblical message in a variety of different contexts, have come to affirm certain things to be true about God, about Jesus Christ, about the world, and about our salvation. These affirmations, later embodied in creeds and confessions, have arisen to counter false beliefs and to confess clearly and concretely what the gospel means in new situations. They clearly show, despite diversity, that there is a strong core of consensus at the heart of historic Christianity which can guide the church in its task in the world. Thus orthodoxy, or the tradition of faith, the cumulative insight of the Christian community, is not a substitute for right action but its guide, and a clarification of its meaning.

Theology acts, as it were, as a bridge between the faith handed down and present Christian action and reflection on the Scripture. But, as liberation theologians argue, it makes a great deal of difference *how* that task is undertaken, and more especially, from what perspective. For those who reflect on the meaning of the gospel in the midst of struggle against poverty and injustice, the good news concerning Jesus Christ will take on a significance and meaning that will not be obvious to those in more comfortable, middle-class environments, or those with wealth and power. This has always been true ever since the Magnificat was first sung. Hence liberation theology is not simply the restatement of traditional orthodoxy, but its retrieval in a new, often radically different perspective. In Nouwen's phrase, liberation theologians have lived themselves into a new way of thinking about the gospel. What matters ultimately is not simply believing in the resurrection of Jesus Christ, but in being risen together with him in the newness of life. To believe in justification by faith without really obeying Jesus Christ as Lord is, as Dietrich Bonhoeffer described it, nothing but "cheap grace" because "only he who is obedient can believe."[7]

In rejecting liberal Christianity and in seeking to restate the historic Christian tradition, liberation and black theologians are clearly not the proponents of a "dead orthodoxy." Indeed, their rejection of liberal reductionism is not for the sake of defending an orthodox traditionalism. For them, much of traditional Christianity has become a problem because it has provided religious sanction for unjust social structures, such as slavery in the past and apartheid in the present. Latin American theologians are fully aware of the extent to which traditional Catholicism has given support to oppressive governments; South African theologians are equally aware of the extent to which traditional Protestantism sanctions the status quo. The problem, as they see it, is the way in which the gospel has been understood and embodied. Much traditional Christianity has in fact, if not in theory,

become a reduction of the gospel because it has denied the socially liberating character of the biblical message. Liberation theologians seek the
liberation of historic Christianity from such bondage so that the Bible may
speak with transforming power to a new day and situation.

THE SOCIAL REALITY OF SIN

Liberation theologians are accused of reducing sin to social and political
oppression. According to this critique, sin is no longer seen as human
alienation from God which needs to be remedied by the death of Christ on
the cross, but as the product of historical forces which can only be
overcome by political action and revolution. In other words, liberation
theology, it is argued, deals not with the root cause of social oppression, but
only with its symptoms. This is a fundamental misunderstanding of
liberation theology, for it in no way denies that sin is separation from God,
not that personal redemption is totally dependent upon God's grace. But it
does argue that sin has grave social consequences against which Christians
are called to struggle.

Liberation theology further argues that there is not only a distinction but
also an integral connection between salvation by grace and human liberation in its various aspects.[8] The Bible never talks about our separation from
God in vague "spiritual" terms; its depiction of the "wickedness of the
heart" is invariably described in graphic, concrete images that have to do
with human life in its every dimension. There is ample evidence of this in
the prophetic literature in the Old Testament, but consider simply the way
in which Isaiah describes the sin of Israel: "Woe to those who make unjust
laws, to those who issue oppressive decrees, to deprive the poor of their
rights and rob my oppressed people of justice, making widows their prey
and robbing the fatherless" (Is. 10:1-2). Time and again the Bible describes
sin as that which destroys human community, a consequence of alienation
from God and a contributing factor to that separation. So much is this the
case that Jesus' parable of the Last Judgment (Mt. 25:31ff.) indicates that
our relationship to him is bound up with the way in which we have related
to those who are disadvantaged. To reject the latter is to reject Jesus—and
this, according to the parable, becomes the basis for our own rejection by
God. Gutiérrez puts it in this way:

> In our relationship with God and with others there is an inescapable personal
> dimension: to reject a fellow human—a possibility inherent in our freedom—is to
> reject God as well. Conversion implies that we recognize the presence of sin in our
> lives and our world. In other words, we see and admit what is vitiating our
> relationship with God and our solidarity with others—what, in consequence, is
> also hindering the creation of a just and human society.[9]

Liberation theologians believe (and they are not alone here) that it is of fundamental importance not to reduce sin to some vague "spiritual" notion, or only to personal guilt—real as that is—but to describe its reality as it manifests itself. Some critics of liberation theology have no hesitation in doing this with regard to alcoholism or adultery—and rightly so. But why not also give names to the sins of injustice and oppression? And just as the root causes of alcoholism and adultery are spelled out in detail, why not spell out the root causes of injustice and poverty?

It is precisely for this reason that liberation theologians insist on the need for adequate and penetrating social analysis. The analysis of society, the attempt to understand the reasons for its condition—why the poor are poor, why the oppressed are oppressed, why the rich and powerful act in the way they do—is essential if we are really going to speak about sin with biblical authority and clarity. The problem with too much of Christendom is that it fails to do precisely this—it skirts the issues, particularly if facing and struggling against them is costly and contrary to the interests of those in power.

PROCLAIMING NO OTHER GOSPEL

The German movement "No Other Gospel," led by Tübingen theologian Peter Beyerhaus and others, has been particularly critical of liberation theology. In turn, their criticisms have been used by right-wing religious groups in South Africa to attack the *Kairos Document* and other expressions of liberation theology. These critics have, in fact, gone so far as to claim that they stand in the tradition of the Barmen Declaration, that great confession of faith used by the Confessing Church in Germany in its opposition to Hitler and Nazism. In other words, they claim that liberation theologians are guilty of doing precisely what the Nazi theologians did—using Scripture for ideological ends! As Míguez Bonino noted more than ten years ago: "The ghost of 'German Christians' and their monstrous accommodation to Nazi ideology are frequently conjured up in order to anathematize the theology of liberation."[10]

It is strange, to say the least, that the Barmen Declaration, which became the Christian charter against Nazi anti-Semitism and against the attempt to neutralize the church politically in subservience to Hitler, should now be used *against* those who are struggling against racism and oppression. That does not necessarily mean that there is no point to the criticism, but there can be no doubt that Karl Barth, who drafted the Barmen Declaration, would have rejected outright any alliance with right-wing Christianity in South Africa today. That, I suggest, should make Beyerhaus and others think again before they allow themselves to be coopted in this way. But let us examine the classic text used by the proponents of "No Other Gospel": Paul's letter to the Galatians.

Paul criticized the Galatians for turning away from the gospel that he had originally preached to them. They had turned "to a different gospel — which is really no gospel at all" (1:6). The good news according to Paul is that God redeems us not through any merit we have but out of God's boundless mercy, love, and grace. Any reliance we put on our own righteousness, ability, culture, race, or class as a means of salvation is ruled out. We are justified only through our faith in God's righteousness revealed in the death and resurrection of Jesus Christ, and in this way we are set free to be God's children. As a result, "the only thing that counts is faith expressing itself through love" (5:6). Indeed, Christian freedom is about life in the Spirit which, in the end, means serving and loving others, bearing their burdens, and not becoming weary in doing good.

From my reading of liberation theologians, I have yet to come across any who would contradict this brief, but I submit accurate, account of the gospel Paul preached. Of course, the gospel has many other dimensions and emphases, some of which are found in the synoptic gospels and the Johannine corpus rather than in Paul — for example, the emphasis upon the gospel of the kingdom of God, and that upon walking in the truth. The gospel is not exhausted by Pauline theology, and we must be careful not to reduce it in such a way. But having said that, I can think of few liberation theologians, if any, who would not wish to affirm the gospel as Paul expresses it in Galatians, though they may well articulate their affirmation in a variety of ways and in different terms. After all, liberation theologians number among them Catholics and Protestants, including Pentecostalists and evangelicals, and each tradition has its own favored way of stating the truth of the gospel. I am not always in agreement with the way in which Catholic theology relates nurture and grace, but I find Leonardo Boff's exposition of grace (*Liberating Grace*) one of the most profound and helpful discussions on the subject.[11]

Strikingly, it is Gustavo Gutiérrez, the pioneer Latin American Catholic liberation theologian, who claims that our salvation has nothing to do with our merit but everything to do with God's grace. Reflecting on Mt. 25:31-46, a favorite passage for liberation theologians and one that might suggest that we in some way earn our salvation, or at least that love for neighbor is all that is needed, Gutiérrez writes:

> . . . we have also come to understand that a true and full encounter with our neighbor requires that we first experience the gratuitousness of God's love. Once we have experienced it, our approach to others is purified of any tendency to impose an alien will on them; it is disinterested and respectful of their personalities, their needs and aspirations. The other is our way of reaching out to God, but our relationship with God is a precondition for encounter and true communion with the other. It is not possible to separate these two movements, which are

perhaps really only a single movement: Jesus Christ, who is God and man, is our way to the Father but he is also our way to the recognition of others as brothers and sisters.[12]

There is no other gospel. Liberation theology does not reduce salvation to something we can achieve by our effort or merit. On the contrary, the gospel of God's saving grace in Jesus Christ is proclaimed as that power which liberates men and women from sin and enables them to serve others in the struggle for justice in the world.

WITNESSING TO THE KINGDOM

"If you preach the gospel in all aspects with the exception of the issues which deal specifically with your time," declared Martin Luther, "you are not preaching the gospel at all." Much traditional theology does, unfortunately, reduce the gospel to timeless principles. In the process of trying to be faithful to orthodoxy, many theologians likewise reduce the gospel to a set of ideas that do not impinge in any real way on their historical context. As Luther in his own time saw so clearly, that results in no gospel at all. The good news about Jesus Christ is always related directly to the life-situation in which men and women, societies and groups, find themselves. The gospel is not about timeless principles, but about God's Word addressed to us here and now. That is why Christians insist that Word and Spirit belong together—it is the Holy Spirit who enables us to understand what God is saying to us through Scripture in relation to our particular historical context.

How, then, does the good news about Jesus Christ; about God's grace and our response in faith; about God's gift of freedom and our life lived in love; about salvation and sanctification; become concrete and specific today, and especially today in South Africa? How does the gospel address the issues facing us so critically? Or, in other words, in what way does the gospel address the sins of our situation and point us toward salvation, a salvation that is holistic and therefore integrally related to us both as individual people and as a society, a gospel for poor and rich, oppressed and oppressor, black and white?

Liberation theologians have found the key to this question in Jesus' own proclamation about the kingdom of God. The gospel of the kingdom of God is not about a gospel different from that proclaimed by Paul in his letter to the Galatians, but it expresses the good news concerning Jesus Christ in different terms. For Jesus, the good news of the kingdom of God was summed up in Is. 61:1-2, a passage he applied directly to his own redemptive task (cf. Lk. 4:18f.): "The LORD has sent me to proclaim freedom for the prisoners, and recovery of sight for the blind, to release the oppressed, to proclaim the year of the LORD's favor." God's redemption in Jesus Christ addresses human need quite concretely and specifically—the needs of the poor, the blind, and the oppressed are all needs that God seeks to meet and redeem in Jesus Christ.

This raises the question, How does God meet these needs? The biblical answer is that God usually acts through human agency. Consider, for example, the fact that God uses the "foolishness of preaching" to make the good news known to people far and near. Indeed, without a preacher, God's Word would not be made known (Rom. 10:14f.)! In the same way, it is through the witness and action of people "redeemed by grace" that God addresses the needs of the poor, the physically disabled, and the oppressed. Indeed, it is the poor and oppressed themselves, renewed and liberated by grace, whom God uses to work out his purposes. Of course, whether it is in "justifying the ungodly" or "liberating the oppressed" it is all, in the end, the work of God's grace and mercy. But God uses human instruments to witness to his redemptive purposes—that is primarily the reason why he brought a special people into being, the People of God.

Liberation theology has been criticized for reducing the People of God or the church to the community of the poor and the oppressed. There is undoubtedly a danger to avoid here. If we equate the church with any particular group it loses its universal character, its inclusiveness and power to transcend human and social barriers. Moreover, the distinction between the church and world at large may be lost if the People of God is simply equated with an oppressed people or nation. All of this could lead to the religious sanctioning of nationalism, a *volkskerk* and *volksteologie*. Clearly the poor are not to be equated with the church, though there is more biblical support for that than there is for equating the church with a particular nation or racial group.

There is, however, the opposite danger: the church can become unrelated to the cries, struggles, and agonies of the people who are oppressed and poor, and its middle-class members may well be prevented from encountering Jesus in the poor. The church should take its stand clearly on the side of those in need, whether they be Christian or not. But there is another factor here we must take into account. In Latin America it so happens that the vast majority of the poor are, in fact, members of the Catholic Church. Likewise in South Africa it is equally the case that the vast majority of the poor are members of some Christian church or other. For the church to stand aloof from their struggles would not only be a denial of the gospel, but also a denial of itself as their church. In this very important sense, the church is the church of the poor, but that does not imply that it is sectional in any way, for the church includes all who respond to the good news of Jesus Christ.

But let us focus, finally, on Christian hope and redemption. The resurrection of Jesus from the dead is the powerful message that death is not the final word, that sin will not finally triumph. The amazing thing about the proclamation of Jesus' victory over death is, however, that it radically affects life here and now. So much is this the case that John's Gospel proclaims eternal life as a present reality! It is therefore a false reduction of the gospel to see it in terms simply of saving souls for life after death. This is more akin to that early heresy called Docetism and Platonic dualism than the gospel of the incarnation and the kingdom of God.

The final victory over all evil and death is, of course, yet to be, but already we witness some penultimate victories as God works out his purposes of redemption. This is seen, for example, in Jesus' own ministry—casting out devils, healing the sick. And it is precisely what Christians pray for day by day when they ask that God's kingdom will come on earth as in heaven. Liberation theology does not in any way deny the reality of life beyond death, but in accordance with the New Testament, it affirms that God's intention is also for life now in all its fullness. Therefore everything that detracts from such life—including oppression of every kind—is contrary to God's will and must be overcome and transformed. Hence in praying for God's kingdom on earth as in heaven, Christians are called to become the vehicles for the answering of that prayer. To share in God's process of liberating the oppressed is to participate in God's redemptive purposes, to proclaim the good news. Rather than reducing the gospel to some social program, it is ensuring that God's good news is proclaimed concretely here and now.

Liberation theology does not proclaim that the kingdom of God is a form of socialist utopia that can be brought into being through human effort. Liberation theology proclaims that the kingdom of God is always God's reign and rule, and therefore always beyond human control or achievement. But the gospel calls us all to work, witness, and pray in such a way that this kingdom will become a reality in our midst. The struggle for justice and liberation is not the struggle to bring in the kingdom, but a witness to what the kingdom is all about. Any movement toward God's justice, any fresh approximation amid sinful reality of God's reign of righteous peace, is a sign of God's promised reign at the end of historical time.

Whatever its faults and failures, liberation theology seeks only to proclaim the gospel of Jesus Christ "according to the Scriptures." That gospel sets men and women free from all forms of bondage and brings them to the fullness of life. Hence Pope John Paul II's identification with the call for "a liberation theology of universal dimensions." As he put it, "the reality of the 'liberty for which Christ freed us' (Gal. 5:1) is universal. The task of theology is to discover its authentic meaning in its various concrete, historical, and contemporary contexts."[13]

NOTES

1. Two examples must suffice. J. Andrew Kirk, *Liberation Theology: An Evangelical View from the Third World* (London: Marshall, Morgan & Scott, 1979); Dennis P. McCann, *Christian Realism and Liberation Theology* (Maryknoll, NY: Orbis, 1981).

2. *Instruction on Christian Freedom and Liberation* (Vatican City: Congregation for the Doctrine of the Faith, 1986).

3. Juan Luis Segundo, "The Shift within Latin American Theology," *Journal of Theology for Southern Africa* 52 (September 1985):17.

4. I. John Hesselink, "Toward a Seminary that is Catholic, Evangelical and Reformed," *Reformed Review* xxvii (1974):108.

5. See this important study: James Leatt, Theo Kneifel, & Klaus Nurnberger, *Contending Ideologies in South Africa* (Cape Town: David Philip, 1986), esp. part five.

6. Henri J. M. Nouwen, *¡Gracias! A Latin American Journal* (New York: Harper & Row, 1983), p. 158f.

7. Dietrich Bonhoeffer, *The Cost of Discipleship* (New York: Macmillan, 1963), p. 50.

8. See Leonardo & Clodovis Boff, *Salvation and Liberation: In Search of a Balance between Faith and Politics* (Maryknoll, NY: Orbis, 1979).

9. Gustavo Gutiérrez, *We Drink from Our Own Wells* (Maryknoll, NY: Orbis, 1985), p. 97.

10. José Míguez Bonino, *Revolutionary Theology Comes of Age* (London: SPCK, 1975), p. 87.

11. Leonardo Boff, *Liberating Grace* (Maryknoll, NY: Orbis, 1981).

12. Gutiérrez, *We Drink from Our Own Wells*, p. 112.

13. Quoted in Boff, *Salvation and Liberation*, p. 34.

13

WILLIAM E. PANNELL

✛

Evangelism: Solidarity and Reconciliation

THE SALMON WAS GOOD and the wine a soothing elixir. The Boeing 747 lacked the ambience of a restaurant, but at 43,000 feet one can make do. The Aleutians were off to the right—not the average view from any eatery.

Along with a planeload of others we were well on our way to Seoul, and then on to Manila. It was mid-July and already I felt I'd spent the entire summer of '89 in international convocations. First there was the meeting of the World Council of Churches Commission on World Mission and Evangelism (CWME) in San Antonio, Texas. Now the second international gathering, this time with my evangelical brethren (and a few sisters) under the banner of the Lausanne Movement in Manila.

The venues for these conferences were significant. The WCC meeting in San Antonio was a first—the first time such a gathering of the Commission was held in the U.S. San Antonio was selected because of its proximity to the world of Latin America: part of it below the border and the significant Latino presence in the city itself. A statement could be made about solidarity with distressed people from San Antonio that could not be made in, say, Chicago. Perhaps.

Lausanne II chose Manila for much the same reason, although the leadership's first choice was Singapore, in part because that city-state has become a hub of evangelical ministries in Southeast Asia. There are strong Christian churches and other evangelistic ministries there also. But Singapore is in a delicate economic circumstance, almost totally dependent upon outside sources for its critical raw materials. This is especially true in the case of oil supplies, which come from the Middle East where oil-rich kingdoms are Arabic in national origin and Muslim in religious commitment. Muslims, along with all other peoples committed to non-Christian religions, are targets of evangelical ministries of evangelism, a fact not lost on Singapore politicos. They apparently made it clear that they were not willing to risk offending Muslim leaders in these oil-producing countries. It is also reasonable to think that the Lausanne Committee, once it recovered from the disappointment, could see in Manila a venue from which to locate the movement's focus on evangelizing the whole world with the whole gospel.

So on to Manila. The city is a study in contrasts, as is the entire country. High-rise hotels and offices for the wealthy and their foreign benefactors in business tower over hollow-eyed children begging in the streets just beyond reach of the guards at these posh hotels, while young women inside sell themselves to affluent men. Countryside villages suffer the carnage of murder and torture as vigilantes play soccer with the heads of their victims, some of whom were believers and pastors of small churches. Villagers are shot by men brandishing M-16s with "Jesus" emblazoned across their T-shirts.

In a major welcoming address, Senator Jovito Salonga highlighted these contradictions: "Our people have been described as far back as I can remember as 'the only Christian nation in Asia.' We say that with pride since ninety percent of our people profess the Christian faith. But sometimes I wonder whether that is a compliment or a cause for continuing reproach. You see, during the twenty-year rule that ended in February 1986, we were described as 'the most corrupt nation' in Asia. Corruption and Christianity are simply incompatible."[1] That address, more than any other, put the conference in its proper setting. By coming to Manila, the Lausanne Movement gave every indication that it intended to take the world seriously in its attempts at evangelism.

After these sojourns, it seems clear to me that there is much to rejoice over from these two gatherings of Christians. My observation of the WCC over the past twenty years, along with involvement in the Commission over a similar period, leads me to rejoice over the steady movement of this group toward a clearer understanding and practice of evangelism. This was clearly evident in San Antonio. As Dr. Raymond Fung, Secretary for Evangelism for the CWME, stated in his follow-up *Monthly Letter on Evangelism,* San Antonio witnessed the breaking of a "psychological barrier":

> the feeling that in WCC circles and meetings, one simply does not talk the
> language of evangelism, or that one does it only at the risk of confrontation, and
> that even if one does talk about it, one should so load it with qualifications . . . that
> it no longer soars. That barrier has been broken through. In San Antonio,
> Christians committed to evangelism at home were able to express that same
> commitment with no hangups and no apologies.[2]

There is a growing evangelical presence in the WCC, and it is thoroughly biblical and Christ-centered. Thus it tends toward proclamation in evangelism. It was evident that the CWME is acknowledging this evangelical presence and taking it seriously.

The most perplexing issue facing the WCC is a theological one. It concerns the centrality of Jesus Christ in the church's understanding of its mission in the world. The willingness on the part of key leaders in the movement to join the current fascination with "myths" of God is seen within the membership of the CWME as the most critical theological issue in the WCC's turbulent history. Hence the verbal broadsides from Bishop Lesslie Newbigin and others in late spring calling for a repudiation of this trend with the passionate conviction that the future of the organization depends upon its willingness to nip this heresy in the bud: *Now*.

This sense of urgency emerged from plenary sessions and in the sections dealing with the various aspects of mission concerns. The growing consensus among many delegates was that whatever mission and evangelism were, they had to be centered in the uniqueness of Jesus Christ if the enterprise was to remain Christian. A statement from delegates and other evangelicals present at San Antonio was sent to the Lausanne II conference, expressing deeply felt concerns for the total agenda of the church. The statement, "A Letter of Evangelical Concerns," celebrates the positive aspects of the San Antonio meetings and calls for the strengthening of key areas in evangelism and theology. Of the nearly three hundred delegates and four hundred "other participants," almost two hundred persons signed this document. There are strong evangelical stirrings within the WCC.

Lausanne, Switzerland was the site of the 1974 Congress on Evangelism sponsored by evangelicals throughout the world. It was largely stimulated by the same North American leaders who had earlier convened the 1966 Congress on Evangelism in Berlin. This international group, taking its name from the Swiss city, has for nearly fifteen years called itself a movement and now comes complete with a covenant, state-of-the-art techniques and definitions, and money. Since 1974 the movement has spawned numerous smaller conferences focusing on different aspects of the group's interests. Thus a conference in 1982 attempted to deal with the relationship between evangelism and social responsibility, an issue that still nags at the movement's (especially Western) leadership.

In a summer laced with sequels, Lausanne II seemed to fit. Evangelicals gathered under a familiar banner in Manila: "Proclaim Christ until He Comes," with the subtitle, "Calling the Whole Church to Take the Whole Gospel to the Whole World." The subtitle became the organizing framework for the two week-long sessions. Thus we talked about the church, the gospel, and the world.

This framework is clearly related to the initial congress in Berlin. There evangelicals gathered under the banner "One Gospel, One World, One Task." But Lausanne II is a long way from that gathering in its understanding of the church's task. What distinguished the current evangelical under-

standing of mission from both the '66 and '74 meetings is a broader and
deeper knowledge of and sensitivity to the world. In 1966 scarcely any
mention was made of the world, especially at the level of human need. The
world was simply the place where millions of people lived, most of them
without the gospel. Little attention was given to their human condition of
suffering and oppression. The symbol of the world in Berlin was a huge
ticking clock in the foyer *Congresshalle,* each tick representing lost souls
passing into eternity without being saved. The hands, predictably, were
inching toward midnight.

By 1974 such images of the world had changed. The influence of Third
World leaders was strongly felt by then, and their experience of the world
was quite different from those in the West. Nevertheless, that event was
still strongly impacted, and hence controlled by, missiologists and apolo-
gists from the West—from Donald McGavran and Ralph Winter to Francis
Schaeffer. The debates were Western in source and polemical in nature.
They were about theories: of Scripture (the inerrancy debate), of church
growth, of mission strategy. In the shadows lurked the dreaded WCC (the
real enemy of missions advance), located actually and symbolically at the
other end of the lake.

But if Lausanne I witnessed a change in the movement's understanding of
the world, Lausanne II demonstrated that evangelicals have also matured in
their understanding of the gospel. Like their WCC counterparts, the
Lausanne contingent is working seriously on the kingdom motif of Jesus in
the Gospels, especially as this relates to the poor. Evangelicals have
discovered the poor in the Scriptures in their relationship to the good news
of the reign of God, an emphasis also characteristic of the WCC. This
reflects a realization that previous understandings were too narrowly
focused and lacked the overarching, all-encompassing intention of God in
Christ for the world. Previous definitions were also felt by many to be too
dependent upon Western categories to be of maximum use in non-Western
settings.

There is still only one gospel for Lausanne people, and the uniqueness of
Jesus Christ is unequivocally proclaimed, but as the Manila Manifesto
explains, "We have been confronted with Luke's emphasis that the gospel is
good news to the poor (4:18, 6:20, 7:22) . . . and we repent of our
comparative indifference to the plight of the poor and of the preference we
have often made for the rich. We determine to make the needy peoples of
the world our mission priority and like Jesus 'to preach the good news to the
poor' by both word and deed."[3] To a younger group of evangelicals, the
gospel is now seen as encompassing the needs of the whole person,
reconciling persons to God and to each other, as well as the entire creation.
Lausanne II is focused on the church's unfinished task. Although still
strongly influenced by Western categories ("hidden peoples," "people
groups," etc.), the movement is seeking to face into the strong and fierce

winds that blow menacingly across the earth. And these winds are seen as ideological, political, theological, and economic. The Lausanne Movement may be growing up.

Thus occupied, there was little mention of the WCC in the conference. Dr. Eugene Stockwell, general director of the CWME, was present throughout the event, as was his able associate Dr. Raymond Fung of Hong Kong. But aside from one mention of the San Antonio event from the platform, there was no indication that the mentality against the WCC, so much in evidence at other evangelical events, was prominent at Manila. This was salutary in that it suggests that evangelicals are better informed about the Council, and perhaps even better mannered in their relations toward it. It also suggests that evangelicals recognize that the Commission has moved more closely to those understandings of evangelism and mission shared by the Lausanne delegates (of course, many Lausanne believers belong to churches long allied with the World Council). Perhaps this good news heralds the death of an earlier fire-breathing evangelical and missiological presence in these gatherings which, like most fundamentalists, would rather wage war than peace.

Yet if there is much about these two gatherings to celebrate, there is also much to regret—even lament. Neither of these groups has fully arrived. There is nothing strange about this, since the same could be said of every era in church history. There is plenty of evidence that however divine its Head, the church usually has feet of clay. But these meetings were not about heresies or cranking up another crusade (although there will be one of those from within the Lausanne group, urging the evangelization of the world by the year 2000). These latter-day movements are about mission and evangelism, about taking the "Whole Gospel to the Whole World by the Whole Church," about "Mission in Christ's Way." So the lament? In both of these gatherings, there was too much Western influence. This was especially true of Lausanne. (Too much vanilla in Manila!)

Manila was a reflection of Yankee organization. With the exception of the music, intentionally non-Western in focus and scope, the platform was precise and predictable. (The Manila program was reminiscent of old Youth for Christ rallies or revised versions of Graham crusade formats: more sophisticated in the use of media, but basically the same one-to-the-many approach.) The platform was Western throughout: even when non-Westerners spoke, their categories were Western. This confirms what critics of culture have been telling us for years: the onward march of secularism will finally catch up to the entire global population. This secularizing process carries information through technology, sweeping up the church in its momentum. Thus the West exports not only Coca-Cola but also all sorts of categories for formulating everything from theology to mission strategy. This accounts for the wide response of the conferees to the powerful cultural critique from Os Guinness, who laid out the movment of

secularism from Western sources. The speech was often interrupted by
applause, which included the affirmative response of non-Westerners. They
seemed to recognize that what began in Europe had found its way to their
societies.

Unfortunately, even the criticism of Western orientation was couched in
Western thought forms. One could only wonder what such a critique
would sound like from an African perspective. But then even African
thinkers seemed to have been converted to Western categories. What was
missing was some recognition that in accepting these categories of thought
the non-West, especially Africa, was giving up its religious and cultural
history, including elements toward which modern Western science is
moving. T. F. Torrance put it well in his *Theology in Reconciliation*. Noting
that modern science is searching for a way beyond older formulations
which produced a dualist understanding of nature and society, the Scottish
theologian sees a "decisive move away from the dualist epistemologies and
cosmologies . . . and their replacement by an integrative outlook upon
man and the universe in which form and being, or structure and substance,
instead of being torn apart, are found to be indissolubly linked together in a
continuous dynamic field of relations."[4] He furthermore observes that
when it comes to fleshing this out in actual experience, the churches in the
East and in Africa have a decided edge since they have already developed
"ways of thinking, which are more at home, in their distinctive ways, with
natural coherences, intrinsic connections and dynamic transformations."[5]

The West has a great deal to learn from the church in the non-West. But
this partnership in learning can only happen if leaders in the non-West
refuse to give up their assumptions about how things really work. The
implications for theological reflection and dialogue are obvious; but then
Manila had too little to do with theology.

But this was also true in the area of hermeneutics. Non-Westerners
seemed to offer no real departure from Western thought forms when it
came to examining texts or contexts for ministry. I had the eerie feeling
that, in such settings, if you've heard one evangelical you've heard them all.
There was some good speaking and fine exegesis in morning Bible studies.
But Western preaching lacks enthusiasm and passion. This is sad because,
as in the case of the Lausanne movement, preaching or proclamation is still
the key activity. The announced task is "proclaiming Christ." This is
clearly Pauline, of course. The great evangelical always spoke of his calling
as that of proclaiming Jesus Christ, and urged the church to do the same—
for, he asked, "How shall they hear without a preacher?" But for passion
during these meetings one had always to look to the non-West. People of
color have passion, and they made it felt when they had opportunity to
speak.

But there were no speaking opportunities given to people of color from
North America. There were no African-Americans to be seen near the

platform, no Hispanic-Americans, no native Americans—a complete lock-out of these people. Yet if asked, some of the key convenors from North America would admit that the best preaching from that commmunity probably comes from the black church. This points up a key weakness in this gathering: North American Anglo-evangelicals have yet to come to grips with their brothers and sisters of color from North America. This failure constitutes a crucial item on the unfinished agenda of North American evangelicalism. By extension one wonders if this failure affects relations between African-Americans and their black counterparts in Africa and the Caribbean. The omission of people of color from the U.S. did not seem to bother key leaders from Africa. Is the reason for this lack of concern on their part further evidence of the global outreach of a still-alive colonialism?

A further shortcoming among evangelicals—and here I mean the North American contingent, whose definitions seem always to prevail—is that while emphasizing proclamation by word and deed, there is still little evidence on their part of the need for the church to be in solidarity with the world. By solidarity I mean essentially what Karl Barth stated so power-fully in his work on the church as "the society in which it is given to men to know and practice their solidarity with the world." To Barth, solidarity with the world "means full commitment to it, unreserved participation in its situation, in the promise given it by creation, in its responsibility for the arrogance, sloth and falsehood which reign within it, in its suffering under the resultant distress, but primarily and supremely in the free grace of God demonstrated and addressed to it in Jesus Christ, and therefore in its hope."[6] He argued that the church owed the world this expression of obedience because in the church humans "know and practice their soli-darity with the world" and because in the world the church "finds its own cause . . . and that of the world in its own."[7]

Central to Barth's understanding of the church's mission in the world is his grasp of God's love for the world as revealed in Jesus Christ. Says Barth: "First and supremely it is God who exists for the world. And since the community of Jesus Christ exists first and supremely for God, it has no option but in its own manner and place to exist for the world. How else could it exist for God?"[8] Then in a most profound Christological statement Barth argues that the church for the world is the consequence of God being in Christ: "For in Him God is not for Himself, but for the world. In Him God has given Himself to and for the world to reconcile it to Himself. In Him God, supremely and truly God, has become man. This decides the orientation, meaning and purpose of community."[9] This is surely the meaning of the church as the body of Christ.

This radical solidarity is risky. For this reason we need to hear Barth's cautionary words about the church's separation from the world. His watchword is "solidarity with the world, not . . . conformity to it!"[10] It is this separation from the world, as a result of being called out of it by Jesus Christ, that enables the church to reflect the glory and mercy of God while it calls the world to obedience inspired by faith in Jesus Christ. "To be sure, the community is the people which is called out of the nations by the Word of God, which is separated from the world, which is separately constituted within it and which is thus set over against it."[11] This is the basis of Barth's contention that the church cannot say yes to the world if it cannot also say no. His reference to the Pharisees at this point is classic. They could not say yes to the world because they were separatists who were unable to see their own mirror image in the misery and corruption of society. They could not acknowledge any responsibility for the ruin and wretchedness of humanity, and thus could not share in its hope. The Pharisees considered themselves the answer, not the problem. Though sincere, they became a hindrance to the possibility of finding joy in the midst of agony, and hope in the midst of suffocating despair.

Hendrikus Berkhof argues for solidarity from a different angle. He begins with the model of the believer's sanctification and thus argues his view of the renewal of the world from a pneumatological understanding. But he begins with an understanding that humankind and the world are indissoluble: "The important thing is man, but precisely for that reason the world is important as well. Man and world are the two sides of the *one* reality. They are not reducible to each other but can only define each other. For that reason Christian conceptions of creation, of renewal, and of consummation are bound to remain abstract unless the world is included in the consideration." From here Berkhof argues that when one faces the full challenge of renewal by the Holy Spirit, both humankind and the world must be included: "If it is God's desire to renew man, it must also be his desire to renew the world. Else he would renew only half a man."[12]

But what of the church in all this? Berkhof faces the often painful question of persons vs. structures in the renewing work of the Holy Spirit. It is evangelical to argue that the Spirit changes people. People can repent and believe. Structures can do neither. This leads Berkhof to observe that it is precisely for this reason that theologians ignore the world in their dogmatics, consigning the topic to the field of ethics. But he argues that "if renewed man is driven to work for the renewal of structures, this is not a personal hobby but a mandate of the Spirit."[13]

Berkhof's use of the work of the Spirit here is encouraging, especially in a time when charismatics, no less than the rest of evangelicals, seem bent on ignoring the world in their attempts to "power" their way through the kingdom. Using analogies from the sanctification process in persons, e.g. "sanctification, freedom, love, dying and rising again, struggle and progress," Berkhof says it can be assumed that "if the Spirit works in the *world,* there are bound to be analogies of these concepts. For the world is the institutional manifestation and extension of what man himself is. Structures, too, can be sanctified by God, that is, made serviceable."[14]

Two things must be said at this point. Berkhof is right when he argues, "the Spirit is not only working through believers in his structure-renewing work. For it is evident that that is to a large extent the work of people other than believers. The renewal of the world is thus not a direct fruit of the renewal of people, but it follows its own ways."[15] The sanctifying work of the Spirit is thus seen working extrinsically to the church, to borrow Barth's language. Yet in the second place, the work of the Spirit is seen in and through the body of Christ. The community of faith is in the world, a part of the world, and is thus the point of contact with its structures which the Spirit seeks to change.

Any discussion of the world that ignores the need to change these structures can only be an exercise in abstraction. People are being oppressed today through the structures of society, not simply by one-on-one encounters with evil people, or by the carnality which rages within themselves. The attempt of evangelicals in South Africa to critique their own theology makes clear that in their experience apartheid has both a personal and a structural dimension. There are evil racists in South Africa whose deeds are demonic in their execution. But apartheid is an institutional problem also. The demons of racism are entrenched in government, business, and ecclesiastical levels. These structures must be changed.[16]

For all the fervor of Western evangelical attempts to change the world, there is still little evidence that their evangelists—or their theologians, for that matter—are prepared to develop paradigms adequate to the realities of most of the world's people. These realities are poverty and political oppression. They are interrelated, largely institutional in nature, and international in scope. I have yet to hear an establishment evangelist deal with the implications of this for evangelism from any platform—none from the white community in North America, at least.

When Tom Skinner and I worked in this area from our platforms in the early seventies we found ourselves charged with being too political and abandoning the "simple gospel." Today's evangelicals are in danger of being redundant and need serious theological overhaul if they are to be taken seriously. Both Barth and Berkhof could be useful in helping them get at the work of the Spirit through the church in changing the world. Barth's definition of solidarity is by far the most useful in the literature. Berkhof's understanding of the Spirit's work of sanctification in changing the world is intriguing and merits much more work. One wonders how praxis based upon his argument could relate to that of John Wesley. The latter proved itself in an amazing way during the era of social reform in the U.S. after the great awakenings. Both these views could provide the necessary antidote to the so-called Third Wave and power evangelism with its willingness to see demons behind every green tree or rock in the world. These solutions prove not to be solutions at all, precisely because they take on the wrong demons. And those who ride this wave's crest have yet to demonstrate their solidarity with the world.

The challenge facing the church, especially its evangelical branch, is to fashion a stylish worldliness that would compel society to take the substance of the gospel seriously. It could not be said better than in Barth's words:

> The solidarity of the community with the world consists quite simply in the active recognition that it, too, since Jesus Christ is the Saviour of the world, can exist in worldly fashion, not unwillingly nor with a bad conscience, but willingly and with a good conscience. It consists in the recognition that its members also bear in themselves and in some way actualise all human possibilities. Hence it does not consist in a cunning masquerade, but rather in an unmasking in which it makes itself known to others as akin to them, rejoicing with them that do rejoice and weeping with them weep (Rom. 12:15), not confirming and strengthening them in evil nor betraying and surrendering them for its own good, but confessing for its own good, and thereby contending against the evil of others, by accepting the fact that it must be honestly and unreservedly among them and with them, on the same level and footing, in the same boat and within the same limits as any or all of them.[17]

Mercy!

Evangelism that takes the world seriously by being in solidarity with it must be based on the gospel of reconciliation. After all, it is the gospel that makes evangelism possible, necessary, effective, and joyful. Evangelism does not create the gospel. Theology does not create the gospel. If Western evangelicalism comes up short in both evangelism and theological paradigms for ministry in a shattered world, it may be because of a shallow understanding of the gospel itself. I suspect that the problem is rooted in hermeneutical systems that do not require responsible action of those who come to understand the text. Anthony Thiselton and his associates, in attempting to get beyond Western attempts to separate ethics from hermeneutics, argue:

> Hermeneutics is not simply a cognitive process whereby we determine the "correct meaning" of a passage or text. Questions of truth and universality are important, but so are questions of cultural value and social relevance. Because the interpretation of texts cannot avoid the historical contexts and actions of both authors and interpreters, questions of ethics and responsible interpretation are as germane to hermeneutics as questions of validity and correctness.[18]

This argument could bring one to the threshold of understanding why an African-American preacher gets into the text of the Exodus story at a different level than his white counterpart in the suburbs; why a Bible study on this Scripture can yield a different understanding in an obscure El Salvadoran village than in a high-rise complex in Washington, D.C.

Writing about the preaching of the late Dr. Martin Luther King, Jr., Richard Lischer notes the tendency to conclude from King's use of classical figures in Western thought that he applied these thoughts to the issues of the day and to an understanding of the meaning of the sacred text. But, says Lischer, "black church-leaders do not operate that way. . . . Life and language are so mixed together that it is impossible to describe how one emerges from the other. It is enough to say that for the black preacher the word does not function as a theoretical base for action. Rather, the word *is* a kind of action that cannot be legitimately separated from the struggles, temptations, suffering, and hopes of the people who live by the word."[19] This sheds light not only on black preaching but also on the actions of black Christians. Among these saints one can scarcely find debates about evangelism and social responsibility, a silence that predates the noisy arguments among their Anglo counterparts around the world. The black church long ago realized, before its preachers ever heard of hermeneutics, that their God is action-oriented in behalf of the oppressed and that this God expects no less of those who belong to him.

But in the light of the cross it is clear that the God who acts does so in order that alienated persons may be reconciled. Reconciliation is a key, if not *the* key, to understanding God's saving intentions in Jesus Christ. God was in Christ reconciling the world unto himself (2 Cor. 5:19). This standard formulation is dear to all evangelicals, yet the reality of this divine provision eludes us. A key reason may be our starting point. Perhaps the place to begin is not with the cross but with the incarnation, with the phrase "God was in Christ." To be sure the focus of this is on the cross, the atoning work of Christ. But the atonement is salvific only because of the incarnation, and here is where many evangelicals have problems. Our inability to be in solidarity with the world reveals a problem with our understanding of the incarnation.

Solidarity with the world and reconciliation of the world to God are both centered in the humanity of Christ. The model for the church existing "in worldly fashion" with the world, "willingly and with a good conscience," is Jesus of Nazareth. Jesus shows the way to reconciliation in his humanity, taking upon himself not only the world's sin, but also its heartbreak and misery, its shattered and broken dreams. He is clearly at home in the world, which means, as Berkhof has stated so well, that Jesus did not come into the world simply to die, but also to live, even if the life he led brought him inevitably to his death. But what a life! How he did live! He knew prostitutes and politicians, aged widows and children, the poor as well as young businessmen on the make, and priests who had lost their way in the labyrinth of ancient tradition. He went about doing good because he *was* good.

It is the *body* of Christ that unites Barth's notion of solidarity with Berkhof's ideas of sanctification as applied to changing systems. Recall

Berkhof's contention that the world's structures can be sanctified by God—that is, made serviceable: "Since this is the work of the Spirit of God the Spirit needs only a body through which to accomplish the work of social change. The Spirit can use nonbelievers to this end, as witness His use of Cyrus."[20]

In a radical statement celebrating the possibility of forgiveness, the writer to the Hebrews reveals the commitment of Jesus the Christ who, when coming into the world, said, "a body hast thou prepared for me," and in that body he did the will of the Father (Heb. 10:5). It was in order to do the will of God that Christ's sacrifice was made and by which believers will be sanctified. Now, this side of Easter and Pentecost, it is still in the body of Christ that the Spirit completes the work of sanctification, only now the church is that body. The church's task is to obey its risen Lord in offering itself for the world so that the love, power, and joy of God can effect transformation where people live out their daily lives.

But again, that body must not only be present in the world, but also in solidarity with it. And if Jesus is our model of ministry, then the starting place for such solidarity is bound to be among the "lowest and the least." Hear Barth again: "The community of Jesus Christ is for the world, i.e., for each and every man of every age and place who finds the totality of earthly creation the setting, object and instrument and yet also the frontier of his life and work."[21] The church, the body of Christ, is a part of the world even as Jesus was. Jesus is the firstborn of all creation, as he is the firstborn from the dead. His body linked him to the totality of creation even as he became the pioneer and perfecter of faith. The paroxysm that shook the earth and darkened the heavens at the offering of that body was the assurance that one day all things will be shaken and a new order will replace the old. The kingdoms of this world will become the kingdom of our God and of his Christ. And in that triumph, believers find their ultimate victory. Where the Head is, there also will be the Body. The effect of Christ upon creation confirms the insight that the goal of creation is Christ, and he is the way back to its final restoration.

This entire discussion rests upon Christological issues. For many evangelicals, especially in North America, this is the stumbling block. In short, how human was Jesus, and what did it mean for God to become a man, to become part of the created order? Was Jesus really flesh and blood, or, as the Gnostics held, merely a spiritual being of the highest order? It seems clear that most of the evangelical church has a gnostic Christ as its leader, which gives this branch of the church every reason to abstain from involvement in the world's pain. This explains why the Scriptures are spiritualized, and the relief of pain and oppression relegated to another time and place where God reigns in celestial bliss.

This failure of the church to accept its incarnational task in the world in behalf of the oppressed inclines the church toward what Helmut Thielicke calls a "false conservatism" in which the plight of the poor is seen as some expression of God's providence. Logically, then, to interfere in their situation would risk frustrating God's plan for those in misery, and perhaps cut short their full reward for faithfulness in the hereafter.[22] Thielicke is right in arguing that this attitude has betrayed the poor into the hands of Marxists the world over, and placed liberation squarely in the hands of the oppressed themselves. Ironically, when the oppressed begin to formulate their own theologies of liberation, it is these very "conservatives" who oppose their efforts.

The cure for this condition is exploration of the relationship between the incarnation of Jesus Christ and his atoning work. Until the Christian community in any and all of its forms, from the World Council to those whose covenant is called Lausanne, explores this relationship there will be no resolution to the ongoing debates over evangelism and social responsibility. And it is getting late.

NOTES

1. Jovito Salonga, address at the Lausanne II Congress on Evangelism, Manila, Philippines, 11 July 1989.
2. Raymond Fung, *Monthly Letter on Evangelism* (September 1989).
3. *Manila Manifesto* (Manila, 1989).
4. Thomas F. Torrance, *Theology in Reconciliation* (Grand Rapids: Eerdmans, 1976), p. 11.
5. Torrance, *Theology in Reconciliation,* p. 13.
6. Karl Barth, *Church Dogmatics,* ed. G. W. Bromiley & T. F. Torrance, trans. G. W. Bromiley (Edinburgh: T. & T. Clark, 1962), IV/3, p. 773.
7. Ibid.
8. Ibid., p. 762.
9. Ibid., p. 763.
10. Ibid., p. 773.
11. Ibid., p. 763.
12. Hendrikus Berkhof, *Christian Faith: An Introduction* (Grand Rapids: Eerdmans, 1979), p. 503f.
13. Ibid., p. 505.
14. Ibid.
15. Ibid.
16. "Evangelical Witness in South Africa: Evangelicals Critique Their Own Theology and Practice," in *Concerned Evangelicals* (Donsonville, 1985).
17. Barth, *Church Dogmatics,* IV/3, p. 774f.
18. Introduction to *The Responsibility of Hermeneutics,* ed. Roger Lundin, Anthony Thiselton, and Clarence Walhout (Grand Rapids: Eerdmans, 1985), p. x.
19. Richard Lischer, "The Word that Moves," *Theology Today* 2 (July 1989):170.
20. Berkhof, *Christian Faith,* p. 505.
21. Barth, *Church Dogmatics,* IV/3, p. 762.
22. Helmut Thielicke, *Theological Ethics,* ed. William Lazareth (Philadelphia: Fortress, 1969), vol. 2, p. 627f.

14

WALTER C. WRIGHT, JR.

✛

The Ministry of Leadership: Empowering People

ROGER AND NANCY ARE average people. There is nothing about them that would necessarily commend them to you over anyone else. If you were selecting a team, you might not choose them last, but you probably would not choose them first. They are ordinary at best.

Along comes George. He has a dream. He visions a new kind of program that takes the services and products of his organization to the customers where they live, a dream that most think is not practical. He needs a team to make this happen.

So what does George do? He chooses Roger and Nancy and four other ordinary people just like them. People laugh. He has gathered nondescript people with no known expertise or experience and grouped them around him, and they look more like a rabble than an efficient team with structure and organization. Most people think his mission is doomed.

But the critics are surprised. George shares his vision, and his team takes ownership for it. George encourages them to contribute what they can to make it happen. They try, sometimes effectively, sometimes quite poorly, usually unprofessionally. He praises their efforts. They try again, helping one another, putting in long hours. He works with them sometimes, leaves them alone other times. He encourages them, he praises them, he believes in them. To everyone's surprise, they succeed. Explanations don't indicate anyone or anything in particular beyond the shared vision. But they pull it off.

George and his group developed a new program that is now well into its second decade of effective operation. This rag-tag bunch of average people took a dream and made it reality. No single person stood out; the team together believed the dream and believed in each other. And they accomplished what everyone else believed was impossible. Today each member of that original team is off somewhere else, successfully leading other teams to accomplish more than they could as individuals.

Now consider the case of Sarah and David. Sarah is bright, articulate, attractive. She works in a small organization that uses her obvious gifts. She is a valuable member of the team and she knows it. Each year her job description is rewritten to take advantage of her continual growth and improvement. And there is David, also bright, articulate, attractive, and gifted—an energetic young man one cannot help but like immediately. He works with Sarah and a group of people just like them. They are good, they own the mission of their organization, and they live its values, whether their manager is present or not. They enjoy their work.

This is an effective group. It is clear that they can tackle any assignment they choose, and that each will succeed as an individual. They are working well together and running an effective organization, even when their manager is promoted and transferred to another division. They are one of the most effective units in their organization.

Then along comes Robert, who has a dream. Even though it's a little different than the mission of Sarah's and David's group, he becomes the new manager of their team. He believes in his vision, and he believes in himself.

But Robert does not share his vision. He simply tells his team members what they must do to make it happen. He doubts their ability to implement his vision. He criticizes their efforts. He doesn't trust them when he is not around, and he communicates it to them.

David is leaving to take another job elsewhere. Sarah is starting to look. So are the other members of their group. The group is still functioning at a minimal level because of their personal commitments to the values of the organization, but it is falling apart. Neither Sarah nor David looks forward to work anymore.

What made the difference in these two cases? In *both* cases the manager responsible exercised leadership. In one case the leadership style empowered Roger and Nancy to perform beyond their usual capacity. In the other, the leadership style decreased the effectiveness of Sarah and David and drained their enthusiasm. Is one an illustration of leadership and the other not? Or is it a difference of leadership style, and one style is more effective than others in building people and getting the job done? And what does any of this have to do with theology, ministry, and the Christian?

These are the questions addressed in this essay. The focus is on the *leadership relationship,* the relationship between the individual leader or manager and the individual follower, because it is precisely at this point that leaders have the most significant impact on the life and mission of the organization and, *more importantly,* on the development and growth of the person with whom they are working. It is also a place of beginnings—a place where every person can start, a place where one's theology can be immediately and visibly applied regardless of vocational calling in life. It is a place where the individual can make a difference.

George Eldon Ladd, the late professor of New Testament theology at Fuller Theological Seminary, used to pace back and forth before his classes articulating his views on the kingdom of God. According to Ladd, the kingdom of God—the future reign of Christ—has reached back into this present age and through the power of the Holy Spirit offers the Christian hope. It is not a hope that waits for the future to be experienced, but a hope that brings with it a present reality as it anticipates and appropriates the reign of God for this age—a reign that will be fully realized at the *parousia*. The kingdom of God, claimed Ladd, is present in part, in the power of the Spirit, today, and it should make a difference in the life of the Christian. Kingdom values should be reflected in the attitudes and actions of Christians as they live and work in the world. And this difference, these values, should impact the way Christians invest in every relationship they enter.[1]

Ladd's point underscores one of two theological assumptions that form the foundation for the thesis presented in this essay. The presence of the kingdom, the acknowledgment of and commitment to the lordship of Jesus Christ and the power of the Spirit at work in us, now empowers Christians today to make a difference in the marketplaces of this world in which God has placed them. We have the power and thus the responsibility to make a difference. Within the context of organizational life in the marketplace, this empowerment, I believe, can be applied most effectively to the leadership relationship. The *personal investment* in this relationship is the subject of this essay.

The second theological, or perhaps strategic, assumption upon which this essay is based is that *the most effective way to change the culture of an organization in today's society is to change the leadership*. It does not take much study of organizational life and culture to find examples of destructive systems at work in contemporary organizations—systems that dehumanize people, misuse the environment, and contribute to the secularization of society. The potential dangers of organizational life are acknowledged here without debate. The question remains, however: How does one initiate social change in organizational life today? How does one change the system? Do we attack the system, strike, picket, boycott, etc.? Or do we change the people who shape and direct the organization? My assumption is that lasting change in the system is accomplished by changing the people who reinforce the culture and shape the organization.

Edgar Schein, professor at MIT's Sloan School of Management, argues that organizational planning and change are constrained by the culture of the organization—the basic assumptions and beliefs that are shared by members and operate unconsciously. Schein sees the creation, management, and change of the culture as the one thing of unique importance that leaders do.[2] Long-term change within organizations in society today is best accomplished by addressing the values and behaviors of those individual leaders whose decisions, policies, and actions will shape future organizational culture. Lasting change, then, is most effectively accomplished by attempting to transform the leader first.

The thesis of this essay is that *effective leadership is empowering leadership, and empowering leadership is an expression of Christian ministry.* Leadership that nurtures and develops people, exercised intentionally by a leader who follows Christ, is ministry. The personal investment of a leader in a follower, a ministry of nurture and caring, seeks to increase the maturity of the follower as one loved by God.[3]

Ray Anderson examines this same concept in relationship to the Christian organization when he writes,

> The character of a Christian organization is rooted in its quality of life as measured by the love of God in Christ displayed in the basic human and personal relations that constitute the daily life of the organization as a community.[4]

I believe that Professor Anderson's statement can be applied equally to the secular organization in the marketplace when Christian leaders seek to impact the character or culture of the organization. The *Christian* character or culture of *any* organization "is rooted in its quality of life as measured by the love of God in Christ displayed in the basic human and personal relations that constitute the daily life of the organization as a community."

A friend of mine, a consultant to corporate leaders, once said, "I spend all my time with presidents and senior management. God has called me to be a minister to multinational corporations: *train* me! The church doesn't respect my gifts or my calling. They put me out with the tax collectors and sinners."

My friend is a minister of leadership looking for affirmation. Do we have anything to offer him?

WHAT IS LEADERSHIP?

Let's start by defining terms. What *is* leadership? According to current literature, leadership is "the process of influencing the activities of an individual or a group in efforts toward goal achievement in a given situation."[5] Given a specific situation and desired outcome, leadership is the process of influencing others, seeking to direct their behavior or modify their values or way of thinking.[6]

Max DePree, chairman of Herman Miller, Inc., sums up this process by its first and last responsibilities: "The first responsibility of a leader is to define reality. The last is to say thank you."[7] Between these two poles lie three other key responsibilities of leadership: reinforcing the culture or the values of the organization,[8] contextualizing the contribution of the members of the organization,[9] and providing the resources that make the members' contribution possible.[10]

Leadership, then, is a relationship between two persons engaged in a process of influence in which the leader seeks to: articulate the vision and mission of the organization for the follower; shape and reinforce the culture, values, or beliefs of the organization, as well as the character of people within the organization; contextualize the follower's contribution to the organization, showing how it fits and why it is important to the mission; provide the resources and the power to make the contribution possible; express thanks on behalf of the organization, affirming the follower's value as a member and conveying appreciation for the follower's contribution. This is the essence of the leadership relationship.

In an organizational setting the leadership relationship has *meaning* only as it has *purpose*.[11] Normally, that purpose is the accomplishment of specific organizational tasks: namely, the mission and objectives of the organization. James MacGregor Burns, however, in his Pulitzer-Prize-winning book *Leadership,* argues that there are at least two different purposes to leadership, which he labels *transactional* and *transforming*.[12] In *transactional leadership* the leader and the follower exchange something, both parties gaining something from the influence being exercised by the leader. Followers perceive that it is to their advantage to undertake the requested action, and leaders set up the request in a manner designed to accomplish a specific action for which they are responsible. This is a contractual arrangement—a relationship between two persons to accomplish a specific task, in which both parties have their personal needs met.[13]

Burns expects more out of leaders, though. He argues that great leadership is *transforming leadership,* by which he means a relationship in which the leader and the follower grow in the process. The follower is lifted to a higher plane of maturity or morality. It is not enough to have a contractual exchange to accomplish the task. Burns wants the leader to influence the values, the aspirations, the beliefs, the world view of the follower—to help the follower grow as a human being as well as to accomplish the task.

I believe that for Christians, leadership must always seek to be transforming, because even as we provide exchange in order to accomplish the task in the organizational setting, our calling as ministers of Christ demands that we seek to enrich the values, beliefs, hopes, and world view of those with whom we have been placed in relationship.[14] If we are influencing others with transforming leadership, those we seek to lead should understand that God loves them—that they have worth.[15] They should understand that we care for them, valuing them as persons as well as employees.[16] They should believe in themselves, and they should believe that their contribution to the organization is valued.[17] All of this they should understand because they have encountered us in the leadership relationship. Christian faith consistently applied should make a difference in the way leadership is exercised. Leadership emerging from theology makes a personal investment in the people for whose success the leader is responsible. It disciples, in that it seeks the growth and development of the maturity of the follower.

An animated video entitled *Try Again . . . and Succeed* helps illustrate this kind of leadership. High up on the crags of a mountaintop a scruffy little eaglet peers over the edge of its nest, trying to get up the courage to fly. A full-grown eagle descends to the nest and encourages the eaglet to try. The little bird takes one terror-filled look over the edge at the ground far below and scurries to the back of the nest, hiding under its wings. Patiently but sternly the eagle marches the eaglet out to the edge of the cliff and demonstrates how to use its wings, encouraging the little one to take the risk. The eaglet puffs up its tiny chest and jumps off the cliff, wings flapping wildly, scattering baby fluff and feathers.

As the baby bird plummets to the ground completely out of control, plunging toward certain doom, the eagle above swoops down and scoops up the little bird on its back, reassuring it and modeling how to use its wings. After depositing the eaglet safely on the cliff again, the eagle encourages it to try once more.

Again the eaglet awkwardly jumps off the edge, wings flapping wildly, scattering baby fluff and feathers. Again the eaglet plunges to the ground. But then it begins to use its wings to slow its fall and, finally, begin to fly—at first recklessly, like a new teenage driver, and then more regally, as befitting an eagle.

As the little eagle stretches its wings and climbs into the sky, it evolves into a full-grown eagle, gracefully gliding over the mountaintops, diving into the valleys, and soaring up again into the heights. Then it spots a fluffy little eaglet peering over the edge of its nest, trying to get up the courage to test its wings. In the final picture the newly-grown eagle swoops down beside the little eaglet and begins to encourage it as it was encouraged.[18]

Transforming leadership is believing in the potential of a person to be more than what you see today. This is what the Apostle Paul spoke of—seeing each person mature in Christ and coaching the person on how to live up to that maturity.[19] Transforming leadership is believing in the potential of a person to be more than what you see today, and committing yourself to work toward the development of that person.

EMPOWERMENT

Current leadership research has taken this concept of transforming leadership and applied it to organizational life today, describing it as the process of *empowerment*: empowering others in their organizational setting. W. Warner

Burke, a leading management researcher at Columbia University, argues that effective leadership in organizations involves empowering the individual to take ownership for accomplishing the task or living the values.[20] Transforming leadership raises the sights, beliefs, and expectations of individuals. Empowering leadership gives them the authority and the responsibility to live at these higher levels of life and performance—in short, the power to make a difference.

One other component of leadership and empowerment needs to be noted here: *Leadership is perceived from the perspective of the follower.*[21] It does not matter what type of leader I think I am; I am a leader only if someone chooses to follow me. I can influence only if someone *accepts* my influence, participates in the exchange provided, accedes to the vision offered. And it is the follower who determines whether my leadership is transactional or transforming.

It is often assumed that a person becomes a leader when appointed to a position of leadership. That is true only if someone decides to follow. It is the follower's perception that makes the leading a reality. `

LEADERSHIP STYLE

Leadership style is the pattern of leader behavior, words, and actions, as perceived by the follower.[22] Research by Hersey and Blanchard has identified four basic styles or patterns of leadership:[23]

(1) Autocratic or Directive Leadership. Hersey and Blanchard label this *Telling.* Here the leader is very directive about what to do and how to do it. The leader makes all decisions and tells the followers what to do and what is best.

(2) Consultative or Persuading Leadership. This is called *Selling.* Here the leader is more interactive with followers about what needs to be done and how to do it. The leader may consult with followers before making the decision, but then seeks to persuade them to follow the leader's direction.

(3) Participative or Coaching Leadership. This is probably the most popular style in the current management bestsellers. The leader remains highly interactive with followers but lets them participate in determining what needs to be done and how to do it. Followers carry out the assignment while the leader walks alongside coaching.[24] Leader and followers together make the decisions about what needs to be done.

(4) Empowered or Delegating Leadership. Here the leader lets the followers determine what needs to be done and how, in order to achieve the agreed-upon objective. Within the context of the objective or mission, the followers make the decisions that impact their actions. The leader delegates to the followers both the authority and the responsibility to complete the assignment.

An important truth coming out of current research like this is that leadership involves a range of styles related to decision-making.[25] Leadership style is a continuum, measuring the relative involvement of leader and follower in making decisions. Effective leaders adapt their style to the decision at hand and to the followers with whom they are working. For example, a crisis situation may require an immediate decision: "The building is on fire: *Get out.*" An autocratic, directive style of leadership is the only appropriate one. At the other extreme, when the firefighters come there is no need to tell them what to do—just get out of their way. An empowered, delegating style of leadership is the only appropriate one when "followers" have more experience and skills to complete the task than "leaders." Effective leaders are able to range across the continuum of leadership styles, being directive when necessary; consultative, participative, or delegative when appropriate. This brings us to the basic empowering model for leadership.

We noted that leadership is established through the perceptions of the follower. Hersey and Blanchard take this a step further, arguing that effective leadership *style* is determined by the followers. Based on the four common styles they developed the Situational Leadership Model. Their research has found that the most effective type of leadership style is directly related to the maturity of the follower at that time and place.[26] Maturity or readiness is defined as willingness to take responsibility for the job and ability to complete the task involved—or *confidence* and *competence*. They identify four levels of maturity corresponding with the four styles of leadership.

With this model the potential leader looks at the follower in a given situation and determines the best leadership style for this person in this situation. A directive style is most effective with persons whose competence and confidence are low—for example, a new employee, an experienced employee taking on a new assignment, or a problem employee. A consultative style is most effective with persons who lack competence, yet are willing to accept responsibility to learn and complete the job. A participative style is important to persons who know how to do the job but feel a little insecure about running alone. The delegative, empowered style is for those who know how to complete the task and accept ownership for it. The leader needs to get out of their way.

The critical principle of this model is not that there are four different styles, nor that the effective manager should be able to lead with all four styles—although both are true. The key principle here for the selection of leadership style is that empowering leadership seeks to move people up the maturity scale, to *increase* their competence and their confidence. The goal in selecting a leadership style is the growth of the people being led, through helping them mature. To use Burns' term, the follower's increasing maturation is the process of transforming leadership. Ideally, the leader wants everyone for whom he or she is responsible to develop into the highest level of job maturity, an empowered state out of which they can become empowering leaders, transforming others.

If the leader operates within only one style that is personally comfortable, it could indicate effectiveness with one maturity level of followers but a weakness in the ability to lift them up to a new level of maturity. Empowering leadership is continually seeking to increase the followers' maturity level. It seeks to *develop* the people for whose success the leader is responsible. This is important, because many leaders tend to stick to the one style they are most comfortable with. This pattern might be effective with one type of follower, but it does not develop people. To be a transforming leader who empowers people requires the ability to lead them into the next level of maturity.

Therefore, the choice of leadership style is determined by (a) the maturity of the follower—the leaders meets them where they are; and (b) the leader's objective of increasing maturity to an empowered level—the leader sees in the followers the potential to grow and is committed to leading them in that growth, adapting leadership styles as necessary along the way. This is ministry—the process of believing in people and investing oneself in their growth before God. It is the process modeled by Jesus and the task of ministry to which we are called.[27]

The story of Gideon in Judges 6—7 illustrates this empowering process as God develops Gideon into a leader of his people. Compare these two statements:

"But LORD," Gideon asked, "how can I save Israel? My clan is the weakest in Manassah, and I am the least in my family."(6:15)

"Watch me," [Gideon] told [his soldiers]. "Follow my lead. When I get to the edge of the camp, do exactly as I do."(7:17)

Gideon had been transformed from a fearful youth hiding in a winepress into a confident commander of troops. What made the difference? God engaged Gideon as he was, saw in him the potential to be the warrior Israel needed, and led him from insecurity to confidence.

The relationship between God and Gideon follows the same stages of development in leadership style as set forth in the empowering model:

Stage I. God finds Gideon hiding in a winepress, threshing the wheat inside the cramped space, because he is afraid of the Midianites. The angel of the Lord says to Gideon, "The LORD is with you, mighty warrior" (6:12). Gideon sees himself as weak and fearful, but God already sees him in his full potential as a mighty warrior of Israel and tells him, "Go in the strength you have and save Israel out of Midian's hand" (6:14). Gideon's response of protesting his own weakness indicates that he is still at stage one on the maturity scale. God is very directive with him, using specific commands and telling him precisely what to do in offering a sacrifice: "Take the meat and the unleavened bread, place them on this rock, and pour out the broth" (6:20). God then consumes the meat and bread in fire to demonstrate his presence and power, and in this interchange deals with Gideon in the second stage of maturity development, what Hersey and Blanchard call the *telling* or *consultative* stage.

Stage II. Through the sacrifice God patiently demonstrates that he is with Gideon, to raise Gideon's confidence. Then he gives very explicit instructions again:

> Tear down your father's altar to Baal and cut down Asherah's pole beside it. Then build a proper kind of altar to the LORD your God on the top of this height. Using the wood of the Asherah pole that you cut down, offer the second bull as a burnt offering. (6:25-26)

Again God is very directive, but this time he allows personal interaction to teach Gideon and raise his confidence in his ability to do what needs to be done, since God is with him.

Stage III. Participation, the third level of maturity, is illustrated by the Spirit of the Lord coming upon Gideon, so that Gideon leads out and summons the men of Manasseh to arms (6:34). Gideon is now acting, leading out, but God is still visibly present with him, participating alongside as it were, in the power of his Spirit. But even at this stage Gideon still needs his confidence bolstered. Here he tests the reality of God's presence with him twice through the fleece. Gideon is now leading the troops, but God is still patiently coaching him and encouraging him with his presence.

Stage IV. God decides Gideon is finally ready and sends him out to battle. Gideon rounds up thirty thousand men to fight the Midianites. God whittles this number down to three hundred and turns Gideon loose. From this point on Gideon leads out like a confident warrior. He believes that God has empowered him to act and he does so in confidence—a far cry from the frightened youth in the winepress. "Get up!" he tells his band of soldiers. "The LORD has given the Midianite camp into your hands" (7:15). He implements his battle plan with authority and tells his troops, "Watch me. Follow my lead . . . do exactly as I do" (7:17). Gideon leads out, an empowered warrior with just three hundred men, and defeats the Midianites.

God's relationship with Gideon illustrates the four stages of the empowering model for leadership development. All four of the Hersey-Blanchard styles were necessary as Gideon was developed from a youth in

hiding to a confident warrior, leading his troops as an empowered commander. John Gardner sums up this process when he says: "It is not
uncommon that inside a mediocre performer is an excellent performer
awaiting liberation."[28]

Empowering leadership accepts followers where they are but sees in
them the potential to grow in maturity. It adapts leadership style in order to
transform their ability to do the task, their confidence in accepting ownership of the task, and their perceptions of themselves. The goal of empowering leadership is to help every follower grow into an empowered leader
who will in turn exercise this kind of leadership with each person for whom
he or she is responsible.

I now return to my friend, the "minister to multinational corporations."
He is still out there in the marketplace. He still lives in the middle of his
organization, but he owns his ministry and his work. Over the years he has
had an impact on individuals and corporations because he cares for people;
his commitment to God is evident in his leadership. A multinational
corporation revised its advertising campaign to a new level of maturity
because he cared for the chairman. Today he runs leadership networking
groups for CEOs, investing his life in the lives of these corporate leaders,
providing support groups that empower growth in the individuals who can
and will shape the future of the marketplace. To the corporate world, he is
an effective management consultant. From his own perspective, he is a
minister of Jesus Christ, engaged in the marketplace, placed in a position of
leadership, and called to the ministry of leadership.

Leadership is the process of empowering people to live and work as
empowered people who need minimal direction and are minimally dependent upon our support. It is the process of empowering people to be mature
followers, competent to do the job, and confident in their ability. It is the
process of empowering people to utilize the gifts that God has given them;
to have vision, purpose, and meaning in their lives and work; to make a
difference. In short, empowering leadership is the process of empowering
people to become empowering leaders — men and women who will shape
their organizations and make a difference in the marketplaces of the world.

NOTES

1. George Eldon Ladd, *The Gospel of the Kingdom* (Grand Rapids: Eerdmans, 1959),
p. 78.

2. Edgar H. Schein, *Organizational Culture and Leadership* (San Francisco: Jossey-
Bass, 1987), p. 2.

3. Eph. 6:7, Col. 3:23, 1 Pt. 4:8-11, Eph. 4:11-13.

4. Ray S. Anderson, *Minding God's Business* (Grand Rapids: Eerdmans, 1986), p.
106.

5. Paul Hersey & Kenneth H. Blanchard, *Management of Organizational Behavior,* 5th
ed. (Englewood Cliffs, NJ: Prentice-Hall, 1988), p. 86.

6. See also Eric H. Neilsen, "Empowerment Strategies: Balancing Authority and Responsibility," in *Executive Power,* ed. Suresh Srivastva (San Francisco: Jossey-Bass, 1986), p. 84.

7. Max DePree, *Leadership Is an Art* (Lansing: Michigan State Univ. Press, 1987), p. 11.

8. Schein, *Organizational Culture,* p. 2.

9. John W. Gardner, *The Tasks of Leadership* (Leadership Papers/2, Independent Sector, 1986), p. 10.

10. W. Warner Burke, "Leadership as Empowering Others," in *Executive Power,* p. 51.

11. Gary Yukl, *Leadership in Organizations* (Englewood Cliffs, NJ: Prentice-Hall, 1981), p. 5; James MacGregor Burns, *Leadership* (New York: Harper & Row, 1978), p. 251.

12. Burns, *Leadership,* p. 4.

13. See also John W. Gardner, *The Task of Motivating* (Leadership Papers/9, Independent Sector, 1988), p. 4.

14. Eph. 4:11-13, Col. 1:28-29.

15. Gn. 1:26-28; Jn. 13:3-5.

16. Rom. 12:10, Phil. 2:3.

17. Lk. 10:7, Rom. 12:3-8, 1 Tm. 5:18.

18. Warren Schmidt, "Try Again . . . and Succeed," in *Parables for the Present* (Gospel Films, 1980).

19. Eph. 4:1, Col. 1:10.

20. Burke, "Empowering Others," pp. 68-69.

21. Abraham Zaleznik, *The Managerial Mystique* (New York: Harper & Row, 1989), p. 18. See also Yukl, *Organizations,* p. 10; John W. Gardner, *The Heart of the Matter: Leader-Constituent Interaction* (Leadership Papers/3, Independent Sector, 1986), p. 6.

22. Hersey & Blanchard, *Organizational Behavior,* p. 146.

23. Ibid., pp. 173-80.

24. Thomas Peters and Nancy Austin, *A Passion for Excellence* (New York: Random House, 1985), pp. 354-60.

25. Yukl, *Organizations,* p. 205.

26. Hersey & Blanchard, *Organizational Behavior,* pp. 174-80.

27. Col. 4:5-6.

28. Gardner, *The Task of Motivating,* p. 10.

PART III

✠

A Theology of Family Ministry

15

DENNIS B. GUERNSEY

✢

Family Ministry and a Theology
of the Family: A Personal Journey

T HE TASKS I HAVE set for myself in this chapter are both personal and
theological. The personal task involves my journey toward a philosophy of the church's ministry to its families. The theological task involves a
discussion of certain of my theological reflections on the family. Addi-
tionally, I would like to conclude with a discussion about some practical
implications. As for the journey, my colleague Ray Anderson has been an
integral partner on the way. He has influenced me personally as the pastor,
friend, and "older brother" that he is. It is my pleasure to honor him with
these reflections.

HISTORICAL DEVELOPMENT

In the late 1970s Ray Anderson and I decided to organize and team teach a
new course at Fuller Theological Seminary entitled "Theology of the
Family." Our first step was to commission one of Ray's doctoral students to
do a bibliographic search of the literature, expecting to find a substantial
amount in this field. To our chagrin the student returned with a disappoin-
tingly short list of citations. We concluded that our research was missing
something.

Quite by accident, the next day I was standing in a bank line immediately
in front of one of my faculty colleagues. Dr. Colin Brown is known for his
thorough awareness of the literature in his field. I put our dilemma to him:
Where could we find the key material dealing with a theology of the family?
Our British friend furrowed his brow as he contemplated the issue and then
replied, "By jove, I think there's a massive gap." Our worst fears were
realized. We weren't missing the material; the material itself was missing.

Subsequent to that conversation, we decided that our only recourse was
to begin to think and write about the theological issues regarding the

218

family as if we were "first generation" theologians. For Ray, the task seemed reasonable. For me, the task seemed overwhelming.

As our scholarly base we identified less than six hundred pages of substantive literature regarding the family—two hundred of them from one source, Karl Barth's *Church Dogmatics*.[1] Our own contribution to the field came several years later as *On Being Family: A Social Theology of the Family*.[2] The dilemma we faced in constructing a theology of the family was common to all thinking about this field. Other categories of theology, such as soteriology, ecclesiology, or theological anthropology, have a deep and rich history of theological reflection. Much is to be gained from mining the depths of the thinking of those who have gone before. Such is not the case, however, in theology of the family.

This area of a theology of the family is now emerging in much the same way as have other areas of theology.[3] Just as the apostles of the first-century church were practitioners, so those who were among the first to struggle with the problems of the family from a biblical and theological perspective were practitioners in this field—such as psychologists James Dobson and Bruce Narramore, for example. As we searched for what the Bible teaches regarding the family, we were attempting to scratch the church where it was itching. The explosion of popular Christian literature on the family in the last twenty years is the natural consequence.

The early church leaders were preoccupied with doing ministry before they were compelled by the Holy Spirit to write the documents that were later collected as the New Testament canon. Last of all, but still necessary, came the formal theologies necessary to systematize and organize the church's thinking regarding the New Testament, which are still emerging. Those who have the greatest need have the most to gain from a particular theology, and the ones in greatest need are those active in the ministry area relevant to that theology.

A proposition thus emerges, perhaps controversial, but central to my own thinking: *Ministry necessarily precedes theology but is eventually monitored and disciplined by that theology.*

In terms of my own thinking about family ministry and a theology of the family, a second proposition comes into play: *The epistemological assumptions of a theology of the family are most congruent with those of the social and behavioral sciences.* This is contrast with the epistemological assumptions of traditional systematic and biblical theology, philosophy, and literary analysis. For family theology, the epistemological assumptions of General Systems Theory and of social ecology come to mind.[4] In *On Being Family*, I have suggested four key underlying assumptions.[5]

The first assumption is that thinking about the family is deliberately *non-Cartesian* rather than Cartesian. In his book about the influence of General Systems Theory upon the so-called hard sciences, Fritjof Capra describes the failure of a Newtonian understanding of reality and its dependence upon the philosophy of Descartes.[6] In order to explain phenomena at the sub-atomic level, scientists in the field of quantum physics were forced to abandon their previously held reductionistic explanations of reality. Since Descartes, science had attempted to reduce the world to its progressively smaller and more "accurate" properties—the Cartesian approach. The scientists studying subatomic particles began to understand the nature of the reality they were observing only when they began to think in terms of relationships rather than things.

My application of Capra's argument to the family is that you cannot understand the family if you believe it is simply a collection of individual persons and that in understanding, ministering to, or treating individuals you are by extension treating the whole. That is the Cartesian trap. Rather, a non-Cartesian approach assumes that the whole is greater than the sum of its parts.

The second assumption is that an understanding of causality must be *systemic* rather than linear. Traditionally, thinking about the family has been essentially hierarchical and linear. Thus if you want to change the family, you begin at the "top" with the father, assuming that if the father changes so will the rest of the people in the household. A child or an adolescent is always an "effect" and never a "cause." "Chain of command" thinking about the family is necessarily linear.

In contrast, systemic thinking about causality embraces the principle of feedback. Through the process of feedback, what is on the one hand a cause can simultaneously be an effect. Consequently, in terms of the family, an adolescent can be the cause of a parent's low self-esteem as much as vice versa. This assumption leads to an emphasis upon patterns of relationships rather than upon "ultimate" causes.

The third assumption is that thinking about the family must be primarily *relationalistic* rather than reductionistic. The theologian H. Richard Niebuhr refers to this phenomenon as a person's "fitting" behavior. It is the concept that persons are "responsible" to accept their membership in a community (or social system) in such a way as to contribute to the benefit and health of that community.[7] In Christian terms, it is that self-love is hurtful and damaging if it is not balanced by a love for God and a love of neighbor.

The fourth and last assumption is that family systems are essentially *dynamic* rather than static. Process rather than structure is the appropriate focus of attention in a theology of the family. People in their significant relationships are moving, creating, active beings. Life can't be represented on an organizational chart. Adaptation and flexibility are as important as structure and permanence. Change is normal rather than aberrant.[8]

It logically follows that those who are most aware of both systemic and ecological assumptions, if only subconsciously, will be most able to think outside the lines in terms of family ministry and a theology of the family. A cursory evaluation of the literature in the field to date bears out this fact. It is the practitioners, especially the social and behavioral scientists, who are on the cutting edge of both family ministry and a theology of the family.

FAMILY MINISTRY DEFINED

These assumptions form a context for the definition of family ministry. I define the concept as "the church's enabling of the people of God to relate to one another as if they are family, especially if they are." This definition represents a movement away from a static, programmatic understanding to a more dynamic and relational one.

Implicit in this definition is an assumption that in New Testament terms, "family" is primarily a verb rather than a noun. The infinitve form would be "to family" one another. The focus is upon how we as the people of God relate to one another, in contrast to who we are when we relate.

This idea of family has emerged from my personal observation and experience. It first occurred to me when I was participating in the White House Conference on the Family in 1979/80. The goals of the Conference were never met because the participants could not agree upon a definition of the family. Participants from the conservative camp insisted upon a traditional definition equating family with a unit of mother, father, and children — the traditional nuclear family or household. In contrast, participants from the non-traditional camp insisted upon a freewheeling definition almost without boundaries — family was whatever you decided it to be. The two sides were never able to get together, and the noble purposes of the conference were short-circuited.

As I sat in the auditorium of the Executive Office Building listening to the final briefing for religious leaders, it occurred to me that the tension between the two camps could be mediated if the word *family* were thought of as a verb rather than a noun. My systems orientation pushed me to think in terms of the process rather than the content. The imperatives of the Great Commandments, "you shall love your God" and "you shall love your neighbor as yourself," were lost in the debate and conflict about the definition of the family as a noun. In contrast, the Great Commandments of the New Testament are relational and process-oriented concepts. My experiences since that time have only reinforced my interpretation.

A second set of observations and experiences is more cumulative, occurring over a period of years as I have moved about the country pursuing my interest in family ministry. It is my observation that all too often, the practitioners in the church responsible for family ministries tend to focus upon programs rather than process. Successful family ministry is determined by the number of programs the church has implemented in any given year. Thus, in a tangible sense, family ministry is reduced to showing

a film series on Sunday night. It involves organizing Sunday school classes
to deal with family themes such as marriage and parenting.

Though useful and congruent with the idea of family as a noun, a
programmatic approach to family ministry is necessarily flawed: It tends to
perpetuate a static, Victorian ideal of the family. In the crucible of the late
twentieth century the Victorian ideal of mother at home, father as the sole
supporter of the family, and two or more children applies to less than fifteen
percent of the population. Too many people fall outside this definition.
They are the widows, orphans, strangers, and sojourners of the biblical
story as applied to today.

If "family" is primarily a verb, however, all that the church teaches
regarding relationships is legitimately family ministry. Family ministry
becomes the ecclesiastical custodian of relational theology. The mystery of
the people of God as the family of God is integrated into what the church is
about as a whole.

Though often necessarily programmatic, family ministry according to
my definition represents a philosophy of ministry as well as a strategy for
achieving that ministry. The nurture and succor of the people of God one to
another and outward to still others are the legitimate goals of family
ministry, whatever forms the structures take.

THEOLOGICAL FOUNDATIONS

I suggested above that although theology emerges out of ministry, its
ultimate purpose is to organize and discipline ministry. What follows are
five theological principles that seem to me to be central in the formation of
the family.[9]

(1) Human persons are created in the image of God and are of infinite value. Thus
whatever defaces or destroys that image—whether person, laws, or institutions—is not in the will of God and is to be resisted or changed.[10]
According to this principle, family ministry and theology must have an
ethical center. The heart of a theology of the family comes out of an
anthropology that is theologically centered in the *imago Dei*. We are created
in the image of God and have infinite value. Therefore, racism, sexism,
classism, etc. are antithetical to an ethically centered family theology.

*(2) Human persons are created as relational beings to exist in cohumanity as male
and female, male or female.* "God created man in his image, male and female
created he them" (Gn. 1:27). In addition to what has been written about this
principle, I would add an emphasis upon the conjunction *and*. The conjunction is not merely a word linking two nouns; it is pregnant with meaning.
The "and" is the nexus of family ministry. A theology of the family is the
simple but profound exegesis of that conjunction.[11]

A corollary to this principle, if not a logical extension of it, is that both
women and men are equally gifted and fitted by God to minister within the

church and to the world. Most would agree that in general, women are more sensitive to relationships.[12] Therefore, whatever "family" means, those who are most sensitive to relationships—that is, women—become central to the mission of the church. Perhaps it is the chauvinism in the church that keeps and perpetuates the noun forms of the family, the same chauvinism that limits women from freely expressing their gifts in ministry.

(3) The church as the body of Christ is the real presence of the incarnate Christ in the world. The body of Christ is more than a metaphor; it is a mystery. The Apostle Paul wrote, "Now you are Christ's body, and individually members of it" (1 Cor. 12:27). Jesus Christ is alive in the world today not in some ethereal, new-age sense of the term, but in the mystery of the church as the people of God, a people who live in relationship with one another as family and with those in the world around them. Jesus Christ is alive today because we are here. The only Christ some people will ever touch will be in their contact with our hands, our compassion, our ministries, our lives.

A parallel example of this principle occurs in the social psychology of intimate psychosocial networks.[13] Suffice it to say that the secular literature strongly suggests that something important happens when human persons create and maintain intimate, caring relationships with one another. Both help and healing take place. If this is true in human relationships in general, how much more so is it true when the people of God become family to one another?

Unfortunately, in the church's ministry, much of the time when we gather together as the people of God we create a portrait more bizarre than beautiful. In making the body of Christ a vacuous metaphor we empty the image of its meaning and rob ourselves of a powerful truth.

In contrast, when we live together as the body of Christ to one another we experience the vitality of the living Christ. The New Testament emphasis upon family went far beyond the maintenance of the nuclear family—or of the extended family, for that matter. The emphasis was intended to make the body of Christ relevant to real people. The people of God as the family of God were to be the ultimate litmus test for the visage of Christ in the real world. If it is going to be real, Christianity must work in the most intimate of relationships: between husband and wife, parent and child, sibling and sibling, friend and friend, believer and believer, believer and unbeliever. As the people of God we paint a family portrait as we demonstrate the real presence of Christ in the world through our love for one another.

(4) The church is primarily the people of God, and secondarily the place they gather. This idea strikes terror in the heart of every church finance committee—it takes money to pay utility bills, salaries, and "keep the place running." It is also a fact that the people of God both need and want a place to gather. My suggestion has more to do with emphasis.

Wherever the people of God are, the church exists. Thus it is impossible by definition to sustain an incarnational ministry as the body of Christ if the emphasis is disproportionately placed upon where the people of God gather for a few hours per week. If the church is only the *place,* we will subsequently equate family ministry with content, presented on a Sunday morning to people seated in metal folding chairs neatly arranged in rows, talking *about* family rather than *becoming* family to one another.

(5) *Family ministry takes place most naturally wherever and whenever people feel most natural.* Ask yourself how likely you are to be the "real" you when you are sitting in a molded plastic chair in the church basement at ten o'clock on a Sunday morning. It's my belief that there is something innately artificial about how we are when we come to church as it is commonly constituted. Church too easily becomes the place where we dress ourselves up in our finery and present ourselves as having our act together. Rarely do we talk about our failures and our problems in such a context. If I feel like a failure with my teenage daughter, if she is being so disruptive that I am considering finding a place for her to live outside the home, it is almost impossible to raise these issues at church in the midst of a Sunday school study on the kings of Israel. The environment is too easily artificial, too easily manipulated.

I suggest that family ministry is most effective when the people of God come together as the family of God in more decentralized ways—around a kitchen table or a backyard barbecue. Accordingly, family ministry takes advantage of "natural events," such as family rituals and celebrations. We are more likely to deal with real life when we are safe and comfortable than when we are on stage and uncomfortable.

I also suggest that part of the creativity required in family ministry is taking the opportunity to influence the way the people of God and the family of God spend the hours of the week they are not at church. That is, family ministry is particularly relevant to the rest of the week, between Sundays.

CONCLUSION

In an emerging family ministry and a theology of the family, such a developmental approach suggests that a skilled pastor from Seattle, an experienced marriage and family therapist or social worker from Butte, or an astute psychologist from Atlanta do not need permission from a textbook or a systematic theology to tell them what to do in their ministry to the family. Their instincts are probably exquisite.

We (especially the practitioners) have too often turned the process upside down. We search in vain for theological categories that will direct us or at least free us to do the work of ministry. Consequently, the conduct of a ministry to families becomes so narrow and truncated that we get caught in methodological boxes. This is not the way it should work. In my opinion, it is not the way of the Holy Spirit.

However uncomfortable, it is a great privilege to be in the first generation of God's people who seriously consider a ministry task and the theological issues that flow from it. It is also a great responsibility to encode family ministry and theology so that future generations will have a basis for ministry and a means of evaluating that ministry in light of the historical church doctrines. Someone has to dream dreams: It might as well be us.

NOTES

1. Cf. Karl Barth, *Church Dogmatics,* ed. G. W. Bromiley and T. F. Torrance (Edinburgh: T. & T. Clark, 1969), III/1.
2. Cf. Ray S. Anderson and Dennis B. Guernsey, *On Being Family: A Social Theology of the Family* (Grand Rapids: Eerdmans, 1985).
3. My switch to the first person singular signals my intention not to saddle Dr. Anderson with my conclusions. He is released from the burden.
4. Cf. L. von Bertalanffy, *General Systems Theory* (New York: George Braziller, 1968); William Buckley, *Sociology and Modern Systems Theory* (Englewood Cliffs, NJ: Prentice-Hall, 1967); David Kantor and William Lehr, *Inside the Family: Toward a Theory of Family Process* (San Francisco: Jossey-Bass, 1975); Urie Bronfenbrenner, *The Ecology of Human Development* (Cambridge: Harvard Univ. Press, 1979); Dennis B. Guernsey, *A New Design for Family Ministry* (Elgin, IL: David C. Cook, 1982).
5. Cf. ch. 1 of *On Being Family,* written by D. Guernsey.
6. Cf. Fritjof Capra, *The Turning Point* (New York: Bantam Books, 1983).
7. Cf. H. Richard Niebuhr, *The Responsible Self* (New York: Harper & Row, 1953); cf. also Stanley Hauerwas, *A Community of Character: Toward a Constructive Christian Social Ethic* (Notre Dame: Univ. of Notre Dame Press, 1981).
8. For an excellent discussion of this idea cf. P. Watzlawick, J. Weakland, and R. Fisch, *Change: Principles of Problem Formation and Problem Resolution* (New York: Norton, 1974); and P. Watzlawick, *The Language of Change* (New York: Basic Books, 1978).
9. It is at this point that Ray Anderson's theology has most influenced me, particularly his book *On Being Human* (Grand Rapids: Eerdmans, 1982).
10. For this principle and the one that follows I am indebted to the writings of Karl Barth regarding human persons as a divine prototype (i.e. the *imago Dei*) and human persons created as male and female in differentiated unity. Cf. *Church Dogmatics,* III/1, pp. 183-191.
11. The systems implications of the principle are further discussed in ch. 6 of my book *A New Design for Family Ministry.*
12. For an excellent discussion of the unique point of view women bring to society, see Carol Gilligan, *In a Different Voice: Psychological Theory and Women's Development* (Cambridge: Harvard Univ. Press, 1982).
13. Cf. Urie Rueveni, *Networking Families in Crises* (New York: Human Sciences Press, 1979).

16

DAVID E. GARLAND
DIANA R. GARLAND

✛

The Family: Biblical and Theological Perspectives

PROFESSOR RAY ANDERSON raises the question whether a theology of the family ultimately comes to grief over the teaching of Jesus. He asks: "In the final analysis are our own commitments to family life and to Christian discipleship irreconcilable?" (Anderson & Guernsey 1985:139). After all, Jesus did not say, "Go ye into all the world and enrich family life." He never gave instructions on how to make family time more meaningful. In fact, Jesus (and the Bible) had little specifically to say about the family, and what he did say is troubling. Some of the statements recorded in the Synoptic Gospels leave the impression that Jesus had a rather jaundiced view of the family.

To sample only a few of Jesus' remarks, he once warned his disciples that his coming would bring not peace but a sword that would sunder even the most sacred of ties: son would be set against father, daughter against mother. The foe would be in one's own household. He then announced: "The one who loves father or mother, son or daughter more than me is not worthy of me" (Mt. 10:34-39; cp. Lk. 12:51-53). For an Oriental whose life was embedded in family, this would be an especially heavy cross to bear (Mt. 10:38). At another time, Jesus proclaimed to a throng of would-be disciples accompanying him: "If anyone comes to me and does not hate his own father and mother and wife and children and brothers and sisters, yes, and even his own life, he cannot be my disciple" (Lk. 14:26). The startling reference to "hate" is a Semitic overstatement that does not mean we are to despise our family. In this context it means "to love less" (cp. Gn. 29:30-31, Dt. 21:15-17, Mal. 1:2-3). Jesus takes for granted that all will love their families but requires his disciples to love God more.

Even if this statement about hating our family is understood to mean that we are not to put allegiance to family before allegiance to God, it hardly pictures Jesus as a family advocate. Apparently, many took Jesus at his word and left "house, wife, brothers, parents, and children," because Jesus promised these very ones that they would receive manifold more in this life and, in the age to come, eternal life (Lk. 18:29-30, Mt. 19:27-29, Mk. 10:28-30). When Jesus forbade divorce, the disciples responded that it might be best not to marry at all, to which Jesus replied that some will indeed make themselves eunuchs for the sake of the kingdom of heaven (Mt. 19:10-12). One could get the impression from this that a life without the encumbrance of a biological family might enable one to attain a higher spiritual plateau.

Jesus demanded absolute loyalty from his disciples; he did not allow one to return home to bid farewell to his family (Lk. 9:61-62). He told another, who wanted to postpone discipleship so that he could bury his father, to "leave the dead to bury the dead" (Mt. 8:21-22, Lk. 9:59-60). This counsel flies in the face of the command to honor one's parents and crosses swords with universal piety that places utmost importance on burying the dead, particularly one's own family member.

Was Ernest Renan right, then, in claiming that Jesus "cared little for the relations of kinship" and considered them only petty loyalties that hindered commitment to the greater cause of the kingdom (Renan 1897:97-98)? If this is a correct assessment of Jesus' attitude, why indeed attempt a theology of the family?

THE PLACE OF FAMILY IN JESUS' TEACHING

To understand Jesus' statements about the family, one must see them in light of his forceful proclamation of the kingdom of God. Jesus announced that the kingdom of God was dramatically breaking into the world (Mk. 1:14-15) and audaciously implied that something greater than Moses, David, Solomon, and the temple was here. This meant that the world and its values would be turned on their head, and the urgency of the situation called for a commitment surpassing even the bonds of kinship.

For those who heard Jesus, the family was the cornerstone of life; it was the center of all one's worldly goods, security, and hope. Malina notes: "In the first century Mediterranean world, marriage means the fusion of the honor of two families, undertaken with a view to political and/or economic considerations" (1981:117). This fact tended to make the biological family unit geared primarily toward gaining family advantage, and maintaining family honor the primary currency in a shame/honor society. For example, Joseph hoped to avoid shame by divorcing the pregnant Mary (Mt. 1:19). Jesus' mother and brothers resolutely sought to bring him back to his senses and compel him to return home out of concern for the family's honor (Mk. 3:21).

Two problems result from centering life in the family. First, the family can become inwardly directed and clannish in mindset. When dishonored, it wants to wreak vengeance (cp. Lk. 9:51-55). Family members may also seize every opportunity to increase the family's honor. This kind of sentiment can be seen in the mother of James and John, who requested that her sons be appointed something akin to Lord High Poobahs in Jesus' kingdom. She was expecting pork barrel politics as usual and wanted to ensure that benefits and honor would accrue to her family. This perspective tended to exclude doing good to others who could not reciprocate directly with benefits (see Lk. 14:12-14). Why do good to a Samaritan mugged on the Jericho road, since he is not a part of the family? Jesus' values turned this tribal attitude upside down with his story of the Samaritan who was more family to the beaten man than were his fellow Israelites (Lk. 10:25-37).

Second, to emphasize the family as the most important concern in life is to give ultimate importance to something that is not ultimate. Family relationships do not continue on in perpetuity; they are limited to this world. The marriage relationship, for example, lasts "till death do us part" (see Mk. 12:25ff., Rom. 7:2, 1 Cor. 7:39). To invest all of one's hopes in the family is, in the end, to make a bad investment. The kingdom of God, on the other hand, is eternal; and Jesus consistently insisted that our lives in the here and now are to be governed by the values of the life to come. This accords with Paul's view that because the time is "pressed together" ("grown short"), it is best for "those who have wives" to live "as though they had none" (1 Cor. 7:29). The reason is that the form of this world and its institutions are passing off the stage and will be replaced by something new and altogether different (1 Cor. 7:31). One must, therefore, seek first the kingdom of heaven.

Jesus sometimes made dramatic pronouncements to drive home the point that one's ultimate allegiance is owed only to God. This does not mean, however, that Jesus depreciated the significance of the family or the universal need for family relationships. (Cp. Mk. 7:9-13; Lk. 7:11-17, 12:13-14, 15:11-32. For a more thorough analysis of these difficult sayings of Jesus, see Garland 1990.) Jesus' goal was not to dissolve the family but to communicate the pressing nature of the hour. All else, even those things considered to be of utmost significance, including the family, paled in light of the importance of the inbreaking of the kingdom of God. If Jesus had chosen an institution of lesser importance to make his point, the impact of his message would have been weaker. For example, if he had said, "Leave the rest of the garden club to plant the roses and come follow me," or "Anyone who loves boss or work colleagues more than me is not worthy to be called my disciple," no one would have been surprised. Instead, he claimed that his calling to kingdom service superseded the family for the very reason that the family was so valued—not only to his listeners, but to Jesus as well.

FAMILY – A FULFILLMENT OF GOD'S PROMISE

Jesus did not undermine the importance of the family; he transformed it. First, he underlined the significance of family relationships. He then broke through the boundaries of the nuclear family to extend the promises of family living to all of God's children.

The significance of family relationships

Jesus' seemingly cavalier attitude toward family responsibilities shocked many of those who heard him; the sanctity he attached to family relationships shocked just as many, including his disciples. For example, Jesus affirmed marriage as a one-flesh union that could not be dissolved by divorce. To divorce is to presume to disjoin what God has joined together (Mk. 10:2-9). When the Corinthians were entertaining the idea of bailing out of family responsibilities by divorcing, presumably to enhance their spirituality, Paul recalled this teaching of the Lord (1 Cor. 7:10-11): a Christian is forbidden to initiate divorce. Jesus' teaching was not intended to be a club used against those already wounded in destructive marriages but a reminder that God's will intended the marriage bond to be permanent. Marriage is not simply a legal contract that can be dissolved by the courts, or in Jesus' day by a divorce certificate handed to the wife. More significantly, it is a spiritual covenant between two partners, sealed by God (see Mal. 2:14-16).

Although Jesus apparently was not married, many of those closest to him, who lived with him day in and day out, were. These members of the inner circle of disciples did not dismantle their family lives in response to anything Jesus said. According to Paul, the brothers of the Lord, Cephas, and other apostles had wives who accompanied them on their mission trips (1 Cor. 9:5). Peter may have traveled without his wife for a period of time during Jesus' ministry (see Mt. 19:27), but she later went with him (1 Cor. 9:5). Married couples figure prominently in those greeted by Paul in his letters as hosts of churches and servants of the Word, most notably Prisca and Aquila. Clearly, these earliest disciples did not understand commitment to Christ as subverting commitment to family.

Jesus also stressed the importance of filial responsibility when he condemned the practice of dedicating possessions to God so that they were forbidden to be used for parents (Mt. 15:2-6). Jesus reiterated God's command that children are to honor (by providing care for) their parents.

In the incident recorded in Mk. 3:31-34, Jesus may appear to have been less than scrupulous himself in honoring his own mother, however. When told that his mother and brothers were outside seeking him, he asked, "Who is my mother, and who are my brothers?" (cp. Mt. 12:46-50, Lk. 8:19-21). But this startling question was not a categorical repudiation of his own family. First, it must be remembered that this was not a friendly family reunion. Jesus' family had heard the word going around that he had lost his senses, and they had come to seize him with the purpose of ending his ministry and taking him back home (Mk. 3:21). Jesus used this situation as an opportunity to make clear to his listeners that nothing can interfere with the calling of God, not even one's own family.

Second, Jesus used this interruption by his family to make a significant point about his definition of family. With this word, he impressively widened the family circle. No longer was family limited to ties of blood; it encompassed all those who do the will of God. This scene illustrates how the nature of the family has been transformed by the good news of the kingdom of God.

Jesus' love for his mother is revealed in his word from the cross, making provision for her care. Jesus secured a commitment from one of the disciples to care for her (Jn. 19:26-27). In this word, Jesus not only showed the significance family relationships had for him; he also brought new meaning and promise to the very definition of family.

A new family — the promise of God

In his pronouncement that his family is composed of those who do the will of the Father, Jesus radically redefined the family. No longer is the family of the Christian to be limited to those who are related by blood or marriage. As Professor Anderson notes: " . . . Family means much more than consanguinity, where blood ties provide the only basis for belonging" (Anderson & Guernsey 1985:40). A new relationship to one another is possible based simply on one's relationship to God as *Abba,* Father (Rom. 8:15, 1 Pt. 1:17). One is able to become a member of a great family (see Mt. 19:29) that transcends all earthly ties and even death.

In the scene at the cross, Jesus brings to fruition the promise of family. To Mary, he says, "Woman, behold, your son"; and to the disciple, "Behold, your mother" (Jn. 19:25-27). The symbolic significance of this disclosure has evoked much discussion, but only a few have noted its significance for a new understanding of the family. Jesus emphasizes that this disciple has become his true brother by stressing that his mother is now the mother of the beloved disciple and that the disciple is now the son of his mother. He pronounces them family, for better or worse (cp. Rom. 16:13, where Paul greets "Rufus' mother and mine").

John's passion narrative highlights three events that specifically fulfill Scripture: (1) the dividing of Jesus' garments by the soldiers (19:23-25), (2) Jesus' thirst (19:28-30), and (3) the piercing of Jesus' side and the fact that his legs were not broken (19:31-37). In between these events, Jesus speaks the word to his mother and the disciple whom he loves (19:25-27). It is not insignificant that this announcement appears in context of the fulfillment of Scripture. John saw Jesus' death as the completion of Jesus' work and the fulfillment of God's intentions as expressed in God's Word. This new relationship between Jesus' mother and the beloved disciple can be seen as the fruit of the completed work of Christ (Bampfylde 1969:258). Jesus' death enables people to become family to one another in a new and different way.

The new relationship also applies to Jesus' Father. Jesus referred to God as "my Father" throughout the Gospel of John. After his death and resurrection, a change occurs. When Mary Magdalene finally recognizes Jesus, she clings desperately to the one she knows only as "my teacher," hoping perhaps that this terrible nightmare is over and that they can return home to lead normal, peaceful lives. Jesus instructs her instead to inform his "brethren" that he is ascending "to my Father and your Father, to my God and your God" (Jn. 20:17). This is the first time in the Gospel that Jesus identifies his disciples as his brothers (in 15:15, they are "friends") and the first time that he refers to God as their Father as well as his own. His ascension to the Father means that he will draw all to himself (Jn. 12:32) and that they will become one as he and the Father are one (Jn. 17:20-21). Jesus' death and resurrection, then, has repercussions on the nature of the family.

Jesus said that he had come not to abolish the law but to fulfill it (Mt. 5:17). We may also say that Jesus came not to destroy the family but to fulfill God's intention for the family. No longer is the family to be a self-serving kin group intent on feathering its own nest. Instead, it is to be the source of nurture and the channel of God's love for all of God's children. Those who for various reasons have been deprived of traditional family relationships can now belong to a family.

Such a one was the Ethiopian eunuch (Acts 8:26-40), who, according to Scripture, was cut off from the assembly of the Lord (Dt. 23:1). He was reading Is. 53:8 and was puzzled about whom the prophet meant when he wrote of the one whose life was taken up from the earth. But he could hardly have been puzzled about to whom Is. 56:4-5 referred. Here was the promise of family, even for the eunuch: "Let not the eunuch say, 'Behold, I am a dry tree'"; and God promises, "I will give him a name that will not be cut off." This man would have recognized immediately that this applied to him; he was the "dry tree," the one "cut off," the one with no possibility of family. Now he hears news from Philip that nothing hinders him from being a part of the family of Jesus. Jesus has brought to fruition the promise of God. To the eunuch, this must have aroused an even greater joy than that experienced by the unemployed vineyard workers who suddenly found themselves with a day's wages in their pockets (Mt. 20:1-16).

This fulfills in an entirely unexpected way what the psalmist said about God who helps the helpless and sets the lonely ones in families (Ps. 68:6). It is also good news to down-and-out prodigals, who find a father waiting for them with the tokens of sonship and a joyous homecoming party (Lk. 15:11-24). It is good news to up-and-out tax barons like Zacchaeus, whom everyone had written off as a sinner beyond the pale, but who finds someone willing to accept him as part of the family, a son of Abraham (Lk. 19:1-10).

God has created in us a basic need to be included in a family group. It is not good for us to be alone (Gn. 2:18). We need others to share in our lives, to help us with the stress of life, to celebrate its joys. Researchers report that isolation of individuals and nuclear families is correlated with a whole array of problems, including physical illness, suicide, psychiatric hospitalization, alcoholism, accident proneness, difficult pregnancies, depression, anxiety, child abuse, and family violence (Cobb 1976; Colletta & Gregg 1981; Garbarino 1979; Gottlieb 1981; Pilisuk 1982; Pilisuk & Parks 1983; Scheinfeld et al. 1970).

One of the most graphic illustrations of this need for family is illustrated by studies of high blood pressure in mice. Researchers have found that when a mouse is placed in a group of strange mice where all have to eat from the same not-quite-adequate source, the mouse develops high blood pressure. But if the same mouse is placed in a same size group of its own brothers and sisters with the same not-quite-adequate food source, its blood pressure stays normal. Mice can handle stress if they have their families around them but not if they are alone among strangers (Pilisuk 1982). People are the same way.

Jesus did not call us to be loners on some quixotic crusade for a higher cause. As Jesus made a family for the ones he loved dearly, so the church should enable those in the community of faith to care for one another and to belong to a family. To some this may be troubling because it means they have as family people like blind beggars, Samaritans, prodigals, tax collectors, and uncircumcised Gentiles, whom no father would want his daughter to marry; we are all "co-heirs" in God's family (Rom. 8:16-17; Gal. 3:29, 4:7; Eph. 2:19). To others, such as the Ethiopian eunuch, this is the good news they've been waiting for.

Yet the creation and nurture of family relationships raise the question of how we can focus attention on developing the special love that means "family" when Jesus called us to love our neighbor—*all* our neighbors—as ourselves. Can the Christian relate exclusively to particular persons as "special" family without including the entire family of faith? And if not, is it even possible to live as one big family with the entire community of faith?

THE PARTICULAR LOVE OF FAMILY
AND THE UNIVERSAL LOVE OF NEIGHBOR

Family love raises two dilemmas for the Christian. First and fundamentally, Jesus calls us to love all others as ourselves. Does this allow room for "special" relationships? If we are to love all of our neighbors as ourselves, can we love certain ones more? Can we commit more of ourselves to some—our family, for example—at the cost of committing ourselves to all others?

The difference between neighbors and families

We can look at the relationship between love of family and the universal love of neighbor in Jesus' own life. John notes that Jesus loved Martha and her sister and Lazarus (Jn. 11:5). Surely, he loved all of his disciples and demonstrated love for all those he encountered, so why does the evangelist single out these three as those whom Jesus loved? Evidently, these were persons with whom Jesus had a special relationship. He was deeply moved by Mary's grief over her brother's death (Jn. 11:33), even though he knew that he would raise Lazarus from the dead (Jn. 11:23-24). He experienced her pain as his own, presumably because these persons were like family to Jesus. And we see them engage in the kind of plain talk that sometimes characterizes family conversations. Neither Martha nor Mary minced any words in their complaints about Jesus' absence (Jn. 11:21, 32). Clearly, these people were special persons in Jesus' life.

Yet Jesus also taught us that as there is no limit on God's love, there is to be no limit on our love (Mt. 5:44-47). The love for neighbor is to be universal, calling us beyond our individual loyalties and special relationships. The Samaritan was neighbor to the Jew. The only thing he could expect in return for his kindness was perhaps vengeance from the man's family if he should die from his wounds. But Jesus insisted that we are to give to whoever asks and to love our enemies (Mt. 5:38-44). If we love only those who return love to us, scratch only the backs of those who will scratch ours, what have we done that is more than what the average pagan does? What have we done to demonstrate the love of God the Father which we have experienced in our own lives (Mt. 5:45-48)?

Family relationships, on the other hand, are reciprocal. When Jesus spoke to the beloved disciple and told him to care for his mother, he also spoke to his mother, telling her to care for the beloved disciple (Jn. 19:26-27). We can be a neighbor without any expectation of reciprocity. But we can be in a family only with other people who in return see us as family. Family relationships are a covenant between persons, and covenants require commitment on both sides. The particular love we have for one another in families symbolizes our covenant with God, who has chosen us. Covenant love is not indiscriminate. It does not include everything that is human in a social community; instead, covenant love "discriminates one from the other as particular and unique" (Anderson & Guernsey 1985:39). It is therefore appropriate for Christians to have special family relationships characterized by mutual commitment and love, and this need not detract from our call to love our neighbors as ourselves. We are to "do good to all, and especially those who are of the household of faith" (Gal. 6:10).

The relationship between church community and family

A second dilemma is created by the belief that the entire church community should relate to one another as intimate family. Jesus put us on notice that all who do God's will are our brothers, sisters, and mothers (Mt. 13:50). Paul understood the entire church community to be like a family, although he used the metaphor of the body: "If one member suffers, all suffer together; if one member is honored, all rejoice together" (1 Cor. 12:26). Certainly, the reciprocity and mutuality that characterize family love should characterize the relationships between fellow Christians. Is there room for family subgroups within this household of faith, or are we to relate to all others in the church community equally as brothers and sisters in the faith? Many churches with memberships of hundreds and thousands struggle in vain to create a sense of intimate family. Persons who do not know one another's last names, much less their first names, may nod to one another across the parking lot and address one another as "brother" and "sister." But this is hardly a picture of God's intention for the family.

We can gain some perspective on this dilemma from Jesus' relationship with his disciples. Even within the inner circle of the twelve disciples there was yet another inner circle. One disciple was known as the beloved disciple. Peter, James, and John were singled out for special experiences. Mary, Martha, and Lazarus, as we have seen, held a special place with Jesus.

The scene at the cross in which Jesus conjoins the beloved disciple and his mother as family also sheds light on the role of special family relationships within the community of faith. Jesus did not tell the disciple to communicate to the others that they were all to look after his mother. Instead, he singled out this one whom he loved. From Acts we learn that the early Jerusalem church shared all things in common and cared especially for the widows (2:44-45, 4:32-35, 6:1). But Jesus' word to the beloved disciple goes beyond the expectation that the band of disciples would care for one another; *within* the community, Jesus designated a special family relationship.

We cannot create family relationships that incorporate the multitude of persons who make up one local congregation, let alone the countless millions who belong to the church universal. The community of faith, however, does have the responsibility for serving as a network of extended families and nurturing within itself the special relationships of family, whatever the biological or nonbiological foundation for those relationships. No person ought to be family-less in the community of faith.

The role of the family in the church community balances our culture's highly individualistic approach to faith. Jesus' revolutionary definition of the family ought to be the basis for our evangelism. In order to evangelize persons and help them grow in the faith, we have to deal with their relationship with and sustenance by families. The church's responsibility is to develop family relationships—relationships beyond the bounds of kinship—as fertile soil for the germination and growth of Christians. The church is to cultivate relationships through which the Holy Spirit can work. We cannot reach individuals unless we can support them in families. God calls persons into a special relationship with God and others. Newbigin writes:

> God is not solitary — but relationship between Father, Son and Spirit. Interpersonal relatedness belongs to the being of God. Therefore, there can be no salvation for persons except in relatedness. No one can be made whole except by being restored to the wholeness of that being-in-relatedness for which God made persons and the world and which is the image of that being-in-relatedness which is the being of God. . . . If the truly human is the shared reality of mutual and collective responsibility which the Bible envisages, then salvation must be an action which binds us together and restores for us the true mutual relation to each other and the true shared relation to the world of nature. (Newbigin 1978:76)

The role of the church, then is not simply to nurture and support the families that are already members. The church is to nurture and support new families and enable all to be part of a special family: the homeless, mentally ill man; the child with special needs awaiting adoption; the developmentally disabled young adult; the teenage mother; the divorced person. The church is to provide a home for the homeless, love for the unloved, and grace for the disgraced. It is to nurture the kind of grace that transforms someone like Onesimus from a runaway slave into someone whom Paul identifies as "my child" (Phlm. 10). As a slave, Onesimus was a part of the household of Philemon; but as a Christian, he was nothing less than Philemon's "beloved brother" (Phlm. 16). The church is to be the seedbed for relationships in which we can parent and be parented, and in which we can give and receive brothering and sistering, regardless of biological kinship.

By pursuing this vision of a family for all God's children, the church provides for the spiritual guidance and Christian education of the saints. For the Christian, family living ought to be an experience of spiritual discipline. In no other relationship of life is more demanded of us. In no other relationship do we learn more about God than in the attempt to live out the commandments of Christ in the family. Perhaps that is why the parable of the prodigal son has had such an impact on people over the ages.

THE SPIRITUAL DISCIPLINE OF FAMILY LIFE

Augustine believed that the particular love of special persons in our lives schools us for the universal love of all others as neighbors. According to Augustine, "real love for any human being, requiring as it does a disciplining of the selfish impulses, will begin to create in us a new openness toward others" (as noted by Meilaender 1981:31). And Professor Anderson writes, "A person's spiritual life is evidenced most clearly by openness and commitment to others with whom he or she shares domestic space" (Anderson & Guernsey 1985:139). The way in which we live with and love one another not only prepares us to love those outside the family; it is also a fundamental expression of our witness as Christians. Our family lives are to be a demonstration to those with whom we live and to the world beyond of our discipleship. Jesus said that it is in our love for one another that all will know "that you are my disciples, if you have love for one another" (Jn. 13:35). Our family relationships are to be a witness of God's covenantal love. This is why the New Testament exhibits concern that nothing be awry in the family life of a Christian (see 1 Thes. 4:3-8; 1 Tm. 3:5, 12 and 5:4-8, 14; Ti. 2:4-5).

Living together in covenant

The Bible frequently describes the relationship between God and God's people with images from family life: God is bridegroom, husband, nursing mother, and father. We do not have to relate to some distant power in the universe. God is seen in the love and loyalty and acts of devotion that one expects of family—the response of a father to a child who says, "I'm hungry" (Lk. 11:11-13).

In order to be the image of God, we must relate to others in like manner. God created humans male *and* female (Gn. 1:27); it is the *and,* the relationship between us, that marks the image of God in us. God was in relationship with the Son before the beginning of the world (Jn. 1:1-2). We cannot bear God's image alone, because it is a relational characteristic. It is in how we love that we demonstrate our God-likeness: in the consistent, extensive, loyal, sacrificial love of family living. As we love one another as husband and wife, we witness both to one another and to those who know us what the relationship is like that God offers us. According to Ephesians, the marriage relationship is a mirror image of the relationship between Christ and the church (5:29-32). As we are parents to our children, we teach them what the love of God is like, and we model this love for others outside our families. This relationship is not a *quid pro quo* arrangement, where each gives on condition of receiving. It is not a contract but a covenant (Kaplan et al. 1984; Sakenfeld 1985). A covenant is a relationship bound by steadfast love, faithfulness, and devotion. The heart of a covenant is not rights and responsibilities—a contract—but love that endures whatever may assail it. Covenant partners love unconditionally, loyally, and sacrificially (Garland & Garland 1989; Garland & Hassler 1987).

Unconditional love. As Professor Anderson writes, "Family is where you are loved unconditionally, and where you can count on that love even when you least deserve it" (Anderson & Guernsey 1985:40). This is not always true of earthly families. Most fathers do not receive disgraced sons with open arms, gifts, and a celebration as did the father in the parable of the prodigal son. Many would share the attitude of the elder brother, who probably thought the father should have killed the errant *son* rather than the fatted calf, or at least have given more careful consideration to the hired hand option. But the parable illustrates that this unconditional love is always true of God's family. The parable begins, "there was a certain man who had two sons"; and there was nothing the prodigal boy could to do to become an ex-son. And the elder brother, who could not bring himself to say, "this, my brother," had to learn that families do not run on a merit system.

Covenant love is unconditional, but it is not forced. None of the biblical examples of covenant describes persons living out their covenant with another because they have no other choice. Abraham could have stayed home instead of taking off into the unknown. Ruth could have gone back to her people. Even though we live in the same house with one another and are legally "family," we have a choice about whether we will offer to live covenantally with one another. The father did not order the elder brother to get inside and "have fun," which the boy would have obeyed since he never disobeyed his father's commands (Lk. 15:29). Instead, the father entreated this son to join in the acceptance of his brother. The decision was left with him whether he would join the party or stay outside and swell with fury. Partners in covenant are not forced — even God never forces us to enact our covenant commitment with the Lord but leaves us free to choose. In the same way, partners continue to choose one another; it would not be a loving relationship if they stayed together only out of necessity. It is the act of continually choosing to love one another, despite whatever happens, that communicates to our family and to the world the love of God who chooses us and calls us children, no matter how far we stray.

This kind of love is not based on emotion; it is action. We cannot force ourselves to feel "in love," but we can will ourselves to act lovingly. We do not choose our feelings, but we can choose what we will do.

Steadfast loyalty. Covenant love is, in essence, "steadfast loyalty" (Sakenfeld 1985). According to Scripture, God became discouraged, disheartened, even exasperated by the failure of the people, but still continued in the covenant (Ex. 32:1-32). According to Paul, when God was establishing the new covenant of the Spirit, God first offered it to Israel: "to the Jew first and also the Greek" (Rom. 1:16, 2:10).

Covenants are not always characterized by warm, intimate feelings. God's wrath waxed hot against the covenant people. But anger does not dissolve the covenant relationship. The relationships in a family sometimes resemble the relationship between Yahweh and the Israelites in the desert. There was a lot of grumbling, minor rebellion, aimless wandering, and despair. Sometimes a partner groused, "If you had just left us alone in Egypt, everything would be fine." Yet the covenant endured.

Over time the loyalty of covenant partners deepens. God's relationship with the people continued to grow and change as Israel came to know God more deeply. The steadfast loyalty of covenant living holds us in relationship so that family members can grow in a deeper understanding of one another. Alone, we cannot fulfill the commitment to love with steadfast loyalty; it is a call to perfection that is beyond our human capability. It is only through the power of God in us that we can live out the promise of a covenant. Our covenant is a witness to that faith.

Sacrificial giving. The sign of covenant love is our willingness to sacrifice ourselves for the other. The basic principle of Christian living is self-giving (see Mt. 16:25; Mk. 10:39; Lk. 9:24, 17:33; Jn. 12:25; 2 Cor. 6:10). As we serve one another, we learn to be servants in the kingdom. The power in a family of Christians is to be the power of sacrificial love (Eph. 5:24-25), which is power turned upside down. We are to show leadership through service to all, not by lording it over others (see Jn. 13:14-15). Christians should never be concerned with staking out their authority; the message of Eph. 5:22-23 is not about who gets to be president of the family. Instead, the message is that we are to submit ourselves to one another (Eph. 5:21). In our mutual submission to one another we witness in our families to the sacrificial gift Christ made of his life to his bride, the church.

The spiritual discipline of family living is not completed by living out the love of Christ in our family. It is not enough for us to order our family lives rightly and to love one another unconditionally, loyally, and sacrificially. As servants in the kingdom, the family is to be together on mission that goes beyond the immediate family.

Working together in the faith

God's covenants with Israel and with the church through Jesus Christ have had purposes beyond creating intimate fellowship between the people and God. Israel was to be a light among the nations of the world to bring all people into fellowship with God. The church has a mission to bring the good news to all the world. Families are to do more than be intimate with one another and provide support and refuge.

Prisca and Aquila lived out their calling as covenant partners. They instructed others in the faith (Acts 18:26), welcomed Paul (and no doubt others) into their home and enabled him to work with them in their business of tentmaking (Acts 18:3), and hosted a church in their home (1 Cor. 16:9). Paul saluted them as his "fellow workers" who laid their lives on the line for him and said that not only he but all the Gentile churches gave thanks for them (Rom. 16:3-4). Their covenant relationship with one another was the basis for a shared ministry that touched others beyond themselves.

Families are to be more than liberty ports, where members sail in for rest, recreation, and refueling and go back into the world renewed. Families must have a purpose beyond their own survival and well-being. Jesus taught that when we focus only on saving our own lives we ultimately lose them. Similarly, families whose sole purpose is to enrich their own lives with one another are simply building bigger and better barns in which they can safely store the treasure of their family lives—only to find in the end that all their activity is meaningless (see Garland & Garland 1986).

God's call to service can take many shapes for the family. The family of Adam and Eve was called to be environmentally concerned caretakers of the earth—so are we. The family of Abraham and Sarah was called to step out in faith, to parent a people who would live in covenant with God—so are we. The families of the New Testament were called to open their homes in hospitality to the community of faith and to strangers and to teach the good news to others (Rom. 12:13)—so are we. Joy in family living, like personal happiness, comes when we lose ourselves and submit our relationships to the calling of God (Is. 58:10).

SUMMARY

The church needs to offer a re-vision of what can happen to and through the Christian family. The good news is that God offers to be our parent, and Jesus promises to be our brother, if we follow him. When we do, we find ourselves entering a whole new set of family relationships.

The task of the church is twofold. First, the church is to create a network of families within the community so that all can find their place. Evangelism must focus on developing relationships that can reach out to the lost and nurture Christians—relationships through which the Spirit of God can work. Second, the church is to provide a context in which families can see visions of ministry and hear the call of God, and then the church needs to provide the resources that empower families to do the tasks God places before them.

As we live in families, we are schooled in the ways of God; we must learn the disciplines of love, of loyalty, of self-giving, and of shared service. It must be so, for it is by our relationships with our families that the world knows what God is like.

REFERENCES

Anderson, Ray S., and Dennis B. Guernsey. 1985. *On being family.* Grand Rapids: Eerdmans.

Bampfylde, G. 1969. John ix.28: A case for a different translation. *Novum Testamentum* 11:247-260.

Cobb, Sidney. 1976. Social support as a moderator of life stress. *Psychosomatic Medicine* 38:300-314.

Colletta, N. D., and C. H. Gregg. 1981. Adolescent mothers' vulnerability to stress.

Journal of Nervous and Mental Disease 169:50-54.

Garbarino, James. 1979. Using natural-helping networks to meet the problem of child maltreatment. In *Schools and the problem of child abuse,* ed. R. Volpe, M. Breton, & J. Mitton, 129-136. Toronto: Univ. of Toronto Press.

Garland, D. E. 1990. A biblical foundation for family ministry. In *Churches ministering with families,* ed. D. R. Garland & D. L. Pancoast. Irving, TX: Word.

Garland, D. R., and D. E. Garland. 1989. *Marriage for better or for worse.* Nashville: Broadman.

Garland, D. R., and D. E. Garland. 1986. *Beyond companionship: Christians in marriage.* Philadelphia: Westminster Press.

Garland, D. R., and B. Hassler. 1987. *Covenant marriage.* Nashville: Baptist Sunday School Board.

Gottlieb, B. H. 1981. Social networks and social support in community mental health. In *Social networks and social support,* ed. B. H. Gottlieb. Beverly Hills: Sage.

Kaplan, Kalman J., M. W. Schwartz, and Moriah Markus-Kaplan. 1984. *The family: Biblical and psychological foundations.* Special issue of *Journal of Psychology and Judaism* 8 (2).

Malina, Bruce J. 1981. *The New Testament world: Insights from cultural anthropology.* Atlanta: John Knox.

Meilaender, Gilbert. 1981. *Friendship: A study in theological ethics.* London: Univ. of Notre Dame.

Newbigin, Lesslie. 1978. *The open secret.* Grand Rapids: Eerdmans.

Pilisuk, Marc. 1982. Delivery of social support: The social inoculation. *American Journal of Orthopsychiatry* 52:20-31.

Pilisuk, Marc, and Susan H. Parks. 1983. Social support and family stress. *Marriage and Family Review* 6:137-156.

Renan, Ernest. 1897. *The life of Jesus.* London.

Sakenfeld, Katharine Doob. 1985. *Faithfulness in action: Loyalty in biblical perspective.* Philadelphia: Fortress.

Scheinfeld, D., D. Bowles, S. Tuck, and R. Gold. 1970. Parents' values, family networks and family development: Working with disadvantaged families. *American Journal of Orthopsychiatry* 40:413-425.

17

LEWIS B. SMEDES

✝

The Family Commitment

RAY ANDERSON PRACTICES theology as an act of ministry. It is with a fine consistency, then, that he teaches the theology *of* ministry. And at no point is his theology more a theology of ministry than when he addresses the family. For one thing, the family today is a crippled and flawed institution desperately in need of a helping ministry. For another thing, family is for him a theologically rooted reality; it is structured according to the pattern of God's covenant with his human family. Therefore, the propriety of a "theology of ministry" is never more apparent than when we deal with the family.

Anderson is fond of saying, theologically, that "covenant is the paradigm for family." What he means by covenant as paradigm might be developed somewhat as follows.

Covenant reveals who God is in his relation to his children. The family, with its conception of new life and its union of caring parents and cared-for-children, is analogous to God's covenant with his children. Therefore, we can say that God's way of caring for his children is paradigmatic for parents' way of caring for theirs. The counterpart to this thought is that as God's children are called to make a certain commitment in response to God's covenant, so the children within a family are expected to respond with a commitment to their human parents. Telescoping all of this into a phrase, we get Anderson's thought that covenant is paradigmatic of family.

The covenant in both cases, God's and parents' covenants, is rooted in unconditional love. As Anderson writes: "Family is where you are loved unconditionally, and where you can count on that love even when you least deserve it" (Anderson & Guernsey 1985:40).

It is my purpose in this essay to reflect on *the sort of covenant that a family covenant is*. A family covenant is a species of all relationships that are rooted in a moral intention to which we give the generic name "covenant." Thus there are features in the family covenant that embody the features of all covenants and at the same time distinguish it from other forms of covenant. I will poke about in both general ideas and then try to illumine special features of family commitments.

(I will use the word *commitment* instead of *covenant*. I think that the difference between commitment and covenant is mostly one of overtone and feeling, not of content. Covenant, with its solemn and stately overtones, is most at home in theology and statecraft. Commitment seems more at home—today, at least—in interpersonal relationships. Besides, I use *commitment* simply because it comes more naturally to me than does *covenant*.)

I suggest that we look at this question in three stages. First, what does any person do when he or she makes any commitment at all? Second, what sorts of commitments are appropriate to make to other persons—as distinguished from commitments to causes or institutions? And third, what sorts of commitments do parents and children make to each other within a family?

THE NATURE OF COMMITMENT

First, then, what do we do when we make a commitment of any kind? For one thing, *we secure a relationship against change.*

We pit our intentions against the whims of fate, the caprice of desires, the storms of tragedy, and the moods that so easily lead us away from established relationships into new and more comfortable paths. The Jewish philosopher Hannah Arendt, toward the end of her book *The Human Condition,* states: "The remedy for the . . . chaotic uncertainty of the future is contained in the faculty to make and keep promises" (1959:213). We reach out into the uncertain future and say to another person: "I herewith make one thing certain: I will be with you." We set ourselves against all that will change in us and say to another: "No matter how much you and I change, the person that I shall become will be there with you unchangingly."

Commitment is a signal that we are in this respect, too, like God: we can take hold of a future and fasten it down for another person. We can offer each other a mooring in the sea of uncertainty. We can to some extent determine the destiny of a human relationship.

Second, when we make a commitment *we introduce a certain unconditionality into human expectations.*

Commitments have a "no matter what" aspect to them, which distinguishes them from contracts. Contracts are agreements in which conditions are made explicit beforehand. It is set out in advance that persons who make the contract are bound by it only so long as the other meets the expressed conditions. One of many illuminating disclosures of Robert Bellah's *Habits of the Heart* is that Americans really intend a *contract* when they use the word *commitment*. That is, they intend to stay with a relationship as long as the payoffs to which they feel entitled are forthcoming in acceptable quantity.

As Bellah and his associates lament, this shift in meaning has made all personal associations in our culture tentative, insecure, uncertain—which, in turn, sets up profound disturbances both in personal and in cultural existence.

It is misleading, however, to absolutize the difference between contracts and commitments. When we say a commitment is unconditional we usually mean that we do not qualify it by conditions at the time we make it. Our *intentions* are open-ended. A parent does not say to a child, "I will be there with you so long as you accept my values." A spouse does not say, "I will stay with you so long as you make me happy." In this sense, a personal commitment may be called unconditional.

But in this world where betrayal and disloyalty and brutality can and do happen, it may become humanly impossible, or at least unreasonably dangerous, for a person to keep the commitment he or she has made. Conditions can undo the obligations of any commitment, and so it is more strictly correct to say that we do not *intend* them conditionally than to assert that they are in fact unconditional.

Moreover, some commitments form the bond of relationships that are inherently conditional—a friendship, for instance. Aristotle illumined the nature of friendship when he observed that there are three bases for it. One is mutual admiration: friends must discern something in one another that they admire and honor. Another is affection: friends like each other; if they did not they would not be friends. The third basis is usefulness: friends are helpful to each other.

These are all shifting conditions. There is no dishonor in the discovery that a friend no longer likes, no longer admires, or is no longer useful to the other. And there is no dishonor if friends become *former* friends. For whatever commitment a friend makes to a friend has conditions that, if not met, may mark the honorable death of a friendship. The breakdown of friendships is sad, but not necessarily a moral failure; painful, but sometimes advisable.

Yet it is nonetheless true that *when we make commitments* we do not qualify them with conditions. We promise to be and do things no matter what our feelings are or what the circumstances of a later time may be. There is a "certain" unconditionality about them.

The third thing we do when we make commitments is, *we promise to perform certain actions*.

When we make a commitment to anything or anyone, we promise to *do* something—not that we will *feel* something or *think* something or even *be* something. A commitment is a promise to *perform* certain roles, to *do* whatever is indicated by the commitment. We cannot commit ourselves to unchanging feelings. We cannot promise unchanging passion. These things are changeable in the nature of their case. But what we can promise is that our *behavior* will be consistent with what we promise.

These, then, are three characteristics of any commitment: *First,* a commitment secures the future against change. *Second,* a commitment is a promise that is made without stated conditions and is, to that extent, unconditional. *Third,* a commitment is a promise of behavior — of action, not of feelings.

THE NATURE OF COMMITMENT TO PERSONS

What are the characteristics of commitments made to persons?

We make commitments in many contexts besides person to person. Individuals make commitments to movements such as the pro-life network or to causes such as the preservation of the grey whale or to institutions such as the church. They make commitments to truths and to ideals. They also make commitments to themselves — to their sobriety, for instance, or to their physical health.

In all of these commitments, a person pledges to *act* in certain ways, not simply to agree with the cause or the institution. Even a commitment to truth is felt to be a commitment to act in ways that commitment to this truth entails. For instance, a commitment to the truth that God loves and forgives sinners implies an intention to respond to God with freely given obedience. Thus, a *commitment* to a truth is different from an *opinion* that such and such is true. I could hold the opinion that there is sentient life in outer space, and not be obliged to act on my opinion. But if I am committed to the proposition that all persons are created equal, then I am obligated to act toward people as my equals.

Commitments to things other than persons are like resolutions. The person who makes them feels responsible for keeping them. But the force of the responsibility lies within: that is, one is not held accountable by the thing to which one is committed. And therefore one is not obligated by a commitment to an ideal in the same sense that one is obligated by a commitment to a person.

Let us, then, go on to examine some of the things we do when we commit ourselves to another human being.

(1) We create a new structure for an existing relationship. Let us imagine two close friends, not yet married, who are consumed by passion and want to love each other as long as they live. Until they change their desire into a commitment made before society, family, and God, they can stop being friends, cool their ardor, and agree never to see each other again without being open to criticism that they have broken their commitment. But once they commit themselves publicly and become married, their loving inten-

tions are set within a new and different structure with new and different presuppositions, with a new moral basis, with new moral obligations.

(2) We give another person a claim on us. In human relationships, once a mutual commitment is made, each person has a *claim* on the other. A commitment confers certain rights. The other person can call us to account somewhat the way a creditor can if we do not meet our pledge of payment— the difference being that the creditor may have a legal as well as moral claim. In both cases we, by our word, give another a right to hold us to what we promise. And the claim of the other upon us constitutes a moral obligation to honor it.

In a marriage ceremony, we give a ring as a signal of our acceptance of that claim. The ring is not a wedding gift; it is a signal that we are pledging a troth, which means we turn over certain rights to the other person. Even in friendship, we implicitly give a friend the right to expect certain things of us simply on grounds of the implied commitment of friendship. One might say, in response to a request: "Why should I?" And the friend may answer: "Because you are my friend." And that's that.

It may seem inappropriate to say that God put himself under obligation by making a commitment to us, as if we have rights that we can claim over against God. His covenant is, after all, a covenant of grace, freely given. Yet once having made it by grace, he gives his children a right to appeal to it, to hold him to it. In the Old Testament, the people remind him of his promise. And sometimes, in the Psalms for instance, there is a hint that if God absents himself he is not fulfilling his obligations: Now, Yahweh . . . "Respect the covenant! We can bear no more" (Ps. 74:20).

(3) We entrust ourselves to another. When we commit a prisoner to jail, we entrust that person to the jailer's keeping. When we commit a sick person to a hospital, we entrust that patient to the care of doctors and custodians. And, in a different but parallel sense, when we commit ourselves to a friend, to a child, to a spouse, we entrust ourselves to that individual.

Trusting always makes us vulnerable to the possibility that our trust will not be honored. Commitment gives us no contractual guarantee. And there is nothing written in the character of fallen humanity to assure us that a fallible human being will never betray our trust. In this sense, a commitment by its very nature makes one deeply vulnerable. Commitment is always an adventure that requires the peculiar kind of hope that dares to risk deep pain for the sake of the abiding relationship it is meant to create.

(4) We surrender important segments of our individuality. There is no committed relationship without surrender. Once committed, I am no longer indentifiable—to others or myself—as an isolated individual: I am a parent, a spouse, a friend. I surrender aspects of my freedom. Once committed, I can no longer move about freely, unattached; I make all decisions with respect to their effect on the person to whom I am committed.

I also surrender something of my control. Once committed to another, I give that person considerable control over my actions. The control is exercised by two simple words: *you promised.*

(5) We pledge presence as well as predictability. It is of the nature of any commitment to introduce predictability into a life that has an inherent element of unpredictability in it. And let no one discount the importance of predictability in human associations. If the best we could ever get from anyone were, "I'll be there if I feel like it, but don't count on me," life would be sold into anxiety.

But commitment to persons needs more than predictability. It needs presence. In his book *Creative Fidelity,* Gabriel Marcel uses the terms *constancy* and *presence.* To commit is to promise, as we say, to "be there" with someone. It is not only a promise that we will predictably perform certain acts at predictable times in order to keep the form of the relationship intact. It is a promise to be personally present and available to another person, to invest oneself in another, to give heed to, to care for, to put oneself at the disposal of another. Predictability without presence is empty; presence without predictability is unsure.

THE NATURE OF FAMILY COMMITMENT

What is there about a family that distinguishes the commitment appropriate to it? All the characteristics of commitment in general will of course apply to the commitments we make within the family. But there must be certain characteristics of family commitment that set it apart as a species from generic commitment.

Within a single family, there are several sets of relationships, each calling for its own sort of commitment. There is, for instance, the commitment of parents to one another. There are commitments of parents to children. And there are commitments that children make to parents. These will be the focus of my discussion. But we should remember that siblings make commitments of a sort to one another. And then there is a commitment all members may make to the family itself, distinct though inseparable from commitments they make to one another. Thus the family is a complex network of relationships calling for a complex set of commitments.

Let us consider, briefly, the commitment of parents to one another. A marriage is not a family. I will not argue that family is the central reason for marriage. But I will assume that, if family is one reason for marriage, that fact tells us something important about the sort of commitment marriage partners make to each other.

If marriage were simply a two-person relationship and only accidentally the means for family, it would lose the most important rationale for commitment. Indeed, in a sense, marriage would be an institutionalized friendship. And there would be little warrant, beyond our psychological needs for lasting intimacy, for interpreting the marriage commitment as anything other than a conditional contract.

But if marriage is intended for family, even though not only for family, we have a powerful moral reason for saying that the marriage promise is a permanent commitment without intrinsic conditions. Further, we have warrant for saying that the commitment is not only partner to partner, but partners to the children they may have together. Our commitment to each other extends beyond ourselves, beyond our relationship, beyond our satisfactions, beyond our happiness. We are committed, implicitly, to stay together for the sake of the family that marriage has as its end.

But what if two people marry with no intention of having children? The answer is very simple: to marry without intending to have children is like planting a garden without intending to have flowers or fruit. There is something pleasant and interesting about cultivating a garden. But the proper end lies in the harvest. So there is something pleasant and interesting about being married. But the proper end lies in family. If this is so, we have a warrant for saying that a marriage commitment entails an obligation to be married enduringly. If it is not so, we lose a rationale for contending that the marriage commitment is unconditional.

We could summon the Word of God at this point, in a somewhat nominalistic way, and say that marriage should be permanent simply because it is the will of God that it be permanent. But then we would be left with the question of why God should command something for which there seems to be no intrinsic warrant. For without reference to family, a marriage is essentially an intimate friendship.

In any case, the family provides at the very least a clear warrant of utility for saying that a marriage commitment obligates partners to remain married even when their companionship does not provide the personal satisfactions they anticipated. Chief among the obligating circumstances, of course, is the injury children suffer from divorce. They experience grief at their loss of a parent, guilt at the hunch that they must be the reason their parents cannot stay together, fear for the uncertain future that the new situation creates for them, and almost certain depression because of their loss. Such injury and pain suffered by innocent victims of divorce is enough to warrant the assumption that a marriage commitment entails an obligation to remain married even when conditions are unfavorable to personal happiness.

Let us now ask about the sorts of commitments parents make to the children in their family.

I am interested in the sorts of commitments that all parents make to their children—and, conversely, the sorts of claims that all children can make on their parents. Privileged parents may make generous promises of all sorts to their children that are not implicit in parenting, and rich children can make claims that poor children cannot make. But I am looking for commitments that are implied when anyone at all becomes a parent.

I will set my observations under three headings: the general characteristics of parental commitments; several specific obligations entailed in parental commitments; and the obligations a family commitment entails for a child.

General characteristics of parental commitments

Parental commitments are unconditional. Perhaps no commitment on earth comes as close to being unconditional as does this one.

In a sense, mothers and fathers cannot unparent themselves. Nobody ever really becomes an ex-parent. A friend can withdraw whatever commitment she made to a friend. A spouse can become an ex-husband or ex-wife. But the parent is forever parent.

In another sense, however, parenthood begins with commitment, not with birth. Two people can conceive a child, be unable to keep him or her, and surrender the child to others. Two people who produce offspring are not thereby parents. It is the *committed* parent who is parent for life.

What do we mean when say that the parental commitment is unconditional? We mean that the *intention* to be parent to a child is without conditions. When we commit ourselves to a child, we say in effect: "Nothing you could ever do and nothing you could ever become can disqualify you from being the object of my presence and care."

Parental commitments are unilateral. A parent's commitment to a child gives the child no choice but to be committed too. In making the commitment, the parent exercises a God-like determination over the child's future. The parents usually determine the genetic, and always determine the psychological, moral, religious, and cultural, environment of the child. The parent creates the covenant; the child is brought into it without option.

What is a parent committed to do?

Provide survival needs. The lengthy dependence of a child within a family entails a parental commitment to provide a child's survival needs. But the nature of modern life creates two complexities in this commitment.

First, the parent must be able to discern the difference between a child's survival needs and the desires that the culture has taught the child to feel as needs. A child's survival needs are biological, of course, but they are also psychological, and it is on the psychological side that desires are often confused with needs. Thus the commitment requires discernment as well as dedication.

The second complexity is that many parents are too poor to provide even what the children need for biological survival. The parental commitment then becomes society's commitment. Commitment to family in a world of poverty becomes part of certain social and economic commitments.

Nurture memory. A family *is* a community of memory. And children gain their identities in vital contact with family memories. We know who we are only if we have a memory of who we were. But who we were is normally who we were as children in a family. So in order to secure an identity, we need to know the family memories as well as our private memories within the family.

A family is more than a current affair; it is a continued story, with earlier and later chapters. To provide a family setting for a child we need to keep memories alive. In this respect, the family is like any significant community. Consider a nation, for example. Citizens need to share the nation's memory, which is why its history is celebrated in national holidays, portrayed in pageants, conveyed to emotions through symbols. The same is true of membership in the church; we celebrate the Eucharist as a *memorial* of Christ's death.

To be a family is to keep memories alive: memories of the days of childhood, but memories, too, of the family's history. Parents are committed to providing children with memories because parents are committed to giving children the raw materials they need to create their identity as a genuine self within a community.

One of the evils of child brutality includes the theft of memory. Brutalized children dare not remember and so suppress their past, therewith losing a vital part of who they are. They cannot find themselves until they regain their memory by confronting their hatred for, and forgiving, the brutal parent(s). The tragedy of a lost memory only underscores how important it is to keep memory alive in celebrative ways, at birthdays and anniversaries, and simply by telling the family story to children.

Teach moral convictions and religious faith. I will not speak here of a commitment to teach the child the *true* faith and correct morality. I will speak only of a commitment to teach the child what the parent believes is the true faith and the correct morality.

As we have noted, a commitment to a person gives that person a right to make a claim on us. A child has a right to know what a parent believes simply because the parent believes it and because presumably what he or she believes profoundly affects the child. If a parent hides or disguises genuine convictions, a child will grow up assuming that the parent believes nothing, and that therefore *whether* one believes or *what* one believes does not matter. The risk of neutrality is not simply that a child may grow up to choose the wrong faith or live by inferior moral principles; the greater risk is that a child may grow up with the conviction that nothing is really worth believing and no principles are valid and binding.

In the Reformed tradition, this responsibility is the one explicitly articulated commitment that a Christian parent makes. The parent vows at the child's baptism to nurture the baptized child in the fear of the Lord. More specifically, the commitment is to teaching the child the true faith through the means of both church and home. In the Christian Reformed Church, the church of my own affiliation, the commitment meant that the parent was obliged to take advantage of *all* available means of Christian instruction, which included tuition at a Christian day school and, where none was available, to do what was possible to establish one. It stretches the point to assume that obligation to provide education at a Christian day school is intrinsic to parental commitment; but, within a secular community in which public school may subvert the parents' faith and convictions, a case could certainly be made for it.

Nurture into freedom. This task is one of the paradoxes of parental commitment that is inherent in human development. The goal of human development is personal and social responsibility. It follows that the parents' commitment to a child is to free the child from dependence on that commitment.

The way to freedom is the way of doubt and conflict, a way filled with alternating currents of pain and joy. Every child passes through certain rituals that mark subtle stages on the way: the first day of school, the beginning of menstruation, the first date, the first summer away from home, the first wage-earning job, graduation from high school—these are all moments that signal a new step into freedom from parental commitments.

The variations are endless. But the process is inevitable: the parents lose power as the child gains power. And, losing power, the parent also loses functional authority. Along the way toward the child's independence, both parent and child need to create new styles of commitment that fit the changing nuances in their relationship.

For many parents this is the most difficult of all commitments to keep: to let a child be free to write his or her own story. Perhaps to write the kind of story the parent had not intended or even dreamed of. Perhaps to reject the parents' values, even the parents' faith. Perhaps to fail. How full of hazards is such a commitment.

The temptation is not so much outward as inward. Most parents have no choice but to watch the offspring fly away. The difficulty lies within their own heart, in trusting the child to be free, in trusting the child to God—willingly, gladly, inwardly, releasing the child into the future. This commitment is harder to keep than all the others.

Establish fairness. In God's covenant family, justice was of the essence. Just treatment of the weak by the strong was to reflect God's just treatment of all his weak children. It follows, therefore, that parents are committed to seek justice for their children.

I will speak of fairness rather than justice because the latter has taken on a juridical and philosophical flavor that narrows its focus and defines the term abstractly in terms of rights and deserts. Fairness is a more flexible and delicate notion. The abstract notion of justice—that each person should get what he or she deserves—does not work well with family. For we must be fair to each other even in situations where it would be absurd to speak of deserts and rights.

Fairness is required even where no one, strictly speaking, merits what is given. In the family circle, for instance, we need to be fair even when we give gifts that no child can claim as a right. If one child receives it, the others should receive it also.

Fairness is not achieved by distributing everything evenly. A handicapped child may need more of something than the other, and therefore it would be fair to give it. Nor is fairness achieved by distributing the same things to all children; to give a small girl the same thing one gives an adolescent boy would be unfair to both. And so establishing fairness always depends on one's discernment of what is appropriate to each. And fairness is always approximated, never achieved perfectly.

Difficult as it is to provide, and difficult as it is to discern, parents are committed to treating their children fairly. The theological background to this obligation rests on sheer faith, for the unequal distribution of God's largesse seems often whimsical and arbitrary, and to that extent unfair. At this point, faith ascends above sight and sets itself in the conviction that God is fair in spite of our lack of clear evidence.

In sum, a parental commitment seems to obligate the parent in at least these five ways. Beyond them, of course, parents are free to promise anything that their resources and status permit.

What do children commit to parents?

Do children make commitments to their parents? If so, what sorts of commitments might they make?

According to the Bible, the dependent child is obligated to honor and obey the parent. But Scripture does not speak of this obligation as rising from a free commitment. The child obeys because the parent has authority over him; the child has no choice. When a child asks, "Why should I do what you tell me to do?" the parent does not answer, "Because you promised." But the parent might well say, "Because I told you to do it."

This resort to authority is a legitimate reflection of why every human being is obligated to obey the law of God whether or not he or she chooses to do so. The obligation of obedience does not arise from our commitment, but from the fact that God is God and we are his creatures, whatever we may think about it.

But it does make sense to say that as children develop into decision-making persons they make their own commitments to their parents, and are obligated to keep them simply because they made them. That is, as they become aware of their parents' commitment, and as they develop, as we say, a mind of their own, the situation calls for a response appropriate to the commitment their parents made to them. In short, the child honors the parents not simply because they are parents, but because the child has made a commitment to them. And at a given moment, the parent may stake a claim not on the sheer fact of being a parent, but on the memory that the child has made a promise.

There is a divine precedent for this way of thinking. When God made his original commitment to his human children, it came unilaterally, without stated conditions, to persons who themselves had no voice in the arrangement. Abraham heard it as a promise without conditions: "I will establish my covenant between me and you and your descendants after you through their generations for an everlasting covenant, to be God to you and to your descendants after you" (Gn. 17:7). And yet, later on, the Lord says: "Now therefore, *if* you will obey my voice and keep my covenant, you shall be my own possession among all peoples . . . and you shall be to me a kingdom of priests and a holy nation" (Ex. 19:5).

The tension between God's unilateral commitment and the required human commitment in response as a condition for the blessing of God's commitment has not been relieved by two millenia of Old Testament exegesis. But the tension is necessary to the situation. Without the response of freely committed obedience, the covenant could be made, but the covenantal relationship could not be effected. Is the family situation not parallel? Can a parental commitment that entails the exercise of moral authority be creatively kept with an adolescent child if the child does not respond with a commitment of obedience?

The commitment, of course, is usually implicit; the child does not take a public vow to honor parents. But parental commitments, for the most part, are also implicit; what a parent commits to remains unspoken. But in both cases, the commitment is no less real for being unarticulated.

And here, too, the commitment is not unconditional. No child is committed to obey when directed by a parent to do evil. No child is committed to submit to a parent's sexual abuse. There comes a time when a child may and even must say *no*.

The commitment to *honor* parents is broader and richer than the obligation to *obey* them. The forms of honor change as the child grows. And there are vast areas where the meaning of commitment can be known only at the moment and only from within the family itself.

When the adult child becomes the parent to a weak and dependent parent, the commitment to honor carries obligations that can be recognized and responded to without prescriptions that apply to all situations. Every child must write his or her own lyrics to the melody of commitment. In every culture, and in every family with one culture, children and parents develop their own styles of commitment to one another. And yet it should be possible for anyone of any culture to recognize any specific form of honor as a window on the sort of commitment children everywhere are expected to make to honor their parents.

My aim in this essay has been to reflect on the multi-layered claims that a commitment has within the family circle. I have sought to inform with some particulars the belief that family is created and sustained by commitment, that commitment in fact is the moral foundation and the structure of family. What I have shown is that, while commitment is indeed the foundation of family, the commitment is complex because the family is a complex network of continually changing relationships. Further, I have tried to show that the obligations of these commitments are not unconditional, not absolute, not unchanging: that, in fact, keeping these commitments requires discernment of the changing conditions, or the very keeping of the commitment can become a violation of it.

REFERENCES

Anderson, Ray S., and Dennis B. Guernsey. 1985. *On being family.* Grand Rapids: Eerdmans.

Arendt, Hannah. 1959. *The human condition.* Garden City, NY: Doubleday Anchor Books.

Bellah, Robert N., Richard Madsen, William M. Sullivan, Ann Swidler, and Steven M. Tipton. 1985. *Habits of the heart: Individualism and commitment in American life.* Berkeley: Univ. of California Press.

Marcel, Gabriel. 1982. *Creative fidelity.* New York: Crossroad. Originally published as *Du refus à l'invocation.* Paris: Gallimard, 1940.

18

JACK O. BALSWICK
DAWN WARD

✦

The Challenge of Modernity for the Family: False Hopes and Opportunities

T HE CONTEMPORARY FAMILY is an institution of contrasts and contradictions. While the divorce rate has been at the highest level in our
nation's history during the last fifteen years, married couples report that
they are getting more satisfaction out of marriage today than in the past.
Another contrast is that at the very time that millions of children are living
in fractured family situations, there is an unprecedented emphasis on love
and intimacy in family relationships. Just as some are celebrating the
freedom and openness brought about by new family forms, others are
horrified by the decline of the American family.

The contradictory nature of the family can best be understood as a result
of modernity. Our society was traditionally noted for its optimistic view of
the future, based largely upon a faith in modernity, which was thought to
be synonymous with progress. Today, however, this very same modernity
which has been heralded as the path to a utopian future is being blamed for
the decline of not only the family but also much of human life in contemporary society.

THE CRISIS AND CHALLENGE OF MODERNITY

In 1947 Nathan Glazer wrote that to be modern is to experience "a sense of
the breaking of the seamless mold in which *values, behavior,* and *expectations*
were once cast into interlocking forms" (Seeman 1957:411). In observing
the effect of this modern condition upon the family, the authors of *Habits of
the Heart* write that "the family is no longer an integral part of a larger moral
ecology tying the individual to community, church, and nation" (Bellah et
al. 1985:111).

A recurring theme throughout our discussion will be the *disintegrating* effect of modernity upon the family. The awesome realization of modernity is that we are responsible to create our beliefs and institutional structures. Threats of social, moral, and intellectual chaos accompany this opportunity, making the creative task of reconstructing institutions rather overwhelming. In this task, we find ourselves having to choose from such incredibly complex mechanisms as propaganda, administrative planning, ideology, and social technology (Ellul 1976). Having to make such difficult choices tends to focus our attention solely on the threats of modernization, so that rather than confronting modernity we retreat or try to avoid the issues it raises.

Social scientists continue to debate the origins and moving forces of modernization. Some theorists believe that modernization is fueled primarily by economic and technological forces; others argue that ideological changes have made modernization possible. Our view is that modernization unfolds in a dialectical manner, fed by both material and ideological aspects of life. No part of society and culture is autonomous; no area of belief or social organization develops purely in terms of its own internal organization. This is equally true for every one of the major social structural units of contemporary society.

Included in this dialectical view is the observation that in the current era, the economic and technological aspects of Western societies are the most dominating parts of social life. Other social institutions have been cast into responsive, rather than leading, roles. The various internal crises of modernization, however, may lead to changes in this current balance of power. For example, the crisis of moral legitimation in modern society may lead to a new role for religious and moral institutions. Many question whether a society built on moral pluralism and its attendant moral uncertainty can maintain itself regardless of its economic strength.

In developing a framework to analyze the modern situation for the family, we will consider four levels or layers of socio-cultural life. These four dimensions of socio-cultural life, given from the most personal and specific to the most impersonal and general, are: (1) *consciousness,* which consists of the level of experience and understanding; (2) *communication,* which consists of the level of symbolic social interaction; (3) *community,* which consists of institutional and group life; and (4) *commodities,* which consists of economic life. Although the more personal socio-cultural layers are based upon the more impersonal, each level should be thought of as reciprocally related to each other level. We hasten to add that these levels should be considered as analytical constructs only. They should not be reified and considered separate components of reality.

With this basic understanding of modernity, it is now possible to examine the dilemma of modernity for the family as well as the false hopes it has generated within the family institution. After we have described the crises for the family created by each of these socio-cultural layers, we will conclude by suggesting the type of "radical" responses Christians need to make in the face of modernity.

CONSCIOUSNESS AND FAMILY LIFE

The fragmentation of consciousness
Consciousness refers to the individual's subjective experiences, including thoughts, beliefs, images, and emotions. Crises of consciousness occur both within and between individuals—both subjectively and inter-subjectively.

Within the individual we see a fragmented consciousness with diverse "provinces of meaning" from different spheres of life. The individual must negotiate between the intimacy of friendship and family and the impersonal competition of the marketplace; between rationality in the school and faith in the pew; between the fast-paced solutions of TV and the routine open-endedness of daily life. Even the best of minds and the most stable of personalities can, as a result, lose a sense of centeredness—a clear sense of meaning and reality.

This fragmentation of thought and meaning has resulted in a modern *disjunction of thought and life*. Modern people have learned to live in a state of cognitive dissonance by adapting to apparently inconsistent beliefs and a lack of congruency between values and behavior. Interpersonal commitments and intimacy are highly valued, but relationships are unstable. Many Christians value compassion for the poor but avoid those in need of compassion. To paraphrase the Apostle Paul, we live in a kind of "sociological body of death," doing not the good we want but the evil we do not want—and we do not understand our actions (Rom. 7:15-25).

A diversity of world views is available to modern people. The more modern we become, the more we are aware of this diversity and the more relative our own views appear. For some, this opens the door to an experiment with reality—a challenging dialogue with others and a construction of their own meaning system. Others want to mold a new consensus of consciousness either by creating a new synthesis or by cutting short the dialogue and imposing their own beliefs on others. For others, questions of meaning become *subjectivized*: because institutions no longer provide consistent and reliable answers to questions of morality, individuals must necessarily turn inward, or subjectivize, to find these answers. This process of subjectivization is not negative; it is simply a structural feature of modern society. It can, however, foster a general subjectivism in a culture marked by an "incessant fixation upon the self . . . by the abiding absorption with the 'complexities' of individuality" (Hunter 1983:40).

Effect on the family

The fragmentation of consciousness has produced a crisis in morality and authority within the family. Each family is put in a position of having to construct its own plausibility structure, usually without the support of extended family members. The family is especially likely to experience a fragmentation of consciousness when children reach their teenage years and begin to compare their family's system of morality with that of their friends' familes. Parents are put in the position of having to defend their view of morality against the real or imagined moralities existing in the minds of their children's peers.

The crisis in authority brought about by the fragmentation of consciousness includes questions of the authority of extended family over nuclear family, of husband over wife, and of parents over children. The current redefinition of sex roles, for example, reflects this questioning of authority in the family.

In traditional societies there tends to be little separation between work and private life. The primary social unit in both are one and the same—the family, clan, or tribe. The recent separation of work and private life has led to two levels of consciousness. While working, individuals experience others as relatively anonymous impersonal beings and themselves as an "anonymous functionary" (Berger et al. 1973:34). This anonymity may be experienced as a kind of "pseudo-intimacy." People attempt to find genuine intimacy, meaning, and fulfillment in their personal lives. But modernity has so weakened the private institution of the family that we question whether even here there still exists the possibility of a meaningful, coherent social construction of reality.

False hopes

As the Christian community has felt the crisis created by the fragmentation of consciousness, a major response by conservative Christians has been that of traditionalism—an attempt to restore the family to what it was in the past. This is a false hope because it is not so much an attempt to discern a biblical perspective on the family in modern society as it is a defense of what the family has been in the past. It is a common trap for Christians to assume that the particular family form existing in their culture is God's ideal. Persons fall into this trap by reading cultural expectations into Scripture and by accepting all biblical accounts of family life as if they are normative instead of descriptive, as is sometimes the case.

Another response to the fragmentation of family consciousness is reliance upon expert opinion—another false hope. Family members, especially parents, are unwilling to trust their own wisdom out of fear that they may do something wrong. This is especially true in the Christian community, where many parents hold to a social-deterministic view of parenting and wrongly believe that right parenting guarantees God-fearing children. This view is unfortunately reinforced by a variety of self-proclaimed Christian parenting experts, who by proclaiming their methods in infallible terms attract large numbers of parents eager for an expert to relieve them of the agonizingly difficult task of parenting in modern society.

The dichotomy of private and public life has produced many "do-it-yourself families" who consider their own home lives as "real reality," and the public world as "artificial reality" (Walters 1979:49-50). The do-it-yourself family can be described as a false hope to the extent that it creates a consciousness out of touch with external reality. Also, the privatization of family life can easily lead to a type of "amoral familism," where the family is so preoccupied with its own concerns that it fails to serve far needier people. The amoral privatized family dishonors the biblical concept of family life.

COMMUNICATION AND FAMILY LIFE

Complexity of communication

Communication in modern society both shapes and reflects the fragmentation, pluralization, and subjectivization of modern consciousness. "Significant symbols"—symbols with shared, taken-for-granted meanings—are the basis of symbolic communication. In modern society we cannot assume the commonality of symbolic meanings. Even the words *family* and *church* have a variety of meanings that arouse emotional debate. The denotative or referential meanings of words vary considerably—consider the multitude of meanings of the word *love*. The connotative or associative meanings are even more diverse. Lack of consensus in language creates specific dilemmas for modern people. On one hand, our diverse backgrounds and uniqueness as individuals make communication more necessary than ever. On the other hand, our lack of significant symbols makes communication more problematic than ever.

In seeking effective communication in modern society we find a polarization of responses. At one extreme is a proliferation of technical and professional languages that can "mystify" the common person. At the other are attempts to transcend the traditional means of symbolic communication through various forms of nonverbal and extrasensory communication. The general result is an impoverishment of everyday language and conversation. This impoverishment is due to a need to capture and simplify a complex and confusing reality. The diverse means of communication and reality construction have been reduced in our attempt to capture reality in words alone.

Effect on the family

The complexity of communication saps vitality from family life in several ways. The lack of common symbolic meanings for words such as *family, love, intimacy,* and *relationship* complicates family communication. To the extent that a husband and wife come from diverse backgrounds or experience differing patterns of growth, they can experience difficulty in communication. It may very well be that the seemingly unquenchable need for "intimacy" in contemporary society is in actuality an attempt to fill a void resulting from people not sharing common experiences.

Parents with teenage children are quick to realize that a good part of what is typically referred to as the "generation gap" may in large part be a communication gap. With the emergence of adolescent subculture comes not only new meanings to old words ("cool," "hot," "bad," "square") but also new words ("punk," "new wave," "rad"), often with old meanings. To appreciate the complexity of communication among adolescents, one must realize that there is no monolothic adolescent subculture, but rather many adolescent subcultures ("preppies," "mods," "stoners," "rockers," "new wavers," "heavy metals," "straights"), each developing its own style of communication. Families with adolescent members may indeed experience the impact of this complexity of communication.

False hopes
Over-reliance on the techniques of communication is a common false hope response to this complication of communication in the family. One need only glance at the many self-help books written on marital and family communication to realize the emphasis placed on communication techniques.

Ironically, focusing on such techniques can often *reduce* communication. Spouses find themselves talking about talking rather than engaging in genuine dialogue. In the area of sexual communication, couples strive for complete sexual fulfillment by following suggested techniques of lovemaking. Parents "set aside time to listen" to their children rather than having conversations as a natural part of life together. In the end, family communication becomes removed from the natural course of activity and becomes one more task for the modern family to master. This is not to say that family communication cannot be greatly improved by learning communication skills, but that communication must be embedded in common experience and the development of relationships in the family.

COMMUNITY AND FAMILY LIFE

Disintegration of community
The breakdown of traditional (homogeneous and geographically based) community has been lamented by many as the crisis of modernity. Without such community, we lack the traditional means of social control and are thus vulnerable to our own moral laxity and to strangers around us. What is

often forgotten when we lament the loss of traditional community, however, is the provincialism and lack of autonomy in such communities. Isolated villages and tribal groups are noted for their ethnocentrism.

Concurrent with the disintegration of community life is the centralization of economic and political functions in corporate and governmental bureaucracies. The image of the *mass society* emerges — the isolated individual and nuclear family confronted with faceless, remote bureaucracy. The community that once mediated between the individual and the larger institutions is no longer there. Legal and political institutions are called upon to settle more and more family, church, and community disputes. There is a vacuum of social control. Issues of privacy and governmental invasion into areas previously considered private or sacred become serious social questions to which there are no apparent answers.

Some social scientists have suggested that "networking" is the modern substitute for community as a mediating structure. Friendship networks, occupational networks, social service networks, educational and cultural networks, religious networks — together, these networks can provide all or almost all of the individual's needs. However, networks tend to be unstable and individualized and thus lack the values associated with community: commitment and a sense of belonging.

We see a unique range of responses to the disintegration of traditional community. At one extreme is the trend toward an individualistic orientation — a kind of self-contained, possessive individualism that disowns significant dependence on or commitment to anyone else. At the other extreme is experimentation with various forms of intentional communities focused around some common value such as economic sharing, family life, or religious devotion. In between these extremes are people searching for a sense of community in other institutional contexts such as the church, where the "community" metaphor is familiar, or in suburban housing developments, where names like "Homewood," "Pleasantdale," or "Community Heights" imply commonality and identity.

Effect on the family
The extended family has been replaced by the nuclear family system in most societies in which modernity has gained a foothold. With the uprooting of the nuclear family from its extended family, clan, or tribal base comes the loss of community support and control of family life. The isolated nuclear family in modern society is a very fragile system. Gone is the day-to-day emotional and financial support provided by the extended family. With no one to help parents with child care, the absence of one or both adults from the home can be severely disruptive.

It can be argued that the isolated nuclear family is most functional for modern industrial society. At a time when others were announcing the decline of the American family due to its loss of functions, some sociologists proposed the rather optimistic assessment that the family is not in a state of decline, but rather is becoming more specialized. Along with this specialization, they foresaw the "beginning of the relative stabilization of a new type of family structure" (Parsons & Bales 1955:9). Although these analysts may have envisioned small community-based organizations such as churches, neighborhood schools, clubs, and voluntary associations assuming the traditional family functions, the family in modern society has become increasingly dependent upon mass economic and governmental institutions. Gone are the smaller, community-oriented mediating structures between the nuclear family and the impersonal, centralized, bureaucratic structures of the modern mass society.

The lack of community moorings has freed family members to become part of social networks over which the family has very little control. So teenagers become part of adolescent subcultures, and all family members participate as individuals in a variety of specialized interest groups. Although most groups are not likely to foster intimate community ties, even those that do promote such connections have the effect of further disintegrating the family as a community.

William Goode (1963) has identified three components of the modernity ideology that values individualism over community: (1) the primacy of industrial growth over the importance of tradition and custom; (2) the idea of equality between the sexes; and (3) the primacy of the conjugal relationships over extended family relationships. Goode sees the emergence of this individualistic emphasis as freeing the individual from both the domination of the extended family and from the bonds of tradition.

Goode also claims that societies affected by modernity are moving toward a conjugal family system characterized by: (1) a bilateral method of reckoning kinship ties; (2) parents and other kin having relatively little stake in marriages; (3) mate selection being participant-run; (4) the absence of customs like the dowry and bride price, which traditionally served to unite extended families; (5) the diminishing of parental authority over children and husbands' authority over wives; and (6) the equalization of power within the family and the emergence of negotiation as a means of decision-making (Goode 1963:7-10). Goode is right in his observation that these changes have served to free the individual from the dominance of the extended family. However, modern ultra-individualism with its lack of community-based accountability causes us to wonder if too high a price is being paid for this freedom.

False hopes

There are at least three false hope responses to the disintegration of community as it affects the family.

The first false hope is that the family will become a self-contained, do-it-yourself unit. The self-contained family attempts to meet its every need within the family unit. The family develops its own "family ideology," strives for economic self-sufficiency, and becomes deeply enmeshed (turned in on itself). The self-contained family is an unrealistic ideal that is doomed to fail in modern society. As we will see later, it is also inconsistent with Jesus' emphasis on the inclusivity of family life.

Out of necessity, other families in modern societies are turning to extra-familial institutions for the care of their dependent members. The family often exists as a fractured unit without necessary resources to provide adequate care for children, the elderly, or the handicapped. In other instances, the stress on individualism and personal self-fulfillment prevents family members from actively assuming caretaking responsibilities for dependent members. The quality of care that mass institutions are able to give needy persons rarely measures up to the New Testament standard of *koinonia*.

Most Christians agree that family forms must change in response to modernity. Yet Christians must critique the range of alternative family forms currently suggested—homosexual marriage, communal group marriage, planned single parenthood, non-marital cohabitation. Largely as a result of modernity's secularizing influence, there currently exists a relativistic predisposition to recreate the family in any form that might appear best suited to both the personal demands of individual self-fulfillment and the public demands of modern society. Such reasoning constitutes a third false hope, for it ignores not only scriptural authority, but also the possibility that it might just be the felt needs of the individual and the structures of modern society that should be changed for the sake of the family.

COMMODITIES AND FAMILY LIFE

Dominance of commodities

In advanced or monopolistic capitalism the economic sphere has been largely secularized. Economic life develops unguided by any particular religious ideology. Disruptions of consciousness, communication, and community make a kind of integration around economic life seem viable. Richard Fenn (1972) argues that religion does not provide the cultural integration of modern society and that uniformity or consensus will most likely be limited to issues related to the political and economic aspects of modern society. Remaining unanswered is the question of whether a society based solely on economic and political consensus can maintain itself.

Economic life and its principles of organization do dominate modern social life. Jacques Ellul has described the technological society (1964) as one in which the principle of technique or rational efficiency has moved from the economic realm to all other areas of life, including the political, educational, and interpersonal. As the principles and values associated with economic life have entered other areas of social life we can see an emerging pattern of the *commodification of social life* (Wexler 1983).

Karl Marx developed the concept of commodities to describe the alienation of modern workers. In modern society, workers lose the intrinsic
meaning of their work. Work becomes only a means to secondary ends—
making money. Once this occurs, workers begin to define themselves and
others in terms of cash value—the ability to make money. As a moral value
criterion for judging people and their activities, money becomes a spiritual
force in society (Ellul 1984). At this point, social interaction and the life
experience are commodified—the ends of efficiency and production have
totally dominated the means (the creative process). The twin phenomena of
careerism and *consumerism,* two evidences of this commodification, are found
at the intersection of economic, church, and family life.

Effect on family life
The major effect of the dominance of commodities upon the family has
been to change it from the basic unit of production to the basic unit of
consumption. It is rare to find family members together for the purpose of
producing, just as it is equally rare to find family members together for any
purpose other than consuming. The world of work and family life are
therefore separated, leading to the fragmentation of consciousness.

Not only has the economy taken over the family's lack of production, but
it now sets the standards determining the worth of individuals and individual families. So dominant is the commodity emphasis in modern society
that not only is our worth in the eyes of others gauged by our success in the
marketplace, but in our own eyes our success becomes simply a reflection
of how much money we earn relative to others.

False hopes
Certain feminists have argued that the only way true equality will be
achieved for housewives in modern society is for the state to pay them a
wage for their work. A less radical suggestion is to assess the market value
of each housewife's work against her husband's earnings. Home economists
estimate that "unemployed" American housewives perform work that has
an average annual fair market value of $32,000. Armed with these figures,
housewives could then bargain for marital power from a position of
strength.

While not negating marital equality as a biblical ideal, we believe that
even this less radical suggestion is a compromise in that it views marriage as
a social exchange whereby partners seek to maximize their gains by getting
more from their spouse than they give up. This may be the basis for many
modern marriages, but it flies in the face of the biblical ideal of mutual
submissiveness.

Some families wrongly believe that they can create a sense of community
purely through consumption. Spending time with each other is defined as

watching television or going to a movie together. Some consuming activities can be community-producing, but we believe that many hold to a false hope that the "family that consumes together blooms together."

In his book *The Third Wave,* Alvin Toffler offers an optimistic view of the future for the family in the technological society. He envisions large segments of work reverting back to the home. Given the current electronic/computer revolution, it is only a matter of time before homes will evolve into electronic-type cottage industries. Toffler believes that the home will come to resemble the medieval guild as the place where work is done, where children learn how to work, and where apprentices will be taken to learn trades. While this delightful image may prove to be a reality for some families, given the multitude of unsolved social problems engendered by modernity it must be viewed as only a false hope at this time.

Over fifty percent of all married women in the U.S. work outside the home. It is unfortunate that some Christians take issue here. We believe that whether the mother has outside employment is not the issue, but rather the adequacy of parental (both fathers and mothers) nurturing of and bonding with dependent children. A structural change is needed in which economic institutions will make provisions for caretaking of children and establish reasonable time commitments from employees who have young families.

The phenomenon of "careerism" needs to be addressed not as a problem arising out of feminism, but as an identity problem for all adults, male or female. Careerism, whether for one spouse or for the dual-career family, promotes the false equation of individual worth with career success. One's career, like money, takes on spiritual significance and detracts from the establishment and maintenance of primary intimate social relationships within the family and society as a whole.

TOWARD A RADICAL RESPONSE TO MODERNITY

The family has been greatly challenged and changed by modernity. The challenges offer us the opportunity to explore fresh insights into how the family might glorify God in modern society. Families of God need to witness to God's nature before the world and show evidence through their family relationships of the salvation and freedom offered in Christ. We have been redeemed at great cost and cannot minimize our call to obedience in all areas of our individual, relational, and collective lives.

It is important to keep in mind that redemption is an unfolding, creative work of God in the lives of individuals, families, and societies. We need a *revolution* of our commodity orientation which, in turn, will enable us to *reconstruct* our communities, which can provide an arena for us to *revitalize* our communication, which will eventually allow us to *reintegrate* our consciousness. We propose a restoration of the family in modern society focusing on each of these themes.

Revolution in commodities

The decommodification of family life cannot be accomplished without its liberation from the pervasive influence of monopolistic capitalism. We are a people for whom the commodification of life has become so all-pervasive that we find it difficult to conceive of any alternative modes of productivity.

As a start, Christian employers can take the lead in a variety of areas. They can make policies that give priority to their employees' family relationships. Such a strategy reversing the two-hundred-year-old trend of economic institutions usurping the parenting role would make a significant contribution to family life.

Such programs would involve maternity/paternity leave policies with liberal time-off compensation, on-site child care, and concessions for difficult pregnancies and family medical problems. Another option is offering flex-time for both mothers and fathers who desire to be with their children during their primary caregiving stages. These policies would inevitably cost the company in monetary profits, but they would result in gains in the strength of family relationships, in employees' personal well-being, and in employee loyalty to a caring, committed company.

Christian employers could also begin to offer opportunities for advancement to those employees who elect not to move their families to a new community. The average young American family moves every three years. It is inconceivable that quality community life can be developed within such a geographically mobile society. Instead, support systems established in family, neighborhood, and community life are critical factors in strengthening families, especially during times of stress and crisis in the family life cycle.

Reciprocal commitments also need to be established: from employers to the welfare of employees, and from employees to their quality of work. The present economic system, which emphasizes the profit motive, works directly against the development of employment loyalty, community building, or pride in the quality of work. In addition to monetary rewards, Christian employers must provide contexts in which individuals are given incentives for taking creative roles in service and pride in production.

Within the family itself, the goals of consumerism and careerism must be replaced by a focus on relationships and on sharing resources with others. This would require attitudes of mutual submissiveness, empowering, and servanthood in work relationships. By developing these attitudes, one is at risk of not achieving the expected degree of socioeconomic status and security. A basic assumption of middle-class America is that all people have the right and privilege to pass on to their children the social status they have achieved. Family life is oriented around this goal. A decision to sacrifice socio-economic status by living according to biblical relational goals can threaten these societal goals. A person's own children, family members, and friends may criticize as radical such behavior as taking a low-paying job so that one can spend more time with one's family or serve one's community, as opposed to making more money to contribute to the welfare of these same persons.

It is not an easy task to buck the system and make personal relationships and serving others more important priorities than making money. Our society awards prestige and respect to persons with high-paying jobs, but very seldom prizes persons who choose relationships as their supreme goal. A typical case in point is parents who choose to stay home with their children because they are dedicated to the parenting role. These parents are often disregarded by others and judged for not being employed outside the home. The single parent has the additional stigma of living at the poverty level in consequence.

The dominance of social exchange theory in family studies, with its emphasis on maximization of social profit, is an indication of the degree to which family life has been commodified. What began as a theory to explain family power has become reified and reflected in family life. Educational materials now *advocate* that persons consciously engage in a process of self-centered bargaining with other family members. This commodified model of family life needs to be replaced by the biblical model of mutual empowering and servanthood.

Reconstruction of community

The typical nuclear family in the U.S. is a partial community at best. It is plundered on one side by the demands and intrusions of a mass society and on the other by an individualism which has become increasingly narcissistic. What is needed most is to recapture a biblical discernment of what it means to be family. In this regard, two points that may at first appear paradoxical need to be made.

First, *the reconstruction of communal aspects of family life will need to take place within a secure environment, made possible by more effective boundaries around the family*. The family needs protection from the intrusion of a multitude of forces currently encroaching upon it which are sapping vitality from family life. In the previous section we mentioned the necessity of protecting the family against the infringement of the economic institution. A similar appeal could be made in regard to the demands of governmental, educational, and even religious institutions. Family members are bombarded with the demands of all these institutions, and the fracturing of the family is a consequence of trying to meet all these demands. Family members need a central place where they can gather together and be nurtured in an environment of acceptance and intimacy by those who care.

In the intimacy of the family community, members have a place where they can be "naked and not ashamed" (Gn. 2:25), a place where each person can be who he or she is without having to meet all those demanding requirements of the outside world. Here is a place where family members can relax and be comfortable in a mutually supporting and encouraging atmosphere. This is a place where a person does not have to hide but can be honest and real before others in the family.

Second, *the reconstruction of community in the family can take place only when the concept of family is one of inclusiveness rather than exclusiveness.* Whereas servanthood and commitment are meant to begin in the family, the Bible presents a moral imperative that will not permit family members to be content with any form of amoral familism. There is much in Jesus' teaching to suggest that loyalty is misplaced if it resides only in the family. Jesus speaks of "leaving," "dividing," "disuniting," and even "hating" in regard to family life. Jesus taught that loyalty must transcend family and reside in the Christian community as a whole. Jesus' attitude toward the inclusiveness of the family is clearly shown in Mk. 3:31-35. The common membership we have in the body of Christ binds all believers to Christ and to one another as family.

Inclusiveness coupled with strong family boundaries in family life are paradoxical only in appearance. It is only the internally strong family that can contribute to the strength of the Christian community, and it is in mutual ministry and reciprocity in the Christian community that the family fulfills its mission.

Revitalization of communication

Communication is vital in reconstructing family life and reintegrating our consciousness. Family communication must be liberated from technique and mere obsessions with words.

First, communication must be contextualized rather than being a separate activity unto itself. Family members, liberated from commodities and living in community, can share more activities together. These activities provide a natural context in which to share and compare experiences and to learn of the other's uniqueness.

Second, families can rediscover other ways of communicating. Creating or rediscovering family rituals for special occasions is a definitive way of breaking down barriers between people and symbolizing family values. At Christmas, for example, it is important that the family diminish the importance of commodities. Celebrating such events with tradition and rituals through music, symbolic acts, art, plays, song, and dance can create a symbolic solidarity in which all members participate. This can become an intimate time of togetherness in which family members express their individual uniqueness in this communal context.

Reintegration of consciousness

Individuals are able to integrate their experiences only if a genuine plausibility structure is available to them. The family and church jointly can provide this coherent structure. The isolated nuclear family is an inadequate basis for maintaining the plausibility of beliefs if it is independent of a wider supporting system. The church can play a primary role in helping the family achieve a reintegration of consciousness. The Christian family is ultimately dependent upon the church to maintain the plausibility of beliefs and values.

Modernity presents the church and the family with the opportunity to be open rather than closed systems. Church and family can have an expanded awareness of and concern for others who might be different in a variety of ways. The nuclear family can develop "fictive kin," or persons who might be of no relation by blood but who are taken in as functional extended family members. Christians in the church have an opportunity to become truly world Christians rather than focusing only on the plight of their own group. The church has the opportunity to learn about Christians existing around the world and respond to them as brothers and sisters in Christ. Where there are poor and oppressed people in the world, the Christian community reaches out in acts of compassion and with monetary and political support.

Family and church must strive together to manifest the value of relationships grounded in a love that is patient, kind, hopeful, and enduring. Only as a concrete witness to this love from God can churches and families enable their members to resist the alternatives provided by the world. The plausibility structures of the world are firmly entrenched, ready at all times to oppose the Word of God. This has always been the case, and the modern situation is unique only in its specific challenges and temptations. The integration of our lives in service and witness to Christ will only be partial, but we have a great hope in Christ and through the wider community.

The disintegrating effects of modernity will be overcome, if now only in part, someday in perfection (1 Cor. 13:9, 13). Christians must not retreat from a radical response to modernity merely because change will only be partial and imperfect in our human social systems. It is essential that Christians neither deny the seriously disruptive effects of modernity nor be petrified by its pervase, disintegrating influence. Christian realism demands that we practice an "optimistic pessimism." Contemporary society is currently staggering from the blows of modernity. It is within this societal context that the people of God, as the "called out ones," must by their example point to the biblical meaning and hope of family life.

A powerful incident in the life of our Lord, as recorded in Jn. 19:26-27, illustrates Jesus' radical redefinition of family:

> Jesus saw his mother with the disciple whom he loved standing beside her. He said to her, "Mother, there is your son," and to the disciple, "There is your mother," and from that moment the disciple took her into his home.

The meaning and hope of family life is that our relationships are conducted in such a manner that Jesus would want to send his own mother to be a part of our own families (Anderson 1985:23).

REFERENCES

Anderson, Ray S. 1985. *The gospel of the family.* Unpublished ms., Fuller Theological Seminary.

Bellah, Robert N., Richard Madsen, William H. Sullivan, Ann Swidler, and Steven M. Tipton. 1985. *Habits of the heart: Individualism and commitment in American life.* Berkeley: Univ. of California Press.

Berger, Peter L, Brigitte Berger, and Hansfried Kellner. 1973. *The homeless mind: Modernization and consciousness.* New York: Random House.

Ellul, Jacques. 1964. *The technological society.* New York: Random House.

———. 1976. *The ethics of freedom.* Grand Rapids: Eerdmans.

———. 1984. *Money and power.* Downers Grove, IL: Inter-Varsity Press.

Fenn, Richard. 1972. Toward a new sociology of religion. In *Religion American style,* ed. Patrick McNamara. New York: Harper & Row.

Goode, William. 1963. *World revolution and family patterns.* New York: Free Press.

Hunter, James Davison. 1983. *American evangelicalism: Conservative religion and the quandary of modernity.* New Brunswick, NJ: Rutgers Univ. Press.

Parsons, Talcott, and Robert Freed Bales. 1955. *Family: Socialization and interaction process.* New York: Free Press.

Seeman, M. 1957. On the meaning of alienation. In *Sociological theory,* ed. L. Coser and B. Rosenberg. New York: Macmillan.

Toffler, Alvin. 1980. *The third wave.* New York: Morrow.

Walters, J. 1979. *Sacred cows: Exploring contemporary idolatry.* Grand Rapids: Eerdmans.

19

FRANCES F. HIEBERT
PAUL G. HIEBERT

✝

The Whole Image of God:
A Theological and Anthropological
Understanding of Male-Female Relationship

THE BIBLICAL CREATION ACCOUNT clearly states that both women and men are created in the image of God (Gn. 1:27), so the complete image must include both female and male. And just as clearly, there is a divine purpose for this arrangement. The image, an Old Testament metaphor for steward or representative, is divided into male and female so that men and women may work in supportive relationship to fulfill the purpose for which they have been created. The mandate to culture the earth and create human cultures in the way God intended requires both male and female participation. Without that reciprocal relationship, the image is ineffective and incomplete.

Samuel Terrien notes that the Bible provides a magnificent but demanding theology of male-female relationship. It guides men and women toward an exhilarating and radiant maturity of relationship between the sexes until, as in Terrien's book title, the heart sings. It culminates, he writes, in the celebration of intelligent love on earth, both human and divine (Terrien 1985:ix). This love is the foundation for covenant community, the first example of which is the covenant between the man and the woman found in Gn. 2:24 and quoted by Jesus in Mt. 19:5.

According to Elaine Storkey, three features characterize a biblical theology of manhood and womanhood: equality, diversity, and unity. Man and woman are created equal, sharing together a distinctiveness from the animals and sharing together in the image of God. Their difference consists in complementing each other's sexuality with different reproductive functions. They are made to be together, united as one flesh, and together as two halves of humankind, providing companionship for each other (Storkey 1985:154).

IN THE BEGINNING

In the first chapters of Genesis, all that God created is pronounced "good" except for one thing.

"Let there be light"
. . . and God saw that the light was good.
God separated water and dry land
. . . and God saw that it was good.
God made the vegetable life and the small seeds that pattern giant oaks
. . . and that was good.
God made the sun, moon and stars
. . . and God saw that it was good.
God created animals for the great world zoo
. . . and that was good too.

Then God made the human—just one, not two
. . . and that was not good.
But God soon fixed that:
. . . God separated the human into male and female.
He recognized his own and she owned his recognition
. . . and what was not good became good.
God gave them equal responsibility for the earth
. . . and that was good.
God turned them face to face for accountability
. . . and that was good sensibility.

It was good, it was good, it was very good.
God's purpose for creation is always good.

(Hiebert 1988:8)

The only time the creation is described as "not good" is when Adam (the human) was alone. Nothing in creation, including the animals which God paraded by him, was able to assuage the man's terrible loneliness.

But then God created the woman, and the man recognized his equal. Bone of his bone and flesh of his flesh, the woman had the same strengths and weaknesses as the man. In other words, they each shared the full spectrum of human characteristics (Terrien 1985:13). But because either of them alone would have been "not good," they were made to be mutually interdependent. They were "for" each other—"for" in the sense of being in support of, not in the sense of being used by. That is the Genesis author's theological foundation for the relationship between women and men.

God's gift of cohumanity brought forth the first shout of human ecstasy. After the disappointing parade of animals, Adam may have fallen asleep thinking that even God had failed to find a companion for him. But when he awoke, and God brought the woman to him, he exclaimed "This one!" As the animals went by him, it had always been, "not this, not this, not this." Now it was, "At last, this one! She shall be called woman because she is just like me — only wonderfully different." Or, as Ray Anderson often paraphrases in his class lectures, "At last, there is someone in my bed!" God, the Helper ('ezer, Ex. 18:4), provided a helper ('ezer, Gn. 2:18) to deliver the man from the void of aloneness and alienation.

The Song of Songs presents a commentary on Gn. 1 and 2 (Trible 1987:146). Like a painting in rich color that is based on an earlier pencil sketch, it shows the joyous revelry in relationship that was made possible by God's gift of the woman to the man.

When everything still was good in God's creation, the man and the woman, thrilled by the discovery of their mutual humanity, were fully equal. They both mirrored the image of God; they both were honored by God with the gift of responsibility for the earth. With singing hearts, they lived in harmony with God, with each other, and with the rest of creation.

THE BROKEN IMAGE

Genesis 1 and 2 present a sublime picture of what the relationship of women and men was meant by God to be. But the disobedience of the first couple changed everything. The image of God was splintered, and the relationship between women and men shattered. The following verses by Ray Anderson poignantly interpret the consequences of the fall.

"Let it be good" —
He breathed, as he kneaded the swirling dust
into every hope and hue of his own image.
And then, stepping back a bit
From his still-new creation
separating its fresh consecration from his older glory,
He whispered again, to no one in particular —
"It is good!"

But even then, as the green world groaned
and stirred to life —
making minor miracles seem common enough,
The image lost its footing
And set the whole plan ajar —

the simplicity of good splintered into a thousand possibilities
of greed, lust, violence, vengeance
and worst of all, unawareness.

And yet, there was a sliver of hope
Prestressed into the likelihood of ungood,
A scalpel-edge of faith slicing through
the senseless flesh to the bone of consecrated spirit.
The creature, still bearing resemblance to the Creator,
Embraces every hope and hue with remembrance
In the prayer of consecration —
"Let it be good."

(Anderson 1975:132)

The world is still reeling from that terrible, cosmic disaster. The alienation and unawareness that imprison individuals within themselves have
shaped the tragic course of human history from that time on. People want
to be accountable to no one and work only for themselves instead of being
co-stewards in the work of God. The image has suffered the fate of
Humpty-Dumpty — without God it cannot be put together again.

The Genesis account leaves no doubt that alienation between God and
"man" and between "man" and "man" are consequences of the fall; Adam
and Eve were alienated first of all from God; but also from each other. What
has not been recognized sufficiently is that the alienation between "man"
and "man" also, and especially, must be understood in terms of male and
female. In the Genesis story, the human actors were a man and a woman,
not two men.

Anthropologists recognize hostility between women and men to be a
universal characteristic of human culture. They usually try to explain this
in terms of culture and socialization. What they are not likely to recognize,
or may refuse to admit, is that there is an inescapably religious and
theological dimension to the problem. The consequences of the fall are
more important than the processes of socialization or enculturation (van
Leeuwen 1987:21).

Throughout church history, however, there have been those who recognize the theological implications of the Adamic fall and have offered various
interpretations of its effect on male-female relationships. These include the
misogynist and sexual-relations-as-sin views.

But theological *interpretations* are influenced by the culture in which they
are formed. Arguing from how things are in a broken world, with its
broken image of God, some interpreters mistakenly exposit that the broken
relationship between women and men is the way God meant it to be. This is
strange because they do not believe that the broken God-human relationship is good or inevitable.

Looking through the lens of the New Testament which focuses on the need for reconciliation, a different, more biblically faithful analysis of the fall appears. The first couple's act of disobeying God resulted in a fall out of love and made conflict rather than cooperation a permanent feature of male-female relationships.

Mildred Enns Toews writes that the "war between the sexes" was initiated by the serpent over the question of whether the image of God was a likeness in character through obedience, or a likeness in power by knowledge. Adam and Eve decided for power, and the die was cast (Toews n.d.). They rejected the rule of God and power struggles became the universal and dominant characteristic of human relationships—including, first and foremost, those between women and men.

Even when culture and society oppress women into submission, women will try to gain their own ground in the war using their own kind of weapons. Men may dominate, but women will manipulate.

THE IMAGE PUT TOGETHER AGAIN

The first sin disrupted male-female relationships not only in marriage, but between men as a class and women as a class. It is important to realize, however, that this is the consequence of sin and not what God first intended for humanity.

Genesis 1 and 2 portray the two sexes in harmonious relationship with God, with each other, and with the rest of creation. But with disobedience came distortion. The theme of Gn. 3 is the theme of spoiled relationships (Storkey 1985:154). According to Helmut Thielicke, the way things are after the fall is the *disorder*, not the *order*, of creation. "The rule of man over woman is the element of *disorder* that disturbs the original peace" (Thielicke 1964:8).

The New Testament, however, is about reconciliation and restoration. This theme is the thread that ties together the Hebrew and Christian portions of Scripture. The Hebrew Scripture, in the third chapter of Genesis, describes (not prescribes) the effects of sin on the man-woman relationship; but it also proclaims the beginning of salvation history. In 3:15, God promises the fallen couple that the seed of the woman will overcome the effects of the fall.

The Christian Testament, in Col. 1:15-20, recognizes the fulfillment of that promise in Christ Jesus. Reconciliation is the heart of the gospel. The broken body and shed blood of Jesus restores the broken image to wholeness; what was lost in Eden is recovered by his life, death, and resurrection. Because of Jesus, it is possible for humans to be reconciled to God and to each other, male and female, and to live in the awareness of what God means by good through the strength of the indwelling Spirit of God.

Although women were segregated and subjugated by the Jewish and Hellenistic cultures of their time, there is firm biblical evidence that both Jesus and Paul lived and worked in the reality of restored relationships between women and men. In the new era inaugurated by Jesus, men and women, rather than being at war for the dominant position, are restored to the position of equality that constituted their life before the fall.

Individualistic equality

But equality in the original image is not the individualistic equality derived from the Enlightenment that is based on what Robert Bellah in his study of North American culture calls "ontological individualism" (Bellah et al. 1985:276). Ontological individualism makes the individual "the only firm reality," which still leaves the self as the highest good and hardly helps to end alienation or promote mutually responsible relationships.

What has happened in the U.S., writes Bellah, is that modernity has produced a culture of separation characterized by the fragmentation of life. What has failed at every point is integration; people have been occupied with their own private interests and have neglected the common good. He concludes that individuals need to rejoin the human race (Bellah et al. 1985:296). Bellah is writing about separation between people in general, but it certainly applies to the situation between women and men. One of the most critical points at which the human race needs to be "re-joined" is at the rupture between the sexes.

Some modern feminists believe that giving women equality with men on the basis of ontological individualism will solve the problem. If, however, that paradigm fails to bring about integration of humanity in general, it surely will fail to bridge the gulf between the sexes.

Biblical equality

A biblical concept of equality is needed for real integration. Equality as it was in the beginning, and exemplified by Jesus as a characteristic of the new era of God's kingdom, means that men and women are free again to be "equal to" so that they can be "for" each other as God originally intended. Jesus used the image of the servant, in contrast to the ruler who lords it over others, to demonstrate this attitude (Mt. 20:25-28). The Apostle Paul spoke of mutual submission and responsibility (Eph. 5:21).

Jesus' treatment of women was a sign of this restored equality and reciprocal relationship between women and men. Not only did he talk with women—strict taboo for a rabbi—he also allowed women disciples to follow him, and in direct contradiction to Jewish law he taught them from the Scriptures. In the parable of the lost coin, Jesus used a woman to represent God. The Samaritan woman was accorded the honor of being the only person to whom Jesus directly disclosed his messianic identity, and she became the first woman evangelist. Jesus appeared first to a woman after his resurrection, and women were sent to tell the male disciples.

John Bristow points out that Jesus' example became the norm within the early church:

> The apostles soon began to speak of the "women of our company" (Luke 24:22). When the apostles engaged in prayer, they did so "together with the women" (Acts 5:14). After the Day of Pentecost, "multitudes, both of men and women" were welcomed into the fellowship of believers (Acts 5:14), and both men and women were baptized (Acts 8:12). (Bristow 1989:54)

The four daughters of Philip, together with Paul and seven other men, are identified as prophets in the book of Acts.

The importance of the place of women in the church is indicated by the fact that Saul (Paul, after his conversion) made no distinction between the sexes in his efforts to oppose Christianity. In the eyes of its enemies, women in the heretical sect were as dangerous as the men. Therefore, Saul persecuted and arrested them both, a fact that he later acknowledged in his defense before the Jerusalem tribunal (Acts 22:4-5; Bristow 1989:55).

Paul's encounter with Jesus converted him to the new relationships prevailing in the apostolic community, and he probably took this radical application of the gospel a few steps further. He preached to women and baptized them without discrimination. Paul recognized women as well as men as leaders in the church and co-workers with him in the gospel. Their mention by name in his letters indicates their importance in the life of the church (1 Cor. 16:19, Rom. 16:1-16, Phil. 4:2-3). Paul describes Junia, one of the nine women he greets in Rom. 16, as one of his kindred and a noteworthy apostle (Bristow 1989:57).

In the last half of the second century, the former pagan Tertullian, who after his conversion retained a rather pagan view of the nature of women, marveled at the mutually equal and responsible relationships among men and women in the church. He wrote that they "perform their fasts, mutually teaching, mutually exhorting, mutually sustaining. Equally are they both found in the church of God; equally in straits, in persecutions, in refreshments. Neither hides from the other; neither shuns the other; neither is troublesome to the other" (Bristow 1989:112).

POST-RESURRECTION CRACKS IN THE IMAGE

What has happened, then, since the time of Jesus and the apostolic church, to bring modern Christianity to the place where inequality—and therefore disharmony and alienation—again characterizes the situation between women and men in many sectors of the church?

A careful reading of church history makes it clear that the wonderful ideal of restored, equal relationships between women and men exemplified by Jesus and his apostles, including Paul, did not last much past the fourth century. And, according to John Bristow, "it all began in Athens." Here lies the source of the Western world's formalized conviction that women are inferior to men (Bristow 1989:3).

The abuse of Pauline theology

From the beginning, the Apostle Paul's grand scheme of equality for Jew and Greek, slave and free, male and female in one family of God met bitter resistance. Deprecation of women was deeply rooted in Greek culture, and Paul's teaching was in constant conflict with the teachings of Greek philosophers and Jewish rabbis of the time. Also, the ideal itself was an easy prey to criticism and fantasizing by a skeptical society in which women and religion were associated with orgiastic rites (Bristow 1989:110).

The mortal blow to sexual equality within the church came when Christianity became fashionable, writes Bristow:

> In the middle of the fourth century, the Emperor Constantine gave his favor to the faith of Christians, and those who would court imperial favor began to join the church . . . —indeed, they may not have cared much at all for the teachings of Christ. As the Church became more and more transformed by society, its life took on more of the characteristics of Hellenized Roman society. . . . Slowly the teachings of Greek philosophy interbred with Christian theology, producing a brood of beliefs that were often pagan in their assumptions. (Bristow 1989:113)

Perhaps with good reason, the inauguration of Christendom is known in Anabaptist-Mennonite theology as "the Second Fall."

But the final conqueror of Paul's ideal of sexual equality, continues Bristow, was Thomas Aquinas. Aquinas, a highly effective Christian apologist and a brilliant and prodigious scholar, used the writings of Aristotle to defend Catholic beliefs. Along with his interest in integrating Greek philosophical method with Christian faith, however—and perhaps partly because of that—he also affirmed the class system of medieval society, the paternal family system, and the authority of church leaders and the nobility.

Aquinas agreed with Aristotle's statement that woman is a defective and misbegotten male, and therefore he could not conceive of woman being equal to man either before or after the fall (Bristow 1989:115). Bristow sees Aquinas as more responsible than anyone else for a misinterpretation of the Pauline writings:

> With Aquinas, the deprecation of womanhood was completely infused into Christian theology, based upon the authority of Aristotle and Augustine and

Aquinas's interpretation of the words of the Apostle Paul. Thus those who have
benefited from the superb scholarship of Thomas Aquinas . . . have also inherited
his Grecian conviction of the inferiority of females. (Bristow 1989:117)

From that time on, Paul has been misused to support a position exactly
opposed to what he intended. Greek attitudes, brought into the church
especially by the church fathers, gradually, and probably unconsciously,
prevailed over apostolic idealism. Paul's own words were quoted in defense
of practices he opposed; they were used as authority to prohibit what he
actually advocated. And according to Bristow, Paul "the Slandered Apostle" is still being slandered today (1989:114).

Inadequate doctrines of creation and incarnation
In addition to the misinterpretation of Paul, inadequate or flawed doctrines
of creation and incarnation both contribute to an errant theology of male-
female relationship. Arthur Glasser, dean emeritus of Fuller's School of
World Mission, says that evangelicals may have a flawed doctrine of
creation because they make the mistake of beginning their theology only
after the fall. They take little account of the fact that there was life before the
fall and that in that life God's original purpose for humanity is revealed.
Unless this is understood, the full scope of redemption will not be
perceived.

According to James Torrance, dependence on Gustav Warneck's flawed
understanding of natural law, which is based on a faulty doctrine of
creation, as well as an inadequate doctrine of incarnation allow for theologies that support many different kinds of human oppression. Some
Christians try to justify unequal and oppressive relationships, including
apartheid and the rule of men over women, on the basis of these theologies.
But in order to do this they must unbiblically divorce the vertical (God-
human) relationship from horizontal (person-to-person) relationships.

An adequate doctrine of creation, on the other hand, takes account of the
original purpose of God in which both vertical and horizontal relationships
partake of the same kind of harmony. Love for God and love for neighbor
are equal parts of the Great Commandment. It is quite impossible to have
one without the other.

A biblically faithful doctrine of the incarnation teaches that because of
Jesus, right relationships of both kinds are possible again. Jesus partakes
fully of ruined humanity and returns it to God without spot or wrinkle. In
return, God restores to humanity its full potential (Torrance 1989). This
understanding of the scope of redemption is stated by the Apostle Paul in
Gal. 3:28. It includes the restoration of equal, harmonious relationships
between male and female. Anything less than that would mean that
Christ's work on the cross was incomplete because it had failed to recover
God's full purpose for humanity.

THE SPIRIT IN THE IMAGE

In the new era inaugurated by Jesus Christ, there is a new availability of the Spirit of God. Whereas under the Old Covenant the Spirit spoke occasionally through individual prophets or kings, the Spirit now has been poured out on all the people of God. The image of God is revitalized by the breath of God's Spirit. As long as it does not hold its breath (quench the Spirit), the image again may function as God's representative on earth.

The gift of the Spirit is accompanied by "gifts" for ministry, and true to God's original intention for God's image, male and female, these gifts are comprehensive and inclusive. None of them is labeled "for men only." Ralph Martin notes that the Greek text of the "gift list" in 1 Cor. 12:4-10 does not have the sexist language employed by the English translations. The gifts are bestowed on the church without discrimination as to gender, social station, ethical maturity, or native endowments (Martin 1984:12).

A proper understanding of the Pauline vision, writes John Howard Yoder, would vaporize the current debate over the ordination of women. In Paul's theology, ministry is not for a privileged few; it is for all, because all have been gifted for ministry. By definition, then, "no one would/could be excluded from a function to which otherwise she/he is called on grounds extrinsic to that function." It is a most basic mistake to try "to open the closed ranks of the tiny clerical minority only to admit the ordination of a few clergy of the other sex" (Yoder 1987:52).

Sadly enough, even in the age of the Spirit, some gifts of the Spirit have lain unopened, collecting dust in the church storehouse. When the gifts to the laity in general or the gifts to women as a class are denied, the image is holding its breath.

History shows, in fact, that whenever God's Spirit is moving freely within the church, men and women begin to relate more as equals. This was true in the apostolic church and was emphasized by Peter's quotation of Joel in his pentecost sermon.

It was true of the Anabaptist women and men in the sixteenth century. Like the women accused of heresy by Saul of Tarsus, Anabaptist women were considered so dangerous to the established churches that they were hunted down, tortured, and killed just like their brothers. *Martyr's Mirror,* a record of Anabaptist martyrdom, comments in several cases on the "valiant manliness" with which a woman went to her death (van Bracht 1951:437, 441). The record also shows that some women carried out their apostolic mission to the very end by trying to convert their captors. Poignant letters to children from mothers awaiting their martyrdom in prison, in which they urge the children to remain constant in their faith, demonstrate the women's remarkable theological reflection and insights.

Wesleyan revivalism in the eighteenth century, the American Fundamentalist revivals, and the early twentieth-century Pentecostal movement with its roots in the Wesleyan holiness tradition also accorded women a place alongside men that was quite extraordinary in Euro-American culture. Charles Finney introduced the controversial measure of allowing women to speak in mixed assemblies that paved the way to the pulpit for scores of turn-of-the-century women (Hassey 1986:8). Frances Willard, founder of the Women's Christian Temperance Union, shared Dwight L. Moody's pulpit; and Moody's associate, Emma Dryer, inaugurated the intensive Bible study and practical training institute that later became Moody Bible Institute (Hassey 1986:33ff.). Early Pentecostalism was partly founded by women, and was eager to use women as preachers and healers (Hassey 1986:xiv).

It seems that whenever the church is focused on its call to mission, as it was in the examples cited above, the scope of the task causes it to unwrap and use all its gifts. When it becomes obsessed with power and internal structures, however, the Holy Ghost is quenched and the old specters of hierarchy and domination are revived.

But God's Spirit never gives up. Although the Spirit may be quenched in one part of the church, it blows where it will to infuse new breath into another. Dry bones are raised and God's image is put together again.

IS THE IMAGE FUNCTIONAL?

Equality and mutual submission between men and women may be God's ideal for humanity. But, some ask, do they work in a world ruled by power-hungry leaders, inequality, and hierarchy? Must not someone have the authority to make the final decisions in a home or church to avoid a deadlock? The social order of the kingdom of God will come when Christ returns as King. Until then, do we not have to live in the world as it is, although we seek to temper the gross evils of its cultural systems?

Family relationships and development
In a comprehensive analysis of socioeconomic development around the world, Emmanuel Todd (1986), a French population demographer, concludes that equality and mutual respect between the sexes, particularly in marriage, are the most important factors in human cultural advancement. Economists look for economic determinants of growth such as resources, productivity, and capital savings; political scientists seek political determinants such as democracy and free markets. None of these, Todd concludes, has been the cause of development in the world in the last two hundred years. Rather, these are all byproducts of that development. The underlying cause, he argues, is the nature of family relationships between the sexes.

Todd defines human development in much broader terms than economic wealth and its equitable distribution. Development also includes political progress such as democracy, the valuation of all persons, freedom, and human rights; demographic progress such as health, long life, and stable populations; and cultural progress such as literacy and generation of useful knowledge. All these, he shows, are rooted in fundamental attitudes children learn through relationships in their home during their early years.

Drawing widely on anthropological data, Todd outlines six fundamental types of families found in societies throughout the world. These types are based on differences in two sets of relationships: (1) that between husband and wife (partiarchal, matriarchal, or bilateral), and (2) that between parents and children (guided or laissez-faire).

The author compares family types with the rates of development of nations around the world since the beginning of the nineteenth century, and finds a consistent pattern. Those in which women and men work as equal partners and parents provide guidance for their children (bilateral-guided) show the greatest development. Next are those in which mothers have a strong public role and train their children (matrilineal-guided). Patriarchal families, in which fathers rule the home, rank from medium to weak in terms of cultural develoment (1986:21).

The reason bilateral and matriarchal families rank high, Todd argues, is that children learn their views of personhood primarily from their mother, with whom they identify in their early years. When they see their mother treated with dignity and acting as an autonomous person, they gain a high view of themselves as persons. This leads them later in life to take control over their own lives and to build institutions and governments in which people are free and empowered to grow.

Equality between the sexes in families is reflected in a number of ways. Girls may be as wanted as boys, children of both sexes may inherit equally, and young couples may live separately, or may choose to live with either set of parents. Todd finds two variables most highly correlated with development. The first has to do with the age at which most women marry, and the age difference between them and their husbands. When women marry after eighteen, they are adults, and they have a greater say in their marriages than those who marry in childhood. Similarly, when the age difference between bride and groom is less than three years, the two are more equal than in marriages where the child-wife is ten or twenty years younger than the husband.

The second factor has to do with female literacy. This depends on the age at which women marry and the willingness of parents to free their daughters from household work and to encourage them to study. Todd writes:

A more detailed examination of the correlation coefficients . . . emphasizes women's specific role in the process of cultural development. The coefficient between age of women at marriage and literacy rate of young people around 1970

(+0.83) is, in fact, much higher than that between age of men at marriage and literacy rate. The age at marriage *of women* is the key variable, rather than the age at marriage of people in general. . . . The woman's cycle of learning appears to be more fundamental than the man's. (Todd 1986:15)

It is primarily women, not men, who teach children to read and respect knowledge in their early years.

The equality of women as reflected in late marriage and literacy correlates highly with political, demographic, and economic development. Literacy—particularly women's literacy—is indeed democracy, for it gives the common people access to information, and therefore to power. It also leads to longer life expectancy, dropping birth rates, and rising income.

Todd does well in defining "human development," but he does not take into account ecological concerns. As Christians we must be concerned not only with the well-being of humans, but also with the earth and its environment. We, women and men, are created in the image of God, and part of that image is to be stewards and caretakers of nature. Walter Brueggemann writes, "[The] image . . . does not have to do with exploitation and abuse. It has to do with securing the well-being of every other creature and bringing the promise of each to full fruition" (1982:32).

With similar concern for human responsibility in the fulfillment of creaturely promise, James Torrance writes:

> God has made all creatures for his glory. The lilies of the field in their beauty glorify God with a glory greater than that of Solomon, but they do not know it. The sparrow on the housetop glorifies God in its dumbness, but it doesn't know it. The universe in its vastness and remoteness glorifies God but it doesn't know it. But God made man [sic] in His own image to be the Priest of creation, to express for all creatures the praises of God, so that through the lips of man [sic] the heavens might declare the glory of God, that we who know we are God's creatures might worship God and in our worship gather up the worship of all creation. Man's [sic] chief end is to glorify God, and creation realises its own creaturely glory in glorifying God through the lips of man [sic]. (1979:348)

This kind of responsibility is learned in the family. Children learn attitudes of nurturing—whether of other humans, animals, or plants—just as they learn competition and conquest: by observing early in life the ways their parents relate to each other and to their children.

Todd does not ask what leads to a high view of women in the family. His data, however, show a high correlation between the dignity of women and Christianity. Europe, North America, Kerala in South India, Korea, and, to a lesser extent, South America have been influenced by Christian values. There are exceptions, of course—notably Japan, which is not Christian and still has a high regard for women. Significantly, Todd points out that in rural areas of Japan, "a radically bilateral variant" of the family, in which both male and female lines are important, may be found (cf. Choi 1970).

Family relationships and church planting
Finally, and most importantly, we need to look at how family relationships affect people's responses to the gospel. Eugene Nida (1978) shows that in Latin America, where the husband is authoritarian, detached from his wife and children, and involved in extramarital relations, children find it hard to think of God with images of "father" and "husband" that have characteristics of love and care. Consequently, Protestant missionaries, particularly evangelicals, often have not been understood or well received there.

In Korea the picture is different. Early Protestant missionaries translated the Bible and printed it in the new, simplified Korean script. Men, by and large, refused to read it because the script did not carry the high regard associated with old Chinese characters. It was a "woman's script." But women used it to learn to read, and they read the Bible to their children. When these children grew up they turned to Christianity in great numbers, igniting the current explosion of the church in Korea.

Equality and mutuality between women and men do lead to better families and societies. This, however, is not the primary reason we as Christians should seek to create such relationships. Rather, it is because these relationships reflect God's created order for humankind and his re-created order for the church. They are a testimony to us that God is in our midst, and to the world that people may be reconciled to God and to each other.

REFERENCES

Anderson, Ray S. 1975. *Historical transcendence and the reality of God.* Grand Rapids: Eerdmans.

Bellah, Robert N., Richard Madsen, William H. Sullivan, Ann Swidler, and Steven M. Tipton. 1985. *Habits of the heart: Individualism and commitment in American life.* Berkeley: Univ. of California Press.

Bristow, John. 1989. *What Paul really said about women.* San Francisco: Harper & Row.

Brueggemann, Walter. 1982. *Genesis.* In *Interpretation: A Bible commentary for teaching and preaching.* Atlanta: John Knox Press.

Choi, J. S. 1970. Comparative study on the traditional families in Korea, Japan, and China. In *Familes in East and West,* ed. R. Hill and R. König. Paris and the Hague: Mouton.

Hassey, Janette. 1986. *No time for silence.* Grand Rapids: Zondervan, Academie Books.

Hiebert, Frances F. 1988. Beginning at the beginning. *The Christian Leader* 51 (10):7-10 (May 24).

Martin, Ralph P. 1984. *The Spirit and the congregation.* Grand Rapids: Eerdmans.

Nida, Eugene A. 1978. Mariolotry in Latin America. In *Readings in missionary anthropology,* vol. 2, ed. William A. Smalley. South Pasadena: William Carey Library.

Storkey, Elaine. 1985. *What's right with feminism*. Grand Rapids: Eerdmans.
Terrien, Samuel. 1985. *Till the heart sings: A biblical theology of manhood and woman-hood*. Philadelphia: Fortress.
Thielicke, Helmut. 1964. *The ethics of sex*. San Francisco: Harper & Row.
Todd, Emmanuel. 1986. *The causes of progress: Culture, authority, and change*. Trans. Richard Boulind. Oxford: Basil Blackwell.
Toews, Mildred Enns. n.d. *Through the lens of Eden*. Typescript.
Torrance, James B. 1989. Informal meeting with students, Fuller Seminary (28 September).
————. 1979. The place of Jesus Christ in worship. In *Theological foundations for ministry*, ed. Ray S. Anderson. Grand Rapids: Eerdmans.
Trible, Phyllis. 1987. *God and the rhetoric of sexuality*. Philadelphia: Fortress.
van Braght, Theileman J. *Martyr's mirror*. Scottdale, PA: Mennonite Publishing House.
van Leeuwen, Mary Stewart. 1987. The Christian mind and the challenge of gender relations. *The Reformed Journal* 37:17-23 (September).
Yoder, John Howard. 1987. *The fullness of Christ*. Elgin, IL: Brethren Press.

20

JUDITH K. BALSWICK

✝

Toward a Practical Theology of Marital Sexuality

THE MYSTERIOUS COMING together of two persons in a "one flesh" relationship involves many aspects of intimacy. Sexual intimacy is an integral part of the consummate intimacy expressed between spouses in marriage. I define intimacy as that process of coming to know and be known by another in deep, caring ways. It involves self-disclosure and the ability to be "naked and not ashamed" in emotional, physical, and psychological interaction. It entails an openness and shared vulnerability between spouses, which is dependent upon the security established in a committed relationship.

The wedding ceremony marks an important event in which two people eagerly promise to remain faithful to each other in the face of the unknown circumstances of physical, financial, and interpersonal stress; in sickness and in health, for richer or for poorer, for better or for worse. These vows of unconditional love are usually made before God and in the presence of family and friends who offer their communal backing and blessing. The bride and groom desire to know and be known in the most intimate ways, including sexual familiarity. They are pledging to grow together in an I-Thou encounter of personal disclosure and vulnerability in their marital union.

Ray Anderson speaks about this encounter in the following way: "For human persons, sexuality becomes a disclosure of the other being in such a way that a complementary relationship results, which both intensifies the 'I-Self' and enhances the 'I-Thou'" (1982:106). According to Anderson, intimacy is discovered when both persons are vulnerable and secure, when each can be defenseless in the presence of the other (1982:64).

Sexual intimacy is not so much a state to be achieved as it is an ongoing growth process. My purpose here is to present a practical theological model that underpins the process of becoming sexually intimate in marriage. The four theological principles of *covenant, grace, empowering,* and *intimacy* form the basis for relational intimacy in marriage. Based on these principles, I will suggest practical guidelines for growth in sexual intimacy.

The foundation for sexual intimacy in marriage is an unconditional love that is cultivated in an atmosphere of grace, forgiveness, and acceptance. Such an environment offers spouses an opportunity to take off their mask of pretense and show their real self to each other. Throughout the marriage, spouses learn about themselves and their partner through a reciprocal empowering process of mutual sharing, listening, understanding, giving, and receiving. Sexual intimacy is a maturing process of knowing and being known in the context of a trusting marital relationship.

THEOLOGICAL BASIS FOR MARITAL INTIMACY

Genesis 1 describes God in plural terms, depicting the relational aspects of the Trinity: "Let *us* make [humankind] in *our* image, in *our* likeness . . . " (1:26). Virginia Ramey Mollenkott explains that we are partakers of the divine nature in which "the equal partner love of one Person of the divine Triad is directed toward another" (1987:70). We are created as relational beings with a capacity for intimacy. This relational aspect of the Godhead has implications for human relationships in general and for marriage relationships in particular.

We can discover a model for intimacy in human relationships in the covenanting God of the Scriptures. Ray Anderson uses the concept of covenant to build a theological anthropology in his book *On Being Human*. He begins with the theological statement, "true humanity is determined as existence in covenant relation with God" (1982:37). He considers the marital relationship a "secondary order, made possible by the primary order of differentiation as male or female" (1982:52). This differentiated creatureliness is a response to the divine Word and results in cohumanity.

Adam is incomplete and cannot know himself on his own. When Eve comes into Adam's life, he recognizes her as "bone of my bones and flesh of my flesh" (Gn. 2:23). Phyllis Trible comments:

> These words speak unity, solidarity, mutuality, and equality. Accordingly, in this poem the man does not depict himself as either prior to or superior to the woman. His sexual identity depends upon her even as hers depends upon him. For both of them sexuality originates in the one flesh of humanity. (1978:99)

Trible contends that sexuality brings about a oneness that is wholeness. The woman is the man's companion, God's gift of life. Man moves toward her for union, and she is the one to whom he cleaves (1978:104). Differentiation and complementarity bring forth the possibility of marital "one flesh" union.

Anderson describes marriage as a covenant partnership that integrates sexuality into total humanity. Spouses commit themselves to a coexistence of surrendering their own cause to the cause of the other. There is a conscious and conscientious "determination to be one for the other and one with the other" (1985:91). Anderson believes that:

> . . . all humans can express a dimension of covenant love because they are created in the divine image and likeness. But God is the source of covenant love, which he expressed through his actions of bonding with Israel and then with all humanity through Jesus Christ. From the human perspective, the essence of a marriage is the social contract explicitly grounded in a relation of human sexuality, male and female, which finds its implicit source of covenant love in God's own commandment and gift of love. (1985:90)

A theology of family relationships has recently been developed that is based upon Anderson's covenant paradigm (Balswick & Balswick 1987). This model incorporates four logical and sequential stages: *covenant, grace, empowering,* and *intimacy.* I will apply these principles to marital sexual intimacy.

THE COVENANT PRINCIPLE

The covenant principle is *to love and be loved.* God enters into and sustains relationships with humankind in unconditional covenant love. In Hos. 11, God is depicted as an intimate, relational God. God is the parent who loves the children of Israel unconditionally and faithfully, and desires a mutual response of obedience and love. God is the Holy One in their midst to teach, lead, feed, protect, and provide. When Israel disobeys they suffer the consequences of their disobedience, yet Yahweh consistently offers reconciliation and restoration to them.

Intimacy requires security. God's covenant love is the secure foundation on which intimacy is built. In marital relationships, trustworthiness and faithfulness provide a secure foundation that motivates spouses to share themselves at deeper levels. Intimacy between partners requires an acceptance and keen desire to listen to, care for, and understand what the spouse is feeling and experiencing. Spouses who cherish each other and communicate this through thought and action provide a place where reciprocal sharing is possible. Spouses who are convinced that they are loved regardless of their failures and flaws can risk being naked and not ashamed. Covenant love in marriage establishes a confidence in which spouses have no need to hide themselves and are free to express their deepest longings, concerns, failures, and needs to each other.

The *unconditional* aspect of a covenant commitment leads to the first guideline: *Partners who feel secure in their commitment to one another will be more responsive sexually.* Research has shown that women are most able to invest themselves in sexual relationships when they feel secure about the relationship. Inversely, women who do not trust their spouse, or have fears that they may lose or be rejected by him, are less able to make an adequate sexual response. When security is lacking in a relationship, the sexual aspects tend to deteriorate.

There is evidence that men also desire such security in their sexual relationship. Males report that they desire sexual involvement because it makes them feel warm, secure, and affirmed in their masculinity. These critical relationship themes of security and trust bring about sexual responsiveness and authenticity.

A second major aspect of a covenant relationship as the basis for marriage is *mutuality*. God enters into and sustains relationships with humankind and desires that we, in turn, be in relationship with him and each other. God initiated this love as expressed in 1 Jn. 4:12, "We love him because he first loved us." God invites a response from all of creation to this unconditional love.

When couples appropriate this unconditional love of God to their marital union, they will have a maturing and deepening love of mutual commitment, acceptance, empowering, and intimacy. The security of such covenant love provides the atmosphere in which sexual intimacy can flourish. The second guideline, *A foundation for marital sexuality is mutuality*, corresponds to unconditional love.

The biblical view of marital sexuality is full mutuality, as seen in 1 Cor. 7:4-5:

> The wife's body does not belong to her alone but also to her husband. In the same way, the husband's body does not belong to him alone but also to his wife. Do not deprive each other except by mutual consent for a time, so that you may devote yourselves to prayer. Then come together again so Satan will not tempt you because of your lack of self-control.

The mutual consent in this verse indicates that the couple must agree together through an awareness of their equality and interdependence. Authentic marital sexuality is based upon the "one voice" of husband and wife in their sexual interaction. There is no room for the misguided view that the husband initiates and dominates while the wife unwillingly submits; the assumption in this scripture is that both partners desire sexual expression. Sexual harmony is possible through the mutuality of two unique persons sensitively expressing and responding to each other's sexual needs and desires.

THE GRACE PRINCIPLE

The principle of grace is *to forgive and be forgiven*. The incarnation is the supreme act of God's unconditional love to humankind. Christ came in human form to reconcile the world to God. This act of love and forgiveness in the Christ event is the basis for human love and forgiveness. We can forgive and accept others as we have been forgiven and accepted.

The love between God the Father and the only begotten Son is tenderly described in the familiar Jn. 3:16 passage, "For God so loved the world that He gave His only begotten Son." The intimacy of the relationship between the Father and Son is again declared in Jesus' prayer in the Garden of Gethsemane indicating the mutuality and reciprocity of that intimate relationship: "I have made you known to them, and will continue to make you known in order that the love you have for me may be in them and that I myself may be in them" (Jn. 17:26).

We are encouraged to love one another with grace and acceptance as we have been loved and accepted (just as we are) in God's grace and acceptability in Christ Jesus. This theme of acceptance suggests a third guideline in marital intimacy: *Partners are to be aware of and accept their own sexuality and the sexuality of their spouse.* The affirmation of one's own sexuality and the sexuality of one's partner comes by accepting sexuality as a gift of God's grace. God pronounced the creation good and acceptable!

When partners are comfortable with their sexuality and body image, they have no need to hide their sexual feelings and desires. There will be a positive attitude about the entire body, including the erogenous zones. Some spouses may try to show signs of interest but then act uninterested when their partner responds because they have difficulty accepting their sexual self.

"Two becoming one flesh" does not eradicate the individual, however. Marital sexuality entails the coming together of two people who are unique in their own sexuality. It is essential that spouses understand and appreciate each other's sexual value system.

An important aspect of accepting one's own sexuality is taking responsibility for one's sexual responsiveness. Instead of blaming the other person, unresponsive spouses need to take ownership and discover ways to increase their own sexual receptivity. If the relationship is pained and hurting on other levels of intimacy, this impact must be addressed. Such action is one way of taking responsibility for what needs changing so there can be a positive responsiveness. It is caring enough about the relationship to bring things out into the open so that change is possible.

It is true that our mind often has more to do with our ability to respond sexually than does our body. It is important for spouses to know their own sexuality and arousal potential in order to find ways to stay responsive sexually. What spouses tell themselves and how they prepare themselves sexually affects their openness to their partner and their own willingness to initiate a sexual approach as well. While all couples will have periodic difficulty with sexual arousal, regular sexual activity and functioning is important for satisfying involvement. Accepting God's good creation of sexuality in oneself and one's spouse leads to personal and mutual expression in sexual intimacy.

Grace also involves *accepting differences*. Differences between spouses are inevitable and must be addressed in a marital relationship. Personal and gender sexual values are developed through early childhood experiences and attitudes learned from the family, church, and community. There will be personal preferences concerning such matters as sexual practices, values, standards, desires, frequency of sexual activity. For example, one spouse may desire a sexual expression that the other partner is uncomfortable with. In this case, an understanding spouse will want to listen to the personal value system and the deep feelings it may provoke. Within the safety of covenant love, spouses will have the freedom to discuss these very personal matters. It will be necessary and appropriate for them to grapple together with these different values and the effect they have on their sexual relationship.

This leads to the fourth guideline: *Couples need to practice the art of forgiveness in their sexual relating.*

Spouses will disappoint one another and make mistakes that hurt their partner and their relationship. An attitude of forgiving and being forgiven can take the edge off disruptions inflicted by blunders, differences, and misunderstandings.

Reaching a mutual decision requires listening to the spouse's point of view in an effort to understand the differences. Sometimes a sexual request will be relinquished for the sake of one spouse or reevaluated for the sake of the other. It takes a loving commitment for the couple to work through decisions that will be right for their relationship and for each individual.

Spouses who put a priority on grace in this process find ways to work out differences in their sexual relationship, to the great benefit of their sexual intimacy. When negative or mixed messages have been given, when mistakes have been made or confusion has arisen out of difference, forgiveness is the ingredient of grace that can keep the couple in a helpful and hopeful growth process.

Persons who have experienced traumatic sexual encounters and abusive sexual situations will often repress or deny their sexuality as a protective measure. Such situations require extraordinary understanding because of the consequent serious damage and distortions. They also require time for sexual wholeness and restoration. Grace (acceptance and forgiveness) will be the environment in which healing is possible.

THE EMPOWERING PRINCIPLE

The empowering principle is *to serve and be served*. Jesus came to empower others, and he came as a servant. These two facts seem contradictory. This is certainly not the conventional idea of power, but a radical redefinition of it. Whereas the Holy Spirit was given to empower the believer to become a child of God (Jn. 1:12-13), Jesus came to empower the powerless. Jesus expresses his mission in Mk. 10:43-45, " . . . for the son of man did not come to be served, but to serve, and to give his life as a ransom for many." Jesus rejected the use of power to control others, but affirmed the use of power to serve others: to lift up the fallen, to forgive the guilty, to encourage responsibility and maturity, and to give power to the powerless.

Empowering is love in action. It involves the intentional process of empowering another person by recognizing and building up his or her strengths and potentials and encouraging the development of these qualities. Those who receive grace in Christ are empowered to act out the command to love and serve others as Christ modeled. These actions produce a maturing and intimate love.

Genesis 2:18 declares, "It is not good for the man to be alone, I will make a helper suitable for him." The word *helper* (*ezer neged*) can be interpreted as an "assistant suitable or appropriate," according to Virginia Ramey Mollenkott (1987:74). She points out that God is referred to as *ezer* sixteen times in the Old Testament as the one who assists those in need. This signifies a relational God not only showing compassion for the created ones but responding in active helping ways. Adam and Eve are partners suitable to help each other, to empower each other.

Phyllis Trible writes that Adam is given a companion who "alleviates isolation through identity" (1978:90). God presents Eve as a person equal to Adam who is created in God's own image and suitable for human relating. Eve is a person like Adam, different from all the other creatures and capable of sharing life in a "one flesh" communion. Adam and Eve are each to be cherished and valued. They are to be co-empowerers of one another's sexuality.

A fifth guideline is, *Spouses empower each other in the mutual giving and receiving of physical pleasure in the lovemaking experience.* The ability for spouses to be open and receptive to each other in a tender interaction of sexual pleasuring is not only mutually satisfying; it also builds a sense of well-being in the individual spouse. This affirmation of sexuality in oneself and the other is an empowering process.

In healthy sexual relationships, both partners view sexual activity as natural and enjoyable. There is a positive correlation between marital sexual satisfaction and a partner's general level of individual pleasure. The mutual, active enjoyment of being erotically attracted to and stimulated by one another is ego gratifying and empowering. Spouses who are keenly aware of their partner's preferences and unique value systems when giving and receiving pleasure will enhance responsiveness.

There will be natural times of ebb and flow in sexual arousal and desire in marriage—e.g. when the demands of child-caring responsibilities are high; during busy and stressful periods; when health problems diminish responsiveness. Other concerns such as anxiety about unwanted pregnancies, value compromises, and inadequate time or privacy will also diminish sexual functioning. Dry spells require patience, restraint, and support so that spouses will be empowered to be responsive once again. Good sexual functioning takes time, energy, and commitment. Couples who keep their relationship a priority and stay flexible in the ebb and flow bring the essential ingredients of grace and empowering into their intimacy.

Marital sexuality involves much more than physical intimacy, as stated in the sixth guideline: *Spouses empower each other by giving and receiving emotionally as well as physically.* The couple's alertness to feelings of closeness and intimacy in nonsexual ways is a reciprocal process. It is extremely important that spouses communicate verbally and nonverbally their expressions of tenderness, affection, understanding, desire, warmth, comfort, and excitement. When spouses take time to communicate and connect in emotional and physical ways, they invite an emotional responsiveness that empowers intimacy.

The self-esteem and well-being felt by spouses in the comfort and joy of simply being embraced by the other brings about a time of deepest intimacy. The vulnerability and love occurring in reciprocal emotional sharing leads to deeper levels of intimacy. It involves a mutual submissiveness in which spouses put the other's needs in a place of priority but express their own needs as well, providing opportunity for a giving and receiving interaction. Serving and being served is a mutually empowering process that deepens love and respect between spouses in their I-Thou encounter. This is an important part of sexual intimacy.

THE INTIMACY PRINCIPLE

The principle of intimacy is *to know and be known.* God knows us intimately! God sees the sparrow fall, counts the number of hairs on our head, knows us in all our ways. This is why the psalmist can cry out in agony as well as ecstasy to God, who knows the innermost parts of his being.

Adam and Eve stood before God completely open and transparent before the fall. They were naked before each other without shame and free to be themselves without pretense or deception. Their relationship with God was gravely disrupted when they disobeyed; they hid from God out of their nakedness and shame, interrupting their intimacy from God.

Fear leads people to put on masks and play deceptive games to keep from being known. The delight of knowing and being known is corrupted by mistrust. The capacity of spouses to communicate feelings with each other freely and openly is contingent upon the absence of fear. John gives us insight when he proclaims, "God is love. . . . There is no fear in love, but perfect love casts out fear" (1 Jn. 4:16, 18).

Our God is not to be feared! We are loved unconditionally, accepted through the atonement of Christ, and empowered by the Holy Spirit to live renewed and regenerated lives. Intimacy with God means that God knows, hears, and is present with us throughout all the unforeseen circumstances of our lives: in sickness and in health, for richer or poorer, for better or worse until our death.

Spouses have the need to be known in intimate ways. Lewis Smedes writes that God made body-persons (male and female) who could be intimate with one another and in the encounter come to know themselves. They were created as sexual beings to be sexual and personal: "They were, then, not to be merely sexual creatures; they were to be sexual persons, responsive to God's will in their development of his garden; and they were to be in personal communion with each other and with their personal creator" (1976:30).

The Song of Songs presents a beautiful picture of intimacy between two body-persons. The sexuality of these lovers is embedded in the loving relationship between the Lover and the Beloved. They are naked and not ashamed in their intimate expression of sensual and sexual love. It is an openly erotic love in which the focus, longing, and attraction is for the beloved him/herself. The mutual responsiveness is enjoyed in a shameless expression of intimacy. Embarrassment has no place because they are comfortable in their one flesh love.

An allegorical interpretation of the Song of Songs declares a bold, intimate love between God and the people of God. It pictures a relational God expressing a compelling love that is responded to and mutually returned by the receiver of the love. Such extraordinary love motivates the receiver to reciprocate by loving others in a similar way. God is the source of personal, intimate, all-knowing love.

The intimacy principle suggests the seventh guideline: *Spouses need to communicate their sexual feelings and desires to each other.* Each spouse needs to know what the other desires sexually, without having to play a guessing game. Often sexual desire is communicated nonverbally, but it is important that the communication be verbalized as well. The couple will do well to find their own special way and the appropriate time to communicate about their sexual relationship so the thoughts and needs that are expressed can be received and responded to.

Guiding each other nonverbally and verbally during lovemaking can be a helpful way to communicate sexually. However, it is also essential to take special time to talk together about the sexual relationship separately from physical involvement. It is useful to have periodic evaluations on how each is feeling about the sexual relationship and to address dissatisfactions so there can be needed adjustment. This is often difficult for couples to put into practice, but if differences are not addressed they tend to take on more dysfunctional patterns of dissatisfaction.

Discussing sexual interaction openly helps in finding ways to improve and reinforce those things contributing positively to the sexual relationship. Areas of disagreement should be expected since spouses come to the relationship with a personal sexual value system. These values need to be honored and carefully understood.

The intimacy principle also suggests an eighth guideline: *Personal involvement is an important part of sexual interaction.* One way to be involved is through a *playful responsiveness.* Playfulness occurs when there is a lack of self-consciousness, embarrassment, or shame about nudity and sexual involvement. Honesty in communication and a healthy view of one's sexual self and one's body are vital ingredients in the freedom to enter into a playful encounter. The opposite extreme of playfulness is making a production out of sex. Controlling the sexual encounter in such a way that it becomes a contrived and serious event takes away important spontaneity and the freedom to be open and responsive to one another.

The other crucial part of involvement is *the ability to give personally of oneself freely and without fear.* It is the ability to be unabashedly responsive to the spouse with body, mind, and soul. Once again, spouses who are comfortable with themselves sexually are not self-conscious during love-making and are free to respond with their whole being. Partners who become self-conscious in how they perform or how they look to themselves or the other assume a "spectator role" during coitus. They tend to remove themselves from the scene rather than participate in it. When this happens the focus on performance inhibits spontaneous personal responses.

We live in a technologically-oriented society which emphasizes the "right technique." This may lead some to reduce intimacy to little more than an exercise of techniques, similar to a paint-by-number kit. Following the specific instructions of a sex manual on every detail forces upon the couple a set of rules or techniques that dictate their lovemaking. The outcome is unsatisfactory because there is no creative personal interaction. In a very real sense, the personhood of each spouse has been lost in the effort to make love "by the book." The intimate response between lover and beloved has been replaced by an effort to be technically proficient.

When people separate themselves from their sexual involvement they focus on their role as lovemaker and fail to be involved in the lovemaking experience itself. This removal of self in the sexual event invariably leads to a self-defeating activity because it reduces personal intimacy and the interactional experience. Authentic sexuality requires that partners freely and naturally express feelings, inclinations, and actions.

In the authentic sexual role, each person is spontaneously involved as an active participator. Healthy marital sex occurs when partners are personally and presently involved in the encounter and are able to "lose" themselves in the moment. Sex becomes a reciprocal giving and receiving activity that increases the one-flesh complementary union.

The ability to be intimate, to know and be known, is a process that grows out of the other three principles. The safety and security of being known comes out of the trust established between spouses in an unconditional covenant love. Covenant love is based on the grace principle (acceptance and forgiveness) and leads to the empowering principle, the mutual giving and receiving that lead to intimacy.

Because God first loved us, we are enabled to love others in a similar way. The security of God's love, grace, and empowering gives us the desire to reciprocate that love and to know and love God intimately in return.

These four dimensions—covenant, grace, empowering, and intimacy— are to be woven throughout the fabric of the couple's whole relationship. Sexual intimacy should be viewed in the context of the overall intimacy between spouses, which is what really determines the overall quality and satisfaction of the marital relationship.

These principles of marital sexuality can be applied to the aspects of relational love, which is grounded in God's covenantal love. A commitment establishes the security that fosters sexual responsiveness. This trust is the solid foundation of healthy marital sexuality. The dimensions of forgiveness and grace allow spouses to accept each other's unique needs and desires and to work through differences and preferences in a loving atmosphere of grace. Disappointments and disruptions in the sexual relationship require a forgiving and accepting attitude.

The serving and empowering principles require that spouses do not make unreasonable demands on each other, but find ways to empower each other through a loving and mutual giving and receiving of themselves. Empowering and being willing to be empowered by the other will result in increased pleasure as the couple knits their lives together in the one flesh sexual union.

Finally, the intimacy dimension involves disclosing, communicating, understanding, appreciating, and cherishing the beloved. Aspiring to know and be known by the other will require that spouses are able to be vulnerable with one another. All aspects of sexual intimacy come through that covenant commitment to the spouse that leads to emotional closeness and oneness. Intimacy is about the beloved, and sexual satisfaction is a wonderful byproduct of the marital relationship. Love deepens as the relationship moves throughout the cycle of covenant, grace, empowering, and intimacy in a growing marriage.

REFERENCES

Anderson, Ray S. 1982. *On being human.* Grand Rapids: Eerdmans.
Anderson, Ray S., and Dennis B. Guernsey. 1985. *On being family.* Grand Rapids: Eerdmans.
Balswick, Jack O., and Judith K. Balswick. 1987. A theological basis for family relationships. *Journal of Psychology and Christianity* 6 (3):(Fall).
Mollenkott, Virginia Ramey. 1987. *The divine feminine.* New York: Crossroad.
Smedes, Lewis B. 1976. *Sex for Christians.* Grand Rapids: Eerdmans.
Trible, Phyllis. 1978. *God and the rhetoric of sexuality.* Philadelphia: Fortress.

21

CAMERON LEE

✦

Toward an Integrative Theology of Parent-Child Interaction

C HRISTIAN AND NON-CHRISTIAN parents alike bring a host of assumptions to the vocation of raising their children. Many of these assumptions, if conscious at all, are vague or unarticulated. Christian parents in particular are often at a loss to understand how their faith relates to this aspect of their lives beyond, perhaps, teaching children proper behavior and the basic tenets of their belief. For this reason, I have attempted an integrative theology of parent-child interaction.

As the title suggests, my focus is *parent-child interaction*: that is, the *relationship* of parents and children as opposed to their characteristics as individual humans. Each partner in this relationship makes demands upon the other to adapt, in what Stern describes metaphorically as an interpersonal "dance."[1] It is the nature and quality of this relationship that I wish to examine. For the sake of simplicity, I will often use the handier word *parenting* as shorthand for this two-person interaction. It must be clearly understood, however, that parenting is not something a parent "does" unilaterally to a child, any more than child development is reducible to a biologically predetermined series of events. "Parenting" denotes a relationship in which, if it goes well, parent and child develop and grow *together*, as each responds to the other's humanness.

My goal is to begin to elucidate a *theology* of parent-child interaction. This is not a study of biblical texts relating to parenthood, whether in reference to human parents or to God as parent. These two topics, worthy of separate treatment, will not be explored here. My purpose, rather, is to examine the broader theological question: "What essential characteristics of created human existence are reflected in the parent-child relationship?" I will address this question by developing an understanding of the parent-child relationship that is founded upon a theological anthropology.

This understanding is to be an *integrative* model: I will make use of knowledge derived from sources other than theology itself. In particular, I will frequently employ the language and perspective of *object-relations theory,* a contemporary offspring of psychoanalysis.[2] Object-relations theory is a critical departure form classical psychoanalysis as espoused by Freud. In general, an object-relations view of human development deemphasizes the role of innate biological drives and assigns more critical importance to the quality of the parent-child (usually mother-infant) relationship. Theorists such as W. R. D. Fairbairn take this further by asserting that the fundamental human drive is not seeking pleasure (or reduction of biological tension), as Freud would have it, but seeking contact and relations with others.[3] As we shall see, such a perspective is relevant to the relational ontology to be developed here.

The primary task, however, remains a theological one. As Emil Brunner wrote, "Man must first of all be defined theologically; only then may the philosopher, the psychologist and the biologist make their statements."[4] The foundation for a theology of parent-child interaction is a theological anthropology that recognizes the importance of *relatedness*—as opposed to locating the essence of the human creature solely in the qualities of the individual. The strands of a fully relational anthropology run throughout the history of Protestant interpretations of two core biblical assertions about humankind: (1) that humans are created in God's image (*imago Dei*), and (2) that humans are nonetheless sinful and fallen. The relational interpretation has been most recently and cogently exegeted by Hall, to whom I am greatly indebted.[5] Due to limitations of both space and competence, I will not attempt a full anthropology: the reader is referred to Hall and others cited in the notes. My goal in the following section is more modest: namely, to discuss briefly the highlights of a relational theology of human nature. This discussion will then form the backdrop for a more specific consideration of parent-child interaction.

THE *IMAGO DEI* AND HUMAN SINFULNESS

In attempting to define the term "image of God," theologians have tried to balance two closely related doctrinal questions. First, what is the content of the concept? In other words, what does Scripture intend by the term? The references are relatively few, and somewhat ambiguous.[6] Although theologians are virtually unanimous in assigning to the image the *sine qua non* of humanity, they differ markedly in their interpretations. The second doctrinal question is, can post-lapsarian humanity be said to retain the image, and if so, how? While most theologians will agree that humanity after the fall still retained something of its essential humanness, they differ here, too, regarding the effect of sin upon the image.[7]

In the brief survey below, I will argue that: (1) the concept of the *imago Dei* points to human being as being-in-relation,[8] and (2) sin is evidenced in the breaking of this essential relatedness.

The image of God: human being as being-in-relation

As Hall notes, theological interpretations of the *imago* can generally be divided into two categories, which he calls *substantialist* and *relational* concepts.[9]

Substantialist interpretations view the image as representing some characteristic that distinguishes the human creature from the rest of creation. This characteristic is seen as a "possession," in principle at least, of every human individual. The early church, for example, often identified the image with human reason or rationality.[10] Substantialist notions such as this are often not derived directly from Scripture, but reflect instead previously held beliefs about the noblest aspects of human nature.[11] Regardless of the characteristic proposed, however, what is important is that these views share this common assumption: the image of God represents human essence defined in the abstract, logically prior to any concrete human existence. This abstract essence is then to be found in each individual instance of humanity.

From a substantialist point of view, actual relationships are to some extent accidents of existence. Relational interpretations invert this emphasis by interpreting the *imago* dynamically as a statement of relationship. The essence of humanness is not an abstract quality which is manifested in isolated individuals, but is inseparably and ontologically bound to the actual relationships of humans to God, to each other, and to the rest of God's non-human creation.[12]

Different writers emphasize different aspects of this threefold relational matrix, though generally viewing the relationship to God as fundamental. Westermann, for example, directly counters substantialist interpretations by arguing that the statement that humans were created in God's image cannot be abstracted from its context: namely, the creation account itself:

> What does the phrase mean? It is not a declaration about man, but about the creation of man. . . . The creator created a creature that corresponds to him, to whom he can speak, and who can hear him. . . . Creation in the image of God is not concerned with an individual, but with mankind, the species, man. The meaning is that mankind is created so that something can happen between God and man. Mankind is created to stand before God.[13]

Brunner takes up a similar theme of divine call and human response, arguing that relationship to God is constitutive of human existence itself:

"Created in His Image, in His Likeness" . . . says that the nature of man . . . is
nothing in itself, and that it is not intelligible from itself, but that its ground of
existence and knowledge is in God. . . . The being of man as an "I" is being from
and in the Divine "Thou" . . . whose claim "calls" man's being into existence. . . . From the side of God this twofold relation is known as a "call," and
from that of man as an "answer"; thus the heart of man's being is seen to be:
responsible existence.[14]

Brunner's phrase "responsible existence" sums up the insight that human
being is indeed being-in-relation, and that the image of God is manifested
in responsiveness in relation.

Human being as being-in-relation entails that responsible (or "response-
able") existence also characterizes interhuman relationships. As Brunner
insists, "Responsibility-in-love first becomes real in man's relation with his
fellow-men."[15] Similarly, Hall interprets the thematic intent of the *imago*
dynamically. The image is not a thing, but a process; it is not a possession or
endowment, but an actual orientation of our very being by which we image
God in *all* our relationships. He summarizes the relational view thus:
"[T]he whole intention of the relational conception of the image of God is
to position the human creature responsibly in relation to other creatures. . . . Relationship is of the essence of this creature's nature and
vocation."[16]

The relational perspective is therefore more than a recognition of the
importance of relationships to individual humans. It is a challenge to an
individualistic, substantialist ontology. Relatedness is not merely an arti-
fact of human existence, it is of the very essence of being human.

This ontological distinctive must be kept clear. Hoekema, for example,
maintains that there are both *structural* and *functional* aspects of human
being — what humans *are* as opposed to what they *do*. He places human gifts
and capacities in the first category; and relationship to God, other humans,
and the world in the second.[17] The question is whether or not relationships
are human "functions" or intrinsic to human "structure." I would agree
with Hall and others in arguing for the latter. The image is not to be
identified with human relationship in a functional sense. Rather, actual
relationships between particular humans are a functional necessity because
the human creature is relational in its very structure.[18]

We must avoid, however, a false dichotomy between structure and
function, or between substantialist and relational options, by making our
ontological assertions clear. A relational anthropology, properly understood, invalidates not the notion of the human as an individual, but an
ontology that limits the human essence to individual characteristics. Even
if the relational exegesis of the biblical statements regarding the image were
completely correct, which is by no means certain, it would still be

indeterminate as to whether these statements should be interpreted structurally or functionally. It may be, therefore, an equal but opposite logical error to conclude that *no* essential aspect of humanness is attributable to individual humans.

The assumption in either extreme, furthermore, is that the image is to be interpreted as exhaustive of anthropology. This assumption lifts Scripture out of its revelatory function and into the realm of a philosophical treatise. A more productive approach would be to articulate the essential "relationality" of human existence more carefully, and maintain a creative tension between individual and relational concerns. In other words, though the I-Thou relationship may be fundamental, there is nevertheless an I and a Thou, neither of which is reducible to the other.

Human sinfulness, broken relatedness

To recognize that humans are created in God's image is to affirm only half the story. Through Christ and the Scriptures, God has also revealed to us our inherent sinfulness. This biblical revelation is more than simply an awareness of the human propensity for evil. The "dark side" of human nature is to some extent common coin among the religious currencies of the world. Rather, what God has revealed is the personal side of sin: that is, our sin is neither an abstract attribute of the individual human, nor a violation of an impersonal moral code, but a personal sin against a personal God, our Creator. As Berkouwer writes:

> All the biblical descriptions of our sins have a single trait in common: *sin is always in relation to God.* Therefore our sin is not an apparent "deficiency" or the result of human, creaturely limitations and the relativities of our living. . . . Man's sin can only be *revealed,* since its origins can only be found in this disruption of the relation of man and God.[19]

The church has traditionally affirmed the universality of sin, and hence the universal need for grace, through the doctrine of original sin. Although the notion was largely discarded by liberal theology during the Enlightenment, postwar theology strongly reemphasized human depravity. Abandoning fruitless speculation regarding the inheritance or transmission of original sin, Neo-Orthodox theologians in particular affirmed the depth and mystery of human sin. The core of the doctrine was declared as the revelation of our solidarity as a sinful race, in personal rebellion against God. Thus Otto Weber interprets original sin as a relational statement:

> If we understand sin basically as the rebellion against God's goodness and the distortion of the relationship between the Creator and creature, then the doctrine of "original sin" can only be properly understood when it is seen, not as a given state alone, but in terms of that relationship.[20]

In relational terms, sin is *personal*. It is an interpersonal affront, an act against our intrinsic being-in-relation. The sin that is originally a sin against God manifests itself in our fallen state as sin against other humans. As Berkouwer notes, the "double command to love" (Mt. 22:37-39) entails an unbreakable connection between these two personal sins.[21] He writes:

> [I]t is impossible, in a scriptural focus, to draw a line between a "real" sinning against God and an "unreal" sinning against our neighbors. Far better to profess that a love for our neighbor is a God-given injunction; therefore an injury to our neighbor is a violation of his command.[22]

Similarly, Weber concludes that the doctrine of original sin teaches that "our existence as sinners is also a social existence as sinners." He continues:

> We have all fallen, are all comprehended within sin, and that means that we now are involved in leading each other astray, in our relationships to one another. . . . "Original sin" is sin to the degree that it defines me totally. As such, it is not a condition, but a relationship, and it is realized in me continually in my relational behavior.[23]

The bipolarity of being-in-relation

These two cardinal doctrines of theological anthropology, that humans are created in God's image and yet are sinful, can be incorporated into a single model of being-in-relation which maintains individual and relational considerations in a mutually interdependent tension. This model, upon which I base a theology of parenting, is suggested by a variety of sources, including Hall's "ontology of communion,"[24] T. F. Torrance's exposition of the double aspect of the contingence of the created order,[25] and John Macmurray's notion of the bipolar nature of personal motivation.[26] Since Macmurray's writing focuses specifically on the mother-child relationship, I will discuss his views in the next section.

As Brunner's terms "call," "answer," and "responsibility-in-love" aptly suggest, the relationships by which humans image God are neither mechanical nor instrumental, but fully *personal*. As Karl Barth argues, covenant is the internal motivation of creation, and the covenant God desires mutual fellowship with his human creatures.[27] Several authors have given the name "communion" to the deeply personal character of this relationship. Hall, for example, borrows the term "the ontology of communion" as he describes creation as a natural outpouring of the divine *Mitsein,* or "being-with":

> The biblical God is busy from the first sentence of Genesis making beings who can participate in his own overflowing *Mitsein.* . . . [N]ot only the steadfast love (*hesed*) but also the anger, wrath, jealousy of this God—all betray God's appar-

ently innate drive towrad an ever more actualized relatedness: "I will be your God, and you will be my people!" God may be transcendent . . . [y]et all of God's otherness is directed to the service of a single biblical theme: the absolute purity and intensity of the divine *agape*.[28]

The creation of the human is an extension of God's own being-in-relation. This creation entails a call to the creature. As Brunner writes, humans are summoned to communion with God:

> The original Divine Word therefore is not first of all a demand, because it is self-communication, a Divine word of love which summons man to communion with Him, the Creator, as the destiny of man. . . . Man is destined to answer God in believing, responsive love, to accept in grateful dependence his destiny to which God has called him, as his life.[29]

Thus, human being is fully human in response to the divine call. It is a response of love to an act of love. In the words of W. W. Meissner, "The loving initiative of God's self-communication through grace is both an invitation and an inner urging of the soul toward union with God."[30]

True humanity, however, is found *not only* in a response of love toward God, *but also* toward other humans with whom we share divine call. For Barth, human being is being in encounter, which entails: (1) a "two-sided openness," embodied in the act of looking each other in the eye; (2) the personal address and reception of mutual speech and hearing; (3) the "being for one another" in the rendering of mutual assistance; and (4) the fact that all these are "done on both sides with gladness."[31]

The converse of this, of course, is sin, which stands over against being-in-relation. If the image of God is manifest in the personal divine-human and human-human relationships of communion, then sin is the personal act that disrupts these relationships. To cite Brunner once again: "The sin of Adam is the destruction of communion with God, which is at the same time the severance of this bond; it is that state of 'being against God' which also means 'being against one another.'"[32] Thus, as noted earlier, because the image of God points to human being as being-in-relation, human sin is not in relationship to God only, but also in relationship to other humans.

I am suggesting that for sinful humanity, theologically, being-in-relation involves a twofold aspect. There is the positive aspect of dependence upon the other, grounded in the image of God. This positive aspect is manifested in a positive movement toward relationship, in response to the call to interpersonal communion. There is also the negative aspect of relative independence as an individual person. When the negative aspect becomes a negative movement away from the other, in rejection of communion, this is in evidence of original sin.

It is important, however, to understand this negative movement correctly. T. F. Torrance asserts that the entire created order, in its contingence upon God, shows a dual positive and negative orientation:

> Contingence has at once an orientation toward God in dependence on him, and an orientation away from God in a relative independence of him. . . . Orientation toward God may be regarded as the positive aspect of contingence, for it is from God that the universe derives its being and order, while orientation away from God may be regarded as the negative aspect of contingence, for it implies that if the universe were left entirely to itself it would be without being or order.[33]

Torrance does not, however, identify negative contingence with sin, though it is a necessary condition for sin to occur. These two aspects of contingence are not mutually contradictory, but complementary:

> [W]hat we have called the negative aspect of contingence in no sense negates the positive aspect but fulfills its function within the positive, thereby contributing itself positively to the full nature of the contingence.[34]

Sin is thus not equal to the human's relative independence as a creature, but is rather the human identification with the negative movement, which severs the creaturely independence from its dependence:

> Certainly evil is found breaking into creaturely being, introducing disorder and bringing about ontological collapse, yet the creature becomes so identified with this evil that it willingly revolts from the Creator in a suicidal movement to *break off its independence from dependence* on him, and thereby lurches toward non-being.[35]

As I said earlier, a relational ontology does not invalidate the notion of the individual. This is important to a proper understanding of the double aspect, the bipolarity, of being-in-relation. As even Martin Buber asserts, it is not possible for a human to live perpetually in I-Thou encounter.[36] There are times of withdrawal from encounter that are legitimate to the existence of individuality, a relative independence characteristic of the negative aspect of the contingence of creation. What is problematic is the *severance* of individuality from relationship, of independence from dependence (or interdependence): the attempt of the I to define itself without reference to a Thou. As Barth writes:

> To the extent that we withhold and conceal ourselves, and therefore do not move or move any more out of ourselves to know others and to let ourselves be known

by them, our existence is inhuman. . . . The isolation in which we try to persist, the lack of participation which we show in relation to others and thus thrust upon others in relation to ourselves, is inhumanity.[37]

Being-in-relation, then, has both individual and relational poles. Being human means that while we exist as individuals, this is only a relative existence; our humanity in the image of God is defined in relation both to God and to neighbor. The shadow of original sin falls upon our contingent individuality as we identify ourselves with this negative movement, ironically cutting ourselves off from the relationships that define us.

BEING-IN-RELATION AND
THE PARENT-CHILD INTERACTION

The theology of the *imago* and of human sinfulness outlined above points to the essential relatedness of human nature. This being-in-relation, which has a bipolar aspect, extends both to the relationship between creator and creature as well as to the relationships between human creatures. How, then, do we proceed to develop a theology of parent-child interaction?

What must be integrated into this theological base is the single but multifaceted concept of *human development*. Children are born with social endowments that orient them toward relationship with their caretakers. Yet while they are born fully human, they are immature. The nascent and inchoate "I" or self of the child encounters a personal limitation in the parent's "Thou," and it is upon this interpersonal foundation that the child's emotional development rests. Parents, therefore, bear the responsibility of creating a proper environment for this development to occur. In this section, I will apply the bipolar understanding of being-in-relation to the parent and child, as a springboard for a theology of parenting.

John Macmurray discusses the bipolarity of the mother-child relationship. His personalistic ontology, applied to the infant, is clearly relational:

> In the human infant . . . the impulse to communication is his sole adaption to the world into which he is born. Implicit and unconscious it may be, yet it is sufficient to constitute the mother-child relation as the basic form of human existence, as a personal mutuality, as a "You and I" with a common life. For this reason the infant is born a person and not an animal. . . . All this may be summed up by saying that *the unit of personal existence is not the individual, but two persons in personal relation; and that we are not persons by individual right, but in virtue of our relation to one another.* The personal is constituted by personal relations. The unit of the personal is not the "I," but the "You and I."[38]

Failures of personal relationship on the part of the parent are inevitable, however, whether or not they are intentional. What follows is a negative movement in which the infant may self-defensively reject this relationship:

> Since the "You and I" relation constitutes both the "You" and "I" persons, the relation to the "You" is necessary for my personal existence. If, through fear of the "You," I reject this relation, I frustrate my own being.[39]

What the infant requires is restored confidence in the relationship, effected by an act of grace on the part of the parent:

> [S]ince it was by his mother's action that the child's confidence was broken, it is only by her action that this confidence can be restored. If we may use the language of mature human reflection which, though its content is much richer, has an identical form, *the child can only be rescued from his despair by the grace of the mother; by a revelation of her continued love and care which convince him that his fears are groundless.*[40]

The restoration of "confidence," in Macmurray's language, is what I would identify as the reestablishment of the positive movement of being-in-relation.

Macmurray's analysis, taken in the present context, suggests a theology of parenting along the lines of the bipolar model of being-in-relation. In outline, such an integrative theology suggests that: (1) the child's intrinsic sociality is a manifestation of the image of God as a nascent being-in-relation; (2) the parent's response of love is a call to interpersonal communion; (3) repeated failures of relationship prompt the child's innate tendency to reject being-in-relation, an act attributable theologically to original sin; and (4) parenting is "good-enough" when the negative experiences of being-in-relation can be contained by the positive, constituting the communication of grace to the child. I will discuss these briefly in turn.

The image of God in the prosocial child

I have argued that human being is being-in-relation. Many child psychologists have insisted, however, that children are not primarily social at birth; the sociality of the child, in other words, is not a human given from the start, but a developmental achievement. Margaret Mahler, for example, though a brilliant expositor of the importance of early parent-child transactions, argues that the infant is autistic at birth, inwardly focused on attaining physiological stability, and oblivious to external stimulation and relationships.[41]

A recent spate of developmental research, however, documents the wide range of prosocial behaviors in the neonate's repertoire, suggesting an intrinsic orientation to human relatedness from the moment of birth.

Reviewing this body of empirical findings, Stern remarks: "The infant comes into the world bringing formidable capabilities to establish human relatedness. Immediately he is a partner in shaping his first and foremost relationships."[42] Similarly, based on her own research, Temeles discards the view that the infant is "an egocentric isolate, requiring considerable maturation and stimulation before he becomes a part of the real world," and asserts instead that "the infant is socially competent from the beginning."[43]

I am suggesting that this intrinsic sociality is an indication of being-in-relation, the child's humanity in the image of God. Once this is recognized, it is still possible to incorporate concepts such as Mahler's "normal autism," provided that the autistic orientation is not held as absolute. In other words, the initial internal directedness which Mahler suggests indicates that interwoven with the child's emotional development is a simultaneous line of physiological maturation. Theologically, however, this may be interpreted as development of the creaturely "substratum," as it were, a necessary but insufficient condition of the image as being-in-relation.

Empathy and interpersonal communion

The relationship between parent and infant, though having instrumental aspects, is primarily *personal*. As Guntrip writes:

> A personal relationship is one in which between persons there is neither constraint nor enforced demand on either side, but freedom. They exist primarily not to serve each other, a Utilitarian value, but to have communion with each other, each valuing the other as an end to himself.[44]

The communion of persons is the positive movement of being-in-relation. This is particularly true in the parent-child relationship, where the parent's ministrations in effect summon the child to a personal relationship that transcends the instrumental functions of child care.

The quality of the parent's interactions is important for the child's subsequent development of self in relation to others. Parents must be able to *empathize* with the self of the immature child, to identify with the child's emotional state without simultaneously losing an adult's perspective. A truly empathic parent responds to a child according to an "insider's view" of what the child is experiencing. Over time, this results in an ongoing relationship of trust, in which the child continues to extend herself personally in relationship to a parent who has proven trustworthy.[45]

In this vein, Daniel Stern has noted an empathic ability of some mothers to perform what he calls "affect attunement."[46] These mothers seemed to able to "get inside" an infant's experience, matching their responses to the infant's emotional state. These types of interactions mesh with and facilitate a child's emotional experiences, rather than interfering with and interrupting them. Stern asked these mothers to explain what they were doing:

> The largest single reason that mothers gave (or that we inferred) for performing an attunement was "to be with" the infant, "to share," "to participate in," "to join in." We have called these functions *interpersonal communion*. . . . Communion means to share in another's experience with no attempt to change what that person is doing or believing.[47]

Thus Stern, also, employs the word *communion* to signify an interaction in which the relationship is an end in itself. The parent's act of love encourages the child's own spontaneous response of being-in-relation.

Failures of being-in-relation and original sin

Not all parental behaviors, of course, are attuned to a child's emotions. Parents sometimes "misattune" purposely to achieve a desired end, such as teaching a child behavioral limits. Or they may misattune unwittingly, by misinterpreting a child's inner state. Either way, such misattunements, which are inevitable in the course of real life, interrupt what Winnicott calls the child's spontaneous "going-on-being," and in excess provoke a reaction of anxiety.[48]

This is not problematic in itself, where the child has a sufficient experience of the parent's accurately empathic care to provide the foundation of trust. Where this foundation is lacking, however, the parent's responses are experienced as either invasive or void. In serious cases, the child, instead of being encouraged to participate in personal relations, chooses against her own being by rejecting relationship. Winnicott describes the child as hiding away her true, spontaneous self, and erecting in its place a "false self," a defensive structure that acts as a decoy to protect the real, vulnerable person inside.[49] This self-protective act must be understood as adaptive in an emotional environment which is hostile to the child's spontaneity. It is, however, an act against being-in-relation, and is therefore an injury to the child's very humanness.

If the earlier relational exposition of sin was at all valid, then the child's innate defensive reaction can be interpreted as a manifestation of original sin. Indeed, Macmurray makes a passing remark that supports such a view. Using the term "hatred" to denote the negative motivation in the bipolar relationship, Macmurray writes:

> This mutuality of hatred as the motive of a negative relation of persons is clearly an evil. Hatred itself, as an original and necessary motive in the constitution of the personal, is perhaps what is referred to as original sin.[50]

This is, of course, quite different from imputing original sin to young children in the sense of conscious moral error. Such interpretations tend to run aground on determinations of a child's "age of accountability," and so on. What I am suggesting here is twofold. First, original sin in the child is demonstrated in the innate yet unconscious defensive reaction that severs individuality from relationship. This is not a conscious choice but an automatic defense. Second, this failure of being-in-relation cannot be imputed to the child alone, but must be understood in the context of environmental deficits. This includes the parent's own failures of empathy, which are just as certainly failures of being-in-relation and hence indicative of sin.

I am not suggesting that sin is a wholly unconscious phenomenon, only that its form is unconscious in the earliest stage of life. The real crux of the matter has to do with how one understands human nature and thus sin in that context. Identifying the human essence with conscious rationality or freedom of choice raises the difficulty of how sin is to be imputed to very young children, whose rational faculties are too immature to bear adult motives. Such a view can wrongly interpret childish behavior as "willful disobedience" at an age when children may be largely incapable of comprehending the alternatives. If, however, the human essence is to be interpreted relationally, then the identification of original sin in the child no longer turns upon the criterion of consciousness. Later, when the child's cognitive capacities have matured, sin will be evidenced in conscious as well as unconscious motives.

Good-enough parenting and common grace

There are good parents, but there are no "perfect" parents. It is not humanly possible for a parent to be perfectly attuned to every emotional nuance of a child. Even if such a parent existed, that child would not be realistically well-adapted to life with others outside the protective circle of home.

This is the implication of Winnicott's phrase, the "good-enough mother."[51] The basic notion is that an infant, in the earliest weeks, needs a nurturing environment that will adapt to *his* needs, rather than demanding that he adapt to it. This provision is the normal and expectable responsibility of the parent. Given such an adequate foundation, the child will eventually learn to tolerate frustrations, misattunements, and environmental demands without resorting to a defensive posture. This suggests that "perfect" parenting is not only impossible but undesirable, for the gradual introduction of frustration into a basically trustworthy relationship is necessary for the infant to adapt realistically to the outside world. The end result is that the child is able to internalize non-defensively both good and bad experiences of being-in-relation. In terms of the model presented above, the child will be able to hold both the positive and negative aspects of relation together, without splitting them apart.

I would argue that from the child's perspective, good-enough parenting is ultimately an experience of grace. The good-enough parent must at some level have experienced what theologians call a "covenantal" kind of love, an unconditional acceptance that transcends the good and bad experiences of the moment. This is the parent's root experience of grace, which is transmitted to the child through the parent's care and ministrations.

This is not, of course, identical with the divine saving grace that God bestows through Christ. It is rather a product of "common grace," of God's continuing covenant love for his creation and his refusal to abandon it, despite its fallenness. It is by common grace that sinful parents are still able to communicate a love to their children that is good-enough. As Reinhold Niebuhr writes:

> [T]he law of love is indeed the basis of all moral life, that it can not be obeyed by a simple act of the will because the power of self-concern is too great, and that the forces which draw the self from its undue self-concern are usually forces of "common grace" in the sense that they represent all forms of social security or responsibility or pressure which prompt the self to bethink itself of its social essence and to realize itself by not trying too desperately for self-realization.[52]

What Niebuhr describes as a desperate bid for self-realization is an ontological impossibility, for self can only be realized in relationship to the other. Good-enough parenting provides the basic security without which a child protectively withdraws from the personal relationships that are the foundation of his being.

CONCLUSION

I have attempted to outline an integrative theology of parenting with an explicitly developmental perspective. This requires that we view the child not as an adult-in-miniature, nor as a non-human bundle of biological reflexes, but as a being who needs a nurturant human environment to grow. The child, as we have seen, is directed toward human relatedness from the outset. Thus, to use Hartmann's phrase, the "average expectable environment" to which the human infant is adapted is an *interpersonal* one.[53] From this standpoint, parenting may be conceptualized in terms of the parent's role in either facilitating or frustrating the developing child's inherent drive for human relatedness.[54]

The relationship established between parent and child is the normative arena for the earliest stages of the development of the child's personhood. The patterns thus established do not, of course, fully determine the child's later adjustment. Where parenting has not been good-enough, however, these patterns will remain a critical factor, especially in the absence of some form of remedial relationship. As Macmurray writes:

> The original pattern of personal behavior is not merely a starting-point. It is not left behind as the child grows up. It remains the ground of all personal motivation at every stage of development. If the *terminus ad quo* of the personal life is a helpless total dependence on the Other, the *terminus ad quem* is not independence, but a mutual interdependence of equals.[55]

The parents' responsibility, in a sense, is to create the original template that sets the pattern for the child's interpersonal relationships. I must emphasize, however, that I view the significance of parenting seriously but not deterministically. The template can be changed, but the cost is often dear. Personal relatedness is forged in an interpersonal context. What has been learned can be unlearned, but such learning may require a relationship equal in significance to that with the parents.

Many parents, especially mothers, have rightly objected to being held captive by the popular prejudice that they are somehow to blame for everything "wrong" with their children. Some readers may feel that the approach I have taken here adds to that burden: that if their children do not develop spiritually, or if they turn away from God, then that deficit stems directly from parental inadequacies. This is only a partial truth, which becomes dangerously distorted if not taken in proper theological context.

It is true that parents bear what I believe to be God-given responsibilities toward their children. It is also true that we are sinful people who live in a fallen world and are constantly in need of God's grace. Much of the blame that has been laid at parents' doorsteps is implicitly infused with the fantasy of perfect parenthood. This is untenable, given the biblical witness to the ubiquity of sin.

The fact that God give parents responsibilities is not a demand for the parents to *be* God to their children. Unwittingly perhaps, parents play God when they search after the formula for turning out perfect children. This may be motivated less by altruism than by an unconscious resistance to come to terms with one's own limitations, or in turn, the limitations of one's own children or parents. Parents must recognize that despite their greater degree of responsibility, they, with their children, share in the fallen humanity that has been redeemed by God's grace. Parents who are dishonest about their own crippledness teach their children, by word and deed, to blind themselves to their own limitations.

What all parents can impart to their children is a realistic love and the common grace of a good-enough environment. What Christian parents in particular can impart is knowledge of the saving grace that gives common grace its depth and meaning. It is not only the children but the parents who must grow and develop, as together they learn both to receive and to give grace anew.

NOTES

1. Daniel Stern, *The First Relationship: Infant and Mother* (Cambridge: Harvard Univ. Press, 1977), p. 1.

2. A good introductory overview can be found in N. Gregory Hamilton, *Self and Others: Object Relations Theory in Practice* (Northvale, NJ: Jason Aronson, 1988). A more in-depth and detailed study is Jay R. Greenberg and Stephen A. Mitchell, *Object Relations in Psychoanalytic Theory* (Cambridge: Harvard Univ. Press, 1983). As Greenberg and Mitchell note, there is a wide continuum of psychoanalytic theory that might be designated "object-relations." Some theorists maintain close proximity to Freud, whereas others radically reinterpret drive theory in relational terms. I have taken the liberty of using the term "object-relations" to designate the relational thrust of the movement, rather than the theory of a particular writer.

3. W. R. D. Fairbairn, *An Object Relations Theory of the Personality* (New York: Basic Books, 1952). See also the summary of Fairbairn's theory in Greenberg and Mitchell, *Object Relations in Psychoanalytic Theory,* pp. 151-187. This is not necessarily a fully relational ontology, since Fairbairn does trace drive for relatedness to the more Darwinian theme of biological survival (Greenberg and Mitchell, p. 156).

4. Emil Brunner, *Man in Revolt: A Christian Anthropology,* trans. Olive Wyon (Philadelphia: Westminster, 1939), p. 102. Note: Brunner, like many other theologians, refers to generic humanity using male pronouns. I have not followed this convention in my own writing, but I have chosen to preserve the quotations as they stand.

5. Douglas John Hall, *Imaging God: Dominion as Stewardship* (Grand Rapids: Eerdmans; New York: Friendship Press, 1986). The end goal of Hall's text is primarily ecological: i.e. to demonstrate that our current state of ecological crisis is due in part to a misinterpretation of the essence of humanity, and more specifically, to a distorted understanding of the *imago Dei*. My focus is upon the interhuman, rather than upon the relationship between the human and nonhuman creation. As Hall insists, however, these two foci can be separated only for the sake of analysis, and such separation cannot destroy what he deems to be their intrinsic ontological connection. See esp. ch. 5, "Dimensions of Human Relatedness."

6. Humans are referred to as being in God's image or likeness in passages such as Gn. 1:26-28, 5:1-3, 9:6; 1 Cor. 11:7; Col. 3:9-10; Jas. 3:9. Similar language is used of Christ: see e.g. 2 Cor. 4:4; Col. 1:15.

7. Good historical surveys of these doctrines can be found in Brunner, *Man in Revolt*; G. C. Berkouwer, *Man: The Image of God,* trans. Dirk W. Jellema (Grand Rapids: Eerdmans, 1962); David Cairns, *The Image of God in Man* (London: Collins, 1953); Anthony A. Hoekema, *Created in God's Image* (Grand Rapids: Eerdmans, 1986); and Otto Weber, *Foundations of Dogmatics,* vol. 1, trans. Darrell L. Guder (Grand Rapids: Eerdmans, 1981), pp. 558-628.

8. Different authors use different terms to denote a relational ontology of human nature. My preference is "being-in-relation," whereas other terms such as "being-with" (Hall), "responsible existence" (Brunner), and "being in encounter" (Barth) are also used when other authors are cited.

9. Hall, *Imaging God,* pp. 88-112. Hall borrows the terms from Paul Ramsey's *Basic Christian Ethics* (New York: Charles Scribner's Sons, 1950).

10. As David Cairns writes, "In all the Christian writers up to Aquinas we find the

image of God conceived of as man's power of reason." Cairns, *Image of God,* p. 110. Quoted in Hall, *Imaging God,* p. 92.

11. Hoekema, for example, suggests that the identification of the *imago* with reason, in the theologies of both Irenaeus and Thomas Aquinas, stems from Platonic and Aristotelian tradition rather than scriptural exegesis. See *Created in God's Image,* pp. 34, 39.

12. For a treatment of all three aspects together, see Hall, *Imaging God,* and Hoekema, *Created in God's Image,* pp. 75-82.

13. Claus Westermann, *Creation,* trans. John J. Scullion, S.J. (Philadelphia: Fortress, 1974), p. 56; cited in Hall, *Imaging God,* pp. 73-74.

14. Brunner, *Revolt,* pp. 96-97.

15. Brunner, *Revolt,* p. 105.

16. Hall, *Imaging God,* pp. 106-7.

17. Hoekema, *Created in God's Image,* pp. 68-73.

18. See Ray S. Anderson, *On Being Human* (Grand Rapids: Eerdmans, 1982), p. 75. See also Berkouwer's critique of Helmut Thielicke in *Man: The Image of God,* pp. 139-40, where he refuses to dissociate the relational from the ontological: "[I]t is actually impossible to describe the image of God as a relation. It is one thing to say that the relation to God is of the essence of the image, but quite another to make the image itself consist merely of a relation."

19. G. C. Berkouwer, *Sin,* trans. Philip C. Holtrop (Grand Rapids: Eerdmans, 1971), p. 255. In a similar vein, Otto Weber writes the following: "Sin is 'personal sin.' It is not 'something' about man, neither a defect nor an attribute nor an act performed by man. It is the comprehensive qualification of his being, in that it defines his direction. . . . [S]in is always missing the way or virtual failure in regard to the relationship to a specific other person." See Weber, *Dogmatics,* vol. 1, p. 592.

20. Weber, *Dogmatics,* vol. 1, p. 596.

21. Berkouwer, *Sin,,* pp. 245ff.

22. Berkouwer, *Sin,,* pp. 242-43.

23. Weber, *Dogmatics,* vol. 1, p. 613.

24. Hall, *Imaging God,* esp. ch. 4, "The Ontology of Communion."

25. Thomas F. Torrance, *Divine and Contingent Order* (Oxford: Oxford Univ. Press, 1981).

26. John Macmurray, *Persons in Relation* (New York: Harper & Brothers, 1961).

27. Karl Barth, *Church Dogmatics,* ed G. W. Bromiley and T. F. Torrance (Edinburgh: T. & T. Clark, 1958), III/1, pp. 228ff.

28. Hall, *Imaging God,* p. 119. Hall borrows the term from Joseph Sittler, who writes, "The only adequate ontological structure we may utilize for thinking things Christianly is an ontology of community, communion, ecology—and all three words point conceptually to thought of a common kind. 'Being itself' may be a relation, not an entitative thing." See Sittler, "Ecological Commitment as Theological Responsibility," *Zygon* 5 (1970):174; cited in Hall, *Imaging God,* p. 115.

29. Brunner, *Revolt,* p. 98.

30. W. W. Meissner, *Life and Faith: Psychological Perspectives on Religious Experience* (Washington, DC: Georgetown Univ. Press, 1987), p. 52.

31. Barth, "The Basic Form of Humanity," in *Church Dogmatics,* ed. G. W. Bromiley and T. F. Torrance (Edinburgh: T. & T. Clark, 1960), III/2, pp. 250-274.

32. Brunner, *Revolt,* p. 141.

33. Torrance, *Divine and Contingent Order,* p. 110.

34. Torrance, *Divine and Contingent Order,* p. 111.

35. Torrance, *Divine and Contingent Order,* p. 118. Emphasis mine.

36. Martin Buber, *I and Thou,* trans. Walter Kaufmann (New York: Scribners, 1970).

37. Barth, *Church Dogmatics,* III/2, p. 251.

38. Macmurray, *Persons in Relation,* pp. 60-61. Emphasis mine. Caution is needed here, along the lines I have already discussed. As long as the interpersonal dimension is given its ontological due, it is not necessary to substitute the "I-Thou" for the "I" as the "unit" of the personal. This is because all such "units" are relative to larger social contexts, if one broadens the horizon of analysis.

39. Macmurray, *Persons in Relation,* p. 74.

40. Macmurray, *Persons in Relation,* pp. 89-90. Emphasis mine. Note: I doubt that Macmurray intended "confidence" to designate a belief that requires greater cognitive sophistication than an infant possesses. The term is used here in a preverbal and existential sense rather than in a cognitive sense.

41. Margaret Mahler, F. Pine, and A. Bergman, *The Psychological Birth of the Human Infant* (New York: Basic Books, 1975). Mahler has since modified her position somewhat, though still asserting that a *relative* phase of normal autism still exists. See Mahler, "The Meaning of Developmental Research of Earliest Infancy as Related to the Study of Separation-Individuation," in *Frontiers of Infant Psychiatry,* ed. Justin D. Call et al. (New York: Basic Books, 1983), vol. 1, p. 5.

42. Stern, *The First Relationship,* p. 33. See esp. ch. 3, "The Infant's Repertoire."

43. Margaret Stewart Temeles, "The Infant: A Socially Competent Individual," in *Frontiers of Infant Psychiatry,* ed. Justin D. Call et al., vol. 1, pp. 179, 186.

44. H. Guntrip, *Psychology for Ministers and Social Workers,* 2nd ed. (London: Independence Press, 1953), p. 331. It is noteworthy that Guntrip, perhaps the most articulate popularizer of object relations theory, was a minister and the son of a minister, was analyzed by both Fairbairn and Winnicott, and began a master's thesis under the supervision of John Macmurray, seeking to translate psychoanalysis into personalistic terms. See Guntrip, "My Experience of Analysis with Fairbairn and Winnicott," *International Review of Psychoanalysis* 2 (1975):145-56.

45. "Basic trust," according to Erik Erikson's well-known model, is the foundational issue of ego development and psychosocial adjustment. See Erikson, *Childhood and Society* (New York: W. W. Norton, 1950). W. W. Meissner also suggests the importance of trust for the child's later relationship to God: "To the extent that the child's early experience with the mother has tipped the balance in the direction of more positive and gratifying experiences, a basic sense of trust is laid down that provides a foundation for the later development of a sense of trusting faith in the relationship to God. Where early infantile experience is discolored with uncertainty, or anxiety, the foundation is laid for a basic mistrust that can contaminate and distort the later experience of God." See *Psychoanalysis and Religious Experience* (New Haven: Yale Univ. Press, 1984), p. 140.

46. Daniel Stern, "Affect Attunement," in *Frontiers of Infant Psychiatry,* ed. Justin D. Call et al. (New York: Basic Books, 1984), pp. 3-14. See also Stern, *The Interpersonal World of the Infant* (New York: Basic Books, 1985), pp. 138-61.

47. Stern, *Interpersonal World of the Infant,* p. 148. Italics in original.

48. See D. W. Winnicott, "Primary Maternal Preoccupation," in *Through Paediatrics to Psycho-Analysis,* rev. ed. (New York: Basic Books, 1975), p. 303.

49. D. W. Winnicott, "Ego Distortion in Terms of True and False Self," in *The Maturational Processes and the Facilitating Environment* (New York: International Universities Press, 1965), pp. 140-52.

50. Macmurray, *Persons in Relation,* pp. 74-75.

51. The term "good-enough" is sprinkled throughout Winnicott's writings, as a catchall symbol for an environmental provision that is adequate to the developing child's emotional needs. The term reflects both the provision itself as well as the child's experience of care in relation to her needs, and thus need not be limited to

mothers. See, for example, "Ego Distortion in Terms of True and False Self" (n. 49 above), as well as the summary of Winnicott's views in Greenberg and Mitchell, *Object Relations,* esp. pp. 196-201.

52. Reinhold Niebuhr, *Man's Nature and His Communities* (New York: Scribners, 1965), p. 125.

53. Heinz Hartmann, *Ego Psychology and the Problem of Adaptation,* trans. David Rapaport (New York: International Universities Press, 1958).

54. This is, of course, only one side of the matter. Developmental and object-relations literature tends to focus primarily upon the development of the child, and the parent's influence upon it. More recently, however, psychologists and psycho-analysts have rightly pointed out that parenting should be recognized as a developmental stage in the life of the parent as well. See, for example, Donald D. Schwartz, "Psychoanalytic Developmental Perspectives on Parenthood," in *Parenthood: A Psychodynamic Perspective,* ed. Rebecca S. Cohen et al. (New York: Guilford, 1984), pp. 356-72.

55. Macmurray, *Persons in Relation,* p. 66.

Bibliography: The Published Writings of Ray S. Anderson, 1964-1990

1964   *Like living stones*. Minneapolis: Free Church Press.

1968   Marriage after divorce. *Eternity* (May).

1973   Toward a theology of celebration. *Christian Scholar's Review* III (1).

1974   Society and culture. *Westmont College News Publication* 26 (1):(January).
        The lengths of God in Christian involvement. *Reformed Journal* (July/
        August).
        Theology as rationality. *Christian Scholar's Review* 4 (2).

1975   *Historical transcendence and the reality of God*. Grand Rapids: Eerdmans;
        London: Geoffrey Chapman.
        Review of *Incarnation and immanence*, by Lady Helen Oppenheimer. *Scottish
        Journal of Theology* 28 (2).
        Review of *True patriotism*, by Dietrich Bonhoeffer. *Scottish Journal of
        Theology* 28 (4).

1976   Review of *Freedom made flesh*, by Ignacio Ellacuria. *The New Review of
        Books and Religion* (June).
        Review of *Theology for a nomad church*, by Hugo Assmann. *The New Review
        of Books and Religion* (June).

1977   Producing doctors for the church. *Theology, News and Notes* (October).
        Review of *Space, Time and Resurrection*, by T. F. Torrance. *Christianity Today*
        (December).

1978   Theologians in life and thought. *Education for Ministry*, APEM (June).

1979   *Theological foundations for ministry* (editor and contributor). Grand Rapids:
        Eerdmans; Edinburgh: T. & T. Clark.

1981   Notations on a theology of the Holy Spirit. *TSF Bulletin* (April).

1982   *On being human: Essays in theological anthropology*. Grand Rapids:
        Eerdmans.
        A theological basis for social justice: The little man on the cross. *Reformed
        Journal* (November).
        Some implications of the "real presence" of Christ in the hermeneutical
        task. *TSF Bulletin* (November).

1984   Burnout as a symptom of theological anemia. *Theology, News and Notes*
        (March).
        Christopraxis: Competence as a criterion for theological education. *TSF
        Bulletin* 7 (3):(January/February).
        Son of God. In *International standard Bible encyclopedia*, vol. 4. Grand
        Rapids: Eerdmans.

1986   *Minding God's business.* Grand Rapids: Eerdmans.
        On being family: A social theology of the family, with Dennis B. Guernsey.
        Grand Rapids: Eerdmans.
        Theology, death and dying. Oxford and New York: Basil Blackwell.
        Karl Barth and new directions in natural theology. In *Theology beyond
        Christendom: Essays on the centenary of the birth of Karl Barth*. Allison Park,
        PA: Pickwick Publications.
        The resurrection of Jesus as hermeneutical criterion: Part one. *TSF Bulletin*
        (January/February).
        The resurrection of Jesus as hermeneutical criterion: A case for sexual
        parity in pastoral ministry. *TSF Bulletin* (March/April).
        Conversion: The essence of the Christian story. *Theology, News and Notes*
        (June).
        South Africa: *Kairos* or crisis? *Reformed Journal* 36 (10):(October).

1987   God bless the children and the childless. *Christianity Today* 31 (28):(August
        7).

1988   Socio-cultural implications of a Christian perception of humanity. *Asian
        Journal of Theology* 2 (October).
        The family as matrix of character. *Theology News and Notes* (Fall).
        Toward a post-apartheid theology. *Reformed Journal* (May).
        Toward a post-apartheid theology in South Africa. *Journal of Theology for
        South Africa* (June).

1989   *Evangelical theology: Heirs of Protestant orthodoxy* (editor and contributor).
        London: Collins.
        Christopraxis: The ministry and the humanity of Christ for the world. In
        Christ in our place: Essays in honor of James B. Torrance, ed. T. Hart and D.
        Thimell. Exeter: Paternoster Press.
        Evangelical theologians. In *The modern theologians*, vol. 2, ed. David Ford.
        Oxford and New York: Basil Blackwell.
        Isomorphic indicators in psychological and theological science. *Journal of
        Psychology and Theology* 17 (4).
        Socio-cultural implications of a Christian view of humanity. *Asian Journal
        of Theology* 17 (4).

1990   *Christians who counsel: A theological approach to wholistic therapy.* Grand
        Rapids: Zondervan.
        Human nature, problems of. In *Dictionary of pastoral care and counseling*.
        Nashville: Abingdon. In press.
        Image of God. In *Dictionary of pastoral care and counseling*. Nashville:
        Abingdon. In press.

List of Contributors

JACK O. BALSWICK is Professor of Sociology and Family Development, Fuller Theological Seminary, Pasadena, California.

JUDITH K. BALSWICK is Assistant Professor of Marital and Family Therapy, Fuller Theological Seminary, Pasadena, California.

GEOFFREY W. BROMILEY is Emeritus Professor of Historical Theology and Church History, Fuller Theological Seminary, Pasadena, California.

JOHN W. DE GRUCHY is Professor of Christian Studies, University of Cape Town, South Africa.

DAVID E. GARLAND is Professor of New Testament Interpretation, the Southern Baptist Theological Seminary, Louisville, Kentucky.

DIANA R. GARLAND is Associate Professor of Social Work, the Southern Baptist Theological Seminary, Louisville, Kentucky.

DENNIS B. GUERNSEY is Associate Professor of Marital and Family Therapy, Fuller Theological Seminary, Pasadena, California.

COLIN E. GUNTON is Professor of Christian Doctrine, King's College, University of London, England.

ALASDAIR I. C. HERON holds the Chair of Reformed Theology at the University of Erlangen, West Germany.

FRANCES F. HIEBERT is a writer and speaker on women's issues from Pasadena, California.

PAUL G. HIEBERT is Professor of Anthropology and South Asian Studies, Fuller Theological Seminary, Pasadena, California.

DAVID ALLAN HUBBARD is President of and Professor of Old Testament at Fuller Theological Seminary, Pasadena, California.

WILLIE J. JENNINGS is Instructor in Systematic Theology and Black Church Studies at the Divinity School of Duke University, Durham, North Carolina.

CHRISTIAN D. KETTLER is Assistant Professor of Theology and Philosophy, Friends University, Wichita, Kansas.

ADRIO KÖNIG is Professor of Systematic Theology, University of South Africa, Pretoria.

CAMERON LEE is Assistant Professor of Marriage and Family Studies, Fuller Theological Seminary, Pasadena, California.

ALAN E. LEWIS is Professor of Constructive and Modern Theology, Austin Presbyterian Theological Seminary, Austin, Texas.

DONALD W. MCCULLOUGH is Senior Pastor of Solana Beach Presbyterian Church, Solana Beach, California.

WILLIAM E. PANNELL is Director of Black Ministries and Associate Professor of Evangelism, Fuller Theological Seminary, Pasadena, California.

LEWIS B. SMEDES is Professor of Theology and Ethics, Fuller Theological Seminary, Pasadena, California.

TODD H. SPEIDELL is Associate Professor of Religion and Philosophy, Knoxville College, Knoxville, Tennessee.

JAMES B. TORRANCE is Emeritus Professor of Systematic Theology, University of Aberdeen, Scotland.

THOMAS F. TORRANCE is Emeritus Professor of Christian Dogmatics, University of Edinburgh, Scotland.

DAWN WARD is Associate Professor of Sociology, Trinity College, Deerfield, Illinois.

WALTER C. WRIGHT, JR. is President of and Professor of Christian Leadership and Management at Regent College, Vancouver, B.C., Canada.

Index of Names

A

Abraham, 65, 237, 239
Adam, 42-47, 53, 56 n, 141, 161, 167, 272, 273, 286, 291, 292, 303
Alexander of Hales, 6
Allison, Dale C., Jr., 76 n
Amos, 169
Anderson, Ray: on the Christian organization, 207; on the church, 66; on the fall, 272-73; on family, 226, 230, 236; on the incarnation, 31 n, 140, 143, 144; life of, ix-xi, xiii-xvii, 175, 218-19; on male-female relationship, 272, 285, 286-87; on marriage, 286, 287; on ministry, 58-60, 98, 110-11, 241; on personhood, 128 n; theology of, xvi-xvii, 98, 241
— works of: *The Gospel of the Family,* 268; *Historical Transcendence and the Reality of God,* 126 n, 127 n, 150 n, 273; "The Little Man on the Cross," 151 n; *Minding God's Business,* 214 n; *On Being Family,* 219, 225 n, 233, 236, 241, 287; *On Being Human,* 128 n, 161 n, 225 n, 285, 286, 313 n; "The Resurrection of Jesus as Hermeneutical Criterion," 151 n; *Theological Foundations for Ministry* (ed.), 31 n, 58, 75 n, 110, 126 n, 127 n; *Theology, Death and Dying,* 76 n. *See also* 317-18.

Anselm of Canterbury, 9, 65
Apollinarius, 155
Aquila, 229
Aquinas, Thomas, 5, 6, 91, 277, 313 n
Arendt, Hannah, 242
Aristotle, 243, 277
Athanasius, xiii, 8, 140, 150 n, 155
Augustine, Aurelius, 8, 48, 91, 235
Aulén, Gustaf, 31 n
Austin, Nancy, 215

B

Bacon, Francis, 14
Bales, Robert Freed, 261
Balswick, Jack O., 287
Balswick, Judith K., 287
Bampfylde, 231
Barth, Karl: on the atonement, 69, 70, 143; and E. Brunner, 32, 56 n; on the church, 8, 197-98, 199, 200, 201, 202; on cohumanity, 148; on community vs. individual, 100; on covenant, 302; on election, 6, 11; his doctrine of God, 2-3, 113; his epistemology, 59-60, 63, 71; on hope, 145; on human being, 303, 312 n; on the incarnation, 64, 67, 147, 149; life of, xv; on the ministry of Christ, 82, 141; on the person, 166, 167; his resistance to Nazism, 139, 185; theology of, xiii, xv-xvi, 5; on the virgin birth, 73-74; on

Index of Scriptures